SEXUAL PRACTICES
& THE MEDIEVAL CHURCH

SEXUAL PRACTICES
& THE MEDIEVAL CHURCH

Vern L. Bullough & James Brundage

Prometheus Books
BUFFALO, NEW YORK 14215

Published 1982 by Prometheus Books
700 East Amherst Street, Buffalo, NY 14215

Copyright © 1982 by Vern L. Bullough
and James A. Brundage
All Rights Reserved

Library of Congress Catalog Number: 80-85227
Cloth: ISBN 0-87975-141-X
Paper: ISBN 0-87975-151-7

Printed in the United States of America

Contents

v

Preface

Though sex and sex activities have been and remain a major force in human history, the subject, until recently, has been ignored by scholars. Since there is and was a demand for information about sex, the interested reader generally has had to either search out the information for himself or herself, or rely upon popular works that have often perpetuated erroneous beliefs. Misinformation about sex, however, is more likely for some periods than for others. Of all periods in Western history, the most neglected and most distorted has been the Middle Ages. This neglect and distortion is due not only to the difficulty in getting at source materials, but also to our general attitude toward our "Christian heritage."

In much of Christian thought sex has been regarded as sinful, except for the purposes of procreation. Thus, many of the superficial historical accounts of sexuality have ignored the Middle Ages on the assumption that nothing happened. Giving impetus to this viewpoint was the lack of source materials in popular vernacular languages. Though the ancient Jews and the classical Greeks and Romans did not write in English, much of what they wrote has been translated. Moreover, the classical writers served as the base of the educational curriculum until fairly recently. In fact, knowledge of Latin and Greek distinguished the educated from the noneducated.

Thus, almost any reader of the Bible has come to realize that sex was a powerful force among the ancient Jews. Sex was at the core of such stories as the expulsion of Adam and Eve from the Garden of Eden, the sins of Onan, the story of Tamar, or the difficulties of David over Bathsheba. No similar stories exist in the New Testament, and what references there are to sex occur in the generally misogynistic statements of Saint Paul, who emphasized the celibate life. Similarly, most educated people came to know something about the sex life of the ancients only because the classics are full of detailed sexual and erotic information. Extensive references to sex can be found in Greek writers as diverse as Lucian, Alciphron, Athenaeus, Demosthenes, Plutarch, and even Plato. As far as the Latin writers are concerned, the gossipy accounts of Suetonius about the sex lives of the Caesars satisfy even the most prurient-minded reader. Through his writings, emperors such as Caligula and Nero achieved a reputation for self-indulgence that remains unmatched outside of the Hollywood of today.

Inevitably, Roman sex became a staple of many pulpit orations designed to bring the good Christians back to their proper senses. The fall of Rome in many peoples' minds occurred because of the sexual excesses of its people, even though individuals such as Caligula and Nero lived at the height of imperial power. Some of this popular morality tale of the evilness of Roman sexuality has even crept into college textbooks. A medieval text of the 1960s stated:

> The civilization of the Roman empire was vitiated by homosexuality from its earliest days. A question, uncomfortable to our contemporary lax moralists, may be raised: Is not the common practice of homosexuality a fundamental debilitating factor in any civilization where it is extensively practiced, as it is a wasting spiritual disease in the individual? It is worth considering that another great and flourishing civilization, the medieval Arabic, where homosexuality was also widespread, similarly underwent a sudden malaise and breakdown. Is there some moral psychological causation, resulting from the social effects of homosexuality that has been ignored?[1]

Only by reading such a paragraph is it possible to realize how ignorant popular writers are about sexuality. Though the writer probably should be congratulated for mentioning sex in a textbook, even in a condemnatory fashion, he demonstrates his total ignorance. First, he advocates the unscientific view that every homosexual is a sick person and homosexuality itself a threat to civilization. There simply is no evidence for such a statement. Second, he is also wrong. Roman society was never vitiated by homosexuality. In fact, the Romans were much more hostile to homosexuality than the Greeks. Moreover, though we know little of the sex behavior of the Roman masses, the Roman ideal never fully accepted homosexuality or, for that matter, any other kinds of nonprocreative sex. Third, as the growth of Roman Stoicism, neo-Platonism, and ultimately Christianity would indicate, the Romans became ever more rigid in what they regarded as the proper sexual code. Thus in the very period that Roman imperial influence is weakening, Roman asceticism is growing. Historically it would be much more accurate to say that Rome fell because they became too antisexual, although that too would oversimplify the issues. The point to emphasize is that there is much misinformation about sex in the early medieval period.

The medieval period has also been more ignored than the modern one. Although some medieval writers such as Chaucer or Boccacio are part of the general liberal education of most of us, Chaucer's descriptions of sexual sins are usually ignored or passed over, except by those who read Middle English. Similarly, Boccacio is regarded as an exception, a throwback to classical times. Except for these brief nods to Chaucer and Boccacio, it is not until Shakespeare's time that the interested reader who can only read English can follow the story of sex. Since this is the case, it becomes not only important for scholars to give accurate information about sex practices of the past, but also to pay particular attention to periods such as the Middle Ages so long ignored. That is the purpose of this book.

It is addressed to those who want to know something about sexuality in the Middle Ages, a period we believe is crucial in the development of Western attitudes. Medieval Christian writers, drawing upon classical, biblical, and Germanic sources, forged a set of attitudes and offered justifications for them. Essentially, these attitudes were what western Europeans have come to call Christian, although it is important to emphasize that there are other attitudes that could equally be called Christian. Orthodox Christians had a different idea about sex than did the Roman Catholics, and still other attitudes were held by the Copts in Egypt, by the Nestorians in Syria, by the Manichaeans in their dispersed communities, and by numerous other Christian peoples.

Though medieval writers looked to the Bible for key concepts, it is important to emphasize that the Bible is ambiguous about sex, and quite radically different ideas could have been, and often were, developed from the same sources. Some writers exercised more influence upon Western attitudes than others, and in the sex field, the most dominant writer is Saint Augustine. What we call Christian attitudes toward sex are really Augustinian attitudes, and not all of the early Church Fathers agreed with Augustine.

Sexual Practices and the Medieval Church indicates how these medieval attitudes, ultimately justified by Saint Augustine, were modified and amplified by canon lawyers who incorporated them into their law codes, and how ultimately these religious laws became not only part of the civil law, but also part of the general cultural inheritance. Little investigation into this topic has been done in the past, with the exceptions listed in the bibliography, and what has been done has usually not been available to the English-speaking reader. No one, as far as we know, has attempted a comprehensive, overall view as we have done here. We set out in this book to examine just exactly what medieval theologians, philosophers, canon lawyers, scientists, and humanists wrote about sex. Some subjects are explored in greater depth than others, and though we have considerable references to literary discussions of sexuality, this topic, except for the introductory essay of Sidney Berger, is not investigated as thoroughly as it could be. Rather we hope to inspire and encourage our readers to explore further into these previously unexamined topics. Interested readers may follow the footnotes for further detailed references and a brief bibliography has been included at the end of the book to serve as further guidance.

Acknowledgments and Identifications

This book grew out of attempts to interest medievalists in the study of human sexuality. Encouraging our efforts were a number of colleagues from around the country, particularly those who regularly attend the medieval meetings held at Western Michigan University of Kalamazoo. Originally we conceived of the book as a series of articles by various contributors, but as the book progressed it came to be the work of the two chief authors and editors, James Brundage, Professor of History at the University of Wisconsin, Milwaukee, and Vern Bullough, Professor of History at California State University, Northridge, who is now serving as Dean at the State University College of New York at Buffalo. Five other medievalists have chapters in the book dealing with themes beyond the competence of the two major authors. Every effort has been made to effectively incorporate their work into our book.

The authors in order of appearance are:

Jo Ann McNamara, Hunter College and the Institute for Research in History.

Grethe Jacobsen, a specialist in Scandinavian literature.

Penny S. Gold, Knox College.

Sidney Berger, Millikan University.

Helen Rodnite Lemay, State University of New York, Stony Brook.

Special thanks should go to all of those who have made this book possible, but particularly to Barbara Bergstrom and Paul Kurtz of Prometheus Books.

SEXUAL PRACTICES
& THE MEDIEVAL CHURCH

1

INTRODUCTION:
The Christian Inheritance

Vern L. Bullough

Sexually, the medieval ideal was that espoused by Christianity, particularly as interpreted by Saint Augustine. Augustine's ideas in turn were influenced not only by biblical concepts, which were often ambiguous in themselves, but also by the philosophical concepts and ascetic practices of the pagan world in which he lived, particularly those advanced by the redemptive cults that were rivals of Christianity. Much of the history of medieval sexual practices discussed in this book represents attempts to interpret the Augustinian ideal and apply it to the lives of medieval people, most of whom came to Christianity with somewhat different sexual attitudes and practices.

Jesus Himself said nothing about sex except that which can be inferred from his references to divorce and remarriage. In the Sermon on the Mount (and elsewhere), He is quoted as stating that it was wrong for a man to divorce his wife except on the grounds of adultery, and that anyone who married a divorced woman committed adultery. He is also quoted as saying that any man who put away his wife and married another also was committing adultery.[1] After hearing Jesus expound on such matters, the disciples wondered whether it might be better to remain unmarried than to chance committing such a sin. He replied:

> All men take not this word, but they to whom it is given. For there are eunuchs, which were born so from their mother's womb; and there are eunuchs, who were made so by men; and there are eunuchs, who have made themselves eunuchs for the kingdom of heaven. He that can take, let him take it.[2]

1

Though this statement apparently satisfied his disciples, later readers still found it ambiguous. Origen (d. c. 251–54), for example, interpreted it literally and castrated himself.[3] By the fourth century such acts of self-mutilation had been forbidden by Church Councils,[4] and instead the prevailing opinion of the Church Fathers* was that Jesus had not called for self-castration but rather for self-imposed continence.

Questions of castration were not the only problems that the early Church Fathers faced. Many other biblical references also seemed ambiguous. Saint Luke, for example, states that a man must hate his own wife and children in order to be a disciple of Jesus.[5] Should this be interpreted literally? Some Gospel writers tended to use a term that can be translated as "leave" rather than "hate,"[6] and by implication, a man is supposed to sacrifice everything for the sake of salvation, yet even this seems a rather strong prescription for a happily married couple. The net effect of the ambiguity, however, was to give scriptural emphasis to a trend towards asceticism, already strongly pronounced in some segments of pagan thought. Obviously a man who had neither wife nor child would be cautioned to hesitate before assuming these burdens.

Other scriptural references causing ambiguity appear in a description of the second coming, a time when, according to Jesus, there would be trouble for pregnant women since, "Woe unto them that are with child, and to them that give suck in those days."[7] This might only mean that pregnant women or women with infants would suffer more general distress or perhaps be too encumbered with earthly concerns to respond properly to the occasion. It has also been interpreted, however, as a divine condemnation of the pregnant and lactating women, a condition that could only result from sexual activity. It is not only the result of sexual activity that is condemned, but even the thought of such activity, since Jesus stated that all who looked on a woman to lust after her committed adultery with her in their heart.[8] Can a male have sex without an erection? And is not an erection itself a sign of lust? Some of the Church Fathers were particularly troubled by this fact.

From these somewhat contradictory statements of Jesus, Saint Paul built his interpretation of the proper sexual conduct for Christians, although his interpretations also often are not clear. For Saint Paul, celibacy was the highest good,[9] although he also pointed out that if a man did marry, he owed certain respect to his wife.

---

*Originally, this term was applied to bishops and witnesses of the Christian tradition, but from the end of the fourth century its use became more restricted—namely, to those whose authority on doctrinal matters carried special weight, a usage established by Saint Basil and Saint Gregory Nazianzus. Generally, the patristic period is considered closed with Saint Isadore of Seville in the West and Saint John of Damascus in the East. Later experts in the Catholic Church are known as Doctors of the Church, a term that also includes some of the Church Fathers. To distinguish various groups we will limit the term to those Greek and Latin Fathers active between the second and seventh centuries. Earlier authorities are usually called the Apostolic Fathers.

Now concerning the things whereof you wrote unto me: It is good for a man not to touch a woman. But for fear of fornication, let every man have his own wife, and let every woman have her own husband. Let the husband render the debt to his wife, and the wife also in like manner to the husband. . . . For I would that all men were even as myself. But every one hath his proper gift from God; one after this manner, and another after that. But I say to the unmarried, and to the widows: It is good for them if they so continue even as I. But if they do not contain themselves, let them marry. For it is better to marry than to be burnt.[10]

Some modern biblical commentators, anxious to defend Saint Paul from charges of misogyny, have gone so far as to claim that this passage established an ethic of mutual obligation. Though this is probably true, marriage is still regarded as little more than a reluctant concession to human frailty. Saint Paul does not make marriage sinful, but he believed that married people had "trouble in the flesh" and were overly concerned with worldly things.[11] Forbidding a person to marry, however, was a heresy.[12]

Apparently some of the early Christians believed that the "day of the Lord" was at hand[13] and took this opportunity to live in idleness and, perhaps, even in sexual promiscuity while awaiting this long expected event.[14] This upset the writer of the Epistle to the Thessalonians and he cautioned his readers that the time of the second coming was not known. In the interval, they were to obey the will of God and try to attain sanctity in sexual matters, even abstaining from fornication:

That every one of you should know how to possess his vessel in sanctification and honour: Not in the passion of lust, like the Gentiles that know not God . . .[15]

If the scriptures were ambiguous about marital sex, attitudes about adultery, fornication, homosexuality, and perhaps also masturbation were more forcefully stated.

But now I have written unto you not to keep company, if any man that is called a brother be a fornicator, or covetous, or an idolater, or a railer, or a drunkard, or an extortioner: with such an one know not to eat.[16]
Know ye not that the unrighteous shall not inherit the kingdom of God?
Be not deceived: neither fornicators, nor idolaters, nor adulterers, nor effeminate, nor abusers of themselves with mankind, nor thieves, nor covetous, nor drunkard, nor revilers, nor extortioners, shall inherit the kingdom of God.[17]

These passages, put in the English of the time of King James I, represent attempts of biblical translators to deal with homosexuality. Two terms, "effeminate" and "abusers of themselves," are used to translate respectively the Greek terms *malakoi* and *arsenokoitai* (Latin Vulgate: *molles* and *masculorum concubitores*), terms distinguishing between those males who engage passively in homosexual acts and those who engage actively in such practices, although it is not clear whether masturbation is included. It is also not clear whether the passage applies to women, an ambiguity that appears elsewhere in the Bible.[18] The most debatable passage appears in Romans:

> For this cause God gave them up into vile affections: for even their women did change the natural use into that which is against nature: And likewise also the men, leaving the natural use of woman, burned in their lust one toward another; men with men working that which is unseemly, and receiving in themselves that recompense of their error which was meet.[19]

It is not clear whether this passage refers to female as well as male homosexuality or whether, as far as women are concerned, it implies the use of orifices other than the vagina for sexual purposes, even though the sexual activity itself is heterosexual.

There are other passages in the Bible that also have sexual connotations,[20] but it would be a serious mistake to regard the very references to sex as a systematic or comprehensive treatment of sexual matters. There is no such treatment in the Christian scriptures: only answers to particular problems that Saint Paul or other writers of the Epistles felt called upon to deal with. Moreover, early Christianity was not a united religion, but a series of local congregations facing different problems that demanded more or less specific answers.

Each congregation was influenced by the local situation in which it found itself and by the cults with which it was competing. In fact, it is not too strong a statement to claim that, within any particular Christian community, the degree of permitted sexual expression was dependent upon the influence of the rivals to Christianity; sexual concepts ranged from permitting copulation, if motivated by a desire for procreation, to an outright demand for celibacy for all Church members. At times, some of the early Christian churches tried to gain status, if not adherents, by outdoing their pagan rivals at ascetic practices. Galen, the second-century A.D. medical writer, commented on this when he observed that the Christian community in Rome included men and women who, like the philosophers, refrained from "cohabitating all through their lives."[21]

One of the cults competing with Christianity was Gnosticism, a movement that represented a syncretism of various religious and philosophical movements of the first few centuries of the modern era. It was both pre-Christian and Christian, independent of Christianity and dependent upon it. Much of the New Testament might well have been written in a reaction to the influence of Gnosticism. In fact, the earliest sources we possess about the Gnostics are the writings of the early Church Fathers who militantly opposed the movement. Gnosticism had many strands, and in some areas it demonstrated greater affinities with ancient Egyptians, Babylonian, and Persian concepts, but all varieties of Gnosticism included elements coming from all of these sources as well as from Greek philosophy.

Central to Gnostic speculation was the conception of dualistic worlds, one evil and material, the other good and spiritual: the same dualistic concept that had such a dominant hold on certain elements of Greek philosophical speculation predating even Plato.[22] Man, according to the Gnostics, had elements of both good and evil; his purpose on earth was to seek redemption, the achievement of the good, and the elimination of evil. Gnostics claimed to possess a saving *gnosis* or knowledge that had been secretly revealed to their predecessors—some of whom were alleged to be the disciples of Jesus—and that could be transmitted to others only by those already initiated. This knowledge concerned the supreme God, superior to the Creator, who was known only to them because, as spiritual beings, they had emanated from Him. Recognition of Him and of themselves would save them so that, after death, they would escape this alien world for the world of their Creator. In the meantime, their spirits had been temporarily imprisoned in flesh bodies. The key to salvation was to free the body from its bondage. Inevitably, such a doctrine led to a stringent asceticism, since the way a true Gnostic could best express his or her alienation from humdrum human existence was by adopting an ascetic life, most particularly by abandoning sex. For this reason Gnosticism has been labeled by John T. Noonan as a special mixture of "Christian theology and sexual morality."[23] Not all Gnostics, however, rejected sex, and some practitioners attempted to show their indifference to the material pleasures of life by engaging in every imaginable kind of sexual practice, arguing that human actions were not subject to moral law and that actions usually considered sinful were not sinful for true believers.

The Gnostics looked to various teachers including Simon, Menander, Saturninus, Marcion, Valentinus, and Basilides. Some of them regarded themselves as Christians, although those who did so believed that Jesus had merely seemed to possess an earthly body and had not really been born of woman. The competition with what became orthodox Christianity is evident from the fact that according to the Christian scriptures, Simon Magus, a Gnostic teacher, was preaching in Samaria where Saint Peter met him.[24] In Revelations there is a fierce denunciation of the Nicolaites,[25] the followers of Nicholas, who was viewed by later Christians as a Gnostic. One of the most important of the Gnostic leaders was Marcion who, after being excommunicated by the Christian congregation in Rome in 144 A.D., set up a competing organization and hierarchy. Clement of Alexandria (second century A.D.) wrote that the Marcionites regarded nature as evil because it was created out of evil matter and, since they did not wish to fill the world with other evil matter, they abstained from marriage.[26] Marcion taught that the highest God, the Father of Jesus, was good, while the Creator-God of the Jews was merely just. Jesus, according to Marcion, came as a life-giving spirit in order to make manifest a new revelation as well as a new way of life. This message of Jesus, unfortunately, had not been written down at first, and, when it finally had been committed to writing, it had been distorted by false apostles under the spell of Judaism. While both Saint Paul and Saint Luke had understood the true gospel, errors had also crept into their teachings, errors that Marcion felt he had to eliminate in order to restore the authentic non-Jewish gospel. Sex, reproduction, and growth were all associated with evil by Marcion, and he was accused by some Christians of denying the birth of Jesus in order that he could claim that Jesus had not come from the flesh of man.[27] Instead, Marcion claimed that Jesus had descended from heaven as a fully formed adult, without undergoing birth, boyhood, or temptation.[28] Marcion and his followers refrained from sexual relations and marriage was prohibited.[29] He limited the sacraments of baptism and Eucharist to virgins, widows, and those married couples who together had agreed to "repudiate the fruit of their marriage."[30]

Another Gnostic leader, Julius Cassianus, taught that men became most like beasts when they practiced sexual intercourse.[31] Jesus had been sent to this earth in order to save men from copulating. Cassianus and other ascetics relied upon a so-called fifth gospel, "The Gospel According to the Egyptians." Clement of Alexandria, who wrote in the second century and from whom we learn the most about this work, accepts it as a legitimate gospel but goes to some pains to provide an explanation for those texts that the Gnostics used to disparage matrimony.

Though Clement of Alexandria and other Church Fathers of the second and third centuries denounced the Gnostic interpretations, the Gnostics nevertheless had great influence upon Christianity. This is evident in their own writings. A good example is the case of Justin Martyr, a pagan philosopher who had converted to Christianity because it was the "supreme and one true philosophy."[32] Justin, deeply influenced by the neo-Platonic dualism of the time, taught that salvation was dependent upon each individual who could choose right or wrong. To illustrate his point, he emphasized the life of the virtuous Christians compared to their heathen contemporaries, and, in one instance, describes approvingly a Christian youth who asked the surgeons to emasculate him as a protection of his bodily purity. Justin also pointed with pride to those Christians who renounced marriage in order to live in perfect continence.[33] So hostile to sex was Justin that he could not conceive of Mary as sexually conceiving Jesus; instead, he argued that Mary had been undefiled, had conceived while a virgin, and he made her the antitype of Eve, the type of woman with whom he associated sexual intercourse.[34] Though Justin did not prohibit marriage, he taught Christians that they should marry only for the purpose of conceiving and bringing up children, and in no case was it a license for sexual activity.[35] In this he followed the teachings of Clement of Alexandria, who said that even though a man married for the sake of begetting children he must practice continence so that it is not desire he feels for his wife, whom he ought to love, and that he may beget children with a chaste and controlled will.[36]

In fact, the Christian ideal of sexual desire was to reach the point at which no desire at all would be experienced.[37] Though marriage had been instituted by God for the generation of children, it was a concession to the inordinate desires of fallen humanity and a refuge for those poor souls who could not bear the discipline of celibacy.

Most of the Church Fathers were bachelors and so, perhaps, are somewhat biased in their attitudes toward marital sexual relations, but even those such as Tertullian, who was married, tended to denigrate marriage. Tertullian in fact came to feel such deep remorse over his lapse into matrimony that he joined the Montanists, a heretical Christian sect far harsher in its attitude toward sexual relations than the more orthodox Christians. In his *Letters to His Wife,* he writes as if there were no sexual element in marriage at all and, in fact, argues that celibacy was much to be preferred.[38]

Tatian became a leader of a sect known as the Encratites, the "self-controlled," after the martyrdom of his teacher, Justin Martyr. Though Tatian is regarded as a heretic today, in his own time he was extremely influential in the development of the Syrian Church, which never regarded him as a heretic. Tatian taught that sexual intercourse had been invented by the devil, and thus anyone who attempted to engage in sexual intercourse, even within the boundaries of matrimony, was serving the devil and not the true God.[39] Tatian was so influential upon the Christian community in Syria that the Christians in that area held that the Christian life was "unthinkable outside the bounds of virginity."[40]

By the end of the second century, Gnosticism was generally looked upon as a distorted expression of Christianity and the organizational ability of the more orthodox Christians appeared to be winning against those elements that denounced sexual relations under any conditions. Still, in struggling against Gnosticism, the early Christian Church came to be deeply influenced by it, and in the long run its attitudes toward sex seem to have been more influenced by the ascetic Gnostics than the more earthly Jews. The extent of the Gnostic influence is illustrated by the fact that one of their most avid opponents, Tertullian, stopped just short of condemning intercourse, even in marriage, and actually seems to be uncertain as to why God had ever permitted such an act.[41]

Not only Christians but non-Christians as well were deeply influenced by such antisex ideas. The general temper of the time tended to emphasize a kind of sexual continence, if Soranus of Ephesus, an influential second-century medical writer, is any example.

Even among dumb animals we see that those females are stronger which are prevented from having intercourse. And among women we see that those who, on account of regulations and service to the gods, have renounced intercourse and those who have been kept in virginity as ordained by law are less susceptible to disease. If, on the other hand, they have menstrual difficulties and become fat and ill-proportioned, this comes about because of idleness and inactivity of their bodies . . . . Consequently permanent virginity is healthful, in males and females alike; nevertheless, intercourse seems consistent with the general principle of nature according to which both sexes (for the sake) of continuity (have to ensure) the succession of living beings.[42]

Even when the competition of Gnosticism began to recede, asceticism retained a strong hold upon the Christian mind. Saint Gregory of Nyssa in the fourth century A.D. dismissed marriage as a sad tragedy,[43] while Saint Jerome (d. 420 A.D.) emphasized its inconveniences and tribulations.[44] His views can perhaps be summarized in an oft-quoted passage:

I praise marriage and wedlock, but I do so because they produce virgins for me. I gather roses from thorns, gold from the earth, and pearl from the shell.[45]

Saint Ambrose (d. 397 A.D.) called marriage a "galling burden,"[46] and urged all those contemplating matrimony to think about the bondage and servitude into which wedded love degenerated.[47] With almost monotonous regularity, the Church Fathers argued that the wedded state was not as good as the single, celibate state. Though marriage was not quite evil, it could only count as thirty-fold, compared to the sixty-fold of widowhood and the hundred-fold of virginity.[48]

There was some Christian opposition to this cult of virginity, but the works of the three most vocal defenders of marriage—Jovian, Helvidius, and Vigilantius—have not survived; their positions in fact are known only through their opponents, primarily Saint Jerome who took great pains to refute their arguments. Saint Jerome, however, was always careful to emphasize that he did not condemn wedlock, even though he admitted he had difficulty in understanding why most people would want to be married.[49] With this half-hearted defense of marriage, celibacy carried the day. It became common practice among many Christian groups to forbid marriage after ordination to the priesthood, although there was, at first, general agreement that a man might be married before ordination. Inevitably also there was an attempt to suggest that matrimonial cohabitation disqualified a person for priestly ministration. The Council of Nicaea specifically rejected an absolute rule of clerical celibacy,[50] but later councils, particularly the Council of Trullo in the seventh century, turned to the subject again. By the fifth century in fact, the western Christian Church tended to hold that bishops, presbyters, deacons, and others employed before the altar were to refrain from coitus, although there were mitigating circumstances that might allow for exceptions.[51] The eastern Christian Church never adopted such a position, and this has been a continuing point of division between Orthodox and Catholic Churches. The Catholic Church, however, has always been willing to grant exceptions and did so in the case of the Byzantine Rite Churches. JoAnn McNamara writes more in Chapter 3.

The growing Western emphasis on celibacy was given final form by Saint Augustine (d. 430 A.D.). It is quite possible that the Christian Church might have become less hostile to sex if it had not been threatened once again by the appearance of a rival that put renewed emphasis on abstention from sexual activity. It was this new rival, Manichaeanism, that Saint Augustine opposed, although he himself had once been a believer. Manichaeanism was a new Christian group based upon the teachings of the prophet Mani (216–277 A.D.) who had lived and been crucified in southern Babylonia. His religious teachings incorporated various aspects of Gnostic, Christian, Zoroastrian, and Greek teachings, and before his death his movement had become influential in Egypt, Palestine, and Rome, and was beginning to spread to Asia Minor, Greece, Illyria, Italy, and North Africa. Manichaeanism had a canonical scripture, the seven books of Mani, and a hierarchy that included apostles and it claimed to be a universal religion. In a sense, it had the same arsenal of weapons as Christianity, and Jesus appeared as equally important. Like Muhammad later did, Mani taught that he was the last prophet in a chain of prophets. Like Christianity, Manichaeanism was a missionary faith and, like Gnosticism, it was dualistic, combining religion, science, and philosophy into a new synthesis. Although claiming the authority of revelation, the Manichaeans also paid deference to reason.

Their universe was divided into two pantheistic portions, the kingdoms of Light or Darkness, that were in juxtaposition with each reaching out into infinity. Light and Darkness were both eternal and uncreated power existing in everlasting opposition and conflict. The God of Light, however, alone was prescient, able to know the future. Eventually, Light would overcome Darkness, but the ultimate victory depended not upon the defeat of Darkness but upon the withdrawal of Light. Originally the two realms had existed without intermingling, but history began when the Prince of Darkness, attracted by the splendor of the Light, invaded the Kingdom of Light. He was met by an evocation of the Father, Primordial Man, a supernatural being of Light. Primordial Man and his sons dueled with the King of Darkness and his sons, but the forces of Light were vanquished and then devoured by their opponents, just as had happened to Dionysus and the Titans. The result was that Light was imprisoned. To rescue Primordial Man the God of Light sent forth his word or the Living Spirit, and after conquering the sons of Darkness, he created the earth, the moon, the sun, the planets, and man, all of which retained some elements of the darkness since, as materials, the God of Light had used the carcasses of the defeated sons of Darkness. Mankind also had both light and darkness, and the purpose of mankind was to follow the path of light.

Procreation, since it kept the light imprisoned, was an evil act to the Manichaeans. The purpose of man was to gain the light, and light could be released by eating bread, vegetables, or fruit containing seeds. The release of light could also be effected or impeded by sexual actions, since the seed of man also contained light. Those entering the Manichaean religion were supposed to have tamed concupiscence as well as covetousness and refused, therefore, to eat flesh, drink wine, or have marital intercourse.

The human race, however, was divided into three classes. The first were the Adepts—the Elect who renounced private property, practiced celibacy, observed strict vegetarianism, and never engaged in trade. The second were the Auditors, or Believers, men and women of good will who could not yet contain themselves and who therefore earned money, owned property, ate flesh, and married but earned high rewards by serving and supporting the Elect in this life. They were also striving to become Elect. Finally, there were the completely sensual members of society, totally lost in wickedness, rejecting the gospel of Mani. At death the spirit of the Elect went directly to the Paradise of Light; the Auditors spent a period of purification in purgatory, while the wicked were doomed to eternal and irrevocable suffering in the three Manichaean hells. The bodies of all returned to dust whence they came.

The soul of God was constantly being freed from its physical fetters by the natural processes of growth and death; unfortunately, through the act of procreation, the spirit was also continually encumbered in the dregs of creation. Sexual intercourse between male and female chained the soul to Satan and denied its rapid progress into the Kingdom of Light. Thus the Manichaeans regarded marriage as a sin and procreation as defiling the birth of the divine substance. Sexual sin not only consisted in the overt act of sex, but also in the impulse: marriage was no greater offence than the desire to marry. Within the Manichaean hierachy, however, marriage was only a sin for the Elect. The Auditors were permitted to follow their natural inclinations, since Christ was the truth, the light, and the way, and no man was to be forced to do what he could not do.[52]

Saint Augustine became an adherent of the Manichaean religion and remained a member for some eleven years but never reached the Elect stage, in part because of his difficulties with sex. He remained an Auditor, living with a mistress and growing more and more uncomfortable with his inability to control his lustful desires. His own ambiguity about the matter is evident from his constant prayer: "Give me chastity, and continence, but do not give it yet."[53] Augustine's mother Saint Monica, though tolerating her son's concubine, and even his son by her, Adeoatus, wanted Augustine to become a Christian and to enter into a regular marriage. Obviously unhappy over his inability to become an Elect, and, perhaps, as a result of pressure from his mother, Augustine reached the conclusion that the only way he could control his venereal desire was through marriage.[54] He sent away his mistress (and his son) and became engaged to a girl who was not yet of age (twelve was the legal minimum). While waiting to be married, however, Augustine found himself unable to refrain from sex and took a temporary mistress. At this juncture he went through a crisis of conscience that ended in his conversion to Christianity and the adoption of a life of celibacy. Triggering the crisis was his reading a passage in Romans:

> Let us walk honestly, as in the day: not in rioting and drunkenness, not in chambering and impurities, not in contention and envy: But put ye on the Lord Jesus Christ, and make not provision for the flesh in its concupiscences.[55]

Augustine interpreted this as a call to celibacy, and conversion for him came to mean the rejection of sexual intercourse.[56] Once he found himself able to accept continence, Saint Augustine found coitus offensive. He wrote that he knew nothing that brought "the manly mind down from the heights than a woman's caresses and that joining of bodies without which one cannot have a wife."[57] He was particularly upset that the act of generation could not be accomplished without what he felt were the bestial movements[58] that inevitably were accompanied by violent lustful desires.[59]

For him sexual lust was the inevitable result of the expulsion of Adam and Eve from the Garden of Eden. In Paradise he believed the two had been able to control their genitals, which had been obedient to the dictates of their will and never stirred except at their behest.[60] Augustine believed that Adam and Eve had not engaged in sexual intercourse before their expulsion, although he believed that if they had chosen to do so they could have managed the affair without lascivious heat or unseemly passion.[61] Once they had fallen from Paradise, however, they became conscious of the new impulse, an impulse generated by their very act of rebellion, and this drove them to an insatiable quest for self-satisfaction.[62] Augustine termed this impulse concupiscence or lust and it was through this that the genitals lost the docility of innocence, were no longer amenable to the will. Inevitably, Adam and Eve had felt shame over their desires, a shame that caused them to cover their nakedness by sewing fig leaves together in order to make aprons with which they could conceal their genitalia. Concupiscence, however, was still displayed through the sexual impulses that proved stronger and less tractable than other passions and that could only be satisfied through an orgasm, something that engulfed the rational faculties in violent, sensual excitement. Though coitus must be regarded as a good since it came from God, every concrete act of intercourse was evil, with the result that every child, literally, could be said to have been conceived in the sin of its parents.[63]

Venereal desire, since it had been implanted by God for encouraging the increase of mankind, must be regarded as blameless but the same desire, corrupted by concupiscence, was to be regarded as shameful and sinful.

Since generation could not occur unless the carnal union of husband and wife was motivated by the stimulus of lust, it must therefore be a sin.[64] Did this make marriage an evil in itself? Augustine tried to distinguish between matrimony and sexual intercourse, but his answers were rather contradictory. He concluded that concupiscence could not take away the good of marriage and that marriage somewhat mitigated the evil of concupiscence. "We ought not to condemn marriage because of the evil of lust, nor must we praise lust because of the good of marriage."[65] Although marriage managed to transform coitus from a satisfaction of lust to a necessary duty,[66] it was only when the act was employed for human generation that it lost some of its inherent sinfulness.[67]

Even this, however, served as the channel, transmitting the guilt of concupiscence from parents to children, a guilt that could only be removed by a baptismal regeneration.[68] Saint Augustine concluded that marriage guarded wanton marital indulgence from the graver sinfulness of fornication or adultery and that, even though nuptial embraces were not always intentionally destined for procreation, the sin that resulted from this was only venial, providing there was no attempt to frustrate the natural consequences of coitus.[69] All intercourse between the unmarried was condemned by Augustine, although he did hold that true wedlock could exist without a ceremony.[70] In short, Saint Augustine concluded that procreation was the only justification of sexual intercourse by a husband and wife.[71] Celibacy was the highest good, while intercourse in itself was only an animal lust. In marriage and only in marriage, was it justified because of the need for procreation. Marital intercourse could be either good and evil, and it was only through procreation that the evil became good and evil. It was this concept that the Christian Church attempted to establish for the medieval world.

Section I

Putting Christian theories into practice was not easy. Complicating an already difficult task were the basic contradictions in Christian teachings, contradictions that ultimately led to major divisions within the Christian Church. Gradually, idealized concepts such as a chaste marriage were abandoned, but often only after they had aroused suspicion and cynicism. Still, the Church came to terms with the real world and, in the process, often improved the lot of stigmatized sexual groups such as prostitutes. One of the interesting by-products of the basic Christian hostility to the woman as a sex object was the development of the transvestite saint, a woman who gained holiness by living and acting as a man.

Christianity ultimately grew to incorporate large numbers of people from quite different backgrounds. Each of these peoples brought attitudes with them that had to be modified if the Christian ideal was to mean anything. A good example of the difficulties in "Christianizing" the various peoples is indicated by the chapter on sex in medieval Scandinavia. Essentially, however, the ideas developed in the early Church came to be the dominant concepts of the Western world, as the discussion of the sin against nature demonstrates.

2

Formation of Medieval Ideals: Christian Theory and Christian Practice

Vern L. Bullough

Though Christian theory was extremely hostile to human sexuality, it did not always coincide with actual practice. The potential for conflict between the two was exacerbated when Christianity changed from being just one of a number of competing religious groups within the Roman Empire to the official religion of the state. Since Christians came from disparate backgrounds and cultures, it was inevitable that they disagreed with each other. Though common areas of agreement eventually were hammered out in a series of Church Councils, not all segments of Christian society accepted these decisions. Conflicts over sex appeared very early in conciliar history.

Even before Christianity had been officially tolerated, there were disputes about clerical celibacy. Most Church Fathers were willing to recognize marriage for purposes of procreation, but there was a strong feeling that clerics should be a special class set apart from the lay person by their celibacy. A council held at Elvira in Spain in 305–306 had attempted to impose a rule of sexual abstinence upon all bishops, presbyters, deacons, and others employed in the service of the altar.[1] The first ecumenical council, held at Niceaea in 325, debated imposing clerical celibacy but in the end failed to do so because of the opposition to it led by Paphnutius, an Egyptian bishop. Paphnutius carried the day, partly because he was a celibate opposed to compulsory celibacy and partly because, in the eyes of many delegates, he was an authentic Christian martyr who had suffered the loss of his right eye rather than recant his faith during a period of persecution prior to the reign of the Emperor Constantine.[2]

14

The rejection of clerical celibacy by the Council of Nicaea, however, did not end the discussion. In the West Siricius, bishop of Rome, soon revived the subject by issuing a decretal on it in 385 A.D. A request for his assistance by Hermeius, Archbishop of Tarragona in Spain, prompted his action in enforcing the celibacy concepts established at the Council of Elvira. Siricius threw his influence behind the necessity of clerical celibacy, prohibiting all coitus by presbyters and deacons, even those who were already married.[3] A succession of western synods, including those held at Carthage in 390, at Toledo in 400, at Turin in 401, and at Rome in 402,[4] further reinforced clerical celibacy. Though Leo I, Bishop of Rome (440–461) allowed married clergy to retain their wives, he stipulated that they should have wives as though "they had them not." To emphasize the importance of celibacy, he extended the prohibition against sexual intercourse to subdeacons, as well as to presbyters and deacons.[5] Still, in spite of such conciliar and ecclesiastical actions concentrated almost entirely in the West, it was not until the thirteenth century that the Roman Church was able to enforce the concept of clerical celibacy.[6]

One of the reasons for the difficulty in enforcement was that the Eastern Church had a different view, and until the Eastern and Western Churches had separated the West was unable to impose its own view. As far as the Eastern Church was concerned, the most complete statement on the matter was given in 692 at the Council of Constantinople where it was stipulated that a lawfully married man might become a subdeacon, deacon, or priest. They had to be married before ordination since only minor clerics could marry after ordination. Bishops, however, were supposed to be celibate and if, per chance, a married man was advanced to the episcopate, his wife was to be separated from him and retired to a monastery.[7]

The Christian Church had split on many other aspects of sexual behavior, not only on clerical celibacy. In sexual matters the Eastern Church tended to look more to Saint John Chrysostom, while the West looked to Saint Augustine. Though Chrysostom, like Augustine, held that marriage had been established to prevent fornication, Chrysostom then went on to state that intercourse was permissible with one's spouse even when procreation was not possible—as when she was sterile, when she was old, and when she was pregnant. He had apparently arrived at this position from his conviction that intercourse in and of itself was not what produced children; rather, it was the word of God that caused men to increase and multiply. Undoubtedly he had observed that not all acts of intercourse led to pregnancy; something more must be needed. As proof of his need for God's intervention, he observed that many men entered into marriage for the purpose of procreation but did not become fathers.[8] Chrysostom, however, opposed the use of contraceptives and classified them as worse than homicide.[9]

Official positions of the Church, however, even the more liberal position of the Eastern Church, remained an ideal and did not necessarily coincide with reality. A good example of this is the discussion of contraception in the medieval medical literature, particularly by Aetio of Amida, a Byzantine court physician of the sixth century. Since Chrysostom and, in general, the Eastern Church opposed the use of contraceptives, it would seem that the wise physician would avoid the subject. Aetio, however, discussed it matter-of-factly. He recognized a safe period and urged those who wished to avoid pregnancy to engage in intercourse either at the beginning or end of the menstrual cycle. He also reported that smearing the cervix with astringent or fatty or cooling ointments would close the orifice of the womb and prevent semen from entering the uterus. Most effective, in his mind, were those ointments that so irritated the womb that liquid came from the uterus (infection?). He also advised males to wash their genitals with vinegar or brine prior to coitus if they wanted to avoid conception.[10] Those males who followed his advice probably would not have lessened their chances of impregnating their female partners; yet, his recommendation might have been slightly more effective if the female had used a vaginal douche from the same solution.

Another medical writer, the seventh-century Paulus Agineta, taught that coitus was the best remedy for melancholy since it restored reason to those afflicted with mania. Paulus did advise moderation in the frequency of sexual activities if only because, like any other kinds of labor, it was best not to overdo it. He also believed that certain times were better for sexual activity than others. He advised his readers to engage in sex after a meal, when one was ready to retire, since this allowed the male to relieve the "lassitude" resulting from the orgasm by going to sleep. It also ensured procreation since, according to Paulus, the "woman falling asleep is more likely to retain the semen."[11]

The Church did not prove particularly effective in forcing the state to adopt some of its other attitudes about sex. This difference in theory and practice appears rather openly in the utilization of eunuchs by the Byzantine state. Organized Christianity had come out against self-castration at the Council of Nicaea and had prohibited the ordination of eunuchs.[12] Roman law had a long tradition of prohibiting involuntary castration by anyone, including slaves; this prohibition was reaffirmed in the sixth century by the Emperor Justinian who went so far as to give freedom to all slaves who had been castrated.[13] In spite of such prohibitions, slaves continued to be castrated, and many rose to be bishops and even patriarchs, since, despite the ecclesiastical and secular prohibitions, eunuchs served an extremely important function in the Byzantine state. In fact, one writer has gone so far as to call the Byzantine Empire a "eunuch's paradise."[14]

Though eunuchs were also important in China and in the Islamic world, they had more influence in Byzantium than anywhere else. In the sixth century, one of the greatest of Byzantine generals was a eunuch. By the tenth century, eunuchs were so powerful in the imperial court that a eunuch took precedence over non-eunuchs, and many of the most prominent men, both in the state and in the Church, were eunuchs. Castration, far from being a stigma or a sin, was sought by parents in order to secure advancement for their sons.[15] The key to the eunuch's power lay in the fact that they were forbidden to serve as Prefect of Constantinople, Quaestor, Domestic of the four imperial regiments, or, more importantly, as emperor. Thus, they could be appointed to powerful positions by emperors who knew that they could never wear the imperial crown nor could they pass on their offices to their children. Eunuchs thereby became the safest and most desirable of civil servants—the bulwark of a strong central bureaucracy that served as an effective counterfoil to the power of a hereditary nobility. While a powerful eunuch could (and did) advance his favorites, even the most powerful had to be content with being the power behind the throne rather than taking the throne himself.

Nicetas, the young son of the Emperor Michael I (811–13), was castrated when his father fell from power and, as a eunuch, he rose to become patriarch of Constantinople, taking the name of Ignatius (847–58, 867–78). The Emperor Romanus I (920–44) castrated his bastard son Basil, who, as Paraceonmomenus the Great Chamberlain, ruled the empire in everything but name for several decades. Romanus also castrated his younger, legitimate son, Theophylact, whom he intended to make patriarch.

Eunuchs served in the armed forces: Narses in the sixth century and Nicephorus Uranus in the tenth were brilliant examples of successful eunuch commanders. In the eleventh century, Nicephorus the Logothet, a eunuch, reformed the army after its disastrous defeat at the Battle of Manzikert in 1071. Eustathius Cymineanus was a leading admiral during the same period. Eunuchs also served as palace servants, as keeper of the wardrobe, manager of imperial estates, captain of the body guard, keeper of the privacy purse, and major domo of the palace. Ranking above the major domo was the senior eunuch and, above him, the superintendent of the bed chamber.[16]

Since many emperors lived in a rather secluded state with only limited contact with their subjects, the eunuchs, by their access to the emperor, could not only give him advice but control which outsiders he would see. As early as the fourth century, Constantius II (337–61) was reported to be entirely in the hands of his eunuchs. For a brief period during the reign of the Emperor Arcadius (388–408), the eunuch Eutropius was the virtual head of the government, while during the later years of the reign of Theodosius II (408–450), the eunuch Chrysaphius controlled affairs.

If official Christian teachings were unable to prevent castration, the results of which were usually fairly obvious, it seems clear that the Church would have difficulty in enforcing their strict teachings about sex. Inevitably, Byzantine history abounds with references to all kinds of forbidden sexual behavior.[17] This can be illustrated by a brief overview of homosexuality in the Byzantine Empire.

Though Saint John Chrysostom (d. 407) was more tolerant of heterosexual activities than Saint Augustine, he was almost paranoid about homosexuality. He cautioned parents not to let their male children's hair grow long because this would make them look effeminate, and such boys were particularly attractive to sodomists. He went so far as to caution parents about allowing pretty, young boys to go to church, since pederasts often came to church to look with lustful curiosity upon such handsome youths.[18] Any attempt by a male to enhance his appearance was regarded by Chrysostom as dangerously effeminate, and he cautioned parents to have their young sons always accompanied by an attendant, in order to shield them from "lurking" pederasts in public squares and open alleys.[19]

Somewhat less paranoid on the subject was Saint Basil (d. 379), but he urged that those men who "committed indecencies" with other men be disciplined in the same way as those who committed adultery,[20] that is, that they be excluded from the sacraments for fifteen years. Saint Gregory of Nyssa (d. 398) agreed with this severe punishment, since both adultery and homosexuality involved unlawful pleasures.[21] Because of the continual repetition of references to pederasty and to homosexuality, M. L. W. Laistner concluded that there was a "prevalence of pederasty" in the Greek Christian Church.[22]

What influence did the Christian Church, the source of such fears, have on imperial legislation? As far as actual legislation was concerned, the state attempted to respond to Christian anxieties. Pederasty, the "corruption" of young boys, was regarded as a capital crime at least by the third century A.D., and under the Emperors Constantius and Constans, homosexual relations between consenting adults were also included.

> When a man "marries" in the manner of a woman, a "woman" about to renounce men, what does he wish, when sex has lost its significance; when the crime is one which it is not profitable to know; when Venus is changed into another form; when love is sought and not found? We order the statutes to arise, the laws to be armed with an avenging sword, that these infamous persons who are now, or who hereafter may be, guilty, may be subjected to exquisite punishment.[23]

Obviously the wording of the law is ambiguous. It might describe a kind of homosexual marriage,[24] but there is no other similar reference to such marriages. It has been suggested that the law was enacted in a "spirit of mocking complacency,"[25] but this ignores the reality of lawmaking. Any ambiguity was removed in 390 A.D. when the Emperors Theodosius, Valentinian II, and Arcadius prescribed burning for those found engaging in anal intercourse.

> All persons who have the shameful custom of condemning a man's body, acting the part of a woman's, to the sufferance of an alien sex (for they appear not

to be different from women), shall expiate a crime of this kind by avenging flames in the sight of the people.[26]

Was the law effectively enforced? Chrysostom does not mention it, and with his paranoid feelings about homosexuality it would seem he would. A tax collected from homosexual prostitutes undermined the effect of the law, at least until the reign of the Emperor Anastasius (491–518).[27]

The most definite regulations on the subject were those issued by the Emperor Justinian in the sixth century and included in the *Corpus Iuris Civilis.* Each of the four sections of the *Corpus* includes references to homosexuality, although most references are to pederasty rather than to sexual activity between consenting adults.[28] The most concise summarization of the basic law is found in the *Institutes* that states that homosexual conduct is to be regarded the same as adultery—deserving of the death penalty.[29] This essentially is an extension of the Lex Julia passed under the Emperor Augustus that, by the third century A.D., had been interpreted as applying to homosexuality,[30] and in the *Institutes* it is clearly applied to those who practice "lewdness with their own sex."

Justinian, however, went further and specifically incorporated the implications of God's anger with those who violate Christian teachings on sexual behavior. Since God in his anger would strike out not only at the guilty but at those innocent bystanders who had remained silent, a 538 edict clearly intended to involve the whole Christian community.

> Since certain men, seized by diabolical incitement, practice among themselves the most disgraceful lusts, and act contrary to nature; we enjoin them to take to heart the fear of God and the judgment to come, and to abstain from such like diabolical and unlawful lusts, so that they may not be visited by the just wrath of God on account of those impious acts with the results that cities perish with all their inhabitants . . . . For because of such crimes there are famines, earthquakes, and pestilences; wherefore we admonish man to abstain from the aforesaid unlawful acts, that they may not lose their souls. But if, after our admonition, any are found persisting in such offenses, first they render themselves unworthy of the mercy of God, and they are subjected to the punishment enjoined by the law.[31]

In this instance the law seems to be used more as a teaching than an enforcement mechanism. Obviously, in spite of the death penalty for sodomy, enforcement was lax. The Emperor seems to be trying to arouse people to pay more attention to such activities, indicating that such conduct is even dangerous to those who do not report it. The opportunity to drive this message home further came in the aftermath of a plague that devastated Constantinople in 544. Justinian stated:

> We have provoked Him to anger on account of the multitude of our sins. And though He has warned us and has shown us clearly what we deserve because of

our offences, yet He has acted mercifully towards us, and, awaiting our penitence, has reserved His wrath for other times . . . we ought to abstain from all
base concerns and acts—and especially does this apply to such as have gone to
decay through the abominable and impious conduct deservedly hated by God.
We speak of the defilement of males *[de stupro masculorum]* which some men
sacrilegiously and impiously dare to attempt, perpetrating vile acts upon other
men.

For instructed by the Holy Scriptures, we know that God brought a just
judgment upon those who lived in Sodom, on account of this very madness of
intercourse, so that to this very day the land burns with inextinguishable fire.
By this God teaches us, in order that by legislation we may avert such an
untoward fate.

And we . . . entreat God the merciful that those who have been contam-
inated by the filth of this impious conduct may strive for penitence, that we
may not have to prosecute this crime on another occasion. Next, we proclaim
to all who are conscious that they have committed any such sin, that unless
they desist and, renouncing it before the blessed Patriarch, take care of their
salvation, placating God during the holy season for such impious acts, they
will bring upon themselves severer penalties, even though on other counts they
are held guilty of no fault . . . . If, with eyes as it were blinded, we overlook
such impious and forbidden conduct, we may provoke the good God to anger
and bring ruin upon all—a fate which would be but deserved.[32]

These edicts of Justinian represent the ambiguity inherent in the Christian
position. Technically, homosexual activities were deserving of the death
penalty, but Christianity taught that even the greatest of sinners could be
forgiven. Thus there was a reluctance to give the ultimate penalty for sexual
sins, although Justinian did castrate some of those found guilty of homosexual activities.[33] What we have is the threat of the law trying to impose
Christian ethics; only rarely was it enforced and then, mainly, when the person involved posed a political rather than a moral threat. Still the death penalty remained on the law books. In the tenth century the collection known
as the *Basilica* reiterated that such activity was to be punished by death.[34] In
the fifteenth century George Gemistus Pletho continued to urge the death
penalty upon all those found guilty of sexual aberration and misconduct,
particularly those engaged in homosexual activity.[35]

If the Church had to resort to the threat of a death penalty to impose its
sexual norms on the Byzantine state, its task in controlling sexual activities
in the West would have been more difficult, in part because of the conflicting Germanic law codes.[36] In general, sexual morality was regarded by the
Germans as falling under the control of the family, not criminal law. When
the law did allow intervention in these areas, its purpose was to replace individual acts of retaliatory violence with symbolic payments in order to curtail
blood feuds and secure peace. The sexually related crime most often mentioned in the various Germanic codes is adultery, but it was the adultery of
the wife rather than the husband. In Germanic law, however, adultery was

not so much a sex crime as a violation of property; the husband, in most cases, had the right to kill his wife and her accomplices if he caught them in the act.[37] Males, married or unmarried, on the other hand, were free to fornicate, providing they did not violate the prerogative of some other male. Female chastity had a property value to a father, a brother, a male guardian; anyone caught as a trespasser in carnal intimacy with a female relative could be punished by the male relatives without fear of retribution.[38]

Thus in dealing with the Germans, the Christian missionaries had to start with considerably more disadvantages than they had with those people who already had some semblance of Roman law. The Germanic toleration of most forms of sexual activity that did not violate property ran into conflict with Christian attitudes towards sex in general, and most of the variant forms of sex in particular. The Church faced the problem of imposing its moral standards upon communicants, particularly in areas where Germanic law did not enter. The same fear tactic adopted in Byzantine law about collective guilt could be used, but the Church lacked the enforcement power of the state to back it up. Ultimately the Church was able to assert its own control over family faith and morals, but it had to do so with an educational campaign based partly on fear, partly upon teachings. In this last case the lives of saints proved particularly important in conveying certain concepts. The Church also used penance and confession to communicate certain ideas. Ultimately, canon law developed to emphasize them. In the next four chapters we will look at detailed examples of the formulation of attitudes on chaste marriage and clerical celibacy, on prostitution, on transvestism, and on homosexuality.

3

Chaste Marriage and Clerical Celibacy

Jo Ann McNamara

The early Christian Church viewed marriage as a divinely ordained institution designed by God and strengthened by Jesus for the licit expression of the sexual impulse, the procreation of children, and the mutual pursuit of salvation.[1] Ultimately it was enshrined among the seven sacraments of the Church. But this straightforward endorsement of marriage was, from the beginning, complicated by Paul's observation that married persons were bound to take thought for one another, while the celibate were free to pursue the service of God. Paul admitted that he had no divine warrant for his belief that sexual continence was superior in virtue to conjugal enjoyment. However, his conviction took hold, spread over several centuries, and received general acceptance among the most influential Church authorities of the fourth and fifth centuries.

From these two seemingly irreconcilable principles, the idea of chaste marriage—marriage without marital relations—came to enjoy a surprising popularity for many centuries. The prestige of this peculiar institution was largely attributable to the fact that it was adopted by the councils of the early Church as a desirable solution to the problem of a married clergy, whose sexual purity was commonly seen as desirable to the perfect administration of the sacred rites. It was, however, popular among the laity who saw it as a means of avoiding the burdens marriage imposed, especially upon women who encountered difficulties in attaining a celibate life.

With the institutional and legal reforms of the late eleventh and early twelfth centuries, the anomaly was viewed with increasing disfavor. The imposition of celibacy upon the clergy removed its principal support and thereafter it was discouraged among the laity.

During the first generation, certain persons were evident to whom the administrative and liturgical leadership of the newly established Christian communities had been entrusted. These were married persons whose households served not only as gathering places for Christian worship but as hospices for itinerant or fugitive Christians.[2] As an identifiable clerical class of persons entrusted with the administration of the sacraments emerged, the *Apostolic Constitutions* recommended that the fitness of a clergyman to govern his Church be judged by his success in governing his household and his family.[3] In the late second century, Polycratus of Ephesus could take pride in the boast that he was the eighth man in his family to hold the bishopric in direct succession.[4]

Except for the Pauline command that a bishop should be the husband of one wife, this married clergy was apparently governed by no other law than the ideal of mutual and exclusive love lain down for all Christians. He and his wife and his children could readily be expected to set a model for the lives of their congregation. There is even some fragile evidence that the priest's wife may have been vested with some ecclesiastical functions. A long-persistent tradition has connected the priests' wives with the office of deaconess, which appears in early Church literature, though there is no clear text to prove the argument. This may be the meaning of the mysterious closing phrase in a letter of Gregory of Nazianzus describing the deceased wife of a priest as "truly sacred, truly consort of a priest, of equal honor and worthy of the great sacraments."[5] In any case, it seems safe to assume that many of the subsidiary and nonsacramental administrative functions must have fallen on the marital partners of clergymen, giving them at least an unofficial role in the direction of the early Church.

Marriage, for clergy and layfolk alike, was viewed as a sexual partnership. Rather grudgingly, Paul argued that "It is better to marry than to burn," and advised both partners that in marriage they had given control of their bodies to one another. The duty to guard one another from the temptations of the flesh generally took precedence over all other requirements made for married persons. Nevertheless, the suspicion that sexual indulgence, however licit, was dangerous and faintly reprehensible pervaded Christian thought. "For in setting out beforehand the fear of fornication, he [Paul] surely did not give a precept to those who stood on their feet, but pointed out the bed to such as were falling, lest they should perhaps collapse to the ground."[6] Accordingly, abstinence was often imposed on married persons for penitential reasons.[7] During Lent and at other significant points in the religious year they were advised to refrain from enjoyment of their conjugal rights; Gregory the Great reinforced this principle with a cautionary tale of a young woman who was possessed by a demon while attending the dedication of an oratory, because she had not been able to refrain from her husband's embraces the night before.[8]

If the sexual relationships of married laity were thus subject to suspicion, those of the married clergy posed more tangible problems. Control of the appetites, particularly the sexual appetite, was commonly viewed as a necessary component in the training of God's athletes. Ritual purity, represented by ablutions, fasting, and sexual continence in preparation for certain rites or the observance of sacred seasons, was prescribed in Jewish law, despite its overall adherence to the divine commandment to be fruitful and multiply. Though the Christians readily discarded most of the ritual practices of the parent religion, they preserved a sentiment that the sexual restraints recommended in Leviticus should not be entirely jettisoned.[9] But as Christian sacraments became more clearly defined and as they came to be administered on a daily basis, the demands of ritual purity and the conjugal duty appeared to be irreconcilable. At least the higher echelons of the clergy were partially submitted to some degree of celibacy by interpreting Paul's advice that a bishop should be the husband of one wife as a prohibition against second marriages, effected as law in the third century.[10] Enforcement was not, however, very enthusiastic, as indicated by Hippolytus's criticisms of Callixtus.[11] Moreover, until the fourth century when the Church was legalized by Constantine, all Christians remained under laws penalizing celibacy enacted by the Emperor Augustus.[12]

The abrogation of these laws by the Christian Empire gave free rein to the growing sentiment that communion with God was best achieved by the sexually pure. It was not forgotten that marriage was a good, instituted by God, and the proponents of virginity who suggested otherwise were swiftly accused of heresy. However, it became a standard practice to rank the virtuous in a hierarchy, with married persons bringing up last place.[13] Such views clearly reflected hardly upon a married clergy who monopolized the administration of the sacraments. An attempt was made at the Council of Elvira to impose celibacy on them and to separate married priests from their wives.[14] Mindful, however, of Jesus' command that marriage was indissoluble, the Council of Nicaea rejected a similar decree.[15] The Church looked more favorably upon a compromise proposed by Eusebius that the ordained clergy abstain permanently from sexual relations with their wives.[16] The idea was taken up by Ambrose, who added that men unmarried at the time of ordination should remain single on the grounds that they would celebrate the sacraments daily.[17] Such a suggestion would lay the ground for a celibate clergy while retaining the services of the married.

Among the leading clergy of the fourth and fifth century, there were a number of couples who embraced the Eusebian solution. The letters of Paulinus of Nola disclose a whole community of clerical couples who devoted themselves to the ideal of sexual purity after their "conversion." The close partnership enjoyed by these persons is still evident in Paulinus's praise of another priest's wife, Amanda, "who does not lead her husband to effeminacy or greed but brings you back to self-discipline and courage to become the bones of her husband."[18] Much the same formula was employed by Augustine in a letter to Paulinus praising his wife Therasia.[19]

Such a life, shared in spirit and endeavor but not in body, provided an ideal compromise between the demands of purity and the sanctity of marriage. The true partnership that it ensured the clerical couple was reflected in the occasional designation of these women as bishop-ess, priest-ess, deacon-ess.[20] Some rituals of ordination even conferred a special blessing and habit upon the priest's wife.[21] These clerical proponents of the chaste marriage were, however, an elite. They provided an example that could hardly have been expected to suit the vast majority of the clergy. Nevertheless, in a letter to the bishops of Gaul, Pope Siricius commanded priests to abstain from conjugal relations on the grounds of ritual purity.[22] Leo I did not carry the prescription to the lower orders of the married clergy but commanded that on reaching the diaconate or priesthood, "their carnal unions must become spiritual marriages" retaining conjugal love but not exercising the conjugal right.[23] Similar arguments were advanced by Innocent I[24] and Gregory I[25] and reinforced by local councils in Italy, Spain, and Gaul, where it became common to require the wives of priests to take a vow of chastity at the same time that their husbands did so.[26] One council involved the priests' wives so deeply with their husbands' commitments that they forbade priests' widows to marry again.[27] This was accompanied by a more enforceable vow to occupy separate chambers.[28]

In theory, chaste marriage was promoted as a perfect solution to the problem of a married clergy in a world that looked with suspicion on sexual relations. But in practice it was, not surprisingly, greeted with limited enthusiasm by most of the clergy and their wives. As early as 410, Synesius of Cyrene refused to accept elevation to the episcopate of Ptolemaïs on the grounds that he loved his wife, wanted more children, and scorned the alternative of a clandestine relationship.[29] We know that he was ordained in spite of that answer, but we do not know whether or not he finally consented to separate from his wife. When the saintly Bishop Felix conformed to the decrees of the Council of Orléans that clerical wives occupy separate chambers,[30] his wife refused to believe that he was sleeping alone until convinced by a miraculous apparition.[31] The Council of Gerona felt it necessary to demand that clerical couples who remained together supply witnesses to their good behavior.[32]

By the Carolingian age, reformers could perceive all too many couples who were unable to reconcile the contradictions of married life and priestly purity. Hincmar of Rheims recalled the sorry example of a priest who separated from his wife but provided her with two children during visits purportedly devoted to her religious instruction.[33] Similar complaints of clerical progeny appeared in France, Spain, and Italy.[34] Briefly, the reformers of that period, while still attempting to enforce the old legislation commanding abstinence,[35] resorted to an effort to separate the clergy physically from their wives.[36] Some of the married clergy protested openly and appealed for a dispensation to continue their marital relations.[37] But among the less vocal clergy, the evidence is overwhelming and undisputed that priests continued to live with their wives, in the ordinary married state, until the eleventh century.[38]

Despite its signal lack of success in the creation of a sexually pure clergy, the chaste marriage proved to be an enduring phenomenon throughout those centuries. Rejected by the majority of the clergy, it nevertheless enjoyed a continuing modest popularity among certain segments of the laity. The appeal of the virginal life, or of chastity embraced at some later period, was not lost on the nonclerical population. Before the fourth century, its attainment was to some extent frustrated by the threats of the Augustan marriage laws. In addition, it was the common assumption that men could not readily live and function effectively without the services of women, and that women could rarely live at all without the support of men. The Pauline letters suggest that the solution of "spiritual marriage" may have been attempted by some members of the Corinthian community in the first Christian generation.[39] In succeeding centuries, it is certain that some young, virgin men and women undertook the perilous experiment of sharing a common habitation without undertaking the formalities of marriage.[40] The practice, with its inherent dangers of scandal and worse, provoked the severe censures of Irenaeus of Lyons.[41] Though it was recommended by Tertullian for priests as a substitute for the second marriage he so violently abhorred, he felt obliged to caution that the holy virgin or widow invited to undertake the direction of such a household be of such age and demeanor that she could be considered "beautiful only in spirit."[42] In the fourth century, when the Augustan marriage laws had been abrogated, the Council of Elvira prohibited the practice but to no avail.[43]

In addition to securing the services of women in celibate households, practitioners of the spiritual marriage argued that female virgins stood in need of their brotherly protection. Their vows of consecration were apparently seen as a barrier to the contradictory vows of matrimony. The custom provoked a whole series of censures. In 268, the Council of Antioch condemned Paul of Samosata for corrupting the virgins he had taken into his household.[44] Cyprian of Carthage threatened a deacon with excommunication for sharing his house, and even his bed, with consecrated virgins.[45] Basil of Caesarea maintained that the object of celibacy was to live without women and separated a couple who claimed to have risen above carnal desires.[46] In the fourth century, the continuation of the practice provoked a vitriolic treatise from John Chrysostom.[47] He condemned even the successful couples because they scandalized the world with the sight of "wise women" running to the houses of virgins to assure a gossiping neighborhood that they remained intact. Wisely, he pointed to the suspect perversity of those who courted such frustrated propinquity and complained that the men who undertook these relationships might well have offered their protection to women broken by age and infirmity, of whom there were no lack. In the same period, Aphraphat went so far as to suggest that a consecrated monk would be better off to marry in earnest than to try a spiritual marriage.[48] Martin of Tours refused a monk permission to return to a common life with his wife, though he claimed that they had both progressed beyond thoughts of sex, on the grounds that women did not belong on the battlefield.[49] Gregory the Great retailed the legend of a saintly bishop of Fulda who separated from the nun who ran his household when told of a vision in which a group of demons celebrated his coming damnation because he had already been induced to show her a small sign of affection.[50]

One obvious solution to this problem was the cloistering of the consecrated. In the east, Justinian legislated the most extreme penalties for deaconesses who took "agapetes" into their houses.[51] The full penalties of the laws against adulterers and seducers—even the death penalty that had formerly threatened "adulterous" vestal virgins—might be applied against them. Instead, deaconesses and other consecrated women under fifty years of age were commanded to live with their natural relatives or to enter cloisters.[52] In the west, conciliar legislation sought to prohibit such relationships through the eighth century, while the Carolingian reformers sought to separate the celibate into segregated cloisters.[53] It is possible, nonetheless, that the practice of spiritual marriage may have taken shelter under the cover of the double monasteries (both men's and women's) so popular in these centuries.[54]

The monastic system, however, had not yet been established in the fourth century and even later, when it had spread throughout Christendom, the cloistered option was not always readily available to those who wanted it. Thus the chaste marriage, secure from the most obvious dangers of scandal, provided them with an important option. Several Christian apologists of the second century had remarked the presence of married couples in their communities who had turned to the ascetic life.[55] Hermas claimed that he and his wife had resolved to raise themselves above the level of conjugal life through chastity.[56] Tertullian indicated that, by the third century, the practice was widespread in Africa.[57] But these nonclerical couples were greeted with suspicion and hesitation by their ecclesiastical directors. Ignatius advised that they should keep their relations secret from all but their bishop.[58] Accordingly, Amoun of Nitria and his wife lived together as virgins for eighteen years because they had convinced one another that the priest who had married them had mistakenly administered the ritual for consecration rather than for marriage. At the end of that period, they separated so that they might display their virtue to the world.[59] The model of the chastely married priesthood, Paulinus of Nola, wrote a letter of praise to the Bishop of Rouen for his success in spreading the doctrine in his diocese and encouraging married couples "subject to God who secretly live as brother and sister."[60] Even Ambrose, who so enthusiastically advanced the idea of abstinence for his clerical brethren, recommended it to the laity only as a perfection to be achieved through stages in a married life. He urged married persons to turn to chastity only after reaching a ripe age, when neither might be tempted to relapse.[61]

While displaying such hesitation and caution in their treatment of contemporary chaste marriages, this generation of writers supplied the practice with the most powerful of all models in their treatment of the Holy Family. Early writers had argued that, after the birth of Jesus, Mary and Joseph had enjoyed a normal conjugal relationship that bore fruit in "the brothers of the Lord."[62] But in the fourth century, Jerome dismissed Tertullian, the chief proponent of that position, as "not a man of the church" and stoutly maintained that Mary had never lost her virginity.[63] By the fifth century, Augustine could cite Mary as the first exemplar of consecrated, perpetual virginity. Joseph had become the guardian of her chastity, married only to avoid a scandal in Israel.[64]

Once credence had been given to the chaste marriage of Mary and Joseph, a new definition of marriage could be developed that would separate the sacrament from the conjugal act itself. Ambrose advanced the idea that marriage consisted in the mutual agreement of the couple, not in their carnal copulation.[65] Augustine added that the indissoluble bond of matrimony could not be broken even when the couple had agreed to abstain forever from the carnal enjoyment of the marriage bed.[66] This led Isidore of Seville to conclude that from the moment of betrothal persons must be regarded as already married.[67] Thus the concept of chaste marriage gave rise to some of the basic questions about the nature of marriage that would concern later generations.

The idea of chaste marriage, moreover, was used to disparage traditional marriage in which the couples continued to obey the ancient injunction to be fruitful and multiply. Jerome, for example, argued that those couples who marry and live chastely together sanctify one another by turning their thoughts to God—a logical extension of Paul's remarks that the married must take thought for one another and were therefore less free to take thought for God.[68] Augustine said that to live as married without copulation is the highest perfection of Christianity, citing the example of Mary and Joseph.[69] The perceptive bishop refined this advice in consideration of the dubious motives that might underlie one party's effort to refuse the marital obligation, condemning a man or woman who abstained in order to keep faith with an adulterous lover, cheat the spouse of the conjugal right, or maintain purity in the service of demons.[70]

This last warning introduces a question crucial to the whole question of chaste marriage. When two people have entered into the compact, which of them introduced this fundamental change in its nature? In the case of clerical couples, it was likely to have been the priest, respectful of the demands of ritual purity. Certainly, in later ages, it was the Church itself that tried so unsuccessfully to impose the practice on these couples. When the women agreed, it must have been due to their own spiritual or clerical ambitions. It was understood that, like the marriage vow itself, the vow of chastity within marriage must be taken only by mutual consent. Even the stern Tertullian had stressed that cancellation of marital obligations must depend on the agreement of both partners.[71] Paulinus of Nola reprimanded a young woman who made a vow of chastity without consulting her husband because such an act was contrary to the nature of the nuptial pact.[72] However, he advised the couple to make a temporary trial of the chaste marriage with a view to future commitment. Augustine found it difficult to prevent a young man from seeking release from a vow of continence to reclaim his rights over his wife.[73]

In these nonclerical marriages, the impulse appears to have come from the wife. This was likely a common condition and may explain the hesitation of bishops to encourage the chaste marriage for the laity. Men who sought lives of chastity were most likely to remain free and unmarried, as did most of the proponents of chaste marriage whom we have cited. Augustine, indeed, preferred to continue a relationship with a concubine until he felt able to embrace a life of chastity. Fulgentius, while giving full credit to the mutual quality of the marriage contract that gave the spouses power over one another's bodies, suggested that it might be cancelled by a vow of continence.[74] But once the marriage had occurred, it was the general view that the option was no longer available. Though praising the greater perfection of chaste marriage, Gregory the Great refused to allow a man to leave his wife and children in order to lead a celibate life.[75] Similarly, wifely opposition prevented Sebbi, King of the East Saxons, from entering a monastery until he had begun to suffer from his last illness.[76]

Women rarely had so clear an option. Consecrated virgins continued to be dependent on their families for shelter and support and, even when convents were gradually established in the fifth and sixth centuries, access was severely restricted. Though the laws of Theodosius[77] gave strong support to those who aspired to the pure life, the ability of women to avoid marriage was not very great. A father could no longer bring the forces of the state to bear against her, but he still commanded many means of pressuring a daughter into marriage. Despite her desire to remain a virgin, Saint Macrina was forced into a betrothal. Relying on the Ambrosian view that the exchange of promises, rather than consummation, constituted a marriage, she took advantage of her fiancé's untimely death to proclaim herself his faithful widow and refused to marry "again."[78]

But few young women could count on such a fortuitous resolution to the problem, and some sought to gain their ends by applying pressure to their young husbands when they could not prevail upon their parents. Palladius praised the guile with which Saint Magna preserved her virginity until widowhood freed her from the marriage into which her parents had forced her.[79] On her wedding night, Saint Melania sought to secure her husband's agreement not to consummate their marriage. He was willing to undertake a life of continence only after both of their families had been satisfied by the provision of two children. After Melania had nearly died giving birth to the second child and then lost them both to death, she reopened the question and offered her husband her entire fortune in exchange for her freedom. Cowed by agonies of her second childbirth, he agreed to join her in the ascetic life and they travelled together for some years before separating to enter the cloister.[80] Saint Etheldreda insisted on the preservation of her virginity as a condition for both of her marriages. When her second husband attempted to gain release from his oath, she fled to a convent and was miraculously rescued from her pursuing mate.[81]

For women, the chaste marriage had the clear advantage of relieving them of the burdens of unwanted marriages or from the perils of childbirth present in even a happy relationship. Moreover, the brother and sister model upon which it was based carries with it none of the subjection that Christians always applied to the conjugal relationship. Indeed, a recent investigation of modern, unconsummated marriages concluded that they are frequently characterized by "the immense power that a number of these women apparently exert over their menfolk."[82] Laudable as sexual abstinence might seem to be, the proponents of virginity understood that it released women from their normal inferior status, lifting them to the status of a man.[83] It is unlikely that so disruptive an arrangement would have won much favor in the eyes of the early Christian writers if it had not provided so convenient a solution to the problem of the married clergy. Even in the early period, as we have seen, they encouraged its lay practitioners to keep their vows secret.

Chaste marriages continued to constitute a stumbling block to later legislators in their efforts to define marriage and provide a ready test of its validity.[84] When Carolingian judges applied themselves to an effort to enforce Jesus' command that marriage be made indissoluble, they faced the question of determining whether or not a marriage existed in the first place. Repeatedly, they returned to consideration of the sexual act as the central point. When consummation had occurred, following the customary exchange of promises and other rites, the marriage was uniformly considered to be both valid and indissoluble. Carolingian councils twice prohibited the dissolution of a marriage that had been consummated, even when one or the other spouse had entered into religion.[85]

Occasionally, however, Carolingian judges appear to have been uncertain as to the validity of marriages in which consummation had not occurred. In one instance, Gregory II tentatively wavered in favor of such a solution.[86] In another case, Hincmar of Rheims allowed nonconsummation as a valid reason for annulment when a young man claimed that he had been forced to marry a woman after he had secretly enjoyed sexual relations with one of her relatives. To be sure, Hincmar was anxious to save the man from the threat of committing incest. But, in justifying his decision, he stated unequivocally that the union of the sexes, and nothing else, whether promises exchanged or financial arrangements completed, made a marriage valid.[87]

In the end, however, the tradition within which chaste marriages flourished reasserted itself. Nicholas I attempted to deal with the question of consummation but finally concluded that it was not necessary to validate a marriage.[88] In another case, Hincmar also disallowed the dissolution of a marriage, even though it had not been consummated for two years because of mutual, ineradicable hatred. The husband appealed for relief lest he murder his wife and was told that he was a victim of the Devil's wiles and must return to his wife and persevere in the effort to achieve marital happiness.[89]

One of the most desirable effects of chaste marriage, when applied to clergy, was its sterility. A chastely married clergy would not encumber the Church with the embarrassing claims of the children of priests to property, dowry, office, or support. Had the effort been successful, the Christian community may well have been more than content to continue to benefit from the services of clerical wives without being moved to complain against the burdens they imposed. Conversely, as the dynastic system became ever more clearly organized as a means of imposing regularity on European political institutions in the eleventh and twelfth centuries, the chaste marriages of some lay persons became increasingly intolerable.

We can hardly be surprised at the lack of warmth accorded the dubious piety of Edward the Confessor and his wife who entered into a chaste marriage. It was conceded that Edward had indeed been a saintly man who kept himself physically unsullied throughout his life, but his motives for failing to consummate his marriage with Earl Godwin's daughter were forthrightly impugned by William of Malmesbury. Since the childlessness of the marriage resulted in a succession dispute culminating in the Norman Conquest, we can well understand the chronicler's hesitation to praise its spiritual merits. Indeed, public gossip went so far as to charge the queen with dishonoring her marriage bed, though William granted that she had successfully purged herself by a deathbed oath.[90]

Similarly, Raoul Glaber was hesitant to ascribe the childlessness of the German Emperor Henry II and Cunegonde to their spiritual excellence.[91] Cunegonde's biographer stated unequivocally that their mutual embrace of perpetual chastity was a powerful argument for her canonization.[92] But it is understandable enough why others might have more interest in a secure succession than a monarchy subject to such exalted personal ambitions.

Certainly, the thinking of canon lawyers in these crucial centuries tended strongly in the direction of making marriage and its conjugal responsibilities synonymous. The old Augustinian definition of marriage as a combination of mutual faith, sacrament, and progeny appealed to jurists ever more deeply involved in the real and present questions presented to their courts. Special difficulties, however, remained in reconciling the marriage of Mary and Joseph, a problem that is discussed in greater detail later on in this book.

In general, the path to an unmarried life of chastity was far more readily available to men than to women, whether in the fourth or the twelfth century. In the early medieval period, women had been able to turn to chaste marriage in order to preserve their purity, but the trend of the laws in the Middle Ages was to deprive them of the support to escape the burdens imposed by marriage that they might otherwise have gained from religion. In part, the tendency to make married couples conform to the responsibilities of parenthood was strengthened because the Church ultimately abandoned the ideal of fourth-century clerical couples. Instead, churchmen had come to see the superior virtues of celibacy as an ideal to be monopolized by the clergy. Seemingly in their zeal to secure clerical celibacy, they abandoned the care with which their predecessors had defended the sanctity of the marriage bond. Even at the risk of denigrating a divinely ordained sacrament or even the security of marriage as a protection from fornication, they pressed for an ecclesiastical order of men married to the Church alone. In the eleventh century, clergymen were ordered to dismiss any women they kept in their houses, including their lawfully wedded wives.[93] In 1059, Nicholas II promulgated decrees imposing clerical celibacy, enforced by prohibiting the faithful from attending masses celebrated by priests who retained women in their homes.[94] By 1123, the First Lateran Council was prepared to bring an end to the struggle by annulling the marriages of clergymen.[95] Finally, the Second Lateran Council of 1139 determined that Holy Orders constituted an impediment that automatically invalidated the marriages of clergymen.[96] Even nonclerical persons who had taken the vows of chastity were urged to separate themselves from their spouses and enter the cloister.[97]

Even the unrelenting champion of clerical celibacy, Peter Damian, hesitated to extend the advantages of sexual continence to the laity. When his friend Beatrice of Tuscany informed the Cardinal that she and her second husband had determined to take vows of chastity, he expressed great reluctance to encourage her. He bade her, despite her relatively advanced age, to reconsider the desirability of having further offspring.[98] Similarly, Gregory VII urged his friend and staunch supporter Matilda of Tuscany (Beatrice's daughter) not to separate from her husband, though the marriage had probably not been consummated and had been undertaken only for the political benefits that it would bring to the papacy in its struggle with the German Empire.[99] Though Matilda, throughout her lifetime, was the secular mainstay of the reformed papacy, her admirers were silent on the subject of her probable sexual purity. The Church that was willing enough to accept her final legacy of her vast Tuscan inheritance never praised the apparent sexual restraint that kept her heirless through two marriages.

This generation of the great reformers of the late eleventh and early twelfth centuries still enjoyed the benefits of communion with members of the opposite sex that distinguished the life of the early Church. Through correspondence and frequent meetings, the men and women of the reform movement supported one another emotionally as well as politically. The letters of Damian to the Empress Agnes, with their combination of exalted religious sentiment and extravagant flattery, have even been taken to foreshadow the courtly love poetry of the next century.[100] Gregory VII enjoyed such intimacy with Matilda that he could propose that she and the Empress join him in a crusade to the Holy Land, expressing the hope that the move would ensure their companionship throughout eternity.[101]

Chaste marriage had always been an uncomfortable anomaly in Christian society, a shadowy zone between the world of the procreative, married majority and the celibate elite. It had been encouraged only so long as it might be expected to provide a solution to the problem of a married clergy. But once they had been legally constrained to occupy the unmarried sphere, the laity were increasingly pressured to see the conjugal bed as their proper sphere. Chaste marriages and even spiritual marriages continued to occur, especially among such fringe groups as the Third Order of Franciscans, but they were treated with suspicion and cynicism. Increasingly, the life of the laity was measured by the ordinary norm of marriage and parenthood, and lay women were subjected to those requirements. Concurrently, the clergy were deprived of their wives and their disappearance, whether by design or not, closed an avenue whereby women were indirectly enabled to participate in the ecclesiastical life.

4

The Prostitute in the Early Middle Ages

Vern L. Bullough

One of the assumptions of this book is that there were different attitudes towards sex in the Middle Ages than in the classical period. The change from one area to another, or over time, can be gradual or almost imperceptible or it can be rapid and quite radical. One rather radical change of concern in this chapter is, namely, the difference between traditional Roman and early medieval attitudes toward the prostitute, and how these ideas were disseminated to Christian Europe. While both Roman and medieval writers tended to regard prostitution as a necessary evil, the Roman tendency to look upon the prostitute as a low-status creature, not fit for the company of proper people, was replaced by the medieval tradition of regarding the prostitute as a weak and strayed person who could be saved in spite of herself. Such a change in attitude had implications for the overall view of women, since instead of establishing a dichotomy between the good and bad woman, it recognized that women, like men, could be part good or part bad.

To illustrate Roman attitudes toward prostitution, it is not necessary to dig very deeply into the sources. Horace (d. 8 B.C.) recounts how Cato the Censor gave his blessing to a young man coming from a brothel, since by his visits there he insured that he and other young men who followed his example would not be tempted to tamper with "other men's wives."[1] This might be called the standard male attitude, one often repeated in the U.S. Army during World War II when the chaplain first advised the troops to keep themselves pure, after which the medical officer offered advice on the proper prophylactic measures. There were, however, limits to the Roman toleration, since, when Cato saw the same young man repeatedly leaving the same brothel, he allegedly remarked: "I praised you then, since I assumed you came here now and again, not that you lived here."[2] Cicero (d. 43 B.C.) perhaps summed up the attitude by stating that while male continence might be a worthy ideal, it was difficult to achieve since it was a Roman custom for males to visit prostitutes.[3]

In spite of these rather tolerant attitudes toward prostitution (and the list of references could be vastly expanded),[4] the Romans traditionally were hostile to the prostitute as a woman. Prostitutes were regarded as women different from other women, a fact evident in the vocabulary of prostitution. One of the terms applied to a prostitute was *meretrix*, technically, she who earns; this was regarded as a term of derision since the proper Roman woman did not have an economic existence independent of her men folk. Similarly, the Romans used the term prostitute derived from the verb *prostituo* (to expose publicly), by implication to dishonor or to defame oneself. *Lupa* was both a term for she-wolf and prostitute. It is at least worth a comment that the Roman traditionalists preferred to regard the foster mother of Romulus and Remus as a she-wolf rather than as a prostitute. The list of euphemisms for prostitute could be extended but the implication is the same: the prostitute in Rome was a low-status person, vile, conniving, not suitable for other tasks.

Similar concepts about the prostitute as woman are conveyed in the literature. Propertius (d.c. 16 B.C.), for example, put women into one of two categories, the devoted wife and mother who dedicated her life and energies to her family, or the others, those who took as much from the male as they could get.[5] Latin literature in general is more or less devoid of the kind of joyous celebration of the courtesan so typical of Greek literature. In fact, the courtesan prostitute is usually taken to represent all that is wrong about women. The Clodia of Catullus (d.c. 54 B.C.), the Nemesis of Tibullus (d.c. 19 B.C.), or the Cynthia of Propertius can all be berated for their faults without impugning the good women, the proper wives and mothers.[6] Whenever an author wanted to blacken the reputation of a woman, he portrayed her in sexual terms. Valeria Messalina, the wife of Nero, is a good example of such a portrayal,[7] while conversely her opposite is the legendary Lucretia, who killed herself after being forced to "betray" her husband.[8] Apparently the Roman writers, consciously or unconsciously, followed the recommendation of the poet Lucretius (d.c. 55 B.C.) who held that the best way a man could free himself from any woman was to continually remind himself that physically one woman was like all other women.[9]

The low status of the prostitute is further emphasized by the fact that no woman whose husband, father, or grandfather was, or had been, a Roman knight could be licensed as a prostitute.[10] Women of this class who were judged promiscuous were fined or banished,[11] while men who engaged in sexual relations with such women were liable to charges of unnatural vice *(stuprum)* or of adultery.[12] Prostitutes, regardless of class, were forbidden to approach the temple of Juno for fear that they would pollute it.[13] Roman citizens were prohibited from marrying slaves who had been prostitutes, while Senators were forbidden to marry anyone descended from a woman who had earned her living with her body.[14]

The Germanic law codes expressed similar attitudes and probably represented traditional German attitudes. In the Visigothic kingdom, for example, a judge who through negligence or bribery permitted a prostitute to ply her trade was not only fined thirty *solidi,* but could be given a hundred lashes as well.[15] Women who lived in illegal liaisons or lived immoral lives were to be flogged. Prostitutes received 300 lashes, the highest number given to any crime in the Visigothic code.[16] Prostitutes could have their hair cut off, or if they continued in their ways, they could be sold into slavery.[17] So degrading was the status of a prostitute that even accusing a woman unjustly of prostitution was a punishable offense. In the Lombard code a person found guilty of making an unfounded charge had to pay twenty *solidi.*[18] Similar harsh punishments were given to men who unjustly cut a woman's hair, apparently in the belief that women who had their hair cut were looked upon as prostitutes.[19]

The Church Fathers held more or less the same ideas about prostitution as did the Romans, although they expressed somewhat different ideas about the prostitute. Saint Augustine, for example, found nothing more sordid, more void of modesty, more full of shame than brothels and prostitution; yet if brothels were to be removed from human affairs, he believed that everything would be polluted with lust, a lust at least equal to the act of fornication.[20] Inevitably most Christian writers agreed that, while prostitutes were to be excluded from the Church as long as they continued their profession,[21] prostitution itself had to be tolerated as a necessary evil. In fact, Saint Augustine argued that if prostitutes were not available, established patterns of sexual relationships would be endangered. In his mind it was better to tolerate prostitution, with all of its associated evils, than to risk the perils that would follow the successful elimination of the harlot from society.

In the thirteenth century, Saint Thomas Aquinas threw his weight behind similar concepts. Though agreeing that fornication was sinful, he felt that prostitution could not be entirely disallowed. He compared it to a sewer in the palace: if the sewer was removed, the palace would be filled with pollution; similarly, if prostitution was prohibited, the world would be filled with "sodomy" and other such crimes. While the money paid to a prostitute was used for an unlawful purpose, the giving itself was not unlawful and the woman was entitled to keep what she had received.[22] The medieval canonists wrestled with the problem and came out with answers similar to those of Saint Thomas Aquinas. As James Brundage demonstrates later in this book, medieval canon lawyers regarded sexual intercourse as part of the natural law, although they emphasized that sexual desire could and often did lead to sin. Complicating their view of prostitution was the fact that most of them strongly believed that the sexuality of women differed from that of men, since women had not been created in the image of God as a man was, but out of a rib of man to serve as his companion and helpmate. This lesser creation, so to speak, made women more susceptible to sexual temptations, and their chastity, therefore, was more likely to be suspect. Since women were sexually weaker creatures, great care had to be taken to confine their sexual activities within a properly structured marriage relationship. In such relationships, husbands had a moral obligation to keep their wives sexually satisfied lest they be tempted to stray to other beds.[23] Modesty was the true glory of a woman. By implication, an immodest woman, one who was sexually desirous and ardent, was a whore at heart, though she need not legally be classified as a prostitute as long as she remained faithful to her husband.[24] The woman as prostitute had little social status. In fact, her status was so low that she was not even required to obey the law; this was because she was beneath the law's contempt.[25] She was so base that canonically she was debarred from accusing others of crime; she was also forbidden to inherit property. If charges were brought against her, she was not allowed to answer in person but had to employ a representative to respond for her. Still, the money she received for her body belonged to her. In spite of these attitudes, which in many ways were similar to those of Rome, there was a difference in attitude toward the prostitute herself, and this new attitude had implications for attitudes toward women in general.

The change appears as early as the Theodosian Code (438 A.D.) when the Christian Emperor Theodosius deprived fathers and mothers of their legal right to compel their daughters or slaves to prostitute themselves.[26] During Justinian's administration (527–65), though prostitution was officially tolerated, there was a concentrated effort to curtail the abuses of organized prostitution by banishing procuresses and brothel-keepers from Constantinople.[27] Moreover, motivated by a concern for the poor and helpless who became entrapped in prostitution, the Empress Theodora opened up a convent, *Metanoia* (Repentance), for former prostitutes. During her lifetime more than five hundred women were relocated there.[28] This tradition of helping prostitutes continued throughout most of the Byzantine history. For example, the Emperor Leo VI Wise (886–917) turned a former house of prostitution into a reformatory institution for fallen women.[29] Later the Emperor Michael IV (1034–1041) established a similar institution. According to Michael Psellus,

> Scattered all over the city was a vast multitude of harlots, and without attempting to turn them from their trade by argument—that class of woman is deaf anyway to all advice that would save them—without even trying to curb their activities by force, lest he should earn the reputation of violence, he

built in the Queen of Cities a place of refuge to house them, an edifice of enormous size and very great beauty. Then, in the stentorian notes of the public herald, he issued a proclamation: All women who trafficked in their beauty, provided that they were willing to renounce their trade and live in luxury, were to find sanctuary in this building; they were to change their own clothes for the habit of nuns, and all fear of poverty would be banished from their lives forever, "for all things unsown, without labour of hands, would spring forth for their use" [Homer, *Odyssey*, IX, 108–109]. Thereupon a great swarm of prostitutes descended upon this refuge, relying on the emperor's proclamation, and changed both their garments and their manner of life, a youthful band enrolled in the service of God, as soldiers of virtue.[30]

Underneath this Byzantine concern for the prostitute as a person lay a new attitude toward the woman who happened to be a prostitute. Probably the most significant factor in the development of this compassion is the importance of Mary Magdalene in Christian thought. A one-time harlot, Mary Magdalene became the great example of a converted sinner in the Scriptures. Although the Gospels tell us very little of her background as "a woman of the city, which was sinner,"[31] legends developed that gave her a lengthy and interesting history. A typical one dating from the ninth century portrayed Mary as the widow of a rich landowner in Magdala who had sunk into prostitution after squandering her inheritance on frivolous pleasures. Her equation with prostitution is significant since she is second only to Mary, mother of Jesus, in importance as a female role model in early Christianity. It was Mary Magdalene who first discovered that the tomb of Jesus was empty. She was also the first to witness the reappearance of Jesus. Perhaps because of her influence, the Gospel writers are careful to portray prostitutes as poor and exploited women, more to be pitied than condemned. This portrayal is evident in the dispute of Jesus with the Pharisees when He is reported to have said that harlots would enter the kingdom of God before they did.[32]

This paper is not the place to amplify on the biblical exegesis of the figure of Mary Magdalene or of the prostitute. Rather the point is to emphasize the biblical base for later medieval attitudes. These attitudes were not without ambivalence, since the prostitute usually is seen both as temptress and as a possible convert. An example of the first is the story told by Saint Jerome (c. 342–420) of a young Christian who was punished for his beliefs by being put in the midst of a lovely garden and beguiled by a beautiful courtesan. Fearful that he would not be able to withstand her blandishments, he preserved his faith by biting out his tongue and spitting it in her face.[33] The more usual story, however, is of dedicated missionaries who pretend to be prospective customers of prostitutes in order to convert them. As soon as they found prostitutes willing to leave their life, the young men exchanged garments with them so they could leave immediately.[34] Perhaps from such a venture a courtesan was able to accuse Saint Gregory Thaumaturgus of having been her lover but of refusing to pay her the sum he had promised. Rather than argue with the woman, Saint Gregory paid her what she asked, but his innocence was demonstrated when the woman almost immediately was possessed by a demon.[35]

One of the more popular stories is that of Saint Mary the Harlot. According to the account of Saint Ephraem of Edessa, a hermit ascetic named Abraham found himself the guardian and protector of his seven-year-old niece. Unwilling to give up his ascetic holy life but conscious of his responsibilities to his orphan niece, he solved his dilemma by adding a room to his desert cell in which the young girl could live and which enabled him to observe her through a windowlike opening. The young Mary quickly adapted to her cell, learned passages of Holy Scriptures, prayed, in fact, imitated her uncle in everything he did. Her reputation for holiness grew as she matured into a beautiful woman. Observing the changes in the young woman was a young monk friend of Abraham, who increasingly turned to calling upon Mary for help. He became so enamored of Mary that he set out on a campaign to entrap her. Besieging her to pray for him, he pleaded for help with such fervor that the innocent Mary, ever anxious to assist a troubled soul, consented to leave her cell in order to console him. When she came to her senses, she found that she was no longer a virgin. Weighed down with the anguish of betrayal and unwilling to face her saintly uncle, she set out for the city, where a fallen woman such as she could survive.

Abraham at first failed to note the absence of his niece, since he thought she was engaged in a period of intense meditation. Eventually, when he realized she was missing, he began to ask his infrequent visitors if they knew of her whereabouts. After two years of questioning, he found out she had become a prostitute in Alexandria, whereupon he immediately resolved to rescue her. Casting aside his ascetic garments, he dressed himself in military garb, took a gold piece that a devoted disciple had given him, and headed for the city. When he found Mary, he bargained with her for her services, then proceeded with her to her house. Though Mary at first failed to recognize her uncle, memories of him came back to her since her visitor had an "ascetic smell" similar to her beloved uncle. To cheer her up, her uncle, still unrecognized, ordered a supper for the two, thereby breaking a fifty-year fast. After the dinner, Abraham went with Mary to her cell where he revealed his true identity and begged her to come back with him, assuring her that God would accept her atonement if she did penance. Mary was so overwhelmed that she returned with him to the desert. Her prayers became legendary as did her miracles.[36] So great was her miraculous ability that upon her death she was recognized as a saint.

This story, like that of Mary Magdalene, emphasized the good in the prostitute; it also gives some evidence of the helplessness that women who had lost their virginity might feel. The dedication of the converted prostitute is also emphasized by yet a third Mary, Saint Mary the Egyptian, who achieved sainthood in spite of the fact that she had spent seventeen years of her life as a harlot in Alexandria. Upon her conversion, she isolated herself for another seventeen years in order to purge herself of her sins. During this time she miraculously lived on only three loaves of bread and wild herbs. So holy had her repentance made her that when she made the sign of the cross, the monk Zosimus was able to walk on water. When she did, her body was placed in a lion's cave, but the lion allegedly left the cave in order that her body remain undisturbed.[37]

Saint Afra was another prostitute saint. After her conversion, she was caught up in the Diocletian persecutions at the end of the third century, but so devout had she become that when she was ordered to sacrifice to the pagan idols, she refused. Though taunted by her persecutors with her past life as a whore, she remained steadfast to her new faith, dying as a martyr. Her nude, exposed body was rescued by her mother and three of her former companions in prostitution, Digna, Eunomia, and Eutropia, whom she had converted. They too suffered martyrdom for their act of charity.[38] Saint Pelagia, a *hetaira* of the grand tradition in Antioch, was so beautiful that even the saintly Bishop Nonnus, a most ascetic monk, was moved to remark on her beauty, much to his own discomfiture. After hearing Nonnus preach, Pelagia became converted; he acted as her patron for her baptism. After being baptized, Pelagia left the city disguised as a man, dressed in the tunic and cloak of the blessed Nonnus, which she had borrowed without asking. She ended up in Jerusalem where she became known as the eunuch monk Pelagius, admired throughout the Holy Land for his ascetic habits and holiness. Only after her death was the secret of her sex revealed, whereupon she took her place among the female saints.[39]

Saint Thais was a former Christian turned prostitute, one of many famous courtesans to bear the name Thais. She was reconverted to Christianity by a holy abbot who deliberately paid a fee to enter her chambers in order to convert her. To do repentance for her sins, she had herself walled up in a cell in a convent, in which there was but one small opening through which she received a little bread and water. After living this way for three years, she was thoroughly cleansed of her sins; later, she too became a martyr.[40] The list of prostitute saints could be extended. In fact, the early Christian stories about the famous courtesans are as plentiful as those told by the Greeks, but the Christian stories usually had a moral: the conversion of the lost and forsaken to Christianity and their ultimate salvation. It was stories such as these that inculcated a different attitude toward the prostitute, as a woman to be pitied more than condemned, and as an ever-present possibility for conversion. These stories also emphasized that there was no dichotomy between the whore and other women: all equally were women, and the whore, with conversion, could become like other women.

This moral continued to be emphasized during the medieval period. Hroswitha (c. 932–1002), the Gandersheim nun, for example, retold the story of the prostitute saint Thais whose wondrous beauty was matched only by her horrible impurity. Thais was so evil that she was not satisfied "to ruin herself with a small band of lovers" but sought to "allure all men through her marvellous beauty," to "drag them down with her." Dismayed at the evil success of Thais, the holy monk Paphnutius resolved to save her from her wicked life. Disguised as a would-be lover, he gained admission to her house in order to engage in a dialogue about Christian salvation with her. So successful was he that she converted and entered a convent where she lived the rest of her life, confined to a small cell. Though Thais grieved that she had to attend to all the needs of her body in the cell where there was not one "clean sweet spot" in which she could call upon God, she lived there for three years before "angels led her to paradise."[41]

To institutionalize such ideals, from at least the twelfth century onwards, if not earlier, religious houses were established in Western Europe with the particular purpose of serving as asylums for reformed prostitutes.[42] In 1198 Pope Innocent III urged that all good citizens make every effort to reclaim prostitutes. In 1224 a concentrated effort was mounted to create a special religious order of penitential nuns to harbor reformed prostitutes, and in 1227 Pope Gregory IX gave the highest ecclesiastical sanction to the Order of St. Mary Magdalene, which subsequently established convents in numerous cities. The sisters wore a white habit, from which they were sometimes known as "the White Ladies."[43] Subsequent official patronage and encouragement was given to the Magdalenes by the fourteenth-century popes,[44] and convents for reformed prostitutes, not necessarily affiliated with the Magdalene order, received endowment and support from monarchs such as Louis IX of France.[45] One of the most famous of the Magdalene houses was established in Vienna at the beginning of the fourteenth century. Known as the Soul House, it was organized like a convent, although its inmates were not required to take a vow of either poverty or chastity, and many of the women left the house as brides of respectable citizens in the city. In 1480 the Emperor Frederick III granted inmates of the house the right to sell the produce of their vineyards, although allegedly the women, in order to increase their sales, began selling sex on the side, an allegation that led to their removal from the house, which then was turned over to the Franciscans.[46] See chapter 16 for details.

Another way in which medieval authorities tried to emphasize the redemption of the prostitute was to encourage her to marry. Canon lawyers, however, were wary of this solution, with the result that before being eligible for marriage the reformed prostitute had to do public penance for her sins and obtain a special dispensation.[47] That this was not always done is obvious from the fact that a man who accidentally married a prostitute, believing her to be a chaste virgin, was still legally married; only if she continued to practice her trade could the legality of the marriage be challenged. Still the Church encouraged marriage of prostitutes, and in 1109 Pope Innocent II lauded those men who married harlots in order to reform them and described their actions as not the "least among the works of charity." Those who rescued public prostitutes by marrying them could count on their actions to help in the remission of their own sins.[48]

One of the most interesting endeavors to rescue prostitutes was that advocated by Fulk of Neuilly, better known for his association with the Fourth Crusade. He secured an agreement with the Parisian authorities whereby they would give some 1000 *livres,* and he supplemented this with an agreement with the students at the University of Paris to give an additional 250 *livres,* to each former prostitute who contracted an honorable marriage.[49]

In short, prostitution in the medieval period was a way of life; it was tolerated, even regulated, in most of the areas of Europe, and almost all attempts to eliminate it during the Middle Ages had failed. The Church and the authorities continued to condemn prostitution, but the prostitute herself was not treated so harshly. There was always hope that she would abandon her ways, either through becoming a nun, entering a Magdalene house, or by marrying. In fact, the salvation of a prostitute became a great challenge. This toleration of the fallen woman was inculcated through stories about the saints, through canon law, and through Church pronouncements, some of which appear in later chapters. The result was to weaken the dichotomy between the good and bad woman, so often present in the Roman literature, and in the process, to extend the potential of women, since a prostitute, from being the worst of women, could also become the best of women. In short, in spite of an inherent misogyny, medieval men recognized women as individuals with potential for either good or bad, but even the bad were never regarded as hopeless.

5

Transvestism in the Middle Ages

Vern L. Bullough

The factors that make for transvestism, the desire to dress in the clothes and even assume the role of the opposite sex, are so far little known or little studied. The very term was not coined until 1910,[1] although Havelock Ellis had studied the same phenomenon under the term eonism.[2] Since then there have been several studies,[3] but most explanations have been in terms of psychopathology and have concentrated upon male transvestites. Stoller summed up much of the current thinking on the subject. He felt there was as yet no genetic, constitutional, or biochemical evidence to explain the phenomenon but, nonetheless, male transvestites had several etiological factors in common: (1) the mother's unconscious wish to feminize her little boy, perhaps as an unconscious expression of her own homosexuality; (2) in such cases, the father is either a coconspirator by being silent and passive about the matter or is altogether absent; (3) transvestites themselves suffer from castration anxiety for which they compensate by making themselves into phallic women; (4) transvestism actually is an efficient way of handling very strong feminine identification without the patient having to succumb to the feeling that his masculinity is being submerged by feminine wishes. In effect, it allows him to channel these feelings through his cross dressing and still, when dressed, be acutely aware of the insignia of his maleness, a penis.[4]

Those sociologists who have examined transvestism have done so in terms of deviant organizations[5] but have not attempted to offer a sociological analysis of the phenomenon itself. This chapter argues that Western attitudes towards transvestism have been strongly influenced by status concepts about the role of the sexes. The result has been a differentiation in attitudes concerning women who dressed as men versus men who dressed as women. Women transvestites were tolerated and even encouraged since they were striving to become more malelike and therefore better persons. Male transvestites, on the other hand, were discouraged not only because they lost status, but also because in the past most writers could find only one possible explanation for a man adopting woman's guise, namely, a desire to have easier access to women for sexual purposes. If this explanation has any validity, then it is important that researchers in the field take into consideration historical and sociological as well as psychological variables in their explanation of transvestism.

One of the richest sources for examining Western attitudes and conceptualizing the phenomenon of transvestism are the lives of the transvestite saints. A survey of their lives gives the foundation for Western attitudes, and more than anything else shows the status concepts associated with transvestism inherent in Western attitudes. In theory, Western society has been hostile to transvestism although it has always tolerated impersonation at certain periods or events such as Halloween, carnival days, and masquerade parties. The source of this hostility has been traced to biblical statements, particularly to a passage in Deuteronomy:

> The women shall not wear that which pertaineth unto a man, neither shall a man put on a woman's garment; for all that do so are an abomination unto the Lord thy God.[6]

In spite of the emphasis on women wearing men's clothes, Christianity at least has always been more hostile to men wearing women's clothes. This in part can be explained by medieval Christian attitudes toward women. In general, medieval society adopted the view of the Greek philosophers that women were inferior to men,[7] although Christianity insisted that women as much as men were a special creation of God. This view is perhaps best summed up by the thirteenth-century theologian Saint Thomas Aquinas, who wrote:

> Good order would have been wanting in the human family if some were not governed by others wiser than themselves. So by such a kind of subjection woman is naturally subject to man, because in men the discretion of reason predominates.[8]

Overlying this view of women as creatures who were subordinate to men was a kind of mystic view of the inferiority of the females. This attitude, as it entered into Christianity, was exemplified by the Alexandrian Jewish philosopher Philo who taught that the reason the male was superior to the female was because he represented the more rational parts of the soul, while the female represented the less rational. For him progress meant giving up the female gender, the material, passive, corporeal, and sense-perceptive world, and taking the active, rational male world of mind and thought. The easiest way for women to approach the male level of rationality was for them to deny their sexuality, to remain virgins, and the words virgin, virginity, ever-virginal occur continually in Philo's references to the best kind of women.[9]

It would seem logical then to argue that the female who wore male clothes and adopted the role of the male would be trying to imitate the superior sex, to become more rational, while the man who wore women's clothes, who tried to take on the gender attributes of the female, would be losing status, becoming less rational. This seems to be implied as early as the fourth century by Saint Jerome, who wrote that:

> As long as woman is for birth and children, she is different from man as body is from soul. But when she wishes to serve Christ more than the world, then she will cease to be a woman and will be called man.[10]

A similar concept was expressed by Saint Ambrose, also in the fourth century:

> She who does not believe is a woman and should be designated by the name of her sex, whereas she who believes progresses to perfect manhood, to the measure of the adulthood of Christ. She then dispenses with the name of her sex, the seductiveness of youth, the garrulousness of old age.[11]

The list of similar statements could be much expanded, but the result is to indicate that the Christian Church might well encourage a woman to adopt the guise of a man and live like one in order to attain the higher level of spirituality normally reserved to the male. Whether this was the actual intention of these saintly Church Fathers is doubtful, but there are numerous stories about saintly women who lived and worked as men. Scholars today might argue that many if not all of these saints were legendary rather than real,[12] but folk belief further emphasizes that transvestism among women was not usually punished but admired. There are no male transvestite saints, not only because the male who cross-dressed lost status, but he was also associated with eroticism. This is most evident by an incident reported in the sixth century by the Frankish writer, Gregory of Tours. He reported that during a revolt of some nuns in the convent of Radegunde, the rebellious faction charged the abbess with keeping a man clothed in female garb and pretending that he was a woman in the convent. Everyone knew, they claimed, that he "was most plainly of the male sex; and that this person regularly served the abbess." The charges led to an investigation that found that indeed there was a male nun. He justified his transvestism on the grounds that

He was unable to do a man's work, and for that reason had assumed this garb. As for the abbess, he only knew her by name and had never seen her or exchanged a word with her, inasmuch as he lived a distance of more than forty miles from Poitiers.

This answer did not satisfy the rebellious nuns, who went on to accuse the abbess of lacking holiness since she made men eunuchs in order to keep them around her. At this juncture a physician by the name of Reovalis stepped forward and explained that he had known the male nun as a little boy, when he

> had a disease of the groin and he was regarded as incurable. His mother went to the holy Radegunde and begged her to have the case examined. The saint summoned me, and bade me give all the help in my power. I then cut out his testicles, an operation which in former days I had seen performed by surgeons at Constantinople, and so restored the boy in good health to his anxious mother. I never heard that the abbess knew aught of the matter.[13]

As a result of this testimony the charges against the abbess were finally dropped. The implication remains, however, that the only reason a man might don female garb and live in a convent was to gain sexual satisfaction from the nuns. A woman who dressed as a man and lived in a monastery, however, was assumed to be innocent of any such intentions.

Probably the archetype for the female transvestistic saints is Saint Pelagia. Her story is rather confused and contradictory, probably because her life incorporates several conflicting legends. She is known both as Pelagia and as Margarito and is confused with another Saint Margarita also known as Pelagius. Pelagia, whom we mentioned in the last chapter, was converted by Bishop Nonnus. To escape from Antioch she disguised herself as a male and with the permission of Nonnus, she wore a haircloth undershirt under her male garments. After much travel she found refuge on Mount Olivet, where she assumed the masculine name of Pelagius, and as a man became much admired throughout the Holy Land for ascetic habits and holiness. It was not until after her death when her sex was revealed that she was placed in the pantheon of female rather than male saints. When Pelagius was found to be a woman, her mourners are said to have cried out:

> Glory be to thee, Lord Jesus, for thou hast many hidden treasures on earth, as well female as male.[14]

In the alternate version, Saint Margarita-Pelagius was not a prostitute but a virgin who held marriage in such horror that, after her betrothal, she fled the nuptial chamber in male dress, cut her hair, and took refuge in a monastery under the name of Pelagius. Her qualities of devotion were such that she was elected prior (a male position) of a convent without a single one of the nuns suspecting her true sex. In fact, she acted the part of a man so well that when the portress (door keeper) of the convent became pregnant and accused Margarita-Pelagius of being the father, the charge was believed. After being expelled from the convent, Margarita-Pelagius sought refuge in a cave, living the life of a hermit. Only at her death, when her true sex was discovered, was she proclaimed innocent of the crime of which she had been accused.[15]

A somewhat similar story is told about Marina, the daughter of a Bithynian called Eugenius who had entered a monastery after his wife had died. Eugenius had only been in the monastery a brief period before he began to worry about the welfare of his daughter Marina, whom he had left in the care of a relative. He confided his concerns to his abbot but, in the process of telling the story, changed his daughter into a son, Marinus. The abbot urged him to bring Marinus into the monastery with him, whereupon Marina, with her hair cut, joined him in the monastery, continuing to live there after Eugenius died. One of her jobs in the monastery was to drive a cart down to the harbor to fetch supplies, an act that necessitated she stay over night in an inn. After one such visit a pregnant girl accused Marinus of seducing her, and Marinus, true to the code of the transvestite saints, suffered ostracism from the monastery rather than admit to her true sex. After her expulsion she lived as a beggar at the gate of the monastery, pleading to be readmitted. When her "son" had been weaned, the child was thrust into her arms and she continued to beg with the infant at her side. After some five years of this, the monks at the monastery successfully pleaded with the abbot to readmit Marinus and "his" son. The austerities that Marina imposed upon herself, however, led to her death shortly after her readmission. Inevitably, when the monks came to prepare her body for burial, they discovered her true sex. True to form, the abbot of the monastery was overcome with remorse, while the woman who had falsely accused her became possessed by demons that were only repulsed when the woman confessed her sin and then called upon Saint Marina for intercession in heaven.[16]

Though all of these stories differ slightly, there is enough similarity that the German scholar Herman Usener felt that they, as well as others, were simply Christian survivals of the legend of Aphrodite of Cyprus, in which women sacrificed to the goddess in men's clothing and men in women's.[17] He emphasized that Aphrodite was known also under the names of Pelagia and Marina, which would seem to give some sort of proof to his arguments. Not all scholars, however, accept such identification and Father Delehaye in particular would argue against it.[18] This chapter does not decide one way or another but emphasizes that through such stories female transvestism was given popular sanction in the Christian West. The stories, however, seem to have implications that go beyond mere human interest. For example, in almost all of the stories of transvestite female saints, the woman dons male clothing at a time when she is undergoing a crisis in her life, and transvestism seems to denote a breaking with her former existence. Some of the saints go to extremes at such time, burning their old clothes and even visualizing themselves as males. Saint Perpetua, for example, in a dream saw herself borne into an amphitheater, stripped of her clothes, and changed into a man.[19] Women were encouraged to visualize themselves as attaining the merits of the higher sex.

Apollinaris (in Greek, Syncletica), the daughter of the legendary "Emperor" Anthemius, ran away from home, disguising herself as a man with the name of Dorotheus. Living the life of a simple hermit, she acquired such a reputation as a healer that when her sister was "possessed by the devil," the holy monk Dorotheus was sent for. Dorotheus exercised her miraculous powers to drive out the evil spirits, but "owing to the machinations of the devil," Dorotheus was charged with improper conduct and brought before her own father. In order to prove her innocence, she revealed herself to her father, who immediately realized that the accusations against her were the work of the devil. Dorotheus then retired to the desert where her true sex was only discovered by her fellow hermits after her death.[20]

Athanasia of Antioch represents still another variant of the standard story of the transvestite saints. Athanasia, the wife of Andronicus, a silversmith, was the mother of two children named John and Mary, to whom she was devoted. When John and Mary both died suddenly and unexpectedly on the same day, Athanasia began spending much of her time praying in a neighborhood church. One day she encountered a stranger who assured her that her children were both happy in heaven, but before she could ask more the stranger disappeared. She felt she had seen a vision of Saint Julian the martyr, in whose memory the church in which she was praying was dedicated. When she told her husband of the vision, the two decided to renounce the things of this world. Leaving everything behind in their house with the door standing open, they set out for Egypt to serve under Saint Daniel, famed for his ability to work miracles. Saint Daniel sent Andronicus to the monastery of Tabenna while Athanasia, dressing in men's clothes, became an anchorite. After some twelve years of isolation in the desert, Athanasia decided to make a pilgrimage to Jerusalem. During her travels she fell in with another monk, actually her husband Andronicus, who was also making the pilgrimage. The two performed religious exercises together, visited the holy places together, and became so attached to each other that when they reached the place where they had met on their way to Jerusalem, they were reluctant to be parted. Together they were admitted to a monastery near Alexandria where they were assigned cells near each other. Here they joyously fulfilled their monkish duties until Athanasius (her male name) felt death approaching, whereupon she began to weep. When asked why she was weeping when she was about to go to God, she said she grieved for her fellow monk Andronicus who will "miss me." The monks were asked to give Andronicus some writing of hers, which they did, and then

Andronicus, her friend and companion, suddenly realized that his friend Athanasius was really his wife.[21]

There are still others whose stories have only slight variations: Saint Eugenia,[22] Euphrosyne,[23] Saint Theodora,[24] and Saint Anastasia Patricia.[25] In two other cases the transvestic experience is only incidental and temporary, Saint Thecla[26] and Saint Natalia.[27] The transvestic saints exist not only in the early Christian Church but also throughout the medieval period. Perhaps the most famous of the later medieval saints is Saint Hildegund (1188), who is the subject of many conflicting accounts. She is usually portrayed as the daughter of a knight of Neuss on the Rhine who, after the death of his wife, decided to make a pilgrimage to the Holy Land. Unable to find anyone with whom he could leave his twelve-year-old daughter Hildegund, he solved the problem by dressing her as a boy, calling her Joseph, and taking her with him. The two traveled together to Jerusalem where the knight died. Before his death he managed to commend a fellow knight to care for and protect his "son," but the protector first robbed the "boy," then deserted him at Tyre. Somehow Hildegund, still masquerading as Joseph, managed to find her way back to Europe. On her return she (still as Joseph) became a servant to an old canon of Cologne, accompanying him on a visit to the pope in Rome. Again she went through a series of extraordinary adventures that seemingly ended with her being condemned to death as a supposed robber. She proved her innocence by undergoing the ordeal of the red hot iron, but she then fell into the clutches of the robbers who actually hanged her. Their technique was so slipshod that Hildegund-Joseph was cut down before she expired. After finally meeting with the pope, she returned to Germany where she entered a monastery at Schonau, remaining there until her death. Only then was it discovered that the famous monk Joseph was actually a woman.[28] In spite of the romantic insertions, the story is believed to contain an essential element of truth.

Another variation of the legends of the transvestite saints is those of bearded female saints of whom the most famous is Uncumber of Wilgefortis. According to tradition, Wilgefortis was one of septuplets (some would say nontuplets) born to a non-Christian ruler of Portugal and his Christian wife. Wilgefortis early decided to devote herself to Christianity by remaining a virgin, but her father had different ideas. When her betrothal to the king of Sicily was announced, Wilgefortis protested to her father, but he ordered her to marry anyway. In desperation, after praying for help, Wilgefortis found her prayers answered by the sudden growth of a long, drooping mustache and a silky, curling beard. In spite of this disfigurement her father pushed on with the marriage plans, but when the king of Sicily managed to see his future bride without her veil, he refused to proceed with the marriage. In a fit of rage her father then had her crucified. The story has been described as having the "unenviable distinction of being one of the most obviously false and preposterous of the pseudo-pious romances by which simple Christians have been deceived or regaled."[29] In spite of this, Wilgefortis was much venerated under a variety of names, usually derived from the term *Liberata,* the deliverer. Thus, in France she became *Livrade,* in Spain *Librada, Debarras* at Beauvais, *Ohnkummer* in Germany, *Ontcommer* in Flanders, and Uncumber in England. Cumber, possibly derived from the German *kummer,* meaning trouble, is now an archaic form, although the word encumber and its antonym disencumber is still used. At any rate, in England Uncumber became the patron saint of married women who wanted to rid themselves of their husbands.[30]

Uncumber is not alone in the bearded-saint category. There are at least two others. Saint Galla, according to the legend, had been left a widow after only a year of marriage and, though she was young and healthy, she refused to remarry because she felt that though matrimony "always begins with joy," it "ends with sorrow." Her physicians warned her that if she did not marry again she would grow a beard, but she refused. When her beard grew she joined a band of religious women who lived close to the Basilica of St. Peter and spent their lives taking care of the poor and needy.[31] The third bearded saint, Paula, a virgin of Avila, fled from a suitor she did not want. In desperation she threw herself at the foot of a crucifix, imploring Jesus to disfigure her. Her prayers were answered so rapidly that her suitor passed by without noticing her, disguised as she was with a full beard.[32]

The most famous transvestite in the medieval period, and the one who perhaps has caused the greatest anguish to Catholic historians, is the legendary Pope Joan, who supposedly ruled under the name of John Anglicus.[33] Several thirteenth-century chroniclers wrote about her life in great detail since, during much of the later medieval period, her existence was accepted as fact. A statue of her was included among the popes in the Cathedral of Sienna in the fourteenth century, while in the fifteenth century John Hus the Bohemian heretic reproached the delegates at the Council of Constance (1415) for allowing a woman to be pope. In the sixteenth century, when her existence was seriously disputed, she became relegated to legend rather than history. Occasionally, however, even today she has her supporters, although few in the scholarly world would now accept her existence.

The legend is so complicated that it seems difficult to believe that people were convinced of its authenticity, but believe they did. Though there are various forms of the legend, Joan is usually said to have been born in England (hence the title Anglicus that is often included in the legend). As a child she was taken by her father, a learned man, to Mainz, where she was taught to read and write. While in Mainz she fell in love with a monk from nearby Fulda, Ulfilias by name, and with his help she disguised herself as a man in order to enter the monastery. Later she (still in men's dress) and Ulfilias traveled together as pilgrims to Athens, where they began to study philosophy, theology, holy and humane letters. They stayed in Athens for ten years, acquiring great reputations as scholars. The sojourn came to an end with the death of Ulfilias, whereupon Joan decided to return to Mainz by way of Rome. When she visited Rome some of her former classmates urged her to lecture there, which she did with great success. As her reputation spread she rose rapidly in the Church hierarchy, becoming first a notary, then a cardinal, and on Pope Leo's death in the 850s, pope under the name of John VIII, Anglicus. Unfortunately she still had a woman's heart, which left her always grieving for her beloved Ulfilias. This made her susceptible to the charms of a Spanish Benedictine monk by the name of Bonaventura, who looked much like her dead lover. Bonaventura took advantage of her, causing her to become pregnant. She gave birth to a child while riding in the papal procession, whereupon she died. One version has her child becoming pope later, under the name of Adrian III. A vast amount of scholarly research has been expended on searching out the history of the period, and this chapter is not the place to examine it in detail. The point to emphasize is that there seems to be no real hint of censure for her donning of the male clothes, and her downfall came about not because of her transvestism but because of her womanly weakness. The legend has also been used to justify an equally fallacious legend that since her time all popes have had to prove they were males by sitting in a special chair.

None of the women so far discussed have basically assaulted what men regarded as their prerogatives. Pope Joan perhaps came the closest but, in the final analysis, she proved no match for the "superior" male. When women attempted to meet men as equals, however, they were in trouble. This appears most obviously in the account of Joan of Arc, since her transvestism was one of the major reasons for her execution. In the original complaints against Joan it was charged that she had

> a male costume made for her, with arms to match. . . . When these garments and these arms were made, fitted and completed, the said Jeanne put off and entirely abandoned woman's clothes; with her hair cropped short and round like a young fop's, she wore shirt, breeches, doublet, with hose joined together and fastened to the said doublet by twenty points, long leggings laced on the outside, a short mantle reaching to the knees, or thereabouts, a close cut cap, tight fitting boots and buskins, long spurs, sword, dagger, breastplate, lance, and other arms in the style of a man-at-arms, with which she performed actions of war and affirmed that she was fulfilling the commands of God as they had been revealed to her.[34]

Later the various charges against her were summarized in twelve articles, two of which dealt with transvestism, as did two of the six admonitions directed against her. When Joan recanted she promised not to wear male clothing. It was her resumption of male dress that led to her execution. When asked why she had resumed it, Joan answered that

> She had taken it of her own will, under no compulsion, as she preferred man's to woman's dress. She was told that she had promised and sworn not to wear

man's dress again and answered that she never meant to take such an oath. Asked for what reason she had assumed male costume, she answered that it was more lawful and convenient for her to wear it, since she was among men, than to wear woman's dress.[35]

After her execution when her trial for rehabilitation took place, it was stated that she had been forced to assume the male dress. It was claimed that when she had arisen in the morning she found that her woman's clothes had been taken away and only her male clothes left behind. She had asked her jailers for her woman's clothes, since she knew the male costume was forbidden her, but they refused to give her clothes to her. She remained in bed until noon when she put on the male garments in order to answer the call of nature. Though the resumption of male dress was not the only reason for her being declared relapsed, since politically the English felt they had to execute her, at least in this one respect her relapse appears to have been engineered.[36] Joan, however, is different from the other transvestite saints in that she never disguised her sex but insisted on wearing men's clothing. Obviously, for a woman to assume a male guise to become more holy was permitted, but to compete with men on masculine grounds, such as warfare, was not permitted.

Compared to female transvestism, male transvestism was nearly nonexistent, but it was tolerated under two conditions: when there was only an illusion of the female, and when the male in drag was performing a function that no proper woman could do. Status loss was tolerated and encouraged when society might otherwise have been threatened. The most obvious place for such impersonation was on the stage as drama began to revive in the later Middle Ages. In Greek times, most of the women's roles had been acted by men, but the Romans had been much more open-minded on the subject, even allowing women to portray themselves. Actresses, however, were often synonymous with prostitutes, while the theater was equated with the brothel by many Christian writers, who strongly condemned it. Though such condemnation did not entirely eliminate drama in such areas as Constantinople, and plays continued to be written in western Europe by such people as the nun Hrotswitha in the tenth century, professional acting temporarily disappeared in western Europe.[37]

The key forces in the development of modern drama were the medieval mystery play, emphasizing the passion of Jesus, and the morality play, emphasizing the saints' lives. Since these plays were performed in the Church, most of the actors were drawn from the ranks of priests or would-be priests. This tradition continued on well beyond the medieval period, and occasionally we even get glimpses of some of the actors. This is the case with a young barber's apprentice at Metz who is said to have performed the role of Saint Barbara so

thoughtfully and reverently that several persons wept for pity; for he showed such fluency of elocution and such polite manners, and his countenance and gestures were so expressive when among his maidens, that there was not a nobleman or priest or layman who did not wish to receive this youth into his house to feed and educate him; among whom there was a rich widow . . . who wanted to adopt him as her heir.[38]

The youth's reputation as a female impersonator was short-lived because the next year, when he acted the part of Saint Catherine, his voice had changed and the audience was not so impressed. The young man then abandoned his acting career and went off to Paris to study for the priesthood.

Females were not entirely excluded from the mystery or morality plays since there are occasional references to them. In general, however, it was not considered proper for a women to exhibit herself; in most of the plays men kept a monopoly. In the beginning when the priests and acolytes had been the only actors, it was out of the question that women share in the performance. As the more secular plays developed, such as the farces, the actors for the most part were vagabonds, outcasts who traveled around the country. Few women appeared in these companies either. This meant that men almost exclusively played the woman's role, an action for which they were not condemned but praised. The organized minstrel companies were also usually all male[39] until the sixteenth century in Italy, when women began to appear as characters in plays portraying themselves. From surviving references it is almost possible to trace the replacement of men by women in the women's parts. For example, in Lyons, the first professional actresses appear in 1548.[40] In general, the movement to use women spread from Italy to France, and thence to Spain and eastward on the continent until the movement reached England. It was not until the seventeenth century that the English fully accepted women playing women's parts. Even then, however, many of the female parts were still enacted by men. As late as the seventeenth century, Nicolo Barieri wrote that he would not follow the custom of having boys play the part of women or young girls because they did not know how to dress or carry themselves. Inevitably, he said, they are dressed at home by their women or "flirting servant-girls" who frequently make fun of them. Then

those whose senses are not calmed by age or by assiduous work may easily become vain and conceited for thus disguised in female attire, these children go out and present themselves in the town, chatting and joking with everybody, and they arrive at the theater in an untidy, disorderly state, so that their friends or teachers have to comb their hair again, paint them afresh, and arrange their collars and ornaments. If only they arrive in time, one must be contented.[41]

Most of the traveling companies continued to include only one or two females in their entourage, making it necessary for men to play most of the female parts until well into the sixteenth century. In sum, the prohibitions against transvestism, which seem to have been socially more enforced for males than for females, did not apply to the stage because society put a higher value on women keeping their place in society than they did realism on the stage. Here again, transvestism was utilized to emphasize a higher virtue in society.

How much then did medieval society move against transvestism? Apparently very little, although, obviously, female impersonators offstage would be frowned upon because they lost status. Nevertheless, even here medieval society allowed an outlet for those men or women who occasionally liked to change roles in the various medieval carnivals. Few of these have been studied in detail, in part because the surviving materials on them are so difficult to deal with, but in Nuremberg we know that there were a number of male dancers who wore feminine masks and probably dressed as women during the Schembart carnival. In fact, it seems so common that one authority has said that disguising as the opposite sex is a custom that seems "peculiar to all carnivals." Some of the carnivals were restricted to women or to men, and apparently each dressed in the clothes of the opposite sex. A standard feature of the Nuremberg carnival was the Wild Woman, probably a man impersonating a woman, who appears in several illustrations of the fifteenth century.[42]

Transvestism in theory might well have been prohibited by the medieval Church, but in practice the Church did not seem to be too concerned about it, providing it took certain socially desirable forms. Under such circumscribed conditions it was institutionalized. Only when it went beyond tolerated levels and threatened the status quo, as happened with Joan of Arc, or might have had too much erotic appeal, as in the case of a man disguising himself as a woman in order to live in a convent and sleep with the nuns, was there reaction to it.

If this analysis is correct, then the root cause of Western hostility to transvestism should not be found so much in the biblical prohibition, but in status loss. This explains why there are so few female transvestites in psychological literature, since society in fact encourages women to assume male roles as a sign of their superiority to other women and does not regard such women as abnormal. Only when they threatened the male establishment by taking too overt a masculine role have they been ostracized in the past; until then, they were accepted. By implication then, if an undercurrent of status loss in assuming a woman's role still prevails in Western society, and studies of women's occupations such as nursing would indicate that it does,[43] then we must also take into account a desire for status loss and inability to adjust to the male role as a possible explanation for male transvestism today.

6

The Sin against Nature and Homosexuality

Vern L. Bullough

The concept that certain sexual activities were against nature developed during the early Middle Ages and was based upon both scriptural references and philosophical assumptions. Once established, such a belief became a dominant factor in forming Western attitudes about sex not only in the religious sense but also in a legal sense, since what ultimately was defined as a "sin against nature" also came to be regarded as a "crime against nature."[1] Though homosexuality was considered to be against nature, so were a number of other sexual activities.

Basis for the medieval belief is derived from the Pauline Epistle to the Romans, where it is reported that God had given up on some idolatrous pagans who in their lust had dishonored their own body:

> Who changed the truth of God into a lie, and worshipped and served the creature more than the Creator, who is blessed forever. Amen. For this cause God gave them up into vile affections: for even their women did change the natural use into that which is *against nature;* and likewise also the man, leaving the natural use of the woman; burned in their lust one toward another; men with men working that which is unseemly, and receiving in themselves that recompence of their error which was meet.[2]

Modern biblical scholars are not certain of the meaning of the passage. Some have contended that the exchange of "natural use" for "unnatural" was aimed at anal intercourse within marriage, others that it included coitus *interruptus,* and others that it was aimed specifically at homosexual activities.[3] The subject of this chapter is not the debate among biblical scholars, but the use of nature as a criterion for right action. Such a usage assumed that man by observation of the world around him could discover the basis for right conduct, a concept that had been an essential part of the teachings of the Stoic and neo-Platonic philosophers contemporary with the emergence of Christianity and discussed in chapter 1. Inevitably many of the early Church Fathers turned to these philosophers for an understanding of what sexual activities were contrary to nature.

Among these philosophers were the group known as the Stoics, who had used nature as a guide for conduct and had assumed that the natural law could be discovered through the reasoning process. The Stoics had also taught that men should be rationally self-sufficient, not dependent upon the body, if only because bodily activities in themselves were so irrational.[4] Inevitably, the Stoic emphasis on nature, virtue, decorum, and freedom from excess proved attractive to the formulators of Christian doctrine who incorporated these concepts into their interpretation of the ideal Christian life style.

As far as sex was concerned, the Stoic emphasis on self-sufficiency and moderation was viewed as a justification for a belief that marriage was only allowed because it served to propagate the race. This meant that intercourse for pleasure was not only morally reprehensible but also contrary to reason and nature since it did not lead to offspring.[5]

Similar concepts appeared in the teachings of those neo-Pythagoreans and neo-Platonists centered at Alexandria. Philo, the Jewish philosopher and one of the most influential of the group, may be used as illustration. While accepting the traditional Jewish belief in the divine command to procreate and replenish the earth, Philo also held that sexual intercourse could remain blameless only if the goal of the husband and wife was procreation of offspring. Males who mated with barren women were deserving of reproach; in their seeking after mere pleasure they destroyed "the procreative germ with deliberative purpose" and by so doing acted contrary to nature.[6] Perpetrators of such acts were bad husbandmen who let the "deep-soiled and fruitful fields lie sterile" and spent all their time and activity on "soil from which no growth" could be expected.[7] Philo's beliefs were echoed by others.[8]

When Christian writers turned to the subject of sexual intercourse, inevitably they looked to their pagan predecessors for guidance. Generally a three-pronged analogy with nature came to be favored. In the first category the sexual processes were compared to the sowing of a field. In the second sexual behavior in animals was compared with that of humans, while in the third there was an attempt to determine the natural functional structure of the organ and accepting as natural what was self-evident. In each case, as John T. Noonan has pointed out, what constituted natural was selectively chosen.

An agricultural phenomenon was considered where human effort was completed by physical forces; the example of human beings damming a river to prevent a flow was not used as an example of "nature." Not all animal behavior was found appropriate to follow; the hyena, for instance, popularly supposed to have a set of organs serving a sexual but not a generative purpose, was an example to avoid. The human sexual organs function for a variety of purposes; some of them were "unnatural."[9]

In effect, the appeal to nature was a teaching device used to reinforce theoretical assumptions. It was not really based upon observations of what took place in nature since anything contrary to the preconceived notions was ignored. Procreation was the chief criterion for judging whether sexual activity was natural or unnatural, and anything that did not lead to procreation was regarded as unnatural. Thus, Christians, according to Justin Martyr, married only for the purpose of bringing up children. Otherwise they abstained from marriage and were completely content.[10] Clement of Alexandria added that those men who intended to beget children should approach their wives with a chaste and controlled will;[11] to engage in intercourse for purposes other than procreation was to do injury to nature.[12]

Many of the Church Fathers with such absolutistic positions were celibate and unmarried but even the married Fathers such as Tertullian agreed. Tertullian wrote that those "frenzies of passions" beyond the laws of nature should be banished from the shelter of the Christian Church because they were such monstrosities.[13] Inevitably, the codes of conduct such as the third-century *Didascalia (Apostolic Constitutions)* incorporated the idea that Christians abhorred "all unlawful mixtures," and that all activities "contrary to nature" were "wicked and impious."[14]

The only disagreement among the Fathers was whether simple fornication in itself was unnatural. Saint John Chrysostom, for example, held that while fornication was a sin, it at least was natural. Chrysostom also adopted a double standard: he put sexual activity by women in a lower category than men since women by their nature ought to have more shame than men.[15] Any uncertainty about what constituted unnatural sex was settled by Saint Augustine, the key formulator of the Western concepts of "unnatural" sexuality. Augustine saw nothing rational, spiritual, or sacramental in the act of intercourse. He admitted that since Jesus had sanctioned marriage, sexual intercourse in marriage must also be accepted but only when and if it led to offspring.[16] Although he recognized that intercourse existed for other purposes, he was not happy about it.

> For what food is to the health of man, intercourse is for the health of the race, and both are not without carnal pleasure, which, however, when modified and put to its natural use with a controlling temperance, cannot be passion. However, what unlawful food is in sustaining life, this is the intercourse of fornication or adultery in seeking a child; and what unlawful food is in the excessive

indulgence of stomach and palate, this is unlawful intercourse in a passion seeking no offspring; and what is immoderate appetite for some as regards lawful food, this is that pardonable intercourse in spouses.[17]

He further stated:

For although the natural use, when it goes beyond the marriage rights, that is, beyond the need for procreation, is pardonable in a wife but damnable in a prostitute, that use which is against nature is abominable in a prostitute but more abominable in a wife. For, the decree of the Creator and the right order of the creature are of such force that, even though there is an excess in the things that have been granted to be used, this is much more tolerable than a single or rare deviation in those things which had not been granted . . . when a husband wishes to use the member of the wife which has not been given for this purpose, the wife is more shameful if she permits this to take place with herself rather than with another woman.[18]

Augustine was particularly opposed to those sexual acts which he said had been committed in Sodom and which

ought everywhere and always to be detested and punished. If all nations were to do such things they would (equally) be held guilty of the same crime by the law of God which has not so made men that they should use one another in this way.[19]

Nowhere, however, did Augustine define the acts committed in Sodom.

Corresponding with the attempts of the Church Fathers to put limits on man's sexuality was a similar movement among secular officials led by the early Christian emperors. One of the earliest documented enactments dealing with "deviant" sexual practices is that of Constantius and Constans in 342 that made those men who marry "in the manner of a woman, a 'woman' about to renounce men," subject to "exquisite" punishment.[20] In 390 the Emperors Theodosius, Valentinian II, and Arcadius II prescribed burning for "all persons who have the shameful custom of condemning a man's body, acting the part of a woman's, to the sufferance of an alien sex. . . ."[21] These laws seem to refer to homosexuality with some degree of specificity, but such specificity soon disappears to be replaced by the concept of acts against nature. One of the *Novels* of Justinian, for example, referred to certain types of men who

seized by diabolical incitement, practice among themselves the most disgraceful lusts, and act contrary to nature, we enjoin them to take to heart the fear of God and the judgment to come and to abstain from such like diabolical and unlawful lusts, so that they may not be visited by the just wrath of God on account of these impious acts, with the result that cities perish with all their inhabitants. For we are taught by the Holy Scriptures that because of like impious conduct cities have indeed perished, together with men in them.[22]

Any doubt about whether the reference to Sodom was meant to include homosexuality is removed by a later enactment *de stupro masculorum* (defilement of males) in 544 where such activity is equated with the sins of Sodom. Though the term contrary to nature is not used in this second statute, it is stated that such activity is regarded as so base and criminal that even brute beasts avoid it, perhaps a close approximation to the same concept.[23]

Though the Justinian legislation is important for its influence upon laws of the later medieval period, more immediately important in the West as far as secular legislation is concerned were the law codes of the various Germanic groups. The earliest of these laws does not include any concept of a crime against nature and in fact ignores almost all sexual activities except for adultery, a crime against property. As the Christian influence becomes more pronounced, the hostility to sex becomes more evident, as demonstrated by the Visigothic laws dating from seventh-century Spain. Under King Chindaswinth (c. 642–53) special laws were enacted that for the first time include a reference to those males who lie with other males,[24] but without including any reference to nature. By the time of King Egica (687–701) this oversight had been remedied and a special canon was enacted providing for the degradation of clergy found guilty of committing the "vile practice against nature with other males."[25] By the time of the Carolingian legislation the sin against nature had been extended to include all sexual activities not leading to procreation.[26]

The growth of this idea can be seen in the penitential literature that underwent considerable change in its definition of sin and the importance ascribed to various sins.[27] Generally, the earliest penitential literature was quite specific about sexual sins but gradually the sin against nature was extended until it became a catch-all category. In fact, the earliest literature was so blunt about sexual activities that some of our scholarly predecessors were quite embarrassed about the whole matter. Plummer, the Victorian who edited Bede, for example, gave thanks that he was not compelled to believe that Bede had anything to do with the penitential literature. He consoled himself with the belief that the penitential book attributed to Bede could not possibly have been written by him simply because Bede, as a proper gentleman, would have refused to discuss such topics.

The penitential literature is in truth a deplorable feature of the medieval Church. Evil deeds, the imagination of which may perhaps have dimly floated through our minds in our darkest moment, are here tabulated and reduced to a system. It is hard to see how anyone could busy himself with such literature and not be the worse for it.[28]

Such a reaction is not confined to the Victorians but appears in slightly different form in later medieval writers. This is because there was a difference in intent between the sexual descriptions in the early penitentials and the later ones. The early writers regarded themselves as preparing handbooks for the physicians of the soul, while the later ones also began to be concerned that specific descriptions of sexual activity might well encourage the penitents to discover activities that they had not known before. Though the early penitential writers were not aware of such difficulties, they felt the confessor had to probe the hidden recesses of the human mind, just as the physician had to probe the hidden part of the human body.

> For no one can raise up one who is falling beneath a weight unless he bends himself that he may reach out to him his hand; and no physician can treat the wounds of the sick, unless he comes in contact with their foulness. So also no priest or pontiff can treat the wounds of sinners or take away the sins of their souls, except by intense solicitude and the prayer of tears. There it is needful for us, beloved brethren, to be solicitous on behalf of sinners, since we are "members one of another" and "if one member suffers anything, all the members suffer with it."[29]

The penitential that went into the greatest detail was that promulgated by the *Synod of the Grove of Victory* (c. 547), whose author(s) gave different penances for adultery, incest, copulation with animals, and various kinds of other sexual activity. *Coitus in ano* was punished by a four-year penance, *coitus in femoribus* three years, and *coitus in manu* two years, although there was no distinction between homosexual or heterosexual partners.[30] Saint Columban (543–615), in a penitential attributed to him, urged that clerics committing sodomy be forced to undergo a ten-year penance—the same as if they had committed murder. Laymen engaged in sodomitical activity were to do penance for only seven years.[31] The most specific listing of possible sexual acts in the early penitentials is in that attributed to Cummean Fota (the Long), a possibly legendary seventh-century Irish abbot. The writer, whoever he was, included a discussion of oral-genital contacts, bestiality (a less serious sin), interfemoral intercourse (either between members of the same or opposite sex), adultery, nocturnal emissions, and *coitus in ano*. Also included is a section on the sinful playing of boys.[33]

At first the penitentials did not categorize sins, but ultimately the belief in seven cardinal sins was adopted by the penitential writers, whereupon sexual sins were classified in the seventh category under lust or lechery.[34] Agreement on classification did not lead to agreement on penances, which varied so much from penitential to penitential that Peter Damiani (1007–1072) was aroused to wrath over the contradictions. In his *Liber Gomorrhianus* he tried to bring some order to the system by classifying sexual sins in a kind of ascending order of sinfulness beginning with masturbation, followed by mutual masturbation, then interfemoral connection, and finally sodomy, defined as *coitus in ano*.[35] All these activities came under the general classification of sins against nature. Damiani believed sodomy was the worst of the sins because it implied lust for lust's sake, and once the biblical sodomites had turned to sodomy, they performed all sorts of other vile acts upon themselves and others.[36] Peter addressed his treatise to Pope Leo IX (1049-54), the only ecclesiastical official whom he believes had both the power and wisdom to deal with the problem. Damiani emphasized that the problems he discussed were shameful topics but argued that he had to discuss them for if "the physician shrinks from the plague poison," no one else would be there to apply the remedy. Pope Leo accepted the dedication of the work to him, commended Peter for raising the arm of the spirit against obscene license, but also emphasized that it was necessary for a pope to season justice with mercy. This made him reluctant to accept Peter's assessment of the measures required to stamp out such activity.[37] Leo also cautioned that not all sins against nature were equally sinful and considerable investigation was needed to document any charge. Only those clerics who proved to be hardened in their practice deserved maximum penalties.[38]

Peter, nonetheless, by questioning the contradictions in the penances, had raised an issue that no longer could be ignored. Particularly important in formulating new standards was Ivo, Bishop of Chartres (1091-1116).[39] Ivo, however, by adopting the Augustinian formula of using a "member not granted for this" as a definition for unnatural intercourse, helped perpetuate the ambiguity that some of the penitential writers had labored to correct. Ivo wrote that

> a use which is natural and lawful in marriage is unlawful in adultery. To act against nature is always unlawful and beyond doubt more flagrant and shameful than to sin by a natural use in fornication or adultery, as the Holy Apostle contends as to both men and women.[40]

In effect, almost everything is "unnatural intercourse" to Ivo. As John T. Noonan has pointed out, Ivo covered not only the use of the unnatural parts of the body for intercourse but included coitus interruptus and masturbation. The effect of the passage was to give legal sanction to the condemnation of all intercourse in which there was not the possibility of conception.[41] Though the *Decretum* of Burchard in the early eleventh century was somewhat more specific,[42] it was the ambiguous concepts of Ivo that were carried over into Gratian, the Camaldolese monk who completed his *Concordia discordantium canonum* in about 1140 and to whom posterity has given the title of "Father of the Science of Canon Law."[43] Gratian, conceiving his work as a universal treatise on the institutions and problems of canon law, based it upon his researches into Roman law, canons of the Church Councils, particularly those of the fourth and fifth centuries, papal and royal ordinances, biblical, liturgical, patristic, and penitential texts. When he came to the question of sexual intercourse, Gratian, following the example of Ivo, relied upon Saint Augustine. What were "acts against nature?" Augustine said they were those acts committed in Sodom that were transgressions of the command to love God and one's neighbor.[44] In *Contra Jouinianum,* a pseudo-Augustinian work Gratian believed to have been written by Augustine, acts *contra naturam* were described as always unlawful and without doubt more shameful and filthy than fornication and adultery;[45] still, just exactly what constituted the sexual sins against nature remains somewhat ambiguous in spite of the distinctions made between the levels of sexual sins. Gratian wrote that the evil of adultery surpassed that of fornication but was in turn surpassed by incest, since it was worse to sleep with one's mother than with another man's wife. The worst sin of all, however, was that which was done contrary to nature, defined in the Augustinian sense as a man using a member of his wife not conceded for that purpose.[46] In addition to the broad categories of sins against nature, Gratian also includes a specific reference to *stuprum pueri,* the sins of boys, based on the *Digest* reference attributed to the third-century jurist Julius Paulus. Included in the category *stuprum pueri* were both the abduction and corruption of boys, an activity that merited capital punishment if the offense was *perfectus* but only banishment if it was *imperfectus.* This qualification might be an attempt to distinguish between those acts definitely performed and completed as against those that were only attempted, but this is by no means certain.[47] Scholars today regard the original Roman enactment somewhat different than Gratian did, namely, as an effort to extend the scope of *Lex Julia de adulteriis* to the protection of minors.[48] Anyone reading Gratian, however, could not be certain just exactly what constituted the crime of nature or even the crime against boys. By the twelfth century the phrase "what is done against nature" had become a euphemism adopted to explain all kinds of forbidden sexual activities. Though this originally might have been done in order not to disclose ways of sin to the innocent, once such a euphemism was adopted many of the later writers were not at all certain about what activities should or should not be included. To be safe, almost everything from failure to use the "normal" position in intercourse (female on her back), to any attempt to avoid conception (i.e., coitus interruptus or intercourse with a partner of the same sex) came to be looked upon as a sin against nature.[49]

Even the term sodomy was ambiguous since its meaning was not always confined to *coitus in ano.* This can be illustrated by the action of King Henry I of England in 1102 who that year summoned a council of lay and ecclesiastical leaders to Westminster to deal with the alleged moral abuses in his kingdom. Among the canons that this Council of London enacted were two that mention sodomy but do not define it:

> In this council, those who commit the shameful sin of sodomy, and especially those who of their own free will take pleasure in doing so, were condemned by

a weighty anathema, until by penitence and confession they should show themselves worthy of absolution.[50]

The canon goes on to state that if the person found guilty was an ecclesiastic he should be deposed, and if a layman, deprived of his legal status and dignity. Only a bishop was entitled to give absolution, unless the guilty person was a member of the regular clergy whereupon his superior was allowed to give the necessary dispensations. It was further stipulated that news of the excommunication of the guilty be published in all the churches in the realm in order that no one be ignorant of the censure passed by the leaders of the Church and State upon the vices of the last reign (William Rufus).[51] All we can say with certainty from such enactments is that the average Englishman had a dread of the horrors of sodomy, but it is not at all clear that this average Englishman knew what it entailed.

The most extensive series of enactments against sodomy resulted from the action of the Council of Napolouse held on the site of ancient Sichem in January, 1120, under the joint direction of Baldwin II, King of Jerusalem, and Garmund, patriarch of that city. Both king and patriarch seemingly believed that the Christian hold upon Jerusalem was precarious, in part because of the evil living of the Crusaders. To raise the level of morality, the council enacted twenty-five canons, most of them directed against the sins of the flesh. For the first time in medieval law the punishment for sodomy is listed as burning, although if any

sodomist, before he is accused, shall come to his senses, and having been brought to pentence, shall renounce that abominable vice by the swearing of an oath, let him be received into the Church and dealt with according to the provisions of the canons. But if he falls a second time into such practices and wishes again to do penance, he may be admitted to penance, but let him be expelled from the kingdom.[52]

The reference to the death penalty probably reflects the secular rather than religious character of the council, since in its general tenure the legislation is dependent upon the Justinian legislation.

Later canon law on the subject tended to ignore this action in Jerusalem in favor of that taken at the Third and Fourth Lateran Councils where the words "activities against nature" were used. The Third Lateran Council held in 1179 under the direction of Pope Alexander III included a canon directed against "that incontinence which is against nature, by reason which the anger of God came upon the children of disobedience, and consumed five cities by fire."[53] Though this equates the sin against nature with the destruction of Sodom and the other cities, it still remains undefined. Later enactments adopt the same phraseology. The Council of Paris in 1212, for example, repeated the statement from the Third Lateran almost verbatim.[54] Since the Council of Paris also extended the provisions of the Benedictine rule preventing monks from sleeping two in a bed to convents, and further stipulated that a lamp be kept burning in a convent dormitory at night, it might be interpreted as referring to homosexuality. The intent remains ambiguous, however, since this provision appears in an entirely different section. There also is no evidence that the council delegates were particularly concerned with female homosexuality in convents.[55] Similar provisions concerning incontinence against nature based on the example of the Third Lateran were enacted at the Council of Rouen in 1214.[56]

The Fourth Lateran Council in 1215 more or less repeated the wording of the Third Lateran on incontinence. Although the term against nature was not used, it was understood.[57] Synodical legislation for the next century or so essentially repeated the actions taken at the Councils, with each emphasizing that the sin against nature was a reserved sin, one that had to be referred to a higher authority such as a bishop for final decision.[58] The wording of the Third and Fourth Lateran Councils was incorporated into the *Decretals* issued by Pope Gregory IX in 1234 as an official and authoritative collection of rulings on questions of canon law decided since Gratian wrote.[59] These *Decretals* remained the final legal word of the Church on the subject until the end of the Middle Ages. Quite clearly the Church was opposed to the sin against nature, but just exactly what this constituted was more and more left up to individuals to interpret.

The ambiguity in the law was reflected in the theological discussion. Peter Lombard (c. 1100–1160) in his *Sentences* referred to the "sin against nature" but explained such activity, following Ivo and Saint Augustine, as using a member of a wife for a purpose other than procreation. In his list of sexual sins he classified it as worse than fornication, adultery, or incest.[60] By Peter's definition any act not leading to procreation could be included in his category of sins against nature. Somewhat more precise was Albertus Magnus (1206–1280), who went so far as to state that there could be no sin at all in matrimonial copulation *(nullum autem peccatum concubitus matrimonialis)*.[61] In his category of sins against nature, Albert listed sodomy as the worst possible sin since it was not only a sin against nature but against man. According to Albert intercourse had been invented and the sex organs formed for the procreation of offspring, the natural end of intercourse. As a by-product there was also the human end of intercourse, namely the "end of medicine and of fidelity to bed and of the sacrament." By his definition an act of intercourse within marriage could be one of nature as well as of man.[62] Albert added qualifications, however, since some types of intercourse might serve man's purpose but were against nature and against reason. Of these, the worst was sodomy, which he carefully defined as male with male or female with female *(masculi cum masculo, vel foeminae cum foemina)*. Sodomy, Albert held, deserved special condemnation for at least four reasons: (1) it proceeded from a burning frenzy that subverted the order of nature; (2) the sin was distinguished by its disgusting foulness and yet was more likely to be found among persons of high degree than of low; (3) those who became addicted to such vices seldom succeeded in freeing themselves; (4) and, lastly, such vices were as contagious as any disease and spread rapidly from one to another.[63]

Saint Thomas Aquinas (1225–74), who discussed the subject under "lust," took a somewhat different approach from his teacher Albert. Lust for Saint Thomas was a vice because it exceeded the order and mode of reason as far as venereal acts were concerned.[64] Sins against nature were a species of lust because they were directed solely to the pursuit of venereal pleasure and excluded procreation. This made sexual acts against nature different from other sins of lust such as fornication, adultery, seduction, rape, and incest, since they were not only contrary to right reason but also contrary to "the natural order of the venereal act as becoming to the human race."[65] In effect, Aquinas once again defined the sin against nature in a broad sense, not in the narrow sense of Albertus Magnus. His definition included four different activities: (1) procuring ejaculation *(pollutio)* without coitus, i.e., masturbation—Aquinas also equates this with effeminacy; (2) copulation with non-human creatures, i.e., bestiality; (3) copulation with an undue sex *(concubitus ad non debitum sexum)* that apparently means venereal acts with one of the same sex; and (4) deviation from the natural manner of coitus *(naturalis modus concumbandi)* that was limited to face-to-face contact with the female on her back. By such a definition a wide variety of sexual activities are classified as contrary to nature, not just homosexuality. There were levels—Saint Thomas regarded bestiality as the most grievous, followed by sodomy (the male/male or female/female), then intercourse in an unnatural position, while masturbation *(pollutio)* was the least serious.[66]

Aquinas was concerned that in many ways the sexual activities classified as sins against nature seemingly were not as serious as adultery, seduction, rape, or other sex crimes that not only injured others but were contrary to the virtue of charity. Nonetheless, Aquinas held that since the order of nature was derived from God, its contravention was always an injury done to God, whether or not any offense was at the same time committed against one's neighbors. Thus, even sexual acts against nature agreed upon by both subjects and harming no one were doing injury to God, thereby making them a transgression of the Divine law by which man's sexual nature was governed.[67] Some actions such as touches, caresses, and kisses between persons of the same sex, Saint Thomas recognized as not being mortally sinful in themselves, but they could easily become so by reason of the motive behind them. When such actions were taken for the purpose of enjoying forbidden pleasure, they were not only lustful but gravely sinful. Consent to the pleasure of a lustful act was not less than consent to the act itself. Only those acts between persons of the same sex that did not arouse venereal excitement were to be permitted.[68]

Saint Thomas, in short, had rejected the narrower definitions of Albertus Magnus in order to include in the category of sins against nature all acts in which ejaculation occurred but in which insemination was impossible, including sexual relations between a husband and wife. It was the Aquinas solution that dominated all later religious discussion on the subject. As late as the fifteenth century, for example, Saint Bernardine of Sienna (d. 1444) wrote that the sin against nature included any act of semination committed "wherever" and in "whatever way" that made it impossible to generate.[69] All such sexual activities were against nature since they were not only against the nature of the individual but also against the nature of the rational species, and against the nature of the animal genus.[70]

Not only was there ambiguity about what constituted the sin against nature, there was also confusion about what constituted sodomy. Some, such as Peter Cantor, claimed that sodomites were like Onan who "spilled his seed on the earth,"[71] thereby making *coitus interruptus* sodomy. Others were somewhat more definite but their meanings are not always clear. John Gerson (1363–1429), Chancellor of the University of Paris, defined sodomy to include copulation with a person of the same sex and semination in a "vessel not ordained for it."[72] St. Antonius (1381–1451) in his book for confessors put it quite clearly as "a man with man, a woman with a woman, or a man with a woman outside of the fit vessel is called the sodomitic vice."[73] Similar confusion about sexual activities appears in the popular literature also. Chaucer in his *Parson's Tale* defined sinning against nature ('unkyndely synne') as having intercourse in such a way that "child may not be conceived."[74] He used a similar reference in the *Merchant's Tale*.[75]

The ambiguity that existed in canon law and in the theological writing appears also in the penitential literature of the later medieval period, a literature that is extremely important in establishing popular conceptions since, by a decree of the Fourth Lateran Council, all Christians were supposed to confess annually and receive communion. In this penitential literature, even when sexual activity was defined primarily for the benefit of the confessor, it was defined in the broadest and most ambiguous sense so the penitent might not find new ways in which to sin. Henry of Susa (Hostiensis), for example, simply defined the sin against nature in his *Golden Summa* as any semination "outside the vessel" and any departure from the normal mode.[76]

There is even greater ambiguity in the vernacular penitentials where the layman might read about such things for himself. In the *Instructions for Parish Priests,* attributed to John Myrc and written before 1450, it was emphasized that the wise priest would refrain from preaching or teaching to his congregation what the sin against nature (kynde) would be:

> Also written well I find
> That of sin against kynde
> Thou shalt to thy parish no thing teach,
> Nor of that sin no thing preach;
> But say thus by good advice
> That too great sin forsooth it is.

> For any man that beateth life
> To forsake his wedded wife
> And do his kynde another way,
> That is great sin without nay.[77]

Lechery in most of these vernacular texts was conceived as proceeding in five stages: from foolish looks to foul words to foul touchings, then foul kissings, and finally "cometh a man to do the deed."[78] There were at least fourteen categories of foul deeds: each of these was divided into the imagined and realized, and the last, and therefore the worst of these, was the sin against nature. In the Book of Vices and Virtues it was called the

> sin so foul and so hideous that it should not be named, that is sin against kynde, that the devil teacheth to a man or to a woman in many vices that more not be spoken, for the matter is so foul that it is abomination to speak it; but nevertheless be it man or woman that be guilty thereof he must tell it openly in his confession to the priest as it was done.[79]

In spite of the injunction to confess, it was believed that simple confession of such a sin was so shameful that confession itself was part of the penance. "For in that sin is fouler and more shameful, insomuch is the confession more worth, for the same that he hath in confessing it, that is great part of his penance." So serious is the sin that it cannot be named except by allusions:

> This sin is so misliking to God that he made rain fire and stinking brimstone upon the cities of Sodom and Gomorre, and sunk into hell five cities. The devil himself that purchaseth that sin is squeamish thereof when anyone does it.[80]

The same penitential writer emphasized that married couples could commit the sin against nature "when that one draweth the other to do this thing against kynde in other wise than the nature of man asketh or law of marriage granteth."[81]

As in the earlier conceptions of the Stoics, what was natural was in part defined by selectively observing nature. In the thirteenth-century *Hali Maidenhad* it was pointed out that where beasts copulate but once a year, men were at it almost anytime, everywhere.[82] In this case the unnameable sin seems to be any kind of sexual intercourse unless it was sanctified by marriage; then it was only justified for the purposes of procreation. Young girls were warned of the sorrows of wedlock, since when they marry they will be

> from so high estate alighted so low . . . into the filth of the flesh, into the manner of life of a beast, into thralldom of a man, and into the sorrows of the world . . . to cool thy lust with filth of thy body, to have delight of thy fleshy

will from man's intercourse; before God, it is a nauseous thing to think thereon, and to speak thereof is yet more nauseous. Consider of what sort is that thing itself, and that deed to be done. All that foul delight is in filth ended, as thou turnest thine hand. But that loathsome beast remains and lasts on; and the disgust at long after. . . . Scorn to do what it seems to thee evil and pain to hear of. For when it is such, and by far more loathsome than any well-conditioned mouth for shame may tell of, what maketh it love among beastly man, except their great immorality.[83]

William Langland in *Piers Plowman* also compared man with beasts, but in this case to the advantage of the beasts:

I could see how Reason controlled all beasts in eating, in drinking, in engendering their kind. And after conception none took heed of the other as they did in mating-time; in the time following males went with males.[84]

In his discussion of the fourteenth lechery that, from its place in the listing, would be the sin against nature, Langland implied that the real difficulty with the sin was its association with gluttony.

Moderation is precious, no price too high for it. For the awful catastrophe that came on the Sodomites was due to overplenty and to pure sloth. Laziness and abundant bread fostered the worst sin, for they used no restraint in eating and drinking and did deadly sins that pleased the devil.[85]

Langland felt that the poor as a group found it difficult to actively engage in the seven deadly sins: lechery was particularly expensive, and only the rich could afford to engage in the sin against nature. There is some possible hint that Langland knew of the existence of homosexuality, but he thought such activities were mainly confined to friars, although again he might be referring to gluttony. The passage in question reads:

There's one word they skip over every time they preach . . . Holy Writ bids men beware (I won't write this here in English for fear it be repeated too often and scandalize good men, but scholars should read it): *"Let everyone beware of friars, for there is peril in false brethren."*[86]
Nuns are also cautioned to avoid the unnameable sin. The Scorpion of Lechery—that is, of lustfulness—hath such a progeny, that it doth not become a modest mouth to name the names of some of them; for the name alone might offend all modest ears, and defile all clean hearts.[87]

Since nuns did not need to draw out confessions from penitents, the sexual sins were even more obscure for them than they were among the priests. Nuns, nevertheless, were to realize what the unnameable sin was by reflecting upon their own accursed devices when tempted by concupiscence. For however it is done, willingly and awake, with the satisfaction of the flesh, except in wedlock only, it is a deadly sin.[88]

Here quite clearly masturbation is regarded as the unmentionable sin. This is emphasized by the story of a nun whom the devil rode day and night for twenty years. On the night that the devil first climbed on her back "she committed one particular sin, on the same night, through his instigation, and though she would, on the morrow, make confession of it, but she committed it again and again, and fell into such an evil habit that she lay and rotted in it."[89]

Other writers seemed to distinguish sodomy from other sins, classifying it as the worst of the unnameable sexual sins. The Pearl Poet in *Cleanness* recounted how mankind simply, for no cause, took up certain sexual practices in Sodom and Gomorrah. The reason for this, he said, are unimportant since people simply do this sort of thing now and again. Unclean to him was not unnameable and he wrote that the descendants of Adam and Eve turned filthy by fleshly deeds.

> contriving practices contrary to nature,
> using them basely, each on the other,
> harming one another by their bad habits.
> They fouled their flesh strangely, till the
> fiends saw that the daughters of noblemen
> were delightfully fair, and formed fellowships
> with them in human fashion, thus engendering
> giants by their evil jesting.[90]

As a result God had destroyed mankind through the flood, but He remained troubled by the continuation of "indecent harlotry, self-degradation." The poet then described self-degradation for his readers. God said:

> The great sound of Sodom sinks into my ears,
> and the guilt of Gomorrah goads me to wrath;
> I shall go to that land and look around for myself
> to see what they are doing—the din rises so high.
>
> They have learned a lust that I like ill,
> they have shown in their flesh the worst of faults;
> each man take for mate a man like himself
> and they join filthily, in female way.

The poem then continued with a description of heterosexual coupling that God had intended and preferred over this man-made method, which "spurned my plan and scorned nature, taking up in contempt an unclean custom."[91]

Chaucer, who recognized many sexual sins against nature, held that sexual relations between members of the same sex was one of the primary ones.[92] He recognized that it was usually regarded as the unnameable but since the Bible mentioned it, he felt that men should also be able to discuss it.

> The cursedness doon men and women in diverse entente and diverse manere; but though that hooly write speke of horrible synne, certes hooly write nat been defouled namoore than the sonne that shyneth on the mixne [dunghill].[93]

Dante put all those guilty of unnatural offenses among the Violent in the seventh level of Hell, while those who had expiated their offenses were in Purgatory along with others guilty of various kinds of lust. Nowhere did he spell out just exactly what constituted either violence against nature or unnatural lust, although he implied that it was a crime limited to males. Most of the people put in Hell for crimes of violence, as he himself remarked, were clerks and great men of letters.[94] In Purgatory he classified those whose transgression was "hermaphrodite" with others who acted like brute beasts in indulging their appetites, although he listed only two troubadours, Arnaut Daniel and Guido Gunicellis by name.[95] This listing of Guido and Arnaut in a passage dealing with crimes against nature has led to some confusion. Denis de Rougement, for example, argued that such a listing was to be expected because the narcissism inherent in any "platonic love" involved great temptations for the troubadours,[96] but it is not at all certain that this was Dante's meaning.

Obviously, we can conclude that Dante, like Chaucer, recognized the existence of sexual activity that we now define as homosexuality, but like most other writers he included any number of other sexual activities in his catchall category. What was the result of such confusion? One of the results was to create considerable ambiguity about what constituted the sin against nature. It could thus easily become a kind of catchall category as for example communism did in the United States during the McCarthy period. Just as anyone who disagreed with McCarthy was labeled a communist so anyone who did not conform to the Church standards on sex could be regarded as a heretic. Inevitably, most medieval heretics were accused of committing sexual sins and invariably one of the charges mounted against anyone whom one did not like was that he was a sodomist or that he committed crimes against nature. Witches too fell into the same grouping and, in fact, part of the definition of witchcraft included sexual activities against nature.[97] The equation of heresy and sexual sins became so deeply engrained in Western culture that it carried over into modern laws through the use of such terms as buggery. Buggery today means anal intercourse, but the term itself derives from a French name for the Albigensian heretics and originally had no sexual connotation at all.[98]

The adoption of the concept of sin against nature as a catchall category had still another implication, namely, the creation of anxiety feelings in

Western peoples about any forms of sexual activity not leading to procreation. So deeply rooted were these beliefs about unnatural sex that in the eighteenth century the medieval concepts underlying the sin against nature were adopted by the medical community to posit a model of masturbatory insanity, masturbation being defined in this instance to mean all sexual activity not leading to procreation.[99] Western hostility to contraceptives was also based upon the belief that any form of birth control was contrary to nature, since this made it possible to engage in intercourse for pleasure instead of procreation.[100]

7

Sexual Irregularities in Medieval Scandinavia

Grethe Jacobsen

Society's attitudes toward illicit sex are mirrored not only by laws but by the ways in which laws are interpreted and enforced. Unfortunately few court records from medieval Scandinavia have survived, and it is necessary to rely on laws themselves for evidence about attitudes toward non-marital sex in medieval Iceland, Norway, Denmark, and Sweden. However, the Icelandic family sagas furnish some additional evidence for that region, and the Danish evidence is enriched by the paraphrase of the Danish laws written by the leading clergyman of the Scandinavian church, Archbishop Anders Sunesøn (d. 1228). Since his paraphrase expresses the views of a canon lawyer and cleric, his views often contrast with the information about Danish society furnished by other sources.

This chapter will survey the different attitudes toward non-marital sex reflected in Scandinavian law at the time when the laws of these northern societies were reproduced in writing, the eleventh and twelfth centuries.

Attitudes toward irregular sex in the Scandinavian countries generally paralleled attitudes toward the role of women in society. In Iceland and, to a great extent, in Norway, women enjoyed legal and economic independence and their rights were well protected by law. Danish and Swedish women were much more restricted and they had little recourse against abuse and exploitation.[1]

It is usually assumed that this difference is due to the age of the laws:[2] the Icelandic and Norwegian laws were compiled during the early and mid-twelfth century, whereas the redaction of the Danish and Swedish laws took place during the thirteenth century. Since Christianity had become firmly established in Scandinavia only in the eleventh century, it is argued that the Icelandic and Norwegian laws were least influenced by canonical ideas. This assumption is reinforced by the fact that the Icelandic and Norwegian laws contain a special section called the Christian law *(kristinna laga battr)* that includes part of the regulations dealing with marriage, divorce, and the like. Denmark's laws were redacted under the influence of leading clergymen who were also canon lawyers.[3] Danish law was also shaped by the domestic policy of the Valdemars (1157–1241), who sought to change the structure of Danish society in order to enhance royal power.[4] The influence of canon law on Swedish law varies, but the pre-Christian codes can be reconstructed.[5]

On the surface it would seem that Icelandic and Norwegian laws might mirror the attitudes of a pre-Christian Viking society while the Danish and Swedish laws would reflect the ethos of a Catholic society. This is only partly true, however, since regional and social differences between the Scandinavian nations also account in part for the variance in laws dealing with irregular sex.[6]

Iceland

The oldest Icelandic law code, the *Grágás,* was compiled between 1117 and 1118 "in order to preserve old laws and customs."[7] The *Grágás* continued in effect until 1264, when Iceland was incorporated into the Kingdom of Norway. Christianity had been peacefully established through a decision of the yearly assembly (the *Albing*) in the year 1000, but on Icelandic terms. The proprietary church and the ensuing lay influence in church matters continued during the twelfth century, almost untouched by the Hildebrandine reforms. The Icelandic clergy generally shunned celibacy; clerics either married or lived in open concubinage, while sons often succeeded their fathers in clerical office. This does not mean that the Icelandic clergy were less immoral than clergy elsewhere: their marital (and non-marital) relationships reflected the Icelanders' negative attitude toward celibacy.[8]

One consequence of this situation was liberal provision for divorce, which was permitted as long as the *Grágás* was the law of the land.[9] If the economic situation of one spouse suddenly worsened, the other spouse could end the marriage in order to avoid having his or her standard of living lowered.[10] If a couple gave each other "large wounds,"[11] this was also considered a valid reason for divorce, as was the refusal or inability to have marital relations.[12] In some cases the bishop's permission was required if one or both spouses wanted to marry again.

Adultery was not a valid reason for divorce. This does not mean that adultery was condoned; rather it was considered an affront to the woman's kin.[13] A man who slept with a woman not his wife had to pay a fine *(réttr)* to the woman's law-warden. If she was married the fine went to her husband.[14] The lover also risked conviction of lesser outlawry, *fjorbaugsgaror*. If the woman died in childbirth as a result of the affair, he received the highest penalty, *skóggangr*.[16] Women who did not become pregnant apparently suffered no punishment.

An unmarried pregnant woman who refused to identify the father of her child could be tortured, but only to the degree that there were no bruises on her skin.[17] If she tried to hide her pregnancy from her kinsmen, she lost the right to receive any inheritance to which she might have been entitled.[18] If she did inform her kinsmen, especially her law-warden, of her condition and the name of her lover, the law stated that she "ought not to take inheritance" but nowhere explicitly forbade her to do so.[19]

The code states: "Women . . . should not take inheritance . . . unless they were forced or pressured to it [i.e., to consent to intercourse]."[20] Therefore, if a woman had been exploited sexually she was deemed not guilty by society. Her male relatives were then prohibited from using this as an excuse to disinherit her or prevent her from receiving property to which she was entitled. But if a woman had consented to the affair, she lost personal inheritance rights. The law provides that if the *legoro réttr* was to go to persons (such as her minor children) of whose property she was trustee, or to persons whose heiress she was, she could not administer the fines herself (and therefore not enjoy income from them), nor could she inherit them.[21]

The payment of *legoro réttr* by a man was not a punishment for an immoral act as such; rather, it was compensation to the woman's family for the affront suffered by it and for the expenses incurred in the suit to make him acknowledge paternity. In turn this had economic and legal consequences for mother and child and, by extension, for the kin who had to support them both. One chapter of the *Grágás* declares that an illegitimate child who had been recognized by his or her father should be supported by the father (or the father's kin);[22] this involved payment of up to two-thirds of the expenses of raising the child. The child also became eligible to receive inheritance from him after legitimate children had inherited. An illegitimate son was ninth in line for inheritance and an illegitimate daughter tenth,[23] but they had fewer responsibilities than legitimate siblings. An illegitimate son was expected to support his parents if they were in need of help, but only if he could afford it. A legitimate son, on the other hand, was required to support his mother under any circumstances, even if he had to borrow money and be forced into debt slavery to do so.[24]

The *Grágás* made it easy for Icelandic women to win paternity suits. There was no statute of limitations in paternity cases so long as the woman's law-warden had raised the matter in court within a reasonable period after it became known that she was pregnant.[25] The presumed father might be gone for years, but once the suit had been filed in court in the prescribed manner it would wait for him. If the law-warden did not act in time he had to support the mother and child himself, unless she had enough property of her own to live on. This acted as incentive for him to pursue the case and ensured support for the mother and her illegitimate child under any circumstances. An amendment from the late twelfth century, however, indicates that attitudes had changed by that time, to the detriment of women. The mother's law-warden was given the right to demand a fine of forty-eight *øre* from her or to force her into debt slavery if she could not pay.[26] Paternity could be determined by ordeal by fire more than once, and the most recent test was considered the valid one.[27]

Illegitimate children were the result not only of affairs between unmarried persons, but also of relationships that most medieval societies outside of Iceland considered legitimate marriages. A couple might be forced to separate by their kin if they became destitute. They were then declared divorced. Should they continue to cohabit, this constituted fornication, for which *legoro réttr* could be claimed by the woman's kin. Any children born after the divorce were illegitimate.[28] The reason for this is clearly economic: the families of the couple had to support both them and their offspring and would not want the burden to become larger.

A parent's status also influenced the legitimacy of a child even if the parents were married. A child whose father or mother was an outlaw at the time of birth was considered illegitimate even though the couple had been legally married before the conviction of outlawry. Similarly, a child born to a free mother and an unfree father was illegitimate and debarred from inheritance, even if the mother had given the father his freedom in order to marry him. This last provision was not a leftover from the pagan period but was labelled *nymæli* ('new law'), and was apparently new in the mid-thirteenth century[30] when the surviving *Grágás* manuscript was written.

Children of beggars were also considered illegitimate, even if their parents were legally married. In addition, they had no claim to support from their relatives.[31] All beggars, however, were treated harshly by the law. They were *rétt lausir*, that is, they could not claim compensation if they were attacked.[32] *A ganga mur* ('wandering man') could be castrated, and those who performed the surgery were immune from punishment even if he died in consequence.[33] An unmarried beggarwoman, *gangakona*, could not claim any fine or compensation if she got pregnant, but some mercy was shown her. If she had stayed at one man's farm for an entire month and conception had occurred during that time, the paternity of the owner of the farm was considered reasonably established, and he had to take care of her until she rose from childbed. Should he deny the charges of paternity but be convicted in court, he had to pay a fine and reimburse those who had taken care of the woman during childbirth. If she had been wandering about at the time of conception, however, no one was obliged to help her. Her child was considered illegitimate and had no right to any inheritance from his father, even if paternity had been acknowledged.[34]

Slaves and their children were wholly owned by their masters or mistresses, who could deal with them as they pleased. A master or mistress could kill a slave without being punished—unless the killing took place on a holy day or during Lent.[35] A master apparently could sleep with female slaves at will. A man could even buy a slave woman, valued up to twelve *øre* (the value of forty-eight yards of homespun cloth), specifically for his own pleasure.[36] If a man slept with a slave who belonged to another, a fine was due to the master or mistress.[37]

The punishment for fornication with a woman in temporary debt slavery was a fine and a conviction of lesser outlawry, the same as that for fornication with a free woman. Thus, the woman in temporary slavery was protected from sexual exploitation, whereas the woman born a slave or enslaved as a result of capture enjoyed no protection under the law. Her children inherited her servile status but enjoyed no other inheritance rights.

Icelandic legal provisions concerning irregular sex and illegitimacy were shaped by economic realities rather than by a moral code. The laws established who paid for what and defined illegitimacy and its consequences. They reflect a pragmatic and realistic attempt to settle peacefully conflicts arising from sexual behavior.

This attitude also permeates the *Landnámabók,* the history of the settlement of Iceland. The *Landnámabók* includes illegitimates in its enumeration of the settlers and mentions them as recipients of land and other property. No social stigma appears to have been attached to their illegitimacy.

Saga evidence confirms this attitude. The sagas are not historical accounts in any proper sense; rather they were written to preserve what the Icelanders considered the ideals of a good society. They can, therefore, tell us a great deal about the attitudes and opinions current in Icelandic society during the tenth to twelfth centuries, the period when they were recorded.[39]

Several non-marital relationships occur in the sagas, without condemnation or impairment of the woman's position, if compensation has been paid according to the law. Fighting that results from these relationships is usually due to the lover's unwillingness to acknowledge paternity or to pay the *legoro réttr* but may be caused by the father's or law-warden's refusal to accept him as a son-in-law. In one saga, a young man who openly carried on an affair with the wife of an older man was killed because he refused to end the affair or to pay *legoro réttr* when the woman became pregnant.[40] In another saga a young man acknowledged paternity of the child his mistress was carrying but her father tried to kill him rather than accept *legoro réttr* or a proposal of marriage.[41] In neither case was the woman punished. In the latter saga the pregnancy of another unmarried woman is used simply as an excuse for continued feuding. The woman's law-warden had sold the right to prosecute the case to a friend for use in a legal maneuver designed to avoid a charge of homicide.[42]

Indicative of society's attitude toward illegitimate children is the story of

Steinvor, a young widow, and Grettir the Strong, an outlaw whom many considered an unjustly persecuted hero. One winter Grettir stayed with Steinvor and the following summer she gave birth to a son. At first it was assumed that the boy was the son of the local priest, who apparently had become Steinvor's lover after Grettir's departure. As the boy grew up he looked more and more like Grettir

> and men expected great things from him,
> but he died when he was seventeen years
> old and no saga was to be told of him.[43]

Norway

The oldest Norwegian laws date from the tenth century but survive in redactions from the twelfth century.[44] In the 1270s King Magnus Lagabøter's law superseded the earlier codes. Norwegian law treated adultery much more harshly than it was treated by Icelandic law. Adultery was considered an insult to the husband. This may originally have been resolvable by the payment of a fine (as in Iceland) or by divorce. By the time of the redaction of the laws, the church had persuaded the lawmakers to forbid divorce. The lawmakers, however, condoned violent reprisal by the husband.[45]

The newer parts of the Norwegian laws, which date from the twelfth century, as well as the town law[46] from the same period, give the husband the right to kill his wife's lover.[47] (This is in contrast to Iceland, where revenge killings are allowed in cases of rape but not in cases of adultery.) Not only did the husband have the right to kill his wife's lover if he caught them together, but the woman's brother, father, son, stepson, brother-in-law, and father-in-law had the same right.[48] An amendment from 1260 declares male adulterers outlaws and denies Christian burial to those who have run away with other men's wives, "many of whom have hitherto atoned very little and some not at all."[49]

The church could not condone killings and imposed fines for adultery, which were to be paid to the bishop by the sinning spouse.[50] If the wife was the adulterer, she was required to pay the fine with her own money or property.[51] An adulterous wife could also forfeit the property that she had received from her husband at the wedding and lose control over her other property.[52] An adulterous husband, however, was only required to pay three *mark* to his wife for each time he had slept with another woman, "whether it be inside the house or outside."[53]

These attitudes toward adultery reflect a double standard that was never intended by the church but reflects the social positions of the spouses. A Norwegian wife was considerably less independent than an Icelandic wife. However, the adult, single Norwegian woman, whether unmarried or widowed, held the same free and responsible position in society that was enjoyed by the single Icelandic woman.

Norwegian law treated fornication and illegitimacy in ways strongly reminiscent of those found in Icelandic law. As in Iceland, fornication was considered an infringement of the rights of the woman's kin and complaints were settled with a fine paid by the man to the woman's kin. There was one exception: if a well-born woman slept with a slave she had to pay a three-*mark* fine to the king or work as a slave on his estates until she could pay it.[54]

Illegitimacy was considered an economic rather than a moral problem. If paternity was established, apparently no stigma attached to mother or child. Furthermore, the mother's word carried more weight in court than the word of the alleged father. The man accused of fathering a child was presumed guilty until proved innocent. If he won a paternity suit but the child in question grew up to look like him, he might be held responsible for supporting the child and also be required to pay a fine for perjury.[55]

The laws distinguish between four types of illegitimate children: the *hórnungr* ('corner child'), born to a couple living in open concubinage; the *rísungr* ('bush child'), born of a free couple but begotten in secret; the *pyborinn*, born to a slave woman and a free man; and, at the bottom of the scale, a *pyborinn* child, whose parents were both slaves. The *hórnungr*, *rísungr*, and (if acknowledged by him) *pyborinn* had the right to inherit from their father.

An illegitimate son or daughter ranked seventh in order of inheritance, following legitimate offspring and secondary male kin.[56] Rigmor Frimannslund argues that this represents a deterioration in the status of the *hórnungr* and *rísungr*. According to Frimannslund, Norwegian society in pre-Christian times made a distinction between children according to the social status of the parents, not legitimacy at birth. After the advent of Christianity and the establishment of the church, a revolutionary distinction was made between legitimate and illegitimate children: parental status was ignored.[57] Illegitimate children could, however, be legitimized through a ceremony conducted by their father or legitimate siblings.[58]

Denmark

The chapters of the Danish law that concern adultery are rather brutal and betray a double standard: only a wife can commit adultery; a straying husband commits fornication. The Danish laws also show a stricter attitude toward non-marital sex and illegitimate children, which, no doubt, reflects the views of the church.

This intolerance may not always have been dominant. The ninth-century Arabic poet Al-Gazal (d. 860) traveled as an emissary to the court of a *magus* king who is presumed to have been king of Denmark. Upon his return Al-Gazal regaled his friends with stories of his adventures and conquests, the most notable being the Danish queen. When he became worried about her obvious infatuation and its effect upon the king, he was told by the queen that jealousy was unknown in that country and that women stayed with men of their own free will and left them whenever they wanted to.[59] However, the story is a questionable source for customs in pre-Christian Denmark for several reasons. It is not certain that Al-Gazal visited Denmark, but, even if based on fact, the story could well have been embroidered before being recorded in the late twelfth century. Moreover, Adam of Bremen, writing during the second half of the eleventh century, tells us that women in Denmark who had been violated were immediately sold into slavery. This hardly indicates that the rights of Danish women were much respected or that there was much tolerance for transgressions of the sexual code.[60]

In cases of adultery the husband had absolute power over his wife. Adultery was considered a personal insult to him,[61] and the legal leniency that permitted disputes to be settled by payment of fines rather than bloodshed was suspended in these cases.

If a husband caught his wife in bed with her lover he was allowed to kill them both without being punished. (They were then denied Christian burial because they had died without receiving the last rites.) If the husband spared his wife he could chase her out of the house without any money or clothes and keep all her property until her death, at which time it would go to her heirs—of which he would still be one if they had living sons.[62] Archbishop Anders Sunesøn approved of this.[63] He also approved of the ordeal by hot iron for a wife who had to prove herself innocent of adultery, although in 1215 the Fourth Lateran Council had outlawed ordeals and the Archbishop himself considered their results inadmissible as evidence in paternity suits.

One law only mentions that the husband is allowed to kill the lover.[64] This law also contains provisions that show some women, after being evicted from their houses and convicted of adultery, did remarry and start a new life. If a man married such a woman and they had children together, the children were considered legitimate, whether or not the husband knew of his wife's past. If the clerical authorities forced the couple to separate on grounds of bigamy, they divided their property and children.[66]

All the laws agree—and Anders Sunesøn stresses—that adultery was no reason for divorce, a rule that may not have been much respected. They also agree that only a wife commits adultery, not a husband. If a married man slept with another woman, he paid compensation for fornication to the kin of his mistress. If his mistress was another man's wife, he risked being killed but paid no fines to his own wife.

Despite this severity and bias, the medieval Danish laws themselves and the paraphrase of Anders Sunesøn (both of which date from the late twelfth and early thirteenth centuries), show the influence of canon law.[67] Fornication, however, though not condoned, was treated not as a moral crime but as an infringement of the right of the woman's kin to make decisions concerning her marriage. This could be remedied by the payment of a fine[68] of six to nine *mark* to the woman's kin[69] — "and she shall have nothing of it," admonishes one law.[70] If the woman was illegitimate and had not been recognized by her father, the fine went to her maternal kin.[71] If she was a servant the fine was paid to her master, in which case it was much smaller: two *øre* (equivalent to one-quarter *mark*) for fornication with an ordinary servant and six *øre* for a lady's maid.[72] Paternal kin collected the fine only the first time. If the woman continued the affair or took a new lover, her kin could no longer demand compensation, unless she was raped or abducted.[73]

The woman risked forfeiting her property unless she was having the affair to protest her kin's inaction concerning her marriage. A young woman eighteen years of age or older had the right to sleep with a man without losing her property or right to inheritance if her kin did nothing to find her a suitable husband.[74] (Her lover might have to pay the fine for fornication once, though.)

If she was pregnant, however, she was much worse off than her sisters in Iceland or Norway. It was not up to the mother to point out the father — the man could choose, or not, to acknowledge paternity. She was at the mercy of her lover to recognize her child, and payment of fornication fines did not itself legitimize the child or confer upon the child the right to inherit from the father. The laws further say that if a man and woman who are not married have a child, the father shall pay a fornication fine to the nearest male kin of the mother, but no money to the child itself.[75]

The influence of the church has been seen in this. Anders Sunesøn's attacks on any recognition of illegitimate children would seem to confirm it. He says that in the old days the law demanded that an illegitimate son identify his father; the alleged father then had to disprove paternity by the ordeal of the hot iron. This the Archbishop finds unreasonable; he adds that things are much better now because a man can only be declared the father of an illegitimate child if he openly and voluntarily acknowledges the child at *ping*.[76] Anders Sunesøn also argues that illegitimate children should inherit only half as much as legitimate children, even if the father has later married the mother. This is rather surprising since the Roman law principle of "legitimatio per subsequens matrimonium" had been adopted in 1179 by Pope Alexander III at the Third Lateran Council.[77] Anders Sunesøn's view prevailed in the two oldest of the medieval Danish laws,[78] but later revisions of these laws (as well as the two other laws from the mid-thirteenth century) recognize the principle of "legitimatio per subsequens matrimonium."[79]

If the father did not marry the mother it was, according to all the laws, entirely up to him to acknowledge the child; they all stress that no one can force paternity upon any man.[80] Nor do the laws mention support of the illegitimate child,[81] which was probably the responsibility of the mother alone. Although the laws did grant illegitimate children some rights, they are primarily addressed to protection of the rights of legitimate children from the claims of illegitimate siblings. Even if the father had publicly recognized his illegitimate child, that child could not inherit from him unless the father, again publicly, had given the child some or all of its share in the property,[82] which might or might not have been economically feasible. Promises or intentions of providing for the child were not binding unless acted upon during the father's lifetime.

In two of the laws an illegitimate child could receive as much as a legitimate child, if the father had permitted it,[83] but one law (perhaps under the influence of the Archbishop's antagonism) limits the inheritance of an illegitimate child to one-half the share of the legitimate child, regardless of the father's wishes. (This meant that an illegitimate son received one-half of a legitimate son's share, which was equivalent to a legitimate daughter's share; an illegitimate daughter would receive one-half of a legitimate daughter's share, the equivalent of one-fourth of a legitimate son's share.)[84] However, an illegitimate child inherited from its mother the same portion as her legitimate children, sons receiving twice as much as daughters.

The situation before the advent of Christianity cannot be reconstructed easily. Speaking of Sweden, Adam of Bremen says that all sons born to one of a man's several wives were considered legitimate.[85] For Denmark, however, he mentions only the case of the illegitimate sons of King Cnut the Great, who shared their father's lands with his legitimate sons, "as is the custom with barbarians."[86] But the illegitimate sons of royalty are not necessarily typical of all illegitimate children. (Adam nowhere mentions the fate of illegitimate daughters.) Saxo, a twelfth-century Danish historian, records that the many illegitimate sons of King Sven Estridsøn (1047–1074) inherited his throne in succession,[87] but King Sven had no legitimate children and no other branches of the royal family had candidates to the throne. Furthermore, it is likely that the future of an illegitimate child depended upon the mother's status, and these sons were all children of noble women. After the advent of Christianity, the lot of the single mother and her child worsened because the church insisted on the father's right to choose, or not, to acknowledge paternity, and the church limited the rights of the child to the father's property.

The church did, however, improve the position of concubines by bringing the law into line with the then-current canonistic thinking.[88] The redaction of medieval Danish law that was compiled in 1241 under the bishop of Viborg, a canon lawyer, states that a man and a woman are legally married if they have been living in open concubinage for three years, that is, if they have eaten and slept together and the woman carries the keys to the house.[89] (By contrast, Icelandic law nowhere makes a concubine equal to a married woman, and the Norwegian laws require a relationship to have lasted for twenty years before it becomes a legitimate marriage.)[90]

Sweden

Adam of Bremen is more favorable to the Swedes, even though they were still predominantly pagan when he wrote his chronicle. He does, however, express shock at the sexual appetites of Swedish men:

> Only in their sexual relations with women do they know no limits. According to his means a man has two or three or more wives at the same time . . . but they consider all sons born of these unions legitimate . . . . But capital punishment is the penalty if someone lies with another man's wife or ravishes a virgin.[91]

In the Swedish laws,[92] the child of an adulterous union had no inheritance rights at all.[93] Here the wrath of society came down upon the child, and even more upon its mother. As in the Danish laws, only a wife could commit adultery, and that crime was considered an insult to the husband.[94] If the wife and her lover were caught in bed, the husband was permitted to kill his wife and her lover or drive her out of the house. She also risked having her hair, ears, and nose cut off.[95] It would appear she also forfeited all her property, since all the pertinent laws state that an adulterous woman cannot be required to pay her bishop a fine because she no longer has any property, and her husband should not have to pay for her sins.[96]

If the husband committed adultery, however, the wife had no recourse unless he drove her out of the house, installed another woman in her place, and gave this woman the keys to the wife's coffers. In such a case the husband had to pay his wife a forty-*mark* fine.[97]

The thirteenth-century Swedish laws reflect attitudes toward sexual relations between unmarried persons and toward their offspring that are very similar to those seen in Danish law. As in the other Scandinavian countries, in Sweden fornication was considered an infringement of the right of the woman's kin to determine her marriage, but it was not severely punished.[98] A fine of four and one-half *mark* was due if the couple was caught in the act. The laws also specify something that seems implied in the other Scandinavian laws, that if a couple was not apprehended and pregnancy did not result from the intercourse, no one could demand a fine from the man.[99] Furthermore, the full fine was paid only the first time a man slept with the woman. If she had intercourse with a second, this second man paid a smaller fine of three *mark,* and if she had intercourse with a third man, the fine was reduced to one-half *mark.* Thereafter her kin could demand no fine for fornication.[100] If she became pregnant and her lover was convicted of or acknowledged paternity he paid three *mark* to the child, which the mother kept until the child was three years of age or was weaned. At that time the parent who could best afford it took the child.[101] Thus the illegitimate child was better provided for than in Denmark; by extension so was the single mother. But the child was still discriminated against in favor of its legitimate siblings since the child could not inherit on equal terms with them and received only as much as its father, with the permission of the legitimate heirs, had publicly given it. The illegitimate child apparently received land or property from its parents often enough to cause dispute about who could inherit from an illegitimate child. All the laws specify how such a child's property should be dealt with should the child die without leaving children of its own.[102]

One exception to the Swedish laws is the *Gutalag,* the law of Gotland, an island nation that formed a reluctant part of the Swedish realm.[103] In this society women enjoyed a fairly independent position, not unlike that of the women of Iceland, the other island society of Scandinavia.

In case of adultery the husband could demand forty *mark* from the wife's lover or kill him if he caught the lover in bed with his wife, regardless of the status of the lover—whether he was priest or layman, adds the law.[104] But no punishment is mentioned for the woman.

Gotlander adultery and fornication laws seem designed to protect a mother and her illegitimate child, as long as she was a native of Gotland. This law blatantly discriminates less against those deemed dishonored or illegitimate than against foreigners, including Swedes from the mainland. The fine for fornication with a Gotlander woman was twice the fine for fornication with a foreign woman.

The fine was secured in a quite straightforward fashion. When a man was caught in bed with a woman he was locked up and his kin had to redeem "his hand and his foot" with six *mark* silver; if they did not, he risked having these parts amputated.[105]

If the woman became pregnant, his fine was eight *mark* silver. This was equal to the *hogsl,* the traditional morning gift to the married woman; after that, the woman's kin had to take care of the child if the father did not want to keep it.[106] By giving the *hogsl* the man may have recognized an illegitimate child as his heir, but this is not stated. However, an illegitimate son whose parents were both Gotlanders could inherit along with secondary male kin, such as the uncles, brothers, and nephews of the dead man. His case was strengthened if his mother's mother and grandmother had also been native women. If no legitimate sons were alive when the father died, the illegitimate sons and daughters of Gotlander parents shared the inheritance equally with their parents' legitimate daughters. A child whose father was foreign but whose mother was a Gotlander also enjoyed these rights. But an illegitimate child whose mother was foreign had no right to inherit

its father's property. However, the father had to feed and clothe an illegitimate child until the child reached the age of eighteen, at which time he could
send the child away, a son with clothes and a weapon, a daughter with
clothes and a small dowry.[107]

Gotland law also dealt with lesser sexual matters. In Gotland, as in Iceland, it was punishable to touch a woman against her will. A fine was due
for such offenses, the amount rising the closer the touch came to her lap.
The highest fine was to be paid for touching a woman above her knee but

> if you touch her higher up, then it is a shameless touch and it is called a fool's
> touch; then no fine is payable; most want it when it gets that far.[108]

Here we see an early version of the "she asked for it" attitude, which has not
yet disappeared from Western law.

Conclusion

Scandinavian laws regulating sexual matters diverge most sharply where
they deal with adultery. In Iceland adultery is not distinguished from fornication. Saga evidence indicates that adultery was considered an insult to the
husband, to be settled between him and the lover. The wife apparently suffered no punishment. However, it should be noted that Iceland permitted
divorce for almost three centuries after the coming of Christianity. In Norway (and in Gotland) the husband had the right to kill a man caught in bed
with his wife without waiting for a conviction of outlawry. For the wife,
punishment took the form of economic sanctions, such as a large fine or
temporary loss of property. An adulterous husband, however, only paid a
small fine for each infidelity, albeit to his wife. Danish and Swedish laws
consider only a wife's infidelity to be adultery. Her punishment could range
from permanent loss of property to mutilation and death at the hands of her
husband, but she had no recourse when he had sexual relations with another
woman. Her crime was not considered a violation of the code of sexual
behavior; rather it was seen as an insult to her husband. This suggests that a
strongly patriarchal society existed before the advent of Christianity, as the
church could not condone revenge killings.

By contrast, the laws of medieval Scandinavia concerning fornication are
similar and lenient as long as pregnancy did not result from the affair.
Fornication was considered an infringement on the right of a woman's kin
to make arrangements for her marriage, but this was easily remedied by
payment of a fine. Virginity seems to have been of little importance since
the laws differentiate between married and unmarried women, not between
virgins and non-virgins. (Rape was in all laws considered a crime of violence,
and the punishment was the same whether the victim was a virgin or not.)

If fornication resulted in pregnancy, differences appear. In Gotland, Iceland, and Norway the laws seem designed to protect the rights of an illegitimate child and its mother and enable them to demand recognition and support from the father. Payment by him of a fine for fornication was less a punishment than a public recognition of paternity and its responsibilities. Evidence from saga literature indicates that an illegitimate child's status in society depended on the place of its parents in the social hierarchy and the child's own character and abilities. Illegitimacy itself was not a handicap in Icelandic society. Swedish and Danish laws, on the other hand, seem more concerned with protecting a man from unwanted paternity suits. These laws also protect the property rights of legitimate children; this placed both the illegitimate child and its mother at an economic disadvantage. The influence of the church, which eagerly protected legitimate marriages and their offspring, may be seen here, but this also may simply be a patriarchal society protecting males and their property from any unwanted claims by mistresses and illegitimate children.

These different attitudes toward irregular sex and illegitimacy have had a long career. A recent article on illegitimacy in the Nordic countries illustrates, with statistics and examples, that Iceland has continually had a much higher rate of illegitimacy than the other Nordic countries.[109] Icelandic society also shows a general acceptance of non-marital sex. Only in the more isolated parts of Norway did one find the same pattern, until the last two to three decades when all the Scandinavian countries became famous (or infamous) for their liberal attitudes toward sexual irregularities.

Section II – Sex and the Canon Law

In any discussion of sexual behavior and its regulation in medieval society, canon law will play a prominent role, as it does in the essays in this volume. The reader may very well wonder why this is so. A partial answer is that the canon law courts claimed an exclusive jurisdiction over matters involving the sacraments (including marriage) and over matters involving sin (including sexual sin). Thus the subject matter itself accounted in part for the prominence of sexual matters in the canonical jurisdiction. In addition, canon lawyers claimed that their legal system enjoyed exclusive jurisdiction over all matters involving certain large groups of people, regardless of the type of behavior at issue. These groups over which the canonists asserted sole jurisdiction included the clergy and disadvantaged groups in medieval society—widows, orphans, travelers, and the like. Not all of the canonists' jurisdictional claims were universally accepted; the matter of criminal clerics in twelfth-century England, which was the central issue in the controversy that led to the murder of Archbishop Thomas Becket, is one well-known example of a refusal by secular rulers to agree to the church courts' assertions of jurisdictional competence. Still, despite some areas of conflict over these claims, the canon law courts generally enjoyed a wide jurisdiction in most parts of the medieval West and it was rare to find their competence to judge matters of sexual behavior brought into question. Since canon law generally was a rather efficient type of international law in the Middle Ages, one that functioned in much the same way from one end of Christian Europe to the other, it was an important force in shaping the sexual mores of medieval society.

It is important to keep in mind, however, the further fact that canon law itself underwent change and development during the Middle Ages. Canonistic ideas and institutions in 1400, say, were certainly far different from what they had been in 800. The changes in canon law did not occur in a vacuum, of course. Rather, they responded to and reflected changes both in the Church itself and in European society at large. Still the canonists' role in this process should not be thought of merely as a passive one: they were not simply reacting to events and developments in other sectors in society. Rather, the canonists were themselves an innovating group in many significant areas of human life and institutions. This was particularly true for the period between the mid-twelfth century and the mid-fourteenth century. The canonists who flourished in that period pioneered new ways of looking at society and structuring new models for human institutions by applying to the realities of medieval life some of the conceptual tools that they found in the Roman law, in the scriptures, in the declarations of popes and councils, and in the writings of the fathers of the Church. Scholars in the twentieth century have begun to discover how important the ideas of the medieval canonists were, for example, in creating the ideas of representation and consent that underlay the development of parliamentary government and of the idea of constitutionalism in Western thought. The canonists likewise brought fresh insights and ideas to bear on the perennial problems of human sexuality and family life, as the next series of chapters in this book points out.

8

Sex and Canon Law:
A Statistical Analysis of Samples of
Canon and Civil Law

James A. Brundage

This chapter begins, as historical investigations are supposed to begin, with a question: "How much did medieval canon lawyers—professionally, of course—think about sex?" In its original form the question is unanswerable, for there is no method whereby we can directly scrutinize the thought processes of medieval lawyers. By some slight alterations, however, it is possible to transform this original question into one that can be answered and that can by inference give us a rational basis for an estimate of the answer to the original query. The transformed question, the one we can answer, is this: "What proportion of the legal texts of the medieval canon law deal with sexual topics?" This is something that can be determined by counting and the results of that, in turn, should give us a clue as to how much of the professional thought and training of the canon lawyers had to do with sexual matters.

Any attempt to deal with the questions already posed will be more illuminating if we also subjoin some related questions about the proportions of other topics dealt with in the canon law—how large a part of the legal texts, in other words, treated such matters as sacramental law, liturgical law, clerical status, women's status, contracts, testaments, loans, debts, possession of property, guardianship, *patria potestas,* elections, manumission, and servile status?[1] If we compare the relative frequency with which these matters occur in the legal texts with the frequencies of sexual themes, we will be in a better position to estimate just how prominent sexual topics were in the professional consciousness of medieval canonists. It would also be instructive, while we are asking questions, to put the same set of questions to the civil law texts, since this might give us some basis for comparing and contrasting the differing professional emphases of the practitioners of the two laws in the Middle Ages.

Now it is far easier to ask these questions than to answer them. Anyone who has read through the medieval *Corpus iuris canonici* and the *Corpus iuris civilis* can testify that the legal texts in them are both voluminous and complex, while the meanings of the texts themselves do not always leap immediately to the eye.[2] The prospect of working one's way through each canon, law, and fragment of both bodies of law, classifying and counting the topics dealt with in each, and then adding up the results is daunting. Any mortal is justified in wondering if there may not be a less time-consuming method of finding an answer to the questions raised here.

And of course there is an easier way. If the cost/benefit ratio of a complete examination of the available evidence is too high to justify the procedure, the obvious alternative is to adopt a more economical method, namely, to sample the evidence. This involves some loss of accuracy, to be sure, and one of the first things one has to resolve is how much accuracy one is prepared to sacrifice in the process. This is rather a subjective question. My subjective answer is that I am prepared to tolerate a 5 percent margin of error in order to get an answer to these questions. So long as I can be certain that there are 95 chances out of 100 that my results are correct, it is tolerable to accept the evidence from a sample of the texts as a workable substitute for a scrutiny of the total body of evidence on this matter.[3] And certainly, these are considerably better odds than the ones commonly met in most other intellectual inquiries—or in most other departments of life, for that matter.

What I have done, therefore, is to select a random sample of passages from the *Corpus iuris canonici* and the *Corpus iuris civilis*—400 texts from each body of law, or 800 texts in all.[4] I have then examined each of these texts and noted for each of the categories that interested me simply whether the text dealt with that subject or not. Using an electronic computer, it was then a simple matter to count up the frequencies with which each of the categories occurred in my sample evidence and subsequently to manipulate the data to discover how these frequencies were distributed between the canon and civil laws; it was also possible to determine within each *corpus* how the frequencies varied from one legal collection to another.[5] Beyond that, it was further possible, by slightly more complicated methods, to crosstabulate the data and to produce enormous contingency tables that showed how different topics were associated with one another and to measure the strength and significance of these associations. Finally, by performing an analysis of variance and a multiple discriminant function analysis, it was possible to arrive at some moderately intriguing conclusions about the ways in which the subject matter of the medieval canon law differed from the subject matter of the civil law.

Turning to the substantive issues that I have raised, my examination of the sample texts showed that, as expected, the canon law dealt with sexual themes slightly more often than did the civil law texts—about 10 percent of the canon law texts treated sexual topics, while only slightly more than 6 percent of the civil law texts dealt with sexual matters. Similarly, the canon law laid greater stress on sexual crimes than did the civil law texts in the

TABLE 1

Frequencies of occurrence of sexual topics in canon and civil law

Response	CANON LAW		CIVIL LAW		BOTH LAWS	
	Frequency	%	Frequency	%	Frequency	%
Non-sexual	360	90.0	375	93.8	735	91.9
Sexual, marital	21	5.2	17	4.2	38	4.7
Sexual, non-marital	11	2.7	6	1.5	17	2.1
Sexual, not specific	8	2.0	2	0.5	10	1.2
	400	100.0	400	100.0	800	100.0

sample. It was not particularly surprising to find, more specifically, that the

TABLE 2

Frequencies of occurrence of sexual crime references in canon and civil law

Category	CANON LAW		CIVIL LAW		BOTH LAWS	
	Frequency	%	Frequency	%	Frequency	%
No sexual crime	372	93.0	390	97.5	762	95.2
Adultery	5	1.2	2	0.5	7	0.9
Fornication.............	11	2.7	2	0.5	13	1.6
Bigamy	4	1.0	2	0.5	6	0.7
Incest..................	0	0.0	1	0.2	1	0.1
Rape	5	1.2	1	0.2	6	0.7
Sodomy................	0	0.0	1	0.2	1	0.1
Other..................	2	0.5	0	0.0	2	0.2
More than one	1	0.2	1	0.2	2	0.2
	400	100.0	400	100.0	800	100.0

canon law was more concerned (by a 5:1 ratio) with fornication and rape than the civil law was, but that the frequencies of texts dealing with such matters as adultery and bigamy, which have obvious implications for property and public order, were rather closer in the two laws. Looking at the texts dealing with the clergy and clerical status, it was again no great surprise to discover that about 45 percent of the canon law texts dealt with clerics, whereas only 7 percent of the civil law texts focused on the activities of the clergy. The canon law, naturally, has much more to say about the sexual activities of the clergy than does the civil law. As one might have anticipated, too, the canon law gives much greater attention to matters of

TABLE 3

Frequencies of laws dealing with the clergy

Response	CANON LAW Frequency	%	CIVIL LAW Frequency	%	BOTH LAWS Frequency	%
Not clerical	221	55.2	372	93.0	593	74.1
Clerical, sexual matter	7	1.7	1	0.2	8	1.0
Clerical, non-sexual matter	169	42.2	27	6.7	196	24.5
Clerical celibacy	3	0.7	0	0.0	3	0.4
	400	100.0	400	100.0	800	100.0

sacramental law than does the civil law and the overwhelming majority of

TABLE 4

Frequencies of laws dealing with the sacraments

Category	CANON LAW Frequency	%	CIVIL LAW Frequency	%	BOTH LAWS Frequency	%
Not sacramental	319	79.7	375	93.8	694	86.7
Baptism	8	2.0	1	0.2	9	1.1
Confirmation	1	0.2	0	0.0	1	0.1
Eucharist	13	3.2	0	0.0	13	1.6
Penance	11	2.7	0	0.0	11	1.4
Extreme unction	0	0.0	0	0.0	0	0.0
Holy orders	21	5.2	4	1.0	25	3.1
Matrimony	26	6.5	20	5.0	46	5.7
More than one	1	0.2	0	0.0	1	0.1
	400	100.0	400	100.0	800	100.0

the civil law texts that deal with sacramental matters are concerned with the law of marriage. It is slightly more surprising to find that illegitimacy is more

TABLE 5

Frequencies of laws dealing with illegitimacy

Response	CANON LAW Frequency	%	CIVIL LAW Frequency	%	BOTH LAWS Frequency	%
Does not deal with illegitimacy	399	99.8	393	98.2	792	99.0
Deals with illegitimacy . . .	1	0.2	7	1.7	8	1.0
	400	100.0	400	100.0	800	100.0

prominently dealt with in the civil law than in the canon law, as is also true of matters concerning dowry. Topics dealing with women's status are just

TABLE 6

Frequencies of laws dealing with dowries

	CANON LAW		CIVIL LAW		BOTH LAWS	
Response	Frequency	%	Frequency	%	Frequency	%
Does not deal with dowries	398	99.5	374	93.5	772	96.5
Deals with dowries	2	0.5	26	6.5	28	3.5
	400	100.0	400	100.0	800	100.0

about equal in the two laws, although a slightly higher percentage of texts

TABLE 7

Frequencies of laws dealing with women

	CANON LAW		CIVIL LAW		BOTH LAWS	
Response	Frequency	%	Frequency	%	Frequency	%
Does not deal with women.............	361	90.3	356	89.0	717	89.6
Deals with women	39	9.7	44	11.0	83	10.4
	400	100.0	400	100.0	800	100.0

dealing with women occurs in the civil law than in the canon law. Legal texts concerning corporate bodies also occur with roughly equal frequencies in each of the two laws.

TABLE 8

Frequencies of laws dealing with corporate bodies

	CANON LAW		CIVIL LAW		BOTH LAWS	
Response	Frequency	%	Frequency	%	Frequency	%
Does not deal with corporate bodies	392	98.0	390	97.6	782	97.8
Deals with corporate bodies	8	2.0	10	2.4	18	2.2
	400	100.0	400	100.0	800	100.0

Another group of matters, primarily secular and non-religious in character, show up much more commonly in the civil law than in the canon law. Among these are topics such as testamentary disposition of decedents' estates and intestate succession to estates, each of which accounts for less than

TABLE 9

Frequencies of laws dealing with testaments

	CANON LAW		CIVIL LAW		BOTH LAWS	
Response	Frequency	%	Frequency	%	Frequency	%
Does not deal with testaments.........	397	99.3	325	81.3	722	90.3
Does deal with testaments..........	3	0.7	75	18.8	78	9.7
	400	100.0	400	100.0	800	100.0

1 percent of the canonistic texts and about 19 percent of the civilian texts.

TABLE 10

Frequencies of laws dealing with succession

	CANON LAW		CIVIL LAW		BOTH LAWS	
Response	Frequency	%	Frequency	%	Frequency	%
Does not deal with succession.........	397	99.3	323	80.8	720	90.0
Deals with succession	3	0.7	77	19.2	80	10.0
	400	100.0	400	100.0	800	100.0

Similarly, such matters as contract, sale, guardianship, slavery, manumission, *patria potestas,* loans, ownership, and possession likewise figure much

TABLE 11

Frequencies of laws dealing with contract

	CANON LAW		CIVIL LAW		BOTH LAWS	
Response	Frequency	%	Frequency	%	Frequency	%
Does not deal with contract............	393	98.3	345	86.3	738	92.3
Deals with contract	7	1.7	55	13.7	62	7.7
	400	100.0	400	100.0	800	100.0

more prominently in the civil law than in the canon law.

TABLE 12

Frequencies of laws dealing with sale

Response	CANON LAW		CIVIL LAW		BOTH LAWS	
	Frequency	%	Frequency	%	Frequency	%
Does not deal with sale................	398	99.5	375	93.7	773	96.6
Deals with sale	2	0.5	25	6.3	27	3.4
	400	100.0	400	100.0	800	100.0

TABLE 13

Frequencies of laws dealing with tutorship

Response	CANON LAW		CIVIL LAW		BOTH LAWS	
	Frequency	%	Frequency	%	Frequency	%
Does not deal with tutorship...........	397	99.3	323	80.8	720	90.0
Deals with tutorship	3	0.7	77	19.2	80	10.0
	400	100.0	400	100.0	800	100.0

TABLE 14

Frequencies of laws dealing with slaves

Response	CANON LAW		CIVIL LAW		BOTH LAWS	
	Frequency	%	Frequency	%	Frequency	%
Does not deal with slaves..............	395	98.8	353	88.3	748	93.5
Deals with slaves	5	1.2	47	11.7	52	6.5
	400	100.0	400	100.0	800	100.0

TABLE 15

Frequencies of laws dealing with manumission

Response	CANON LAW		CIVIL LAW		BOTH LAWS	
	Frequency	%	Frequency	%	Frequency	%
Does not deal with manumission	397	99.3	369	92.3	766	95.8
Deals with manumission ..	3	0.7	31	7.7	34	4.2
	400	100.0	400	100.0	800	100.0

TABLE 16

Frequencies of laws dealing with *patria potestas*

Response	CANON LAW		CIVIL LAW		BOTH LAWS	
	Frequency	%	Frequency	%	Frequency	%
Does not deal with *patria potestas*	396	99.0	376	94.0	772	96.5
Deals with *patria potestas*...........	4	1.0	24	6.0	28	3.5
	400	100.0	400	100.0	800	100.0

TABLE 17

Frequencies of laws dealing with loans

Response	CANON LAW		CIVIL LAW		BOTH LAWS	
	Frequency	%	Frequency	%	Frequency	%
Does not deal with loans	396	99.0	371	92.8	767	95.9
Deals with loans	4	1.0	29	7.2	33	4.1
	400	100.0	400	100.0	800	100.0

TABLE 18

Frequencies of laws dealing with *dominium*

Response	CANON LAW		CIVIL LAW		BOTH LAWS	
	Frequency	%	Frequency	%	Frequency	%
Does not deal with *dominium*	382	95.5	359	89.8	741	92.6
Deals with *dominium*	18	4.5	41	10.2	59	7.4
	400	100.0	400	100.0	800	100.0

None of these differences is terribly surprising and one might have expected intuitively that distributions of these kinds would appear. Still, so far as I can discover, no one has ever attempted to measure these differences before and the measurements themselves have a modest interest. But if that were all there were to it, the significance of this exercise would be fairly limited—it would do little more than to confirm one's intuitive impressions, although that is by no means a negligible outcome.

It is possible, however, to carry the analysis several steps further. For one thing, one can measure the strength of association between different topics in each of the laws and this, in turn, should tell us something about the character of the legal collections that we are working with. It is notable, for one thing, that there is a very strong association in the civil law between laws dealing with sexual matters and laws dealing with the clergy—the two themes go together more frequently than would happen by pure chance.[6] There is a stronger association in the civilian texts between laws about sexual crimes and laws dealing with the clergy.[7] In the canon law, on the other hand, the association between laws dealing with the clergy and laws dealing with general sexual matters is stronger and more significant[8] than the association between laws dealing with the clergy and laws dealing specifically with criminal sexuality.[9] Thus, the civil law treats the clergy and sexuality primarily as a matter of criminal behavior, while the canon law regulates the clergy and sexual activities much more commonly outside of the context of sexual criminality.

It is also evident that some of the law books in both laws dwell more heavily than do others upon sexual matters in general and sexual crimes in particular.[10] This again is not a chance association. Likewise, the association between clerical status and the different lawbooks within the two laws is very marked and cannot well be accounted for by mere chance.[11]

TABLE 19

Distribution by source of laws dealing with sexual topics

Source	SEXUAL, MARITAL		SEXUAL, NON-MARITAL		SEXUAL, NON-SPECIFIC		TOTAL	
	Frequency	%	Frequency	%	Frequency	%	Frequency	%
Decretum	11	28.9	8	47.1	6	60.0	25	38.5
Liber Extra	9	23.7	3	17.6	2	20.0	14	21.5
Liber Sextus	1	2.6	0	0.0	0	0.0	1	1.5
Digest	1	2.6	0	0.0	0	0.0	1	1.5
Codex	4	10.5	1	5.9	2	20.0	7	10.8
Novels	12	31.6	4	23.5	0	0.0	16	24.6
Institutes	0	0.0	1	5.9	0	0.0	1	1.5
	38	100.0	17	100.0	10	100.0	65	100.0

These associations suggested to me that there might also be an interesting association between the time dimension and the frequency with which the legal sources dealt with sexual matters. My tentative hypothesis was that the earlier collections in the canon law *corpus* would show a greater number of texts dealing with sexual matters than the later ones and, further, that the civil law texts that originated during the reign of Justinian would show a stronger interest in sexual topics than would the civil law texts originating in earlier periods. To test this idea, I ran a series of rank-order correlations, with the time dimension as one element, arranging the sources from earlier to later in each of the two laws, and with sexual topics and sexual crimes as the other element in the correlation. These tests did not fully bear out my

TABLE 20

Distribution by source of laws dealing with sexual offences

Source N.	ADULTERY		FORNI-CATION		BIGAMY		INCEST		RAPE		SODOMY		OTHER/MORE THAN ONE		TOTAL	
	N.	%	N.	%	N.	%	N.	%	N.	%	N.	%	N.	%	N.	%
Decretum ..	2	28.6	8	61.5	2	33.3	0	0.0	5	83.3	0	0.0	2	50.0	19	50.0
Liber Extra.	3	42.9	3	23.1	2	33.3	0	0.0	0	0.0	0	0.0	1	25.0	9	23.7
Digest	1	14.3	0	0.0	0	0.0	0	0.0	0	0.0	0	0.0	0	0.0	1	2.6
Codex	0	0.0	1	7.7	0	0.0	0	0.0	0	0.0	0	0.0	1	25.0	2	5.3
Novels.....	0	0.0	1	7.7	2	33.3	1	100.0	0	0.0	1	100.0	0	0.0	5	13.2
Institutes...	1	14.3	0	0.0	0	0.0	0	0.0	1	16.7	0	0.0	0	0.0	2	5.3
	7	100.0	13	100.0	6	99.9	1	100.0	6	100.0	1	100.0	4	100.0	38	100.0

TABLE 21

Rank-order correlations of sexual topics and sexual crimes with source collections in chronological order

Variables	CANON LAW				CIVIL LAW			
	Tau	Significance	Rho	Significance	Tau	Significance	Rho	Significance
Source and sexual topic........	-.21	.08	-.22	.08	-.04	.42	-.05	.42
Source and sexual crime	-.22	.10	-.24	.10	.08	.38	.08	.41

hypothesis, however, for the correlation coefficients proved to be fairly modest, especially in the canon law, and they were not statistically significant at the 5 percent level.

After reviewing the evidence further, I decided to try a different approach based on a modified hypothesis. My new hypothesis was founded on the supposition that it would be possible to identify within each of the two laws one set of topics that could be characterized as religious and another set that could be called non-religious. By religious topics I meant laws concerned with sexuality, the sacraments, the liturgy, and the clergy. By non-religious topics I meant such matters as testamentary disposition, contracts, sale, servile status, electoral law, the law of guardianship, evidence, testimony, succession to estates, appellate procedure, *patria potestas,* loans, possession of property, and manumission. Given these two clusters of topics, then, my hypothesis was that the later collections of the classical canon law placed more emphasis on non-religious matters than did the earlier collections. Likewise, I also hypothesized that the civil law as a whole placed greater emphasis on non-religious subjects, but that the legislation of Justinian would show a greater religious emphasis than the earlier Roman legislation did.

In order to test these hypotheses, I performed an analysis of the variance between the two laws on the topics that I had singled out for special attention.[12] This analysis showed that the variance between the canon and civil laws on the religious topics was comparatively slight, but that the variance on seven of the non-religious subjects was particularly striking and important. There were also significant two-way interactions between several of the non-religious variables in the analysis.

TABLE 22

Main effects in analysis of variance

Variable	F	Sig.
Slave	38.618	.001
Succession....	86.988	.001
Dominium ...	12.055	.001
Tutor........	28.724	.001
Contract	39.321	.001
Loan	15.798	.001
Testament	80.681	.001

TABLE 23

Significant two-way interactions in analysis of variance

Variables	F	Sig.
Slave with *patria potestas*	2.323	.011
Patria potestas with tutor	10.014	.002
Slave with succession	4.570	.031
Contract with testament	4.138	.040

In order to explore these findings more thoroughly and to measure more exactly the relative importance of the various topics that I had segregated as particularly important for differentiating the two laws and the different collections within each of the two laws, I then subjected the data to a series of multiple discriminant analyses.[13] This statistical method involves the mathematical manipulation of the scores on a series of variables so as to weight and linearly combine the discriminating variables into patterns that will make the groups being studied as statistically distinct as possible. This method showed that the treatment of general sexual topics more adequately distinguished between the various collections of the canon law than did the treatment of sexual crimes, but that greater discrimination between the individual collections occurred with other variables. The most useful discriminating categories between the canonical compilations in the *Corpus iuris canonici* turned out to be: sacramental law, law of possession, law of guardianship, law of evidence, liturgical law, and law of sexual crimes, in that order.

Thus, sexual matters are relatively unimportant in discriminating between the law books of the *Corpus iuris canonici*. I found that constructing standardized discriminant function coefficients solely on the basis of sexual themes and sexual crimes would enable me to predict correctly the membership of individual canons in the several canonical collections in only 8.5 percent of the cases. By contrast, the standardized discriminant function coefficients based on these same two variables in the civil law sample yielded correct classifications in 40.85 percent of the cases. When it came to differentiating between the civil and the canon law and predicting which *corpus* a given legal text belonged to, the sexual theme and sexual crime variables in my data yielded correct classifications in 51.9 percent of the cases. It is thus clear that the treatment of sexual topics and sexual crimes is relatively uniform between the various canon law collections, but that the treatment of these matters is far more distinctive between the various books of the civil law than it is between the books of the canon law. In addition, this analysis makes it clear that the relative importance of sexual topics and sexual crimes is different, but only slightly different, between the civil and the canon law.

Further analysis showed, moreover, that when it comes to distinguishing between the two laws the non-religious and non-sexual variables are more reliable and more accurate than the religious ones. Constructing standardized discriminant function coefficients on non-religious variables showed that a half-dozen of them were particularly powerful and accurate guides to the differences between the canon and the civil law. The discriminant function coefficients based on these variables produced correct classifications in more than 76 percent of the cases.

TABLE 24

Most successful discriminating variables

Variables	Wilks' Lambda	F.
Succession....	.9049	83.8356
Testament	.9079	80.9049
Contract	.9496	42.3232
Slave	.9546	37.9099
Manumission .	.9699	24.7677
Tutor	.9668	27.4261

Summing it all up, then, what does this mass of numbers, tables, and statistical manipulations tell us? First, it confirms that medieval canon law gave greater emphasis to sexual crimes and other sexual matters than did Roman civil law. Second, it also showed that there is a slightly greater emphasis on sexual matters in the early books of the canon law *corpus* than there is in the later ones, but that this variation is not statistically significant. Third, it showed a substantial tendency of the later canonical collections to treat non-religious matters more frequently and religious topics less frequently than did the earlier books of classical canon law. The civil law, too, placed greater emphasis on non-religious matters than did the canon law, although Justinian's legislation gave greater prominence to religious and sexual topics than had the civil law of earlier emperors.

On the basis of these results one can therefore conclude, with appropriate caution and reservations, that the canon law during the course of its development between the mid-twelfth and the fourteenth centuries tended to become less and less preoccupied with sexual and theological subjects and to give greater prominence to non-religious and essentially secular problems. As it did so, the canon law came increasingly to resemble the Roman civil law in the pattern of topics that it treated.

9

The Marriage of Mary and Joseph in the Twelfth-Century Ideology of Marriage*

Penny S. Gold

Twelfth-century canonists and theologians found the church's teaching on marriage confusing and contradictory, with existing doctrine failing even to specify what acts were necessary to create a marital bond.[1] Without a clear understanding of when, or if, a marriage had begun, the church's ability to decide on cases dealing with marriage was impaired. By the middle of the twelfth century, two basic positions on the problem had emerged: one opinion, stated most notably by Gratian, held that sexual consummation was a necessary part of a complete marriage; the other opinion, elaborated by both Hugh of Saint Victor and Peter Lombard, maintained that only the consent of the two parties was necessary for the formation of the marital bond and that consummation was not a necessary element.[2] This second opinion is the one that came to dominate canon law and it was the example of the unconsummated marriage of Mary and Joseph that proved decisive. This chapter examines the ways in which Gratian, Hugh of Saint Victor, and Peter Lombard came to a definition of marriage, and then compares their solutions to that of Thomas Aquinas a century later.

It should be noted that although the doctrinal debates we examine concerned an institution that affected the lives of most medieval men and women, the relation of these discussions to actual marital customs is tenuous. The development of the doctrine shows clearly the influence of philosophical and theological concerns; the influence of practice is less clear. In fact, the preoccupation of the church with the determination of the existence of a marriage, and the doctrinal emphasis on the sufficiency of consent between the prospective spouses seem contradictory to what little we know of actual marriage practice. Among the nobility, for example, most marriages were carefully planned in order to provide political and economic advantages to the families concerned rather than carried out by the couple alone.[3]

Gratian compiled his *Decretum*, which he entitled *Concordia discordantium canonum* (harmony of conflicting canons), around 1140. Beyond collecting the various canons (laws), he commented upon them in his so-called *dicta*, into which he inserted relevant extracts from more than four thousand texts. Gratian's purpose was to find through the law a means of enforcing obedience to the Church's belief. Canon law gave the Church the exclusive right to try all cases of heresy, schism, apostasy, and simony, and it also left to Church jurisdiction all cases arising out of the systems of sacraments. In this connection its jurisdiction over the sacrament of marriage was all-important, since cases involving adultery, legitimation of children, separation, or dowry came into the Church courts.

The key to any discussion about marriage was a definition of what constituted marriage, which always, in Gratian's mind, had to be measured against the example of Mary and Joseph. Gratian's discussion of marriage begins by examining the difference between marriage and betrothal. Was a girl, betrothed to one person but subsequently married to another, married to the man to whom she was first betrothed?[4] Assuming that betrothal consists of consent, Gratian seeks to establish whether such consent is sufficient to form a marital bond, or whether sexual union is the necessary element.

Gratian first marshals the arguments and authorities supporting the opinion that consent made a marriage. After two canons, he intervenes in a *dictum* to point out that one cannot simply refer to consent; one must specify exactly what kind of consent makes a marriage. It cannot be consent to cohabitation, because then a brother could contract "marriage" with a sister. And it cannot be consent to carnal coupling because then there would have been no marriage between Mary and Joseph, "for Mary had vowed to remain a virgin" (*dictum post canonem* 2).[5] If by marrying, she was consenting to carnal coupling, she would be breaking her vow of virginity even if she never committed the deed, and "it is wicked to think this" (d.p.c. 2). Gratian resolves this for the moment by citing Augustine's work *On Virginity*, since Augustine, in discussing the difficult matter of Mary's vows, holds at one point, that Mary did, in a special way, consent to carnal coupling:

> Blessed Mary intended to keep her vow of virginity in her heart, but she did not express that vow of virginity with her mouth; she subjected herself to the divine disposition, intending to keep herself a virgin unless God revealed otherwise to her. Therefore, committing her virginity to the divine disposition, she consented to carnal coupling, not seeking it, but obeying the divine inspiration in either case (c. 3).

But this was not the consent that made the marriage between her and Joseph. That, Augustine says, was consent to cohabitation and to keep an undivided way of life (c. 3). This commitment to a joined life, "such that in all matters she show to the man how she is, and conversely," is presumed to be different from the simple consent to cohabitation of brother and sister.

Continuing with the view that consent is sufficient for marriage, Gratian again cites Augustine to the effect that one is called "spouse" *(coniunx)* from the first pledge of betrothal, when there has been no sexual intercourse. This principle, as applied to Joseph, led to the conclusion that Joseph deserves to be called a parent of Christ because he was the spouse of the mother (c. 9). The married status of Mary and Joseph is sometimes, as in this canon, part of a problem which stems from biblical practice; in both the Old and New Testaments, betrothed persons are referred to as spouses. This means that even though there might be a juridical difference between betrothal and marriage, the legal status of the relationship could not be determined by the fact that two people were called "spouse."[6]

Mary and Joseph are introduced once more to prove that a union without coitus is a marriage. Once again, the authority cited is Augustine, who had stated that all three goods of marriage were fulfilled in the parents of Christ: the good of offspring was fulfilled by Christ himself; the good of fidelity, because there was no adultery; the good of sacrament, or indissolubility, because there was no divorce (c. 10).

The notion that "consent makes a marriage" is developed further in a group of canons relating cases where a betrothed person and a married person are given the same treatment, or where a betrothed person is called "married." These conclude the consideration that a type of mental state (consent), which to Gratian is implicit in betrothal, is what makes a marriage.

In Part II of this *quaestio* Gratian has selected canons which make sexual union the criterion for marriage. The first canon is unequivocal, and is crucial to the argument that coitus makes marriage. A text of Augustine (now known to be false) is cited: "There is no doubt that a woman does not belong to marriage as to whom it is learned that there was no mixing of the sexes" (c. 16). The next canon provides the basis for a doctrine of marriage which incorporates the physical union of husband and wife. In his letter to the Ephesians, Paul established the analogy between Christian marriage and Christ's mystical union with the Church:

> Wives, submit yourselves unto your own husbands, as unto the Lord. For the husband is the head of the wife, even as Christ is the head of the church: and he is the saviour of the body. Therefore as the church is subject unto Christ, so let the wives be to their own husbands in every thing. Husbands, love your wives, even as Christ also loved the church, and gave himself for it . . . So ought men to love their wives as their own bodies. He that loveth his wife loveth himself. For no man ever yet hated his own flesh; but nourisheth and

cherisheth it, even as the Lord the church: for we are members of his body, of his flesh, and of his bones. For this cause shall a man leave his father and mother, and shall be joined unto his wife, and *they two shall be one flesh. This is a great mystery: but I speak concerning Christ and the church.*[7]

Pope Leo interpreted this passage to mean that without a sexual bond ("they two shall be one flesh"), the marriage does not have in itself the sacrament of Christ and the Church (c. 17).

Pope Leo's opinion asserts the primary importance of the bodily union of husband and wife. This emphasis is further supported by the subsequent canons dealing with the mutuality of the marriage debt and the necessity for mutual vows of continence if one spouse wishes to vow continence or to enter monastic life. The special importance of sexual union to marriage is also demonstrated in canons indicating that a betrothed woman, as opposed to a married one, does *not* need the consent of her betrothed to enter a monastery (c. 27 and 28).

The dissolubility of an unconsummated marriage also indicates that coitus is a criterion of marriage. Gregory had stated that if a woman could prove that her husband had not been able to consummate the marriage, she could leave him and marry someone else. Gratian says that it appears from this that such a couple was never married, "otherwise it would not be lawful for them to withdraw from each other, except on account of fornication, and then withdrawing, it would be necessary for them to remain unmarried or be reconciled to each other" (d.p.c. 29). In this context the situation of Mary and Joseph is brought up again. Just as the separation of the above couple shows that they were not married, Christ's "entrusting of Mary to John (John 19:27) and the withdrawal of Joseph is denied to be divorce because Joseph had not known her. Hence it appears that they were not married" (d.p.c. 29). Gratian then applies the legitimacy of this separation to the original case under consideration: "If blessed Mary, whom Joseph had betrothed and whom he had taken as his own, is denied to be a spouse, much less is one to be called a wife who is simply betrothed" (d.p.c. 29). Here the union of the holy couple is used to make the point that betrothal is different from marriage, that the difference is sexual "knowledge," and that a betrothed couple may legitimately be separated.

Two more situations, dealing with adultery and rape, are included to support the opinion that betrothal is different from marriage. It is shown that the juridical consequences of adultery and rape differ according to whether one of the participants was betrothed or married. It is assumed that if there is a difference between betrothal and marriage, that difference is the sexual union which takes place in marriage.

This brings Gratian to his first attempt at harmony between the two opposing views of what makes a marriage. Canons 16 to 34 have shown that a betrothed woman (a woman who has not yet had sexual intercourse) is not a wife. But how then can the Fathers (following both the Old and New Testaments) call betrothed persons spouses? The solution is to distinguish between the beginning and completion of marriage: "It must be known that marriage is begun by betrothal and completed by mixing. Hence between the betrothed there is a marriage, but only the beginning; between the coupled there is a ratified marriage" (d.p.c. 34).

With this solution in hand, Gratian reintroduces Augustine's statement that there is no marriage where there has been no mixing of the sexes. He comments: "It is understood that this refers to a complete [i.e., ratified] marriage which has in itself the sign of Christ and the Church" (d.p.c. 39). Now, for the fifth time, Gratian must deal with the case of Mary and Joseph, as Augustine also said that there was a complete *(perfectum)* marriage between Mary and Joseph. To reconcile these two conflicting passages, he poses a different standard for completeness, the three goods of marriage: "But complete is understood not from the office [sexual union] but from those things which accompany marriage, that is fidelity, offspring and the sacrament" (d.p.c. 39). This does not agree with the immediately preceding statement that a complete marriage is one which has in itself the sign of Christ and the Church; nor does it agree with the immediately subsequent statement that a complete marriage, one that is to be considered unbreakable, is one which was begun by betrothal and consummated by sexual union, and that a marriage can be considered separable if it was not perfected by its office (d.p.c. 39). According to this distinction, the marriage of Mary and Joseph would have been a "separable" one, which is what Gratian has, in effect, argued previously in his *dictum* following canon 29.

Gratian's *dictum* goes on to deal with the case from another angle. The Scripture calls some people married who are simply betrothed. This can be explained by distinguishing between the name *(nomen)* of being married, which a betrothed person has, and the substance *(res)* or effect *(effectus)* of being married, which a betrothed person does not have. Gratian, quoting Augustine, uses this distinction to explain that Mary was called "spouse" because she was "a future wife" (d.p.c. 39). Joseph's being called husband is given a similar explanation (c. 40).

That is all we hear about Mary and Joseph. In his final *dictum* on the problem of whether a betrothed couple is married, Gratian again states the solution that consent to contract marriage followed by coitus makes a complete marriage:

> Coitus without will to contract marriage and deflowering of virginity without conjugal agreement do not make a marriage. But the precedent will of contracting marriage and the conjugal contract effect that the man in the deflowering of her virginity or in coitus is said to marry the man or to celebrate marriage (d.p.c. 45).

The conclusion is that in the case initially under consideration, the woman is not to be returned to her first betrothed, since there had not been a marriage between them (d.p.c. 49 and d.p.c. 50).

But what of Mary and Joseph? The opinion that consent makes a marriage can quite easily accommodate categorization of their union as a marital one, and in the section of the *quaestio* dealing with that opinion, three statements of Augustine are cited which speak of their marriage in this light. Though it is difficult, if not impossible, to assimilate Mary and Joseph into the ranks of the married if coitus is held to be the determining condition, it is towards this latter opinion that Gratian tends. His difficulty in explaining the case of Mary and Joseph in these terms is indicated by his four *dicta* on the matter. The only direct affirmation of their marriage which he can provide is that their marriage was complete because it contained all three goods of marriage, a criterion not used anywhere else in Gratian's formulation.[8]

Hugh of Saint Victor, on the other hand, was able to arrive at a definition of marriage that was consistent with the special union of Mary and Joseph. Hugh approached the subject in two treatises composed at about the same time, one on the virginity of Mary and the second a general treatment of the sacraments.[9] The treatise *De beatae Mariae virginitate* was written as an attack on those who were so irreverent as to raise doubts about the immutable virginity of Mary.[10] Hugh's defense of her virginity is emphatic. Immediately after the prologue, he states:

> Concerning the uncorrupted virginity of the mother of God, this faith is piously, and this piety is faithfully, confessed, that the consent to marriage in no way diminished its perfection, just as the conception did not violate chastity, nor childbirth do away with purity.[11]

To prove this, Hugh takes up the definition and substance of marriage.

Hugh's definition is similar to Augustine's: when a man and a woman marry, they mutually agree to a life in which they will always be joined to one another.[12] To deal with those scriptural passages that refer to carnal union—"two in one flesh"[13]—Hugh offers a solution which he develops in greater detail in his treatise on sacraments (and which is subsequently adopted, with slight modifications, by Peter Lombard). Hugh posits two sacraments in marriage, one greater than the other. The first is the sacrament spoken of in Ephesians, the sacrament of Christ and the Church, which is made through the carnal union of the spouses. Hugh calls this sacrament the office of marriage. There is, however, a second, greater sacrament, that of God and the soul. This is made in the heart or spirit, rather than the flesh, and consists of the union of two spouses in love.[14] In this second sacrament, sexual union is not a necessity, and thus there is no reason to believe that Mary broke her resolution to remain a virgin when she consented to marry Joseph.[15] In this treatise the unconsummated marriage of Mary and Joseph is tied closely to Hugh's innovative double sacrament of marriage.

His ideas on marriage are developed much more fully in *De Sacramentis,* which is more closely comparable to Gratian's work since its explicit focus is the sacrament of marriage. Hugh states that sacraments were proposed by God to man in order to provide a remedy for the punishments humans have to suffer as a result of the sin of disobedience of Adam and Eve (Bk. 1, Pt. 8, chp. 11). Genesis, however, states that Adam and Eve were associated with each other ("married") *before* the sin, whereas the sacraments were supposedly instituted *after* the sin. Hugh counters this problem by positing that the sacrament of marriage had a two-fold institution: first, before sin, where it was not a remedy but an office, since there was no sickness in man to be cured, only virtue to be exercised; second, after sin, for remedy (1.8.12).[16] Thus there are two things in marriage: marriage and the office of marriage, each of which is a sacrament. Marriage itself consists in the consent of the social pact; the office of marriage consists in the copulation of the flesh (1.8.13). Each sacrament has its own typology, one of God and the soul, the other of Christ and the Church. Both sacraments consist of the union of two into one: just as in the sacrament of matrimony man and woman are made one through love, so in the office of matrimony they are made one through mingling of the flesh. The office of matrimony is ordained so that the conjugal society of man and woman might not be idle, and "so that those joined in matrimony might be exercised through obedience into virtue and might bear fruit through the generation of progeny" (1.8.13).[17] Hugh found what he thought was a similar dichotomy between the office of matrimony and matrimony itself in Augustine's book on *The Good of Marriage,* in which Augustine stated that there is good in marriage not only because of the propagation of children, but also because of the natural association between the two sexes. Otherwise there could not be marriage in the case of old people who had lost the ardor of the flesh.

Following his consideration of the two sacraments of marriage, Hugh addresses the question of what makes a marriage. In the treatise on Mary's virginity he did not consider any serious challenge to his own view; his argument was based entirely on his own logic and an explication of Scripture. In this second treatise, however, he brings in the statement of Augustine: "That woman cannot attain to the sacrament of Christ and the Church with whom carnal commerce is known to have not taken place." For Hugh the intercourse of the flesh (the office of marriage) typifies that union made between Christ and the Church through Christ's assumption of flesh; thus there could be no sacrament of Christ and the Church where there was no carnal mixing. Gratian had made a similar statement, but then had the difficulty of reconciling the necessity of sex for the sacrament of Christ and the Church with the marriage of Mary and Joseph. Hugh does not mention Mary and Joseph explicitly in this context, but in the response to Augustine which follows, he uses material identical to that found in the treatise on Mary. Again there is the division into two sacraments, but also common to the two treatises is a concern with the corresponding division between body and soul, the carnal and the spiritual: "True marriage and the true sacrament of marriage can exist, even if carnal commerce has not followed: in fact, the more truly and the more sacredly it can exist, the more it has nothing in it at which chastity may blush, but has that of which charity may boast" (2.11.3). The woman who has not engaged in sexual intercourse cannot attain to the sacrament of Christ and the Church, but she can yet attain to another sacrament, "not great in Christ and the Church, but greater in God and in the soul . . . . If that which is in the flesh is great, is not this much greater which is in the spirit?" (2.11.3).

For Hugh, then, there is true marriage before sexual consummation, and a marriage can be holy without it. The allowance of sex in marriage is a matter of indulgence, "lest the vice of concupiscence, which took root in human flesh after sin, might pour forth disgracefully into every excess, if it could never have been received licitly" (2.11.3).[18] Hugh goes on to define marriage as an association between man and woman consecrated by a compact of mutual agreement that neither will leave that association—the Augustinian commitment to an undivided way of life. Consent to such an association makes a marriage. If the couple makes reference in this first pact to consent to carnal mingling, then they are reciprocally constrained to that. But Hugh also allows for the situation in which the couple would mutually vow continence from the beginning of the pact (2.11.4). This last refinement—that the couple could decide at the time of marriage whether their marital consent included consent to coitus—was not part of Hugh's other treatise, nor does he explicitly mention Mary and Joseph in the present context. But their marriage would obviously be a perfect model of the couple who mutually vow continence. Hugh's concern to reconcile Mary's virginity and her marital consent—a concern which dominated the treatise on Mary—is perfectly compatible with his commitment to the superiority of spiritual concerns over carnal ones.

There is only one explicit mention of the marriage of Mary and Joseph in the treatment of marriage in *De sacramentis*. In his discussion of the question as to when a marriage begins, Hugh introduces Isidore's statement: "Consorts are more truly so called from the first faith of the betrothal, although as yet conjugal copulation between them is unknown" (2.11.5). Does this mean that a couple is married from the time they are betrothed? Hugh says it is simply a matter of definition. If betrothal is defined as a promise of future consent, then it is not the beginning of marriage. But if by the name "betrothal" is understood as the contract of matrimony, then betrothal can be considered as the consent to mutual association which is called marriage (2.11.5). Hugh then cites a couple of authorities to support this position, including Augustine, who had said that "from the first faith of betrothal she [Mary] was called the wife of Joseph, whom he had not known by coition and was not to know" (2.11.5). We saw earlier that similar statements would set Gratian off on a consideration of the difference between being "called" married and having the substance of marriage.[19] But the marriage of Mary and Joseph presents no problem to Hugh. He has already defined marriage in such a way that a marriage without sex is morally superior to marriage with sex. Now by allowing for two different definitions of betrothal, it is simple to place the betrothal of Mary and Joseph with those in which betrothal consisted of marital consent.

We have seen, then, that although the subject of marriage is central to Hugh's treatise on the virginity of Mary, the marriage of Mary and Joseph is left virtually unconsidered in his treatment of the sacrament of marriage. Their marriage was problematic to Gratian because he was attempting to reconcile the demands of both flesh and spirit in his definition of marriage. As a canonist, he was, perhaps, aware of the need to make legislation in accord with human possibilities, and, hence, the desirability of including sexual intercourse in a definition of marriage. Perhaps more importantly, Gratian needed to formulate a definition of marriage which would be practicable enough to be applied by church officials making decisions in actual cases. Hugh is far removed from these needs. The celibate marriage of Mary and Joseph is no problem to Hugh since he holds that the spirit is so superior to the flesh, that marriage not only can exist without sex, but is better without it. He overcomes one of the obstacles to this solution in Gratian—that without sex there can be no signification of Christ and the Church—by simply going beyond Ephesians to posit a second, more important sacrament, which signifies the union of God and the soul.

Both Gratian and Hugh consider the marriage of Mary and Joseph to be within the same sphere, to be judged by the same categories, as the marriage of ordinary humans. Hugh's concern to fit Mary into the rules that govern other mortals is particularly clear in his explanation of how it was that Mary conceived by the Holy Spirit. In order to account for this case, Hugh posits a general theory of conception that accommodates both Mary and ordinary humans. Hugh says that there is a fetal seed within the woman that is activated by the male seed received in sexual intercourse. This activation, however, can only occur with the presence of mutual love. In Mary's case, the love of the Holy Spirit, and Mary's especially ardent love for the Holy Spirit, brought about the activation of the seed within her body.[20] This treatment of conception, and likewise Hugh's treatment of marriage, thus elevates human relationships, in order to accommodate both ordinary humans and the Virgin Mary into one general theory.[21]

A similar, but less extreme solution to the problem of the marriage of Mary and Joseph is found in Peter Lombard's *Four Books of Sentences,*[22] written fifteen to twenty years after the works of Hugh and Gratian. The Lombard was a theologian, but was less interested in Hugh's speculative concerns than he was, like Gratian, in reconciling differing opinions which had come down in the Christian tradition. The works of both Hugh and Gratian were used extensively by Peter Lombard, and it is interesting to see how he balances their two different treatments of marriage.

The Lombard's basic chapter on the sacrament of marriage is taken almost literally from Hugh's treatment in *De sacramentis,* but his explanation of the sacramental nature of marriage differs slightly from Hugh's. Rather than accepting Hugh's formulation of two sacraments, one of marriage and one of the office of marriage, Peter Lombard describes one sacrament, which signifies the union of Christ and the Church but has two aspects: will and nature, one spiritual and one physical.

> For as between husband and wife there is union in the consent of their souls[23] and in the joining of their bodies, so the Church is joined to Christ by will and nature in that she wills the same as he, and that he himself assumed the form of the nature of man. Therefore the bride is united to the bridegroom spiritually and physically, that is by love and by a conformity to nature. And the symbol of both these unions is in marriage; for the consent of the husband and wife signifies the spiritual union of Christ and the Church which takes place through love; and the union of the sexes signifies the union which takes place through a conformity to nature (Dist. 26, cap. 6).

Thus human marriage has the same two aspects of will (consent) and nature (carnal union) as does the union of Christ and the Church. The Lombard notes that, in apparent accordance with this, some have said that a woman does not belong in marriage who has not experienced carnal union. Like Gratian, the Lombard sees that acceptance of that position would mean that Mary and Joseph were not married, "to think which is a sin" (26.6). This implication, he explains, can only be made if the statement is accepted according to the superficial meaning of the words. The passage from Augustine is, rather, to be understood symbolically:

> Not that a woman does not belong in marriage, in whose case there is no sexual union; but that she does not belong in a marriage which contains the express and full symbol of the union of Christ and the Church. For her marriage represents the union of Christ and the Church, which is in love, but not that which is in a conformity to nature. There is in her marriage a type of union of Christ and the Church, but only of that union in which the Church is united to Christ by love, not of that in which, through Christ's assumption of the flesh, the members are joined to the head (26.6).

The marriage of Mary and Joseph, therefore, had that part of the sacrament formed by will but not that formed by nature. This lack did not make their marriage any less holy. In fact following Hugh, the Lombard holds that "it was the more holy and perfect as it was the more free from carnal acts" (26.6).

Where Hugh had solved the problem of typology (that marriage is a sacrament of the union of Christ and the Church and sexual union the vehicle of the symbol) by formulating another sacrament of God and the soul, Peter Lombard simply states that the union of Christ and the Church is itself both spiritual and physical. His solution is formulated in order to include the marriage of Mary and Joseph within the fold of human marriage. Gratian, in facing the same problem, was either unwilling or unable to exclude sex from the definition of marriage, as did Hugh and Peter Lombard. The result was that Gratian was not able to be as unequivocal as the other two on the completeness of the marriage between Mary and Joseph.

Peter Lombard also follows Hugh on the relative roles of consent and coitus in the making of a marriage. Consent expressed of the present is the efficient cause of marriage. But the problem of sex, and therefore the problem of Mary and Joseph, comes up again when Peter Lombard, following the order of Gratian's work, has to explain what kind of consent makes a marriage. He has already stated that it was not the *act* of sex which makes a marriage but perhaps it is *consent* to (future) performance of the act of sex which makes marriage. Mary's situation, however, would not fit that condition, since she had pledged herself to perpetual virginity before her marriage and so could not have consented to sex when she entered a marital relationship with Joseph. Peter Lombard concludes that marriage is made by consent to conjugal association, expressed through words of the present, "such that the man says: I receive you as mine, not as a lord, not as a servant, but as a spouse" (28.4). This association is not defined further; it is assumed that Mary and Joseph had such a conjugal association. This leaves the problem of explaining Augustine's statement that their marriage was a perfect one. The Lombard has earlier shown that half of the signification of marriage was lacking to Mary and Joseph because there was no physical union between them. How then could their marriage be considered perfect? He concludes, citing Augustine, that the marriage was perfect, not in signification, but in sanctity, "for marriages are more holy by a mutual vow of continence" (30.2). The marriage of Mary and Joseph was also perfect (complete) according to the three goods of marriage. The Lombard concludes the chapter with a repetition of the idea that sex has to do with the completeness of the signification of marriage, not with the truth or sanctity of marriage.

The marriage of Mary and Joseph is brought up once more in the context of the purposes for which marriage should be contracted, which include: to beget offspring, to avoid fornication, to reconcile enemies. He adds that the marriage of Mary and Joseph had other special causes, and cites the following: the marriage gave the Virgin the help of a man for sustenance; it hid the birth of Jesus from the devil; it made Joseph a witness to Mary's chastity and thus defended her from suspicion; and it prevented her from being accused of adultery (20.4). In this context, the Lombard is willing to view their marriage as a special case.[24]

We have seen, then, that the Lombard begins his treatment of marriage with statements on the nature of the sacrament that closely follow Hugh's formulation. He then deals sequentially with the questions brought up by Gratian, including the various problems posed by the marriage of Mary and Joseph. His conclusions, however, are much closer to Hugh's than to Gratian's. Hugh and the Lombard are more successful in dealing with Mary and Joseph because they define marriage in terms of consent, rather than coitus, and because they are willing to leave something out of their marriage (for Hugh, the sacrament of Christ and the Church; for the Lombard, the part of the sacrament of Christ and the Church that pertains to nature). At the same time they both insist that this omission in no way derogates from the marriage, but, on the contrary, makes it more holy.

Peter Lombard's *Sentences* were the subject of a commentary by Thomas Aquinas at the beginning of his career. In the one hundred years between the text and its commentary, a major shift had occurred in Christian attitudes toward the natural world. Rather than the abhorrence of the flesh and distrust of nature so common in the eleventh and twelfth centuries, there was an increased interest in and tolerance of the natural world and man's place in it. This attitude made possible a new acceptance of the human body as something good. Thomas's thirteenth-century commentary on the twelfth-century work of Peter Lombard provides us with an excellent opportunity to view the changes that this new attitude effected in the theology of that institution—marriage—which is so directly involved with the functions of the human body.

The shift in attitude is seen clearly in Thomas's commentary on Distinction 26 of Book IV, where Peter Lombard had stated that the marriage act (sexual intercourse) is excused by the good of marriage:

> If we suppose the corporeal nature to be created by the good God, we cannot hold that those things which pertain to the preservation of the corporeal nature and to which nature inclines, are altogether evil; wherefore, since the inclination to beget an offspring whereby the specific nature is preserved, is from nature, it is impossible to maintain that the act of begetting children is altogether unlawful, so that it be impossible to find the mean of virtue therein; unless we suppose, as some are mad enough to assert, that corruptible things were created by an evil god, whence perhaps the opinion mentioned in the text is derived; wherefore this is a most wicked heresy (D. 26, Q. 1, Ar. 3).[25]

Sex, as part of the creation of a good God, is good simply because it is natural, and Thomas is far enough removed from the attitudes toward sex expressed by Hugh and Peter Lombard to argue that those who claim sex is altogether sinful, and therefore needs to be excused, are guilty of heresy.[26]

Thomas's acceptance of sexual intercourse as a good act and as an essential part of marriage gives his commentary on the Lombard an orientation toward ordinary human marriage lacking in the twelfth-century works. The change is most clearly seen in his consideration of the fundamental question of what makes a marriage. Aquinas agrees with the Lombard that consent is what makes marriage, but he defines quite differently the content of that consent. In order to establish whether consent to marriage is consent to sexual intercourse, it must first be determined what relationship coitus has to marriage. Thomas concludes that marriage is not essentially the sexual union itself but rather a joining of man and woman ordained to sexual intercourse. To consent to marriage is to consent implicitly, but not explicitly, to carnal intercourse. This is a much more developed definition of the content of marital consent than the simple "consent to conjugal association" used by the other authors mentioned in this chapter. What, then, of Mary and Joseph? How could Mary have consented implicitly to sexual intercourse? Thomas does not deal with her case in this *quaestio* but instead refers the reader to a later discussion of Mary's vow of continence. In the later discussion, Aquinas states that Mary's vow of virginity was proper and fitting to her perfection. To the objection that whoever consents to marriage consents implicitly to carnal coupling, a consent which would diminish the purity of Mary's virginity, Thomas replies:

> Carnal coupling belongs implicitly in the consent of the Virgin Mary, just as the act is contained implicitly in potency . . . The potency, however, to carnal coupling is not contrary to virginity, neither does it diminish someone from purity unless by reason of the act itself; which indeed never was intended by the blessed Virgin, but was already certified that the act was never meant to follow (D. 30, Q. 2, Ar. 1, Quaestiuncula 3, Solutio 2, ad 3).[27]

This metaphysical reconciliation of the vow of virginity with consent to coitus, based directly on Augustine,[28] is Thomas's only treatment of the marriage of Mary and Joseph in his *Commentary on the Sentences.* Though Peter Lombard's discussion provided many opportunities for treatment of Mary and Joseph, all were passed over except for the one cited above. This silence about the marriage of Mary and Joseph coincides with Thomas's interest in discussing marriage as an ordinary human institution rather than as an abstract ideal.

Aquinas deals with Mary's marriage at greater length in his *Summa Theologiae,* but this later discussion is in the context of the virginity of Mary, rather than a discussion of marriage in general. In a *quaestio* on the virginity of the mother of God, one article raises the question, "Did the mother of God vow her virginity?" The answer is different from the discussion quoted above from the *Commentary on the Sentences,* but is similar in that it de-emphasizes the absoluteness of Mary's vow, first by saying that she did not vow virginity until the time of her marriage with Joseph, and second, by stating that the vow was at first a conditional one:

We should not believe . . . that the mother of God had made an irrevocable vow of virginity before she was betrothed to Joseph. Perhaps she wanted to, but she also waited on God's good judgement. Afterwards, when she had taken a husband, the acceptable thing to do in those days, she with her husband took a vow of virginity. [In answer to the first objection,] since it did seem that the law was opposed to giving up the things necessary for ensuring progeny on earth, the mother of God did not make an unconditional vow of virginity. Her condition was: if it were pleasing to God. When she knew it was pleasing to him, she made the vow absolute. This happened sometime before the announcement (3a.28.4).

In the following *quaestio* on the betrothal of the mother of God, Aquinas considers whether there was a true marriage between Mary and Joseph. A distinction between form and substance helps him explain the special circumstances of this marriage. He states that a marriage is called true when it is complete, but there are two kinds of completion: one of form which gives the specific character, and a second which is the operation through which the thing achieves its purpose. "The form of matrimony then is an inseparable union of souls in which the husband and wife are pledged in an unbreakable bond of mutual love, and the purpose is the birth and training of children" (3a.29.2). Like Hugh and Peter Lombard, Thomas Aquinas then reasons that the marriage of Mary and Joseph, while lacking in part, contained most of these criteria. Their marriage attained fully the first kind of completion (the form), but with regard to the second, they did not fulfill the begetting of children since their marriage was not consummated. However, they did participate in the training of children, since they brought up Christ. Unlike Hugh and Peter Lombard, Thomas does not go on to assert that their marriage, though lacking, was actually superior to a marriage that incorporated carnal union. Rather, his discussion has an almost apologetic tone. He concludes with the assertion of Augustine that all three goods of marriage were found in the marriage of Mary and Joseph.

The three goods of marriage had also been discussed in Thomas's *Commentary on the Sentences*. The contrast between Thomas and his twelfth-century predecessors, particularly Hugh and the Lombard, is clearly illustrated in their discussions of which of the three goods of marriage is the chief good: offspring, fidelity, or sacrament. Both Hugh and the Lombard stated most affirmatively that sacrament was the chief good of marriage; Aquinas's answer is very different. He says that a thing can be important either because it is more essential *(essentialius),* or because it is more excellent *(dignius).* In terms of excellence, sacrament is in every way the most important of the three marriage goods, since it "belongs to marriage considered as a sacrament of grace; while the other two belong to it as an office of nature; and a perfection of grace is more excellent than a perfection of nature" (D. 31, Q. 1, Ar. 3). But as concerns essence, the good most essential to marriage is the intention of having children, the next essential is the duty of fidelity, and the third essential is the sacrament, "even as to man it is more essential to be in nature than to be in grace, although it is more excellent to be in grace" (D. 31, Q. 1, Ar. 3). The article continues on to describe the ways in which marriage is an institution of nature concerned with bodily acts rather than a spiritual character. It is his commitment to describe marriage as being essentially an act of nature, rather than an act of grace, and his acceptance of nature as good, that distinguishes Thomas Aquinas's ideology of marriage from those of Gratian, Hugh of St. Victor, and Peter Lombard.

We have found that all four authors wanted to develop a consistent theory of marriage. Difficulties arose because of conflicting demands on the theory: it had to have internal logic; it had to be consistent with the traditions of the Church (themselves conflicting); and it had to be able to take into account the marriage of Mary and Joseph. This marriage caused difficulties because it highlighted the question of the role of sexuality in the formation of the marital bond. The differences in the authors' attitudes toward sexuality and its place in marriage can best be understood in the context of medieval perceptions of the natural, physical world. In the twelfth century, a conflict was posited between the bodily nature of human beings (including sexuality) and their spiritual nature (the soul). As we have seen in Hugh of St. Victor and Peter Lombard, there was little doubt that the soul was the better part of human nature, and that the demands and desires of the body should be subordinated to the nurture of the soul. For this reason they de-emphasized the role of sexuality in marriage, arguing that marriage is made by consent alone and that sexuality in fact detracts from marriage. Gratian, on the other hand, incorporated sexuality into his definition of marriage, but his solution was an awkward one which failed to meet his own standards of consistency, particularly with regard to the marriage of Mary and Joseph.

The next hundred years brought a new acceptance of the natural world which is reflected in many aspects of thirteenth-century culture; for example, in the increased naturalism in sculpture and painting and the frank and humorous illustrations of sexuality both in manuscript marginalia[29] and in the popular *fabliaux*. Going beyond the rigid dichotomy between body and soul, Thomas Aquinas reconciled even this opposition, by stating that "the soul is united to the body as its form."[30] He also reconciled the conflict over whether consent or coitus makes a marriage by asserting that consent included an implicit consent to sexual intercourse, since marriage is a joining of man and woman ordained to sexual intercourse. Because of a new acceptance of the bodily nature of man as good, Aquinas was able to conclude that human marriage was, after all, more concerned with the bodily nature of men and women (the intention of having children) than with their spiritual concerns (the sacramental aspect of marriage).

This brings us back to the verse from Ephesians which was, in some ways, the source of the difficulties in defining the nature of marriage. The Vulgate used the word *sacramentum* to refer to marriage:

A man shall leave his father and mother, and shall be joined unto his wife, and they shall be one flesh. This is a great mystery [*sacramentum*]: but I speak concerning Christ and the Church.[31]

The meaning of the term *sacramentum* was less specific in the early centuries of the Church than it was in the twelfth when theologians were concerned with establishing the precise number and definition of the sacraments. Given Paul's use of the term "sacrament," plus the analogy made between man and wife and Christ and the Church, most twelfth-century authors found it necessary to emphasize the sacramental or spiritual nature of marriage. Despite Ephesians' "two in one flesh," they saw the spiritual aspect as antithetical to the physical aspect of the marital union. Their greater valuation of the spiritual meant that the case of the marriage of Mary and Joseph could be accommodated fairly easily. Gratian, concerned to incorporate the physical side of marriage into the sacrament, was unable to include Mary and Joseph in his schema in a coherent way. It is ironic that the two authors who might be considered the furthest apart from each other in time, sentiment, and method—Hugh and Thomas Aquinas—were the two who could leave out a detailed consideration of Mary and Joseph from their general discussions of marriage. Hugh could do this because he was so concerned about the question of the sacramentality of marriage that he posited two sacraments of matrimony in order to separate sexuality, the physical side of marriage, from the essence of marriage. The marriage of Mary and Joseph then fitted easily into his schema and he could quickly pass over it in *De sacramentis*. Thomas Aquinas, on the other hand, chose to play down the sacramental aspect of marriage in favor of the physical side. A treatment of Mary and Joseph would have been awkward in this context (as it had been for Gratian), and was avoided instead with the principal discussion of their marriage occurring in the context of the incarnation of Christ and the virginity of his mother.

10

Concubinage and Marriage
in Medieval Canon Law

James A. Brundage

Nonmarital sexual unions are a fact of life in all societies. This was particularly bothersome for medieval Europeans, whose theological views of sexual morality insisted that marriage must provide the unique situation in which sexual relations could be tolerated—and even within marriage the experience of sexual pleasure was not highly regarded by high-minded celibate churchmen.

But wine and women will make men of understanding to fall away[1] and neither the teaching of theologians nor the preaching of moralists could alter the fact that medieval Europeans engaged in (and presumably enjoyed) nonmarital sexual relationships. This chapter will look briefly at the ways in which the canon lawyers dealt with this situation and at the legal framework in which they treated it. Unlike the theologian, the lawyer cannot dwell exclusively in a world of abstract theories and high principles. Rather, the lawyer must, in the nature of things, work with social realities, although in the process he may try to change them. And like it or not, the medieval canon lawyer had somehow to accommodate his moral principles to everyday life. He had also somehow to work out a legal structure to deal with these realities and to cope with their consequences.[2]

It is well known that from one society to another the institution of marriage varies considerably in the looseness or strictness with which it is structured. Some societies make marriage difficult to contract and easy to terminate; others follow quite different patterns. Social devices to allow variation from the prevailing patterns of marriage also differ markedly in different societies.

One device used by medieval European society in order to lessen the rigidity of formal marriage was concubinage, and it is with this particular variety of nonmarital sexual union that we shall deal here.

In a concubinage relationship, a man and a woman who are not married to each other live together (whether under one roof or not) and habitually have sexual intercourse with one another, usually (but not invariably) to the exclusion of sexual relationships with other parties. The concubinage relationship, then, is relatively stable and often is sexually exclusive.[3] Both the stability of the relationship and its exclusivity differentiate concubinage from prostitution, in which promiscuity is of the essence, at least in the eyes of the law. Although an occasional moralist, such as Saint Jerome (340–420), may speak of concubines as "one-man harlots,"[4] the distinction in law between the concubine and the prostitute is reasonably clear.

Both the stability and the exclusivity of concubinage make the relationship similar to marriage. Accordingly, one problem which the canonists faced in treating concubinage was the difficulty of differentiating this relationship from a marital situation. They sometimes avoided this problem by assimilating the two relationships: by treating concubinage as a second-class marriage.

The distinction between a concubine and a wife is not nearly so easy to draw as that between a concubine and a harlot. The sources of the medieval lawyers' difficulties in dealing with concubinage as a legal institution go far back into the pre-history of Christian Europe. Ancient Jewish law, which was one source from which medieval Christendom drew its social thought, made relatively little distinction between a concubine and a wife[5] and the Scriptures sometimes used the terms interchangeably, a fact which Saint Augustine (354–430), among others, had noted.[6] In early Roman society, too, the distinction between concubinage and marriage was not entirely clear. Only rather gradually did sharp legal distinctions emerge in this area.[7] The classical Roman law differentiated wives from concubines primarily by two criteria: a difference in the social status of the parties to the relationship, and a distinction in the intention of the union. Roman concubines were usually women of inferior status who lived with men of superior social standing. Roman society made marriage between parties of widely disparate social classes legally impossible and long-term unions between them could only take the form of concubinage. It was also possible, however, for Roman men to take as concubines women whom they were legally free to marry. For a variety of reasons many men did so, although they thereby ran the legal risk of being accused of the crime of stuprum.[8]

The second and more crucial distinction between marriage and concubinage in Roman law rested on the intention of the parties. The classical Roman jurists used the term "marital affection" to designate the intention to contract a permanent union. So long as marital affection existed between the parties, they were married; lacking marital affection, the relationship entailed the lesser status of concubinage.[9] This does not mean that a concubine might not be honored and treated with respect and devotion by her consort; but, unless he had the intention of forming a matrimonial union with her, the relationship failed to qualify as a marriage.[10]

In a Christian society the problem of concubinage might, from one point of view, be thought very simple—might be considered, in fact, no problem at all. Saint Paul had declared that those who did not wish to practice sexual continence should marry, which he thought distinctly better than burning (1 Cor. 7:9). From this viewpoint the choice was clear-cut; the Christian had only two moral alternatives: marriage or total celibacy. Concubinage was not a possible moral option for a Christian. This was the opinion, for example, of Saint Augustine, the most influential of the patristic writers on Christian sexual morality. Having lived with a concubine of his own during his youth,[11] Augustine was perhaps more conscious of the problem of concubinage than were some of the other Fathers of the Church. In any event, Augustine's condemnation of concubinage was flat and uncompromising.[12]

Other authorities were not so certain. Late Roman writers had not considered concubinage immoral or disgraceful,[13] and their attitudes may have influenced Christian churchmen to escape the Pauline dichotomy by holding that marriage and concubinage were essentially the same.[14]

The Christian Roman emperors, beginning with Constantine (311–337), had tried to distinguish marriage from concubinage and limited the rights of concubines and their children rather drastically. Justinian (527–565) reversed this trend, however, and sought once more to blur the distinction between marriage and concubinage. His codification of the law reshaped concubinage into an inferior type of marriage.[15] But Justinian's legal reforms, of course, remained largely unknown in western Europe until the Roman law revival in the late eleventh century. During the early Middle Ages in the West, the customary laws of the Germanic invaders introduced a further complicating element. Their social structure allowed no formal place for concubinage; only marriage with full legal consequences was considered a legitimate union. Other unions had no real standing in Germanic law; consequently, concubinage was not a legal institution in Germanic society. Informal, nonmarital sexual relationships did, of course, exist among the Germanic peoples, but for legal purposes they were treated as nonexistent.[16]

The medieval canonists, beginning with Gratian (ca. 1140), inherited this rather confusing group of traditions. Gratian in particular sought to reconcile the conflicting sources which he found, in order to make some sense out of the situation. One very significant modification in the Roman notion of concubinage stands out in Gratian's *Decretum,* for Gratian ascribed to the concubinage relationship the quality of marital affection which the Roman jurists had reserved for marriage unions. As Gratian saw it, a concubine was a woman who united with a man in conjugal affection, but without legal formalities. Gratian, in other words, conceived of concubinage as an imperfect, informal marriage, a marriage which lacked formalities and full legal consequences, but which was nonetheless a true and valid marriage.[17] This meaning of concubinage became the reigning sense of the term among the canonists of the high Middle Ages. It was on the basis of this particular meaning of concubinage that the successors of Gratian elaborated their legal treatment of the concubine's status.[18] At the same time, however, the canonists also continued to use the term "concubinage" in the sense of a temporary, nonmarital union. The canonists' ambivalent terminology in dealing with concubinage was rooted in their even more fundamental ambivalence about the morality of sexual relations. Several influential canonists taught that sexual pleasure was a result of original sin,[19] and hence that the enjoyment of sex, even in marriage, was irretrievably tainted with sin. Those who married solely for sexual fulfillment were validily married, it is true,[20] but the experience of pleasure in coitus was not only treated as essentially immoral by theologians,[21] but was also condemned by many canonists as well.[22] The only exception was intercourse for the purpose of reproduction, and even in that situation some canonists thought that the pleasure derived from the experience was wrong.[23] Given these attitudes toward sexual relations in marriage, it follows that the concubinage relationship, in which pleasure was a primary goal, was even more vehemently suspect.[24] Not even a procreative intention could fully legitimize sexual relations with a concubine.[25]

This same ambivalence toward sex is noticeable in discussions as to what kind of offence it was that concubinous couples committed. One viewpoint, enunciated by Saint Augustine and reiterated by later writers, held concubinage was simply a type of fornication.[26] Some considered concubinage the most heinous form of fornication.[27] Others equated concubinage with the even more serious offence of adultery.[28] Those who thought of concubinage primarily as an informal type of marriage, on the other hand, were inclined to consider that the concubine and her lover were free of any taint of fornication.[29] One key text which Gratian included in his *Decretum* was a canon of the first Council of Toledo (A.D. 400), which stated the rule that an unmarried man who had a concubine should not be forbidden to receive communion, so long as he was content to limit himself to one woman, be she wife or concubine.[30] It has been argued that Gratian quite misunderstood the intent of this canon and probably, in fact, he did.[31] But, misunderstood or not, the canon was included in the *Decretum* and thenceforth stood as witness that concubinage was tolerated by the Church and that it might in fact be considered the functional equivalent of marriage. Another early text which Gratian incorporated in the *Decretum* seemed to make it plain that concubinage was inferior to marriage because the two parties in a concubinage relationship were of disparate social classes, whereas the parties to a marriage must be of approximately equal social standing.[32] As Gratian read the sources, he apparently concluded that marriage and concubinage, although different in some legal effects, were nonetheless essentially the same. Concubinage he seems to have thought a lesser form of marriage, an informal and unstructured marriage, to be sure, but nonetheless a marriage. Provided that marital affection existed between the partners in a concubinage relationship as it did in a marriage, then marriage and concubinage were essentially two forms of the same basic thing. Gratian's misunderstanding of his texts may have been colossal, but it guided subsequent generations of canonists in formulating a new law of concubinage for the western Church.[33]

The decretists who commented on Gratian's treatment of concubinage accepted, for the most part, his basic premise that concubinage was a secondary type of marriage.[34] This was only true, however, if the intention was to form a permanent association, an intention which they understood to be implied in the term "marital affection."[35] If there was no intention of permanence, however, the union could not be considered a marriage in any sense.[36] Other canonists distinguished between the civil law and canon law treatments of concubinage. The civil law, they thought, allowed concubinage, while the law of the Church forbade it.[37] The underlying meaning of these statements, apparently, was that the civil law failed to accept as marriages some unions which, by canon law standards and definitions, were true marital unions, even though informal ones. The civil law treated such unions as concubinage (in the nonmarital sense), while the canon law treated them as marriages and, hence, might be said to allow nonmarital concubinage.

Scattered statements in the canonistic literature, moreover, indicate that some lawyers thought that there was an essential difference between a concubinage situation and a formal marriage.[38] These views, however, were not in the mainstream of canonistic thought. From Gratian onwards, the prevailing view maintained that the fact of habitual cohabitation and the existence of marital affection constituted a marriage, even though that marriage might not be provable at law.[39]

Essentially, the canon law knew only one type of marriage, namely, the union which was distinguished by marital affection.[40] This concept stems entirely from the Roman law.[41] In the law of Justinian, marital affection was the sole requisite condition for constituting a marriage—dowry, ceremonies, and the rest were mere adjuncts to the creation of a marital union, but marital affection was of the essence.[42] For Roman lawyers of Justinian's time, marital affection distinguished a marriage from a mere concubinage situation. Two people who had been living together in concubinage and who began to regard each other with *maritalis affectio* were deemed to have changed their previous relationship into a marriage.[43]

The term "marital affection" was used in different senses at different periods in the long history of the Roman law; yet, by the time of Justinian it had come to mean not only an intention to contract a life-long union, but also to denote a quality in the relationship between the parties, an emotional tie of affection and dependence between them.[44] Marital affection, moreover, was not seen as a single discrete act of the will, a consent that was given at one moment in time, once and for all. Rather, it was described as a continuing consent which must persist, from one moment to the next, so long as the marriage endured.[45]

Now this is a pretty construct, but it presents serious juridical problems. The crucial difficulty, of course, is proof. How does one prove that marital affection has come into existence and that, therefore, a given relationship is now a marriage? Or how does one prove that marital affection does not exist between two given parties and that, therefore, they are not married? And what may be the legal consequences of these facts, assuming one can prove them, for children, for inheritances, for the property rights of the parties, and the like? The Roman jurists had faced these problems and the same difficulties also bothered the medieval canonists when they dealt with informal marriages. One obvious answer to the difficulties, of course, is to create some sort of legal mechanism which requires the contracting parties to exteriorize their feelings—a ceremony, a ritual, a formal exchange of words of consent in the presence of other parties who can bear witness that the couple manifested the intention of contracting a permanent, exclusive marriage relationship, not a temporary, nonexclusive union. This had been the function of the *deductio in domum,* the dotal gift, and other such formal acts in Roman law.[46] In any event, marital affection remained crucial and, provided that its existence could be proved by some external, circumstantial evidence, the presence or absence of ceremonies and witnesses was irrelevant to the legal question of whether this particular union was a marriage or whether it was something else.

The medieval canonists, in turn, adopted the Roman approach as their own. For the canonists, marriage was essentially, as Huguccio expressed it, "a personal relationship."[47] When the canonists speak of concubinage as a type of marriage, they mean cohabitation with marital affection, which entails many of the privileges and consequences of any other marriage.[48] When they speak of concubinage without marital affection, they describe it as an illicit union.[49] This second type of concubinage might be temporary and did not involve any commitment to fidelity.[50] Concubinage in the second sense was a simple liaison for pleasure only and was not in any sense a marriage.[51] All of this seems clear, but the inherent ambiguity in the canonists' terminology when they deal with concubinage can sometimes be very confusing.

The medieval canon law of marriage has been harshly criticized from the twelfth century to the twentieth. Maitland, for example, considered it "certainly no masterpiece of human wisdom" and declared it "not pleasant to read."[52] The early Christian Church adopted without substantial change the Roman law of marriage.[53] The Church wished to make the formation of marriages as easy and simple as possible; for this purpose the Roman marriage law was virtually a formless transaction.[54] Marriage came into existence by the consent of the parties involved and of those who had legal power over them.[55] Sexual intercourse was not essential to constitute marriage.[56] While a few Christian writers argued for the view that coitus was essential to marriage, theirs was a minority position.[57] The theory of marriage adopted by Gratian was one that was apparently first voiced by Cardinal Peter Damian. In Damian's and Gratian's view, marriage came into existence through the exchange of consent between the parties; it was then ratified by intercourse.[58] The canonists felt constrained to assign a secondary role to sexual intercourse in their matrimonial theory because of the theological difficulties posed by the marriage of the Virgin Mary to Saint Joseph. It was necessary to uphold this union as a true marriage, but at the same time it was also necessary to deny that intercourse took place between the parties. Hence, the canonists could not readily accept a theory of marriage which made coitus essential to a true marital union.[59] "A joining of bodies is not marriage, nor does it make a marriage," declared Huguccio, adding that marriage was rather a joining of souls.[60] The essential thing in contracting a marriage was the exchange of consent with marital affection.[61] No special form of words was required, and even unspoken consent was sufficient, provided that it could be proved.[62] From the time of Peter Abelard (1079–1142), it was the common teaching of both lawyers and theologians that the exchange of consent must be made in the present tense or with a present intention,[63] although as Maitland observed, "Of all people in the world lovers are the least likely to distinguish precisely between the present and the future tenses."[64] From the moment of the exchange of the consent the couple were married. Subsequent intercourse was not necessary for the validity of the marriage; neither were publicity, witnesses, or formal rites.[65] Marriage contracted solely by consent was sacramental, at least in some sense of the word, although the notion of the sacramentality of marriage was slow to develop and did not begin to bear the meanings that modern theologians assign to it until late in the medieval period.[66] In contrast to all of the other sacraments, marriage required no special form for validity.[67]

The usage of the Latin Church in regard to marriage ceremonies differed notably from that of the Eastern Churches. The latter from the ninth century onward required a nuptial blessing as a condition for the validity of a marriage.[68]

This is not to say, of course, that marriage ceremonies of various kinds did not exist or were not used in the medieval Western Church. It was, in fact, the usual practice of most couples to exchange consent publicly, to receive a nuptial blessing, and to contract marriage in a ritual fashion of some sort.[69] Nonetheless, such ceremonies were not required for legal validity and marriage could quite easily be contracted in total secrecy, without witnesses or any formalities whatever. Ceremonies were a matter of decorum, but were not essential.[70] Canon law urged couples to contract their marriages publicly, with solemn rites, but stopped short of absolutely requiring them to do so.[71] The fourth Lateran Council in 1215 took special pains to discourage secret, informal marriages, forbade priests to officiate at them, and demanded that couples intending to marry cause a public announcement to be made of their intention.[72] The Council, however, again stopped short of requiring compliance as a condition of validity, and the Council's decree, although incorporated in the *Liber Extra,* proved difficult to enforce in practice.[73]

Given the fact that consent alone created marriage, medieval ecclesiastical courts and lawyers had enormous difficulty in distinguishing nonmarital concubinage from clandestine marriage.[74] Secret marriage was clearly perceived by the canonists as a problem, but it was not a problem that they were really able to solve. Gratian might call such marriages *infectae* or *non legitimum,* but nonetheless he held them valid. Other canonists, such as Rufinus (d. before 1192) might declare that the faithful were forbidden to contract secret marriages; nonetheless, he conceded that if a couple did contract such a marriage they were truly married and should not be separated.[75] The surviving evidence from the medieval ecclesiastical courts emphatically demonstrates that clandestine marriages were extremely common. Recent analyses of records from two English tribunals in the fourteenth century show that nearly 90 percent of the marriage cases handled by these courts involved clandestine unions.[76] Given the fact of clandestine marriage, the canonists lacked any sure or certain criterion whereby a concubine could be clearly differentiated from a clandestine wife.[77]

To complicate matters further, the lawyers established certain legal presumptions about marriage which tended to ensure that under many circumstances a concubinage relationship would be considered a clandestine marriage until proved otherwise. Antecedents of the presumptive marriage can, again, be found in the Roman law; but the Roman law doctrines were radically altered by the medieval canonists.[78] The canonistic doctrine was summed up by Huguccio, who taught that when there had been a promise of future marriage between a couple, any subsequent intercourse created a presumption of consent, not only to sexual relations, but also to marriage, and that the marriage should be reckoned to begin at the time of coitus.[79] This doctrine of Huguccio's, that intercourse following a promise of future marriage established a presumption of consent, was subsequently adopted by Pope Innocent III (1198–1216) and was even more emphatically affirmed by Pope Gregory IX (1227–1241) in the *Liber Extra.*[80] By the mid-thirteenth century the doctrine of presumption of marriage had expanded to the point where jurists held that a man and a woman who cohabited openly thereby established a presumption that they were married.[81] This was a *presumptio iuris et de iure.*[82]

Presumptive marriage further accentuated the ambiguous treatment of concubinage by medieval canonists. They maintained, on the one hand, that nonmarital sexual relations were not legally permissible. At the same time their marriage law, particularly the portions of it dealing with clandestine marriage and presumptive marriage, created a situation wherein virtually any concubinage relationship, whether blatant or furtive, might reasonably be construed as a marriage of some sort, so long as the partners to the relationship did not strenuously insist that they were not married. The ambiguity in the law was further magnified by the way in which the term "concubine" was used to describe both women who were by canonical standards married to their consorts and also those who were canonically unmarried. In the one sense, the concubine had legitimate legal standing and her legal situation was perfectly acceptable. In another sense she was a public sinner, subject to numerous legal sanctions.[83]

This cloud of legal confusion makes it extremely difficult to estimate the frequency of concubinage relationships in the high Middle Ages. Literary evidence indicates that nonmarital concubinage was relatively common in the early medieval period, before the subtleties of the lawyers blurred the distinctions between concubinage and marriage.[84] For the period after the twelfth century, evidence for frankly admitted concubinage among laymen is relatively scarce, although some cases are documented.[85] Clerical concubinage is a special matter whose peculiar complications we cannot explore here. The remarks of the lawyers make it amply plain, however, that clerical concubinage was frequently and openly practiced virtually throughout the medieval period.[86]

Presumably because the canonists were, in fact, so successful in blurring the lines of demarcation between concubinage and marriage, medieval legal writers gave relatively little attention to the legal rights and liabilities of the concubine. The elaborate treatments in the Roman law of the question of what women might legally be kept as concubines, for example, have no counterpart in the medieval canon law and are only briefly mentioned by the medieval civilians.[87] In theory, at least the assimilation of concubinage to marriage worked to improve the status of the concubinage. Whereas the Roman concubine had none of the rights but all of the obligations of a wife,[88] the medieval concubine, according to canonistic theory, should have been entitled to the full legal status that a wife enjoyed. In practice, so far as one can tell from the scanty evidence, the concubine's status was not nearly so secure as that of a wife who was married formally and publicly. The concubine's consort could renounce her at any time and, unless she was in a position to bring proof to show that their relationship had actually been a clandestine marriage, she had no legal recourse against him.[89] The concubine apparently did possess the right to receive and retain gifts and legacies from her consort as property in her own separate name and title.[90] Likewise, she had the right to receive testamentary bequests from the estate of her lover.[91]

The children of a concubinous union presented special problems. The canon law presumed that the child of a concubine was fathered by her consort and applied the same procedural standards to proof of paternity in cases of concubinage as obtained in cases of formal marriage.[92] The children of a concubine who made no claim to marital status were treated as natural children.[93] If the union was treated as a clandestine marriage, however, the children were both natural and legitimate.[94] Natural children, like their mothers, could receive testamentary bequests from the estates of their fathers, although the portion which they could receive might be limited if there were other children who were legitimate. If no legitimate children survived, the father might leave his entire estate to his natural children, according to the canonists.[95] The children of the concubines of clerics were subject to special rules.[96]

Not the least of the anomalies of the medieval canon law was the persistence of lay concubinage throughout the Middle Ages. It was not until the Reformation period that concubinage among the laity was finally and definitely prohibited by the Church. Even the constitution of Leo X (1513–1521) on this matter at the fifth Lateran Council in 1514, while decreeing severe punishment for concubinage, stopped short of prohibiting the practice completely.[97] The final prohibition of lay concubinage did not come for almost another half century, until the Council of Trent in 1563.[98] Even this prohibition was agreed to only after extended debate and rejection of a more severe form of the measure. The abolition of concubinage at Trent was part and parcel of the Council's general overhaul of the Catholic marriage law and was accompanied by the abolition of clandestine marriage as well, without which the reform would probably have been altogether meaningless.[99]

The Tridentine reforms brought to an end, so far as legal doctrine was concerned, the medieval Church's attempts to assimilate concubinage to marriage. There is much to criticize in the record of the medieval Church's efforts to cope with concubinage. Certainly the institution of clandestine marriage, which represented one of the principal means by which the canonists were able to take the position that concubinage was a secondary form of matrimony, created a situation that was very unsatisfactory. When any, or virtually any, sexual union might conceivably be interpreted as creating a marriage, one result was that no marriage relationship could be considered safe or stable. At any time its validity might be challenged by an earlier sexual partner of one of the parties, who could assert (and might be able to prove) that he or she had entered into a clandestine marriage real enough under the canonistic rules prior to the existing marriage. And quite possibly the first marriage might be real enough under the canonistic rules, but still entirely unprovable, which created a seriously troubling ethical situation.[100]

Yet there is something positive to be said for the canon law of concubinage. In its own peculiar way and for its own reasons, the canon law did recognize some basic facts of life—that nonmarital unions do exist, that they may have a great many of the virtues of marriage and yet may satisfy the needs of parties who do not wish to bind themselves publicly in a formal marriage situation. The canonists offered such persons a legal situation which had many of the advantages of marriage, but still stopped short of creating a public marriage situation. In some ways the medieval canon law in this regard was both more flexible and better adapted to the needs and wishes of real people in actual situations than was the far more rigid, inflexible Tridentine marriage law, under which Catholics were either married or not married, with no legally acceptable intermediate situation available to them. The history of post-Tridentine marriage litigation in the canonical courts illustrates, among other things, the problems this system has had in coping with the vagaries of human actions (Noonan, 1973). The inflexible rigidity of the Tridentine marriage law has created countless tragedies. This may have been too high a price to pay for an illusory certainty.

11

Adultery and Fornication: A Study in Legal Theology

James A. Brundage

"Let him who is without sin cast the first stone." These are reported to have been the words of Jesus of Nazareth when he was asked to give judgment upon a woman taken in adultery.[1] The significance of this Gospel episode has been disputed, but whatever else may be said of it, it testifies that Jesus did not regard adultery as a proper cause for the imposition of public penalties.

The medieval Christian Church in the West, however, adopted quite a different policy toward sexual activity outside of marriage. The medieval Church's enthusiasm for sexual expression was, in any case, apt to be less than overwhelming,[2] and sexual relations outside of marriage were the target of a complex set of ecclesiastical laws emphatically designed to discourage such conduct. Monogamous marriage was assumed to furnish the only situation within which Christian society ought to countenance sexual activity.[3] Extramarital sex, although perhaps inevitable,[4] was an activity that the Church wished to suppress whenever possible and to punish when suppression failed to work.

It scarcely needs saying that suppression was not totally effective and, accordingly, the medieval canon law and the ecclesiastical courts which applied that law to individual cases were much concerned with infractions of the laws restraining sexual behavior.[5] This chapter will examine some features of the law itself as it dealt with two of the commonest kinds of sexual delicts, adultery and fornication.

At the outset, let us examine what the canonists meant when they used the terms "fornication" and "adultery." These terms might seem to have very obvious meanings, but in canonistic usage they turned out to bear some complex interpretations.

Gratian (ca. 1140), the father of canon law, furnished a reasonably straightforward definition of fornication. "Fornication," he wrote, "although it might seem to mean any kind of illicit coitus practiced other than with a legitimate wife, is understood especially with reference to [coitus with] widows, harlots, or concubines."[6] Sexual activity of this kind, Gratian further declared, was prohibited by the Scriptures,[7] and he quoted with approval a statement of Saint Jerome that fornication is a crime.[8] To incur the full legal effects of the crime, however, one must fornicate knowingly. Simple coitus with someone whom one believed to be one's wife, for example, did not qualify as fornication in the rigor of the term.[9]

If this were all there were to it, the matter would have been simple enough; but there were other complications. Gratian extended the notion of fornication to include a wide variety of other sexual activities. For one thing, he considered that people who married one another simply for sexual pleasure were fornicators.[10] Some canonists taught that even within marriage excessive intercourse constituted fornication,[11] particularly if the partners had a contraceptive intention.[12] The term "fornication" in fact came to be used to mean any kind of illicit sexual intercourse whatsoever.[13] Matters were not much clarified when the canonists expanded the notion of fornication beyond the area of sexual activity and came to speak of spiritual fornication, by which they meant idolatry, superstition,[14] a relapse into infidel faith,[15] witchcraft,[16] greed, or any immoderate desire for an object.[17]

With such broad scale definitions it perhaps was inevitable that the canonists would consider fornication sinful and taught that no one could commit fornication with impunity,[18] but clearly this was a moral judgment, not a juristic doctrine. Some canonists also held that the circumstances of a particular act of fornication were irrelevant and that distinctions should not be considered in dealing with individual cases.[19] This principle might also have been adequate as a moral position; but as a legal principle, it was simply unworkable and the canonists came to acknowledge this explicitly. They found it necessary as a practical matter to distinguish degrees of guilt and, hence, degrees of punishment, depending upon the circumstances of the case and the parties involved. Thus they treated fornication by two married persons separated from their legal spouses, for example, as a minor offense.[20] Indeed, in some circumstances, as the ordinary gloss noted, the fornicator might be better favored by the law than a person who remained chaste.[21] Even in the particularly sensitive case of fornicating clerics, decretals of both Pope Lucius III and Gregory IX held that the guilty cleric might be tolerated and allowed to continue in his clerical functions, unless his conduct became flagrant and notorious.[22] The husband who took a vow of chastity without his wife's consent, to cite another example, might be considered to have given her a license to fornicate. Her peccadilloes were not totally excusable, but the blame for her conduct lay with her husband.[23] Despite the attitudes of the canon lawyers, however, it was apparently a common belief among the laity that fornication was not really culpable, save when it was indulged in by monks, nuns, or married persons.[24]

Adultery, like fornication, was classed as a crime against the body.[25] The canonists, in dealing with adultery, drew upon a large body of earlier Roman jurisprudence for a surprising number of their doctrines. Nevertheless, one cannot characterize the medieval canon law of adultery simply as an adaptation of the earlier Roman law on the topic, for the canonists differed sharply on several fundamental points from the position adopted by the Roman lawyers.

It is surprising that the Roman law, for all its elaborate treatment of adultery, never really defined what constituted the offense.[26] The medieval canonists were bolder and sought to define adultery with some precision. They did so basically in terms of the violation of the marriage bed.[27] Adultery consisted in sexual relations with a married person other than one's own spouse.[28] Even the consent of the other party's spouse was not adequate to alter the nature of the crime, nor did mitigating circumstances change the character of the offense, although they might lessen its seriousness.[29] At times, admittedly, the canonists drifted away from their definition and spoke of adultery metaphorically when they wished to express deep disapproval of other kinds of activity. Thus, they used the term "adultery" to describe any sort of sexual lust, including excessive desire for intercourse with one's own wife,[30] intercourse with someone else's fiancée,[31] or coitus between a priest and his spiritual daughter.[32] One also finds them treating certain kinds of marriages as adulterous unions: a marriage contracted for a wrongful purpose, for example, may be thus characterized,[33] not to mention clandestine or illicit marriages,[34] or the remarriage of separated persons during the lifetime of their spouses.[35] Still, the notion of adultery was employed with greater precision by the canonists than was the category of fornication and they adhered far more strictly to their definition of this offense than they did to the central, sexual meaning of fornication. As with fornication, one has to be conscious of the nature of one's actions in order to be guilty of adultery[36] and, indeed, an element of malice was held by the ordinary gloss to be essential to the crime of adultery.[37] Thus, sexual intercourse with a married person when accomplished by force was considered adulterous only for the party employing force.[38]

One of the most important differences between the treatment of adultery in the Roman law and in the medieval canon law had to do with the legal parity of the sexes. In the Roman law adultery was treated as a married woman's offense. A married man, in other words, did not commit adultery if he had illicit relations with another woman.[39] For the medieval canonists, however, adultery was criminal whether it was committed by a man or a woman. Both men and women were equally punishable for adulterous acts.[40]

Indeed, there was even some support in the canon law for the notion that adultery was more serious when committed by a man than when committed by a woman. Since the man was the head of the house he was expected to excel his spouse in virtue. Hence, men should be more severely punished for their adulterous affairs than should women.[41]

The canonists elaborated, too, a systematic hierarchy of sexual crimes. Fornication was the category basic to all sexual offenses and, in a generic sense, this term might be used to include them all.[42] Used in a strict sense, however, to denote sexual relations between unmarried persons, fornication was the least serious of the sexual crimes. More serious than fornication was bigamy; still more serious was adultery. Beyond adultery, transcending it in gravity, was incest, while the most heinous of all sexual offenses was unnatural intercourse, whether homosexual or heterosexual.[43]

This hierarchical order of sexual offenses was reflected in the penal system of the canon law. The person guilty of fornication, whether cleric or layman, was classified as infamous and, as such, might suffer a variety of disabilities resulting from that status.[44] In the practice of the courts, the commonest type of punishment meted out to convicted fornicators seems to have been a fine, often a relatively light one.[45] Clerics found guilty of fornication, however, were subject to more severe penalties and, if their delinquency was notorious, they might even be deposed from their clerical positions.[46] A layman convicted of fornication ran the further risk of being sentenced to be married as a result of his offense.[47]

The greater seriousness of adultery, as compared with simple fornication, was likewise reflected in the penal law of the medieval canonists. Still, the canonists rejected in principle one of the strongest and most persistent traditions of secular law systems in dealing with adultery, namely, the right of the injured husband to avenge himself by slaying the adulterer and his unfaithful wife. The Roman law had maintained the death penalty for adultery, allowing the wronged husband the license to kill the adulterer, although the right to kill an adulterous wife was by the *Lex Julia de adulteriis* reserved to her father, rather than her husband.[48] This ancient law, indeed, represented an attempt to mitigate the still older Roman practice of death in adultery cases, for the object of the *Lex Julia* was essentially to ensure public, rather than private, punishment of adulterers.[49]

Although the laws of the Germanic invaders perpetuated the old tradition that the wronged husband had the right to avenge himself by killing his guilty wife and her partner,[50] the Church tried to mitigate this traditional right and rejected the notion that a Christian could kill an adulterous spouse, even one caught *in flagrante delicto*.[51] While medieval secular laws continued to tolerate private homicide in adultery cases, lesser punishments became increasingly more common, perhaps as a result of the influence of the ecclesiastical law.[52] Frequently the lesser punishments involved the assessment of a fine, often quite a heavy one, in addition to some form of public humiliation, such as a whipping or the shaving of the head.[53] Basic to the penal structure, too, was the notion that the offended spouse must in no way condone the actions of the wayward partner. The medieval canonists retained the Roman law principle that the man who kept an adulterous wife after learning of her extramarital adventures became in some sense a party to the affair and should be classified as a pimp.[54] In addition, the condoning husband became ineligible for ordination and advancement in the Church.[55]

The penal sanctions for adultery and fornication in the canon law were especially grave for married persons. While the canonists might insist that extramarital sexual relations did not dissolve the bond of marriage,[56] the fact (or perhaps even the mere suspicion) of extramarital dalliance justified the innocent party in separating from the guilty spouse.[57] This was, in fact, the only reason that the canonists were prepared to countenance for the judicial separation of married persons.[58] Even separation for this cause was hedged about with restrictions. For one thing, the party bringing action for separation must not be guilty of fornication or adultery himself; if he (or she) were, the case was lost.[59] Furthermore, a separation granted because of adultery might be rescinded if the petitioner were subsequently convicted of fornication or adultery.[60] Those separated for this reason were restrained from remarrying during the lifetime of the first spouse.[61] Moreover, the parties were required to remain together during the pendency of the separation case and could not leave the common home until the case was settled.[62]

Married persons guilty of adultery were not, of course, routinely required to separate. Rather the hope was that the guilty party might do penance and that the marriage might then continue.[63] Until penance was done, however, the spouses might not licitly have sexual relations with one another.[64] But while the canonists might hope that an adulterous couple would stay together, they were not prepared to insist upon this and were willing to tolerate separation as a legitimate consequence of adultery.[65] The scattered evidence reported from the actual practice of the courts confirms the statements of the law books: adultery did in fact furnish grounds for marital separation and the courts often did order such separations. On the other hand, ecclesiastical judges seem to have been chary of proceeding to judicial separation and to have sought penance and reconciliation in preference to separation with considerable frequency and apparent success in some cases.[66]

The adulterer, male or female, was further penalized, in a sense, by the barriers that the canon law threw up to subsequent marriage with his or her partner in adultery. The underlying theory of the canonists here was that sexual relations between two persons created a bond of legal affinity analogous to that created by the relationship between a baptismal sponsor and a godchild.[67]

Another difficult problem raised for the canonists by non-marital sexual relations concerned the status of the children of such unions. Although there was an honorable tradition, of which Gratian, for example, was aware, that the sins of parents ought not to be visited upon their children,[68] the general conclusion of the law on this matter was that the children of irregular unions ought indeed to be discriminated against by the law.[69] What saved the canon law on this point from being intolerably harsh was the provision of two means of evading the strict consequences of the general law. One means was the legitimation of the children of irregular unions by the subsequent marriage of the parents when that was possible. Otherwise, the exercise of the dispensing power of the ecclesiastical *magisterium* might exempt the child from the stigma of irregular birth and allow him to escape the strict consequences of his parents' indiscretion.

What I have briefly sketched here is a view of the law dealing with adultery and fornication as it had emerged by the mid-thirteenth century. Two concluding remarks are in order. First, the state of the law as I have described it is the outcome of a vigorous refurbishing of the law during the century that separated Gratian's *Decretum* (ca. 1140) from the promulgation of the *Liber Extra* (1234) (see Appendix). During that century of rapid development, the status of non-marital sexual partners and their offspring was significantly altered as a result of the legislative activity of popes and councils and also as a result of the re-examination and systematization of legal doctrine concerning marriage itself by the canon lawyers, especially the academic canonists who taught in the legal faculties of the universities of that period.[70]

Second and finally, the law of adultery and fornication as it emerged at the end of this process has been remarkably enduring. The law in this area— at least formally—bears a recognizable resemblance to the law on these topics still current in many parts of the Western world. The medieval canon law on adultery and fornication was framed explicitly on the basis of theological doctrines about marriage and sexual relationships current in the late twelfth and early thirteenth centuries. Those doctrines conceived of any sexual activity outside of marriage as not only immoral but criminal. On the basis of such notions the medieval law of adultery and fornication took its characteristic shape.[71] The law on these topics is a reflection of and is based upon theological opinions that are no longer widely shared. One is entitled, I think, to ask if it has not now outlived its usefulness and whether the viewpoint ascribed by Saint John to Jesus may not have something to be said for it.

12

The Problem of Impotence

James A. Brundage

What role should sexual relations play in marriage? Is the sexual ability of the spouses a critical factor in determining whether a marriage exists between them? The answers that medieval canon lawyers give to these two questions are not always clear or consistent. One major factor that complicated their views of the role of sex in marriage was, of course, the theological necessity of framing the definition of marriage in such a way as to preserve the legitimate marital character of the relationship between the Blessed Virgin and Saint Joseph. Given that model, the canonists could scarcely hold that sexual relations were essential to all marriage relationships. At the same time, especially considering the importance that they attached to the procreation of children (Saint Augustine's *bonum prolis*) as one of the essential purposes of marriage, the canonists could scarcely maintain that the sexual relations of the spouses were irrelevant to marriage. Given also the lusty character of the clientele with whom they dealt, the canonists, who unlike theologians necessarily had to take account of the problems of the real world, would have been hard put to ignore the obvious fact that many of the people with whose cases they dealt attached considerable significance to the sexual attractions and abilities of their marriage partners.[1]

Though the terms frigidity *(frigiditas)* and impotence *(impotentia coeundi)* were used almost interchangeably by the canonists to describe the condition of a person who was unable to perform sexual intercourse, irrespective of the person's sex,[2] most of the problems discussed would today be called impotence. The basic rules concerning marriages in which one spouse was impotent were outlined by Gratian in Causa 33, question 1, of the *Decretum*. If a couple were married and the man proved unable to consummate the marriage, they might separate and the wife might remarry. The husband was forbidden to remarry.[3] The attempt should first be made, however, to persuade the couple to remain together and to live as brother and sister. If the woman insisted that she wished to have children, then she should be permitted to separate and remarry.[4] A complaint of impotence must be timely — a couple could not live together for an extended period and then petition for separation on the grounds of impotence.[5] Gratian's text does not specify the time limit involved here, but the ordinary gloss supplies a rule that the complaint must be made within two months of the beginning of cohabitation.[6] These rules applied to situations where impotence was "natural" and hence permanent. The canonists acknowledged the possibility of temporary impotence, and in these cases the situation was more complicated. Temporary impotence was assumed to be the result of sorcery and witchcraft *(sortiarias atque maleficas)*. Hence the attempt must be made in such cases to cure the afflicted spouse by penance, exorcism, and medical treatment. Should these fail to work a cure, however, the couple might separate and, if they wished, remarry. If the impotent partner in the first marriage proved able to have intercourse with his second wife, the second marriage should stand and he should not be compelled to return to the first spouse, even if she petitioned for a restoration of the first marriage.[7] A serious complication in all impotence cases was, of course, the question of proof of the allegation. The canonists were understandably skeptical about the evidential value of *ex parte* declarations, even under oath, by spouses who wished to terminate a marriage.[8] If the woman was a virgin, it was often possible to secure corroboratory evidence through a physical examination by midwives.[9] If she was not a virgin — if, for example, she was a widow — corroboration by this method was not feasible. A physical examination of the husband might or might not produce useful evidence.[10] If no other corroboration were available, the canonists would accept the oaths of seven neighbors as relevant support for the allegation of impotence. Should the allegedly impotent male successfully remarry, however, those who swore to a belief that he was impotent in the first marriage might be liable to punishment for perjury.[11]

The law on these matters as described by Gratian and his commentators was not wholly satisfactory: it failed to cover some situations that might be expected to arise and, moreover, as Pope Alexander III (1159–1181) noted in a decretal letter, there was no uniform policy on the disposition of impotence cases.[12] Both Alexander III and Clement III (1187–1191), moreover, favored a policy of requiring couples to remain together, even if sexual intercourse was impossible. Clement III, in fact, was prepared to insist upon this even if a continuation of cohabitation between an obviously disaffected couple might result in danger to the life of the woman.[13] This ruling apparently seemed excessively rigorous to later authorities; at any rate, the decretal that incorporated it was excluded from the decretal collection compiled by Ramon de Penyafort at the direction of Pope Gregory IX (1227–1241).

Other decretals of the late twelfth and early thirteenth centuries that were included in the *Liber Extra* (1234) (see Appendix) dealt with the evidential problems involved in proving an allegation of impotence,[14] and also sought to clarify the procedures involved in judicial consideration of cases in which impotence was at issue.[15] One of Lucius III's (1131–1185) decretals made it clear that a woman who knowingly contracted marriage with an impotent man was bound to continue in the marriage and could not escape from the relationship on a subsequent plea of nullity based on impotence.[16] A decretal of Innocent III (1198–1216) added a further ground for nullity on the basis of impotence in situations where a disparity of the size of the genitalia of the marriage partners made intercourse impossible or dangerous.[17]

The decretalist commentators further clarified some points in the law that remained obscure. One such matter concerned marriages among the elderly who, because of age or physical infirmity, might not be able to consummate the marriage. Were such marriages to be considered invalid by reason of impotence? The answer of the ordinary gloss was that such marriages were not intended to be classed with those held null because of impotence. Child-bearing was not likely to be expected in marriages between elderly persons, and the lack of ability to consummate the marriage might also reasonably be presumed prior to the marriage; hence, such marriages could not be nullified because of impotence.[18] Another significant concept that emerges from the ordinary gloss is the notion that impotence might be relative, that is, that a man who was impotent with one woman might be able to perform sexually with another. This distinction was grounded on the assumed difference between natural frigidity and impotence induced by witchcraft. The man who was by nature frigid, according to the gloss, was perpetually incapable of intercourse with all women, whereas the man who was rendered impotent by means of sorcery might be incapable of intercourse only temporarily or only with a particular woman. Naturally frigid men, accordingly, could not be allowed to remarry, while those who were rendered impotent by witchcraft might be able to remarry successfully.[19]

One question that taxed the ingenuity of the decretalist commentators involved the situation in which a woman was released from her first marriage on the grounds of her husband's impotence and subsequently contracted a second successful marriage. What should happen if the first husband then sought to reclaim her? Was he entitled to get her back for a second try? Johannes Teutonicus (d. 1245) thought that he was entitled to this opportunity and that if the second attempt was a failure, the woman should be returned to her second husband. Johannes was further of the opinion that the first husband might reclaim the woman subsequently for further attempts to consummate the marriage and that he might do this an infinite number of times. Tancredus (ca. 1185-1234/36), on the other hand, thought that the first husband should be limited to three chances at consummation, but that after the third attempt he should be barred from further trials.[20] If the failure to consummate the first marriage was a result of a disparity of genital size, however, Tancredus believed that the first husband was not entitled to reclaim the woman from her second husband for a further attempt at consummation, and in this conclusion both Johannes Teutonicus and Vincentius Hispanus (d. 1244?) concurred.[21]

Within the general legal framework that I have described, I should like to illustrate the ways in which the courts applied this body of law by taking three cases as examples. The first of the cases comes from the records of the Consistory Court of Ely in the late fourteenth century. This case is an *ex officio* proceeding commenced against John Poynant and Jean Sikon in 1378. The couple had been married publicly, had subsequently discovered that John was unable to consummate the marriage, and had then petitioned the ecclesiastical court to grant a separation, which was done in due course. Jean afterwards married one Robert Toby, while John, her former husband, became involved in an extramarital relationship with a certain Isabel Pybell. In his relationship with Isabel, John proved capable of consummating a sexual relationship — so much so that when Isabel appeared in court, she was noticeably pregnant. This situation came to the attention of the Consistory Court, which then summoned John, Jean, Robert, and Isabel to explain what was going on. John and Jean recounted the history of their marriage, the failure to achieve consummation because of John's impotence, and the subsequent ecclesiastical nullity finding. Jean and Robert gave evidence about the solemnization of their marriage, while John and Isabel confessed to fornication. Isabel was called upon to testify concerning John's sexual prowess and replied that he was plenty potent *(satis est potens)* and that he was the father of the child that she was carrying. She also testified that she and John had contracted marriage after the dissolution of the marriage between John and Jean. The court demanded that John show cause why the earlier nullity decree should not be revoked on the grounds that it had been given in error and why the previous marriage between him and Jean should not be reinstated. He was also required to show whether his current partner, Isabel, was consanguinously related within the forbidden degrees to his first wife, Jean; this, if true, would have constituted an impediment to his second marriage. After some procedural delays, the parties duly produced witnesses to the facts of the case, including John's confessor, who was given permission by John to testify to matters told to him in sacramental confession. The court also appointed experts *(peritos)* to give evidence concerning John's impotence and the alleged consanguinity count. The witnesses were duly produced on 24 September 1379 and their testimony taken, including evidence of a physical examination *(palpacione)* of John to determine whether he was potent. After due deliberation and the consultation of legal authorities, the court determined that the nullity decree concerning the marriage between Jean and John should be revoked, since the impediment of impotence had ceased to exist. That marriage was therefore reinstated. The marriage between Robert and Jean was declared null and they were ordered to separate. John and Jean were ordered to live together once again and to show each other marital affection. Concerning Isabel and her child, the court made no order.[22] The theory apparently applied in this case was that the first nullity decree had been based upon a finding of essential or natural impotence, that this theory had been proved wrong by John's affair with Isabel, and that the impotence which was the basis for the first nullity declaration had either never existed or had now ceased to exist. The subsequent marriage of Jean and Robert was for that reason no marriage at all, since Jean had been legally bound, even though she was unaware of it, to her first husband. Since there is no finding against Robert or Isabel, the court presumably may have believed that they were morally guilty of simple fornication and had been acting in good faith.

A second case from the Ely Consistory Court records shows a very different outcome. This case, which chronologically overlaps the first one, began with a complaint on 9 April 1377 that Jean Pyncote, wife of John Maddyngle, had deserted her husband. Upon appearance, the plea was entered that although marriage had duly been solemnized between the couple, John had proved frigid and was unable to consummate the marriage. Jean therefore requested the court to declare the marriage null, since she wished to have children and would not be able to do so with John. The court ordered the submission of formal complaints and trial upon the issues; meanwhile, Jean was commanded to return to her husband, to live with him, and to attempt to consummate the marriage. At subsequent hearings both parties were ordered to undergo physical examinations in connection with the allegation that John was impotent. Meanwhile, John sought to change the grounds of the nullity suit. He charged in his turn that the marriage was indeed null, but he founded his case upon the theory that he and Jean were consanguinously related within the forbidden degrees of kinship. The court ordered him to produce witnesses to support his contention, which he did. Jean meanwhile vanished and could not be located. After further delay both parties were produced in court, but this time the witnesses failed to appear. Finally, after nearly four years of appearances, delays, exceptions, and miscellaneous procedural entanglements, a decision was rendered in 1381. The court found that the parties were indeed related within the fourth degree of consanguinity and hence that no marriage could have existed between them. They were pronounced separated; the marriage was annulled. John was made responsible for the legal expenses of the case.[23] It can reasonably be inferred from the record of these proceedings that either the proofs of impotence were insufficient, causing the parties to propose an alternate plea to secure the annulment, or else that John preferred to base the annulment on grounds of consanguinity, which would not prevent him from remarrying, rather than on grounds of impotence, which might free him from Jean, but might also have left him legally unable to remarry.

The third case is less amply documented than the first two. It is drawn from the decisions reported by Etienne d'Aufrere, a fifteenth-century counsellor of the Parlement of Toulouse.[24] The relevant facts are these: a thirty-year-old man married a twelve-year-old girl with whom he lived for six years. During that time he was unable to consummate the marriage, even though he asserted that he was sexually potent and substantiated this assertion by the testimony of prostitutes with whom he had consorted. Nonetheless, he found it impossible to have sexual relations with his wife. She petitioned for a declaration of nullity and the husband opposed her petition. Five issues were tried by the court: first, whether the husband should be considered frigid or afflicted with impotence by reason of witchcraft; second, whether the marriage should be declared null by reason of impotence arising from witchcraft; third, whether the witchcraft should be presumed to antedate the marriage; fourth, whether the impotence should be considered permanent; and last, whether the period of the marriage had provided reasonable opportunity for the consummation of the marriage. The findings of the court supported the contentions of the wife. The court determined that this was a case of impotence resulting from sorcery, that it should be presumed to antedate the marriage and to be permanent, that there had been adequate opportunity for consummation, and that therefore the marriage should terminate by reason of the husband's inability to consummate.[25] Thus, in this case impotence was successfully pleaded and the wife secured the nullity decree that she desired, despite corroborated evidence that the husband was sexually adequate in other relationships.

Thus both the law itself and actual cases such as the ones examined here seemed to assume that sexual intercourse was an intrinsic and essential element in marriage. Where intercourse was impossible, the marriage was null. Granted, marriages between the elderly could not be nullified on this ground, but that was so because the couple could reasonably have been expected to know from the beginning that sexual intercourse might be impossible between them. Presumably this same line of reasoning might also indicate that marriages where intercourse was excluded as a condition of the marriage might also be regarded as valid, although this situation was exceedingly complex and had been the subject of conflicting rulings.[26]

But if sexual intercourse was essential and intrinsic to marriage, what becomes of the matrimonial character of the relationship between Saint Joseph and the Blessed Virgin? The way out of this nasty impasse was to distinguish between the right to intercourse and the choice to make use of that right.[27] Thus the canonists simultaneously held that sexual relations were integral to marriage; that where sexual relations were impossible for reasons outside the power of the spouses, a marriage did not exist; and that marriage partners could properly exclude sexual relations from a marriage and still be validly married.

13

Rape and Seduction in the Medieval Canon Law

James A. Brundage

Rape and seduction are crimes in modern European and American law. It was not always thus: European societies have varied greatly over time in the sorts of sexual behavior that they have been willing to tolerate among their members. True, historians have written that the concept of rape has been constant throughout the ages, and courts have held that the word needs no definition because everyone has always known what it means.[1] This simply proves a notorious truism, namely, that courts are as fallible as historians. In point of fact, the crimes of rape and seduction, as they are currently conceived and defined in European and American law,[2] have only gradually become what they now are, and the definitions of these offenses presently in use would have puzzled European courts, say, twenty-five generations ago. This chapter argues that the canon lawyers of the medieval Church between about 1140 and about 1500 played the leading role in shaping the law from which our own notions of rape and seduction derive.

Both medieval and modern notions of rape emerged from the *raptus* — literally carrying off by force — of the Roman law. Thus in ancient Roman law *raptus* consisted in the abduction of a woman against the will of the person under whose authority she lived. Sexual intercourse was not a necessary element of *raptus*. The specific malice of the offense consisted not in the sexual ravishment of the woman, but in stealing her away from her parents, guardian, or husband. *Raptus* might also be used to describe theft of property as well as of a person, so long as violence was employed in the act. In the ancient law, moreover, *raptus* was not a public crime; rather, it was a wrong against the man who had legal power over the woman or property violently seized.[3]

Changes in the ancient law began to appear during the reign of Constantine (311–337). Constantine made *raptus* a public crime, punishable by death.[4] The woman who consented to the abduction was also liable to the death penalty under Constantine's legislation. Two centuries later Justinian (527–565) further revised the law on *raptus,* abolishing all previous legislation on the subject[5] and prescribing confiscation of the property of those guilty of the crime, as well as the death penalty.[6] Further, Justinian specifically described *raptus* as a sexual crime against unmarried women, widows, or nuns.[7] This was significant since at least temporarily it was not only a crime against property but against an individual woman.

The Germanic invasions and the subsequent dislocation of society in the West meant, among other things, the introduction of primitive Germanic legal systems that were not much concerned with the protection of women from violent assault. Consequently, it was the law of the Church that strove to penalize such assaults during the early Middle Ages. Vigorous as these efforts may have been, however, they proved easy to evade and in practice were ineffective.[8]

The canon law did not, in fact, become a well-organized legal system until the appearance, about 1140, of the Decretum of Gratian.[9] For the building blocks of his system, Gratian quarried the rich resources of the Roman law, particularly the law as it had been codified by Justinian, and it was in this way that the older Roman definitions of *raptus* came back into currency in European law. Relying on the summary definitions given by Bishop Isidore of Seville (560–636), Gratian characterized rape as unlawful coitus, related to sexual corruption.[10] In another passage he also indicated that rape involved abduction of the woman in addition to unlawful intercourse with her. He further qualified his definition by adding that rape was committed only if there had been no previous marriage negotiations for the woman's hand.[11] Gratian emphasized that the abduction must be accomplished by violence, whether directed against the woman, against her parents, or against both. He added that a mere intention of marriage did not mitigate the offense and that the rapist might escape the death penalty for his crime by seeking sanctuary in a church.[12]

The lecturers on Gratian's *Decretum* in the twelfth-century law schools were quick to seize on Gratian's treatment of rape, subjecting it to increasingly sophisticated academic analysis. Some of them, more learned in the Roman law than Gratian had been,[13] pointed out that *raptus* could mean the forcible seizure of a thing as well as of a person; they proposed that *raptus* be restricted to the crime against persons while *rapina* should be used to designate the crime against property. The decretist commentators grounded this distinction upon the Roman law analysis that differentiated between appropriating a thing itself and appropriating the use of a thing.[14] For

Gratian and his twelfth-century commentators, rape began to be distinguished from property crimes and to be categorized with crimes of violence against the person.[15] Although moralists treated it as a species of lust,[16] Gratian distinguished rape from other kinds of illicit coitus.[17] It is one thing, he declared, to seduce a woman with promises and quite another to bring force to bear upon her.[18] This distinction, which was not explicitly spelled out either in Roman law or the scriptural sources (especially Deuteronomy 22:28-29 and Exodus 22:15-16) upon which medieval canonists also relied,[19] remains a significant one for the law of sexual relations.[20]

The canonists tried, without complete success, to create a hierarchy of sexual crimes. Seduction, according to one scheme, was less serious than adultery, while adultery was less serious than forcible rape.[21] Other legal writers held that rape of a married woman should be considered more heinous than rape of an unmarried girl, since the former compounded the offense.[22] Rape, of whatever kind, however, was a major crime along with assassination and treason, an *enormis delicta*.[23] It was treated as the most serious sexual offense, one that merited more severe punishment than other violent crimes.[24] By the end of the Middle Ages at least one canonist, Egidio Bossi (1487-1546), argued that the law should extend the definition of rape to include any intercourse, violent or not, with a child under the age of six or seven, since a child of that age could not give knowing consent to the act.[25]

The canonists, from the time of Gratian onwards, gradually defined four constitutive elements of rape in their law. Rape must involve the use of violence, it must involve abduction, it must involve coitus, and it must be accomplished without the free consent of one partner. Let us briefly examine these four facets of the crime.

The obvious problem with violence lies in deciding what degree of force must be involved for a given act to qualify as rape. Sexual advances of any kind, no matter how amiable, involve pressure of some sort by one person on another, and society may choose to draw the line between permissible and nonpermissible pressures at any point along a very wide spectrum.[26] Since so wide a range is possible, it is not surprising to find that the medieval canon lawyers—like modern lawyers, one may add—were far from unanimous in defining just what degree of force must be demonstrated to prove rape. The common opinion of canonists was that moderate force was all that was required. By this they meant something well short of force that created an imminent danger of death or grave bodily harm. The attacker did not have to have his sword at your throat for his menaces to constitute moderate force; a threat to burn your house down, for example, would do, so long as there was reasonable cause to believe that the attacker was able and willing to carry out the threat.[27] Likewise the sight of a group of armed men under the command of the attacker might be held to constitute violent force, even if no physical assault occurred.[28] The violence involved in an act of rape might be described in other terms as force sufficient to move a "constant man," or, as we might say, a solid citizen. The degree of force required to prove rape was, in fact, for most canonists just the same degree as was required to invalidate a marriage contract when it was claimed that consent to marriage had been coerced. A few writers, however, put the standard much lower, holding, for example, that importunate pleading might constitute sufficient violence to warrant a rape charge and that any appreciable degree of physical force would suffice.[29] In rendering judgments, however, the basic principle was that the punishment should vary with the seriousness of the violence proved in the evidence.[30]

The consent issue that medieval jurists addressed in rape cases was not, "Did she consent?" but rather, "Was her consent procured by force, either physical or mental?"[31] The violence or menaces involved need not be directed at the victim personally. Consent induced by violence or threats of violence against her parents or family were quite sufficient to qualify an act as rape.[32] Strenuous resistance was not something that the canonists insisted upon: the victim must at least cry out in protest, but active combat by the victim was not something that they expected; weeping and wailing were sufficient resistance to require, in their opinion.[33]

In addition, medieval definitions of rape required abduction of the victim.[34] This provision of the medieval canon law was clearly derived from the Roman law. Not every abduction, to be sure, constituted *raptus*, but every rape must involve abduction.[35] The abduction, moreover, must involve physical conveyance of the victim from one place to another—it was not enough, for example, to move her a little way out of the street—and it must involve the intention of hiding her away.[36] Abduction of one's own fiancée, however, did not count as rape and the abduction of one's wife by someone else was likely to be treated somewhat differently, as "diversion," for which both ecclesiastical and secular courts offered separate remedies.[37]

As a final constituent of the crime of rape, there must be coitus; violent abduction without the woman's consent for purposes other than sexual intercourse did not qualify as rape.[38] Medieval writers failed to specify the degree of coitus necessary to qualify the crime as rape, but some form of sexual congress was essential. Merely stealing a kiss, for example, would not do.[39]

The canonists also held that only certain women could be raped. Although the Roman law had admitted the possibility that a husband might rape his own wife and provided that if he did so he should suffer the death penalty,[40] the medieval canonists took another view. If the couple were legally married to each other, then consent to intercourse had already been given and a wife could not refuse to have relations with her husband (or the husband with his wife) simply because he took her away from home and was forceful in his approach.[41] Furthermore, the victim of rape must be an "honest" woman, that is, she must be of good legal standing.[42] One could not rape a harlot.[43] As a defense to a rape charge, however, it was not sufficient merely to show

that the victim had a bad reputation; she must be shown to be an acknowledged prostitute whose services were generally available to the public.[44] One
writer nuanced his exposition of the law on this point by adding that if the
prostitute had a just cause for refusing intercourse—for example, if she was
a close blood relative of her attacker—then coitus without her consent and
accomplished by violence and abduction would constitute rape.[45] Another
writer added that if the prostitute had shown signs of repentance and wished
to abandon her wayward life, then any subsequent sexual assault might be
construed as rape.[46] There was little discussion by medieval lawyers of the
rape of a man by a woman, and although they occasionally envisioned the
possibility, they dismissed it as "extremely rare," as they did the rape of a
woman by a woman.[47]

Jurists in the Middle Ages, as in modern times, were concerned to see that
rape was punished by public authorities and disapproved of self-help remedies by which families of victims revenged themselves upon the presumed
attacker without judicial process.[48] How far they were successful in this is
difficult to say and the law itself did not entirely bar self-help remedies. It is
notable, however, that rape cases are comparatively rare in the sample court
records I have examined. Thus, my analysis of the records of the court of
Cérisy in Normandy, for example, shows that rape accounts for less than 1
percent of the 170 sexual crimes tried by that court in the decade 1314–1323.
This suggests either that the law may not have been very successful in preventing self-help, or that many cases of rape simply may not have gotten to
the complaint stage, or both.[49] It is perhaps significant, too, that a considerable number of the cases that did proceed to the complaint stage failed to
show further action, which may well indicate that cases tended to be settled
before trial, often, one suspects, by agreement to a marriage. Undoubtedly,
too, many rape cases ended in the courts under other types of action: in
English common law records, for example, rapes often show up in the plea
rolls as trespass cases rather than as felonies, since the civil action secured a
remedy for the victim and, at the same time, spared the transgressor from a
visit to the hangman.[50] Nonetheless, the church courts asserted jurisdiction
over rape, as they did over other sexual crimes, and a significant number of
these cases found their way to the ecclesiastical bar,[51] sometimes by agreement with the secular authorities.

The Roman law prescribed death and confiscation of property as the penalties for rape.[52] The secular jurisdictions of the Middle Ages often maintained this venerable tradition, although the law was sometimes softened to
permit the substitution of some kind of bodily mutilation—castration was
naturally a favorite—often combined with fines.[53] The ecclesiastical courts,
however, refrained in principle from imposing sentences that involved death
or mutilation. The punishment for rape at canon law, then, involved
excommunication, public penance, imprisonment, whipping, money fines,
and possibly even enslavement, or some combination of these, depending

upon the circumstances of the case.[54] Burdensome and unpleasant as these remedies might be, it was normally to the advantage of the defendant in a rape case to be tried in the church courts. If he were a cleric, he might claim trial in the ecclesiastical courts as a right. If he were a layman, the prudent rapist was well advised to flee to a place of ecclesiastical sanctuary, since this would in principle secure him against death or mutilation.[55] Conviction of rape in the ecclesiastical courts also carried with it the disabilities of *infamia:* the convicted rapist could not accuse another person before the courts, nor was his testimony admitted in judicial proceedings.[56]

One aspect of the law of rape that particularly concerned the canon lawyers was the possible marriage of a rapist to his victim. The Roman law, at least after A.D. 320, had been hostile to such marriages,[57] and the canon law up to the time of Gratian refused to permit them.[58] Gratian's texts show a softening of this attitude, in large part as a result of the influence of Germanic customary law, which permitted such marriages.[59] Although Gratian reproduced some of the earlier prohibitions against the marriage of ravisher and victim,[60] he qualified this position in order to allow such marriages, provided that the rapist had done penance for his offense and both the victim and her parents consented to the arrangement.[61] The decretist commentators were concerned to ensure that the girl's consent to marriage was freely given and also came to see marriage subsequent to abduction as a means by which girls might be allowed to marry men of whom their parents disapproved. Hence, marriage subsequent to a technical rape might ironically allow a woman greater freedom of choice in her marriage than she could otherwise enjoy.[62] This position was officially incorporated into the law by a decretal letter of Pope Innocent III in 1200 that allowed such marriages in the name of freedom of contract.[63] The legal commentators on this new law insisted that the girl's consent to such arrangements must not be forced. The development of the law on this point is consistent with the concern that the canonists frequently expressed to liberate marriage from the constraints imposed by family and parental choices.[64] This new law also opened up an escape hatch for the perpetrators of rape: if they could subsequently persuade their victim to marry them, they stood to escape the more extreme penalties for their crime.[65]

Rape as a juristic category has much in common with seduction. Both offenses involve sexual intercourse secured by taking advantage of a victim. But, while the rapist achieves his goal through the use of force or menace, the seducer, a more cunning type, gets his way by enticement, persuasion, solicitation, promises, fraud, and deceit.[66] Rape is an offense in virtually every European and American legal system, while seduction is more sparingly represented in the penal codes of the Western world.[67]

Seduction is, in a sense, a more modern and more sophisticated offense than rape. Extremely few societies allow men to overpower and ravish women without let or hindrance. But it takes a keener insight and a more acute sensitivity to the notion that women should have an independent choice of sexual partners for a society to outlaw the wilier practices of the seducer. It also takes a degree of legal sophistication to define seduction as a distinct category of offense and to differentiate it clearly from other types of sexual crime.

Ancient European law did not know seduction as a specific offense. The Roman law had no technical term for what we call seduction and subsumed this species of behavior under the more general category of *stuprum* or sexual corruption. *Stuprum* consisted in the sexual use of an unmarried free person and was only gradually distinguished from adultery and concubinage.[68] Roman law also distinguished *stuprum* from sexual relations with a prostitute, which was no crime.[69]

The medieval canon law adopted its definition of sexual corruption from the Roman law.[70] The commentators on Gratian's work discussed the topic of sexual corruption only in passing and did not greatly develop the legal teaching on this theme.[71] By the end of the twelfth century, lawyers were beginning to sense that the canon law on sexual corruption was inadequate and unsatisfactory. Consequently, when new legal collections began to be compiled as supplements to Gratian's *Decretum,* these new decretal collections, as they were called, incorporated material dealing more explicitly with the crime of sexual corruption.[72] Not until the late thirteenth century, however, did jurists commence to perceive that there might be merit in distinguishing between sexual corruption in general and illicit coitus achieved by arts and blandishment. The earliest indication of a dawning perception of this distinction that I have come across occurs in the commentaries of Cardinal Hostiensis (d. 1271).[73] His description of sexual conquest achieved by flattery, lies, and false promises verged upon modern notions of seduction.[74] The gravamen (substance) of the offense lay in the frustration of the victim's free choice through the deception practiced by the seducer.[75] Later writers introduced the further notion of the misuse of authority to achieve sexual corruption, as, for example, when a jailer seduces a prisoner under his control or a guardian seduces his ward.[76]

The penalties for seduction were less severe than the penalties for rape. Although Gratian quoted with approval a Roman law text which prescribed the death penalty for the sexual corruption of boys or girls,[77] excommunication was probably the more ordinary penalty.[78] By the end of the twelfth century, a more practical approach was devised to discourage debauchery, namely, the imposition of a fine of up to one-half of the assets of the offender as a dowry for his victim and, if her parents agreed, also marriage of the victim to the offender.[79] The purpose of the law, as one commentator frankly admitted, was to force marriage between the couple.[80] The seducer who would not marry his victim or who was too poor to give her an adequate dowry was flogged.[81] In actual practice, the courts were often content to levy a small fine for such offenses.[82]

By the end of the Middle Ages, then, the main elements of the law of rape and seduction had been spelled out in ways that are perceptibly similar to the concepts of these offenses in most modern European and American legal systems. Modern penal law may be less draconian in its punishment of the offenses than the medieval law, but both the conceptualization of the offenses themselves and the punishments prescribed for them in late medieval law bear a strong family resemblance to more modern treatments of them. The development of this area of the law from Gratian to the end of the medieval period tended to secure a greater personal autonomy for the individual and, most particularly, for the woman in late medieval society.

14

Prostitution in the Medieval Canon Law

James A. Brundage

Prostitution has the name of being the oldest human profession,[1] and it is certainly true that virtually every known system of positive law has had something to say about the harlot, the pimp, the procurer, and the conduct of their curious, if elemental, business.[2] This paper will examine the treatment of the harlot and her trade by the lawyers and lawgivers of the medieval Church.

One difficult question must be faced at the outset: the definition of the term itself. What is prostitution, so far as the medieval canonists were concerned? The answer to this fundamental question involves two strands of thought. Prostitution may be treated as a moral category, in which case the element of sexual promiscuity will be prominently emphasized in the definition. Or prostitution may be treated primarily as a legal category, a type of trade that has implications for public order and policy. In this case, the element of gain, the cash nexus of the transaction, will tend to be emphasized in defining prostitution. The moralist will mainly be concerned about the ethical problems of indiscriminate intercourse for the sake of gain; while the jurist will tend to analyze prostitution in terms of the hire-sale situation, will be concerned about the quasi-contract established between the harlot and her customer, and will have something to say about the property rights conveyed in the transaction, the price paid, and the value received in the exchange. It is precisely this contrast in viewpoints that makes the treatment of prostitution by the canonists particularly intriguing; for the canon law grew out of moral theology and never quite discarded its moralistic heritage. Yet the canonists also drew upon the Roman law as a major source of their arcane science and tended to think in terms of legal categories as well as in moral ones.[3]

How, then, did the canonists define prostitution? As one might expect, both of the basic criteria, promiscuity and gain, were involved. The fundamental definition that they employed was coined by Saint Jerome (ca. 342–420) and borrowed from him by Gratian (ca. 1140), the author of the *Decretum*: "A whore is one who is available for the lust of many men."[4] Gratian, then, relying on Saint Jerome, considered promiscuity the controlling factor in determining who is a prostitute. There is much sense in this: it may be possible to be promiscuous without being a prostitute, but it is hardly possible to be a prostitute without being sexually promiscuous. The notion of promiscuity was further defined by the decretist writers in the ordinary gloss (first redaction by Johannes Teutonicus [d. 1245/46]; second redaction by Bartholomaeus Brixiensis [d. ca. 1258]) to the *Decretum*: "Promiscuous: that is, she copulates indifferently and indiscriminately, as in canine love. Dogs indeed copulate indifferently and indiscriminately."[5] Other canonistic writers mentioned some additional considerations in their discussions of what prostitution meant. Hostiensis (d. 1271) gave some stress to the element of notoriety: a prostitute was not only sexually promiscuous, she was openly and publicly promiscuous.[6] Both Hostiensis and Joannes Andrea (ca. 1270–1348) agreed that an element of deception is also involved in prostitution: the harlot systematically deceives those whom she serves.[7]

When the canonists dealt with the element of gain in prostitution, they drew heavily upon the Roman law. The classical Roman law had defined prostitution as the offering of the body for sexual intercourse in return for money or other remuneration, at least so long as the woman made herself available to more than one or two lovers.[8]

It is clear that the widespread practice of concubinage complicated the attempts both of canonists and of Roman lawyers to define prostitution. The Roman jurists had assigned the concubine a status quite distinct from that of the prostitute. They considered the concubinage relation a relatively stable one, in contrast to the transient relationship of the prostitute and her customers. Thus, the status of the concubine was commonly assimilated to that of the married woman in the Roman law, and concubinage might be treated as an informal type of marriage. The concubine and her lover were considered bound to one another, not simply by lust and sexual attraction, but also by "marital affection." The lawyers used this latter term to signify either an intention eventually to contract marriage or else an emotional quality, not wholly unlike the concept of love.[9] Marital affection, in fact, was treated in Justinian's legislation as excluding promiscuity, which was essential to the definition of prostitution.[10] Thus concubinage and prostitution were mutually exclusive.

The medieval canonists, although conscious of these Roman law texts, faced a theological problem in adopting wholesale the Roman law definitions. By the lights of Western theology in the twelfth century, all extramarital sexual relations involved fornication, which was a species of sin. Concubinage, from this viewpoint, was an aggravated type of fornication, since it implicitly involved a long-term, continuing, nonmarital sexual relationship.[11] On the other hand, some of the decretists preferred to treat concubinage as a type of marriage,[12] a temporary marriage, perhaps, as Rufinus (d. 1192) called it,[13] or an informal, clandestine marriage, as Huguccio (d. 1210) and the anonymous author of the *Summa Coloniensis* (redacted ca. 1169) thought of it.[14] The canonistic doctrine on concubinage, in short, was not wholly clear or consistent. Yet although the canonists clearly thought concubinage undesirable, it was less undesirable than prostitution, and they felt it necessary to draw a sharp distinction between prostitution and concubinage. The distinction that they drew was based on the element of promiscuity, not on the element of gain in the relationship.[15]

When one looks beyond the matter of definition, one finds other anomalies in the ways in which the canonists dealt with prostitution. On the one hand, they flatly disapproved of prostitution. It was morally offensive, theologically repugnant, and ought to be repressed. For these views they could find adequate basis in the Scriptures,[16] in the natural law,[17] and in the Roman law.[18] Yet the medieval canonists' treatment of prostitution was strangely ambivalent. Although they disapproved of it in principle and thought that it should be prohibited, still, in practice, they were prepared to tolerate prostitution and to justify its toleration in a Christian society.

The origin of this policy of practical toleration seems to go back to Saint Augustine (354–430), who observed that if prostitutes were not available, established patterns of sexual relationship would be endangered. Therefore, he thought, it was better to tolerate prostitution, with all of its associated evils, than to risk the perils that would follow the successful elimination of the harlot from society.[19] In Augustine's attitude one can arguably find the wellsprings of later medieval and even modern attitudes toward prostitution: the notion that it is a necessary evil and that its elimination, if possible at all, would disturb and dislocate the social order.[20] Augustine's views on prostitution, as on other matters of sexual conduct, were accepted by theologians as well as by the canonists. Some of them even made the argument that prostitution was necessary for the public good.[21]

But there is more to it than this. The practical toleration of prostitution, coupled with the moral condemnation of it, was also rooted in medieval notions about the nature of sexuality itself. The medieval lawyers construed sexual intercourse as a part of the natural law, a notion that stemmed from the Roman jurists.[22] Although they knew that sexual urges are strong and universally shared, the canonists were also aware that sexual desire could lead to sin—and usually did. Few adults are not guilty of fornication, they observed,[23] and the ordinary gloss to the *Decretum* noted that people are commonly more inclined to fornicate than to steal.[24] The canonists also suspected that sexual desires might be of diabolical origin, a product of original sin and man's subsequent fallen state.[25] While they taught that the only legitimate outlet for sexual desire was to be found in marriage, some canonists believed that even in marriage sexual pleasure was sinful.[26] The major difference of opinion among them on this matter concerned the question of whether intercourse was sinful if the reason for the sexual act was enjoyment, rather than the procreation of children. Huguccio thought that even procreative sex was morally wrong; his more liberal brethren allowed that sexual relations might be morally admissible between married persons when the object of their relations was to beget offspring.[27] There was general agreement, however, that excessive intercourse, even within marriage, was sinful, although there was some dispute as to whether the sin involved should be equated with simple fornication or with the more serious sin of adultery.[28] Sex outside of marriage, however, was clearly wrong and intercourse with a prostitute compounded the wrong: it involved the bad use of an evil thing, as the ordinary gloss put it.[29]

The canonists were further conscious that the sexuality of women differed from that of men. For this they found a theological reason: woman was not created in the image of God, as man was.[30] The chastity of women, particularly young women, they held, was always suspect,[31] and women, they observed, are always ready for sexual intercourse. Hostiensis illustrated his comments on these points with the story of a priest who was journeying with two girls, one riding in front of him, the other behind. The priest, said Hostiensis, could never swear that the girl in back was a virgin.[32] Young girls were thought to be particularly susceptible to the call of sexual desire: the less they knew about it, the sweeter they thought it, as Saint Jerome put it.[33] Since women were considered so susceptible to sexual temptations, great care had to be taken to confine their sexual activities within a properly structured marriage relationship. Women usually sigh when their men are not available, Hostiensis observed,[34] and so husbands had a moral obligation to keep their wives sexually satisfied, lest they be tempted to stray to other beds.[35] The canonists treated this obligation as a debt and, like other debts, it was enforceable at law.[36] Nonetheless, women commonly yielded to stray sexual desires for a variety of reasons: they were overly trusting and put faith in the dubious promises of unworthy men; they were ignorant, sometimes so ignorant that they were unaware that adultery was sinful; or they might be separated from their spouses and despair of their husbands' return.[37] Morever, they were fickle and inconsistent creatures by nature,[38] soft of heart,[39] and susceptible to sensual stimulation, which easily led them into sexual sins.[40] In addition, the canonists were aware that females reach the age of sexual readiness earlier than males: girls are *viripotentes* from age twelve, according to Hostiensis, who cited the Roman law to prove his point.[41] They reach sexual maturity earlier than males, he thought, because they are warmer and quicker by nature than men and hence reach their natural perfection at an earlier age. Hostiensis also observed, rather ungallantly, that women are like weeds, which mature earlier than desirable plants — he quotes Plato to prove this point — but also die earlier.[42]

Despite all these handicaps — and one might have thought from some of the discussions that chastity in a woman was virtually impossible — women were nonetheless expected to observe a more austere standard of sexual conduct than were men, as at least some of the canonists were quite aware. They taught a double standard of sexual morality: they were aware of it and they had reasons for it, mainly theological.[43] Modesty, they taught, was woman's glory.[44] Therefore, a woman who was sexually desirous and ardent, who did not blush at sex, was at heart a whore, though she need not legally be classified as one so long as she remained faithful to her husband.[45] The adulteress, on the other hand, was more reprehensible than her partner in sin, and sexual promiscuity was considered more detestable in women than in men, according to Johannes Teutonicus in the ordinary gloss on the *Decretum*.[46] Even within the marriage relationship, a woman should not use the sexual wiles of a prostitute, and a matron who dressed like a tart could legally be classed as one.[47]

As for male sexuality, it was no secret to the canonists that men have a natural appetite for carnal relations with women.[48] The lawyers were also aware that casual conversation with members of the opposite sex might easily lead to greater intimacy,[49] an outcome that became even more likely when conversation was enlivened by intemperate drinking.[50] So rampant was male attraction to women that the ordinary gloss to the *Decretum* observed that some scholars even went to church services more in order to ogle the women who attended than to worship God.[51] It was obvious to the canonists, too, that religion and sex did not mix well together: a man who had sexual gratifications readily available could not give his whole attention to God.[52] This being so, clerics were especially exhorted not to have dealings of any kind, even the most innocuous conversations, with women whose morals were suspect. Those who did so were liable to excommunication.[53] Still, the canonists cautioned their students to give a benevolent interpretation to the association of clerics with members of the opposite sex. A cleric found embracing a woman is presumed to be blessing her, according to the ordinary gloss[54] — to which a later commentator jestingly added: "God save us from such blessings!"[55]

Given such views of male and female sexuality, with a far higher standard of sexual conduct demanded from women than from men, it may seem somewhat surprising to find that the lawyers generally, both civilians and canonists, wasted very little time detailing punishments to be dealt out to prostitutes. The prostitute, in the eyes of the canonists, was culpable, but not severely culpable for her conduct. She was, after all, simply acting in accord with her sexual character, as the canonists viewed it. When it came to punishments, they gave most of their attention to the penalties to be inflicted upon those who used the prostitute's services and upon the pimps, procurers, and brothelkeepers who made those services regularly available.[56]

The canonists saw financial need as one root cause of prostitution, but they did not consider poverty or economic necessity as mitigating circumstances.[57] No matter how hungry she might be or how desperate her situation, a woman was not justified in turning to prostitution in order to earn even the necessities of life.[58] Although poverty and desperation might excuse a man who committed theft, for example, and under certain circumstances even homicide could be justified, the canonists admitted no circumstances to excuse fornication and prostitution.[59] Nor was a natural craving for sexual gratification a mitigating circumstance:[60] some theologians indeed taught that the more pleasure a prostitute derived from her sexual encounters, the more serious was her offense.[61] Some authors tended to link prostitution with greed and saw an inordinate desire for wealth and opulence as a cause of harlotry, but this was not a theme on which the legal writers had much to say.[62] The only mitigating situation that the canonists would admit for the prostitute occurred if the girl had been forced into prostitution by her parents or someone who exercised legitimate control over her actions.[63] In such a situation, the prostitute herself was not accountable for her actions, and those who forced her into a life of sin bore the guilt for any actions that she was forced to perform.[64]

Perhaps the principal disability felt by the medieval prostitute was her inability to attain any form of significant social status. This she shared in common with her predecessors in Roman antiquity.[65] It has been suggested that even in modern societies the harlot's loss of social status remains one of the major disabilities adhering to the prostitute's role, and that the fees she receives should be interpreted as compensation not only for her sexual services, but also for her impaired social standing.[66] Certainly the medieval canonists considered the harlot's status debased: it was so vile, according to Hostiensis, that she was not even required to obey the law—the inference being that she was beneath the law's contempt.[67] She was so base that she was canonically debarred from accusing others of crimes, according to one conciliar canon,[68] save for the crime of simony, which the canonists considered a particularly depraved offense.[69] The harlot was also forbidden to inherit property or to be a beneficiary under a military testament.[70] If charges were brought against her, she was not allowed to answer in person but had to employ a representative to respond to them, just as did madmen and monsters.[71]

When it came to dealing with the property and property rights of harlots, the canonists followed very closely the stance of the classical Roman lawyers. Money given to a prostitute could not be reclaimed by the donor, according to this doctrine: the client had no right to take back the money he paid for the strumpet's services. She, for her part, committed no wrong in accepting the money. What she did in return for her fee might be wrong, but the taking of money for it was no crime.[72] The customer who paid the harlot her fee might be held wrong to give money to her, but her acceptance was perfectly legal.[73] Once she had taken the fee, it became her property outright and her rights to it were legally valid, a validity that at least one medieval lawyer sustained because of the harlot's "usefulness."[74] Cardinal Cajetan, incidentally, stipulated that a prostitute, in order to be entitled lawfully to retain what she earned, must charge only a just price for her services. He did not specify how this was to be determined. He also considered it unlawful for a prostitute to practice deception in the display of her wares.[75]

If a whore was legally entitled to retain what had been paid to her, she was on shakier ground in seeking fulfillment of promises made to her. The customer who paid in cash could not reclaim what he had paid to her. The wilier customer, who paid with promises of future gifts, could renege on his promises and the prostitute could not legally secure enforcement of them.[76]

Another vexing question concerned the liability of ladies of joy for the payment of the tithe. On this matter opinions were divided. Some canonists held that since the harlot unlawfully possessed the money she received for her services, she must pay tithes from her earnings.[77] Hostiensis, however, thought otherwise; the earnings of the whore, although lawfully held, were nonetheless the wages of sin and tithes could not lawfully be collected from them.[78] Saint Thomas Aquinas (1224–1274), as usual, distinguished: the harlot must be required to pay the tithe from her earnings – but the Church might not accept the payment until she had reformed.[79]

If the harlot's liability for payment of the tithe was disputed, her ability to give free-will alms was likewise in doubt; most canonistic authorities agreed with Huguccio that the Church could not accept alms from ill-gotten goods, such as the gains derived from usury, the earnings of actors, the stipends of *mathematici,* the profits of extortioners, or the fees of prostitutes.[80] Others distinguished between various types of ill-gotten gains, commonly on the grounds that some were wrongly acquired by force or the threat of force (e.g., the profits of robbers, extortioners, or advocates, who prey on the poor and ignorant), while other ill-gotten gains were derived from more or less generous, if misdirected impulses; the earnings of prostitutes and actors fell into this class.[81] The ordinary gloss distinguished on still other grounds. Alms should not be given from ill-gotten gains if ownership of the goods were retained by the original giver with mere possession passing into the hands of the receiver, according to this view; but, if both ownership and possession passed to the recipient (as was the case with fees given to prostitutes), then alms could be given and received from such goods.[82]

Hostiensis posed a particularly tantalizing case, that of the crusading harlot. What would the legal situation be if a whore took the cross? She would surely be followed by many men, since nothing is stronger than love, and this would clearly bolster the defensive forces of the Holy Land. Should the crusading harlot therefore be obliged to fulfill a crusading vow? Hostiensis thought not: the motivation of her followers, after all, was not likely to be a spiritual one. Should she then be allowed to redeem her vow by making an offering for the defense of the Holy Places? Hostiensis thought that this, too, would be unacceptable.[83] The appropriate conclusion seems to be that harlots should not take crusading vows.

Although prostitutes were acknowledged to have some property rights, their power to protect those rights was extremely limited, so far as the canonists were concerned. A prostitute could not denounce a criminal, nor were the courts to hear a harlot's complaints about wrongs done to her.[84] This attitude was consistent with the teaching of the Roman lawyers.[85] Alberto dei Gandini (ca. 1245–ca. 1310) discussed this situation in the context of a case that is said to have occurred at Mantua. One Armanius, clearly no gentleman, entered the house of a woman and attempted to have forcible intercourse with her, against her will. Charged with this offense, Armanius proved in his own defense that the woman he had assaulted was a public prostitute, of bad condition, ill-famed, and known by many men. Indeed, Armanius himself was one of her regular customers and frequently had intercourse with her. Under these circumstances, could he be punished for attempting to rape her? The subtlety of the question taxed the wits of lesser lawyers and a famous jurist, Dino Mugellano, was consulted on the matter. Dino gave it as his opinion that if it were proved that the woman had put her body up for hire, then Armanius could not be punished for an attempt to rape her.[86] Alberto cited another case: an unnamed man broke down the door of a harlot's house, *libidinis causa*. Thieves subsequently entered the house through the broken door and made off with the furnishings. Was the sex-crazed door-breaker liable for damages for the stolen goods? Alberto thought not—his motive was lust, not theft, and he could not be held responsible for what he had not intended.[87]

If whores abounded everywhere in medieval Europe—and the available evidence strongly suggests that they did—one problem that faced public authorities was how to distinguish them visibly and clearly from respectable women. The canonists tended to think that distinctive dress was the best solution to the problem.[88] Municipal authorities commonly reverted to ancient practice by sequestering their prostitutes in specified portions of their cities and establishing quasi-public control over the practice of their trade.[89] The whores of Paris are even said to have founded a guild—perhaps in an attempt to restrain competition, as other guilds commonly did.[90]

Attempts at regulation, identification, and isolation were made easier for the authorities by the fact that prostitution in medieval Europe was most commonly practiced in the setting of a brothel.[91] Streetwalkers were not unknown, but brothels were everywhere, even in small towns and large-sized villages.[92] In many towns the local brothels were acknowledged civic corporations, regulated minutely by local ordinances, even supervised by public officials: often enough the local executioner doubled as supervisor of whorehouses in his off-hours.[93]

Despite sporadic local efforts to outlaw brothels and prostitution,[94] whorehouses apparently flourished everywhere, often under the guise of bathhouses, and frequently under the supervision of barbers.[95] For this reason, canonists frequently warned Christians in general and clerics in particular not to frequent bathhouses, since they were apt to be morally dangerous.[96] Bathhouses and barbershops might not be the only occasions of sin. Jacques de Vitry, writing in the first quarter of the thirteenth century, gives a vivid description of the Parisian prostitutes of his day. They were everywhere in the city, soliciting passing clerics to sample their delights and crying out, "Sodomite!" after those who passed up the invitation. Both a brothel and a scholar's hall might occupy the same premises: while the master delivered his lectures in an upper room, the trollops exercised their trade below. It is likely that the twain sometimes met, as the arguments between the harlots and their pimps rose to mingle with the disputations of the schools.[97]

Bold and brazen though she might be, the medieval prostitute was largely powerless in the eyes of the law, socially degraded, although tolerated in a practical sense and, to a limited degree, allowed property rights in her earnings. Still, she could redeem her situation through reform. For this there were illustrious examples—had not Jesus himself said to the Pharisees of his time that repentant tax collectors and whores would take precedence over them in the kingdom of heaven?[98] And, the example of Saint Mary Magdalene demonstrated that the believing and repentant harlot could achieve salvation.[99] In some circumstances the Church stood ready to assist girls to leave a life of sin. Involuntary prostitutes, i.e., girls who had been sold into prostitution by their parents or masters, could petition the local bishop or other authority to liberate them from their carnal bondage.[100] Other harlots could also look to the Church for help in efforts at self-reform. Still, the canonists recognized realistically that the chances of successful reform were slim, and that a repentant strumpet might continually be tempted to take up her former life.[101]

Nonetheless, the hope of reform was there. Two major avenues of reform were contemplated. The favorite with most reformers was to induce the repentant harlot to enter the religious life, to become a nun. From at least the twelfth century onward, religious houses were established with the particular purpose of serving as havens for reformed prostitutes.[102] In 1224 an effort began to create a special religious order of penitential nuns to harbor reformed whores, and in 1227 Pope Gregory IX (1227–1241) gave the highest ecclesiastical sanction to the Order of St. Mary Magdalene, which subsequently established convents in numerous cities. The sisters wore a white habit, whence they were sometimes known as "the White Ladies."[103] Subsequent official patronage and encouragement was given to the Magdalenes by the fourteenth-century popes.[104] Similar convents, not necessarily affiliated with the Magdalene order, received endowment and support from monarchs, such as the pious Louis IX of France (1226–1270), who was subsequently elevated to the altars of the Church for this and other saintly actions.[105]

For the harlot who wished to reform but who was not inclined to embrace the religious life, there was another alternative: marriage. The canonists required, however, that a number of conditions be fulfilled before a prostitute might marry. In this area of the law, a gradual change of attitude and policy took place. The doctrine of the early Church had tended to discourage such marriages: one of the canons in Gratian's *Decretum* characterized the man who kept a whore as his wife as idiotic and unreasonable.[106] Even the reformed prostitute, who had done solemn public penance for her sins, might be forbidden to marry, unless she first obtained a special dispensation for this purpose,[107] a provision consistent with Roman imperial law on the subject.[108] Still, marriage to a prostitute, although dubious, was not held to be actually sinful.[109] And a man who married a prostitute, believing her to be a chaste virgin, was held to be validly married by the leading theologian of the twelfth century.[110]

Gratian was inclined to take a cautiously more permissive view of the matter, although he observed gloomily that one could not trust the word of a harlot.[111] He distinguished between the situation in which a man married a whore who continued her trade and that in which a man married a whore in order to reform her. In the first situation the marriage was not allowed; but, in the second situation it was permitted.[112] The decretist commentators accepted Gratian's distinction. They also commonly insisted that the reformed prostitute must demonstrate her intention of changing her ways by doing penance prior to the marriage.[113] Rolandus remarked that in his day it was considered praiseworthy to marry reformed prostitutes.[114] Pope Innocent III (1198–1216), in a decretal issued during the first year of his pontificate, confirmed Rolandus's observations. The pope lauded those who married harlots in order to reform them and described their actions as "not least among the works of charity." Further, he assured those who rescued public prostitutes and took them to wife that their actions would count for the remission of their own sins.[115] Bernardus Parmensis, the author of the ordinary gloss to the *Decretals*, was apparently more dubious about this matter than was the pope: "This [decretal] concerns her who freely wishes to be chaste—if someone can be found who wishes to take her as a wife."[116] Other decretalist commentators also insisted that corrigibility was an essential criterion: the incorrigible prostitute was not allowed to marry, and the man who kept such a one as his wife was classified as a pimp.[117]

The man who wished to marry a prostitute, even one who had reformed her life, also faced certain problems. If he had previously had intercourse with her himself, there was some question whether he could marry her at all:

Gratian raised the matter at two points in the *Decretum,* but left the solution unclear. He apparently believed that such a marriage would be licit, but that the woman must do penance.[118] Once the marriage had been contracted, she could be put away only if she reverted to her old ways and refused to do penance.[119] If the husband were a cleric, he was further penalized for his choice of a wife: he could not be ordained to major orders even after the death of his wife,[120] and he was barred from any sort of promotion in the ecclesiastical hierarchy,[121] although presumably it was possible to receive dispensation in such cases.[122] Even after Innocent III's approval of marriage with harlots for purposes of reform, the ordinary gloss to the *Decretals* continued to classify men who married harlots as bigamists for ecclesiastical purposes.[123]

What does this survey of the canonistic jurisprudence tell us about the theory and practice of medieval prostitution?

The writings of the canonists underscore what other sources indicate about the prevalence of prostitution in medieval society. It is also clear that one reason for the frequency of prostitution in a society that was heavily influenced, not to say dominated, by ecclesiastical institutions and the doctrinal attitudes of the Church may well have been a fundamental ambivalence in the Church's own law about prostitution. Although theologically denounced, prostitution was viewed by the lawyers as an evil that must be tolerated in order to avert the greater evils that would follow from the abolition of prostitution. Further, the medieval notions about male and female sexuality, as reflected in the lawyers' writings, led the Church's legal functionaries to require that women (whom they thought highly susceptible to sensual stimuli) adhere to a higher standard of sexual morality than men. Conversely, however, the woman who fell into a life of prostitution was not overly punished by harshly repressive measures, while men who frequented prostitutes were subject to more numerous and more severe punishments than were the ladies of joy whom they patronized. Ironically, then, the lawyers treated the prostitute as a necessary evil, to be tolerated and dealt with rather leniently, while at the same time they looked upon the use of her services as a relatively serious crime, subject to stringent repressive measures.

The canonistic jurisprudence dealing with prostitution also points up another characteristic of the canon law rather generally, namely, the way in which it accommodated moral principles to the realities of human behavior. This was, after all, the basic service that the canonist performed for the medieval Church and for society at large. The canonist attempted to translate the abstract principles of the theologian into practical, workable behavioral norms. The canonistic treatment of prostitution illustrates this function of the canon law, I think, very well indeed. Without abandoning the moral principle that prostitution was an undesirable form of sexual behavior, the canonists tried to work out a fundamental system of norms that also took into account the existing structures of society, of the family, and the nature of male and female sexuality as they understood them. Many of their fundamental ideas about the nature and function of sexual relations in society are not ones that are nowadays shared by most people in the Western world. But given the data and the assumptions with which the canonists of the twelfth and thirteenth centuries worked, one can hardly fail to admire the ingenuity with which they reconciled reality with high principles in dealing with one of the most intimate and most difficult of all human behavioral situations.

Section III

Historians of sex have difficulties in describing actual sexual conduct. How effective were the Church teachings about sexuality? Answers to such a question are not easy to come by because the sources simply do not permit us to enter into the bedroom of the past; even today we are not certain we can answer such questions. Creative writers, however, often give us insights into sexual practices and beliefs. Sidney Berger examines some of the pertinent medieval literature. His survey is not all-inclusive but rather is intended to indicate areas that need exploration. Another way of examining past sexual practices is to look at the laws and regulations about sex. Prostitution is a good example of secular attempts to deal with what was perceived as a sex problem requiring regulation. But why are people so sexual? Helen Rodnite Lemay examines some of the scientific answers put forth in the Middle Ages, including some of the astrological–astronomical answers that might be regarded as the medieval equivalent of current psychological theorizing. Medieval, like modern, society often had guilt feelings about some of their sexual urges, and this is demonstrated not by its willingness to give a sexual connotation to groups such as heretics or witches that were regarded as threats to societal values. The section concludes with a paragraph assessing the importance of research into human sexuality and emphasizing the need for such research to better understand life in the Middle Ages.

15

Sex in the Literature of the Middle Ages: The Fabliaux

Sidney E. Berger

When one speaks of sex in the literature of the Middle Ages, the first genre that must come to mind is the fabliau, a type of literature akin to the fable (of which word it is a diminutive form). The fabliau is a short tale, usually in verse, and often dealing with some sexual activity. The characters are usually portrayed realistically, speaking an earthy dialogue, performing "natural" acts, and exhibiting, uncensored, their needs and desires with grace, lust, and enjoyment.

This review of the major critical topics will not be definitive but will show some of the areas of the fabliaux thought to be most worthy of discussion by critics. The notes will refer the reader to some of the more recent or important work that has been done on the subject.[1]

Sources

Jürgen Beyer, in his essay "The Morality of the Amoral,"[2] says that the source of the fabliau is the farcical spirit that "pulls every element down to the level of the human and only-too-human, of the physical and worldly, of the drastic and vulgar." Or the source of the genre may be simpler than that—"it may lie where Ranke placed it: in 'a basic drive of our being: man cannot bear the solemn and grave for long.'"[3] These two explanations of the source of the genre are not contradictory. They show the nature of the human psyche in terms of the satisfaction of certain needs. But on a different level, what are the literary sources of the genre? The answer to such a question is important in interpreting medieval sexual activity.

It has been frequently noted that the fabliaux and courtly love literature share many characteristics.[4] In the courtly love system, some commonplace observations are that true love cannot exist in marriage, that, in the standard situation, the man's rank is beneath that of the woman he worships, and that ultimately (as Alexander Denomy points out[5]) courtly love is a heresy because the goal of the lover is adultery. But the defenders of courtly love say that even if the goal of the lovers *is* illicit love, the man never expects or perhaps even wishes to get there. The woman cannot risk the consequences of being caught by her husband in an affair; the lover glorifies in the pain and deprivation he must suffer in his lady's name. Though this is something of a simplification, one fact remains: the emphasis is on the man's striving; it is on the ennobling effects that such a love has on the man. I contend that in true courtly love the striving of the man *must* fall short of consummation. When the striving goes beyond the pristine and ennobling relationship of pure courtly love, it takes two different paths: (1) it could turn to romance, in which the characters are motivated by genuine and deep affection (as in *Tristan and Iseult*); or (2) it could turn into fabliau, in which the love is more accurately depicted as lust, and this lust is consummated in any of a variety of bizarre or acrobatic ways in order to amuse us. Thus the genre of the fabliaux often parodies courtly love. Paul Theiner — writing about "Aloul"[6] — uses the apt phrase "the parodic echoing of courtly values" (p. 134). Unquestionably, the writers of fabliaux were intimately familiar with courtly love literature, and they seem to have taken every opportunity to parody it.

Constituent Parts and Structure

Along with the elements of courtly love discussed briefly above, there is also a large number of motifs and of stock characters that all fableors drew upon. There are naturally a man and a woman, frequently not married to one another. There is the woman's husband — unsuspecting or suspicious — who gets cuckolded, and usually deserved to be. The young lover is usually of the lower classes or of the priesthood; if he is a priest, he is more likely to fail in his courtship of the woman than if he were simply a "lovere and a lusty bacheler,"[7] a phrase accurately describing the third member of the lovers' triangle as this triangle is normally depicted in the fabliaux. For some reason, the low level of the characters seems to give the author a loose rein in the actions he may have his characters perform. This laxity yields a tremendously varied array of means of arriving at sexual satisfaction or of revealing erotic situations. Two examples should suffice: Damian and May in Chaucer's *Merchant's Tale* consummate their love in a pear tree, while January, May's jealous (and blind) husband, stands below with his hands awaiting the fruit May said she wanted to get in the tree; and the knight in "The Knight Who Conjured Voices" ("Le Chevalier Qui Fist Parler les Cons")[8] could make vaginas and rectums speak.

Unquestionably, the writers of the fabliaux drew upon the system of courtly love for their plots, their stock characters, and the spirit of sexuality implied in courtly love. In *The Reeve's Tale* Chaucer tells us that Symkin's wife is high-born.[9] And in *The Merchant's Tale* May is the wife of a knight while Damian is a lowly clerk. The writers of the French fabliaux rely on the same courtly love situations, though for them actual sexual intercourse is not necessary; humiliation because of sexual matters may be the source of their humor. [Absolon in *The Reeve's Tale* is humiliated when he is duped into unknowingly kissing the lady's crotch.] In "Beranger Longbottom" ("Béranger au Lonc Cul") by Garin,[10] the cowardly knight—like Absolon— is humiliated by being forced (this time knowingly) into kissing his wife's crotch. Similarly, humiliation in sexual matters is the source of the humor in "The Knight Who Conjured Voices" and in Jean de Conde's "The Beaten Path" ("Le Sentier Battu").[11] In the former, a knight embarrasses a haughty woman by forcing her anus to tell him why her vagina could not reply to his question (because the woman had stuffed it full of cotton so that it could not speak); and in the latter, a proud-spirited queen who has embarrassed a young knight by revealing his lack of experience in sex (she says, " . . . it is easy to judge from the state of the hay [his sparse beard] whether the pitchfork is any good"—p. 24) is herself embarrassed when he in turn reveals her excessive sexual proclivities (she is forced to tell him in front of the court that she has no hair between her legs, to which he replies, " . . . grass does not grow on a well-beaten path"—p. 25). Even in "The Partridges" ("Les Perdriz")—which has to do with the way a gluttonous wife saves herself from an angry husband after she has eaten the two partridges he has caught— sexual matters enter almost as a necessity: the angry husband is chasing after a priest who, the wife has said, took the two birds; the wife has told the priest that her husband was going to castrate him; so the humor rests on the *double entendre* yelled by the husband, chasing the priest with a knife in his hand, "You won't get away with them like that . . . . You're carrying them all hot, but you'll leave them here if I catch you!" (p. 125).[12]

The courtly love elements, even in very rudimentary form, are present in all these tales. In "Beranger Longbottom" and "The Knight Who Conjured Voices," there is a knight whose very title should indicate the courtly code he should adhere to. In "The Beaten Path" the roles of queen and knight are appropriate for a courtly love relationship.[13] And in "The Partridges" we have a (brief) triangle when the priest propositions the wife. In "William and the Falcon" the young squire, William, loves his lord's wife, though she did not even know of his love.[14] Typically, the courtly lover should keep his feelings to himself for a time. Just the phrase "He was in the power of the God of Love, who made his life a martyrdom" (p. 82) signifies the courtly element; Hellman and O'Gorman themselves call it "a little satire on the conventions of courtly love" (p. 93). Despite William's sincerity in his love for the lady, the facts remain that she is married and that the only way he can be relieved of his love pains is if she gives in to him. And, since this *is* a fabliau, this is exactly what must happen; she falls madly in love with him and begins to exhibit the same signs of love that he had. Here the author enters with a moralistic tag to conclude the story, and even though they do not consummate their love in the tale itself, it is clear to us that they will soon do so.

Another fabliau, "The Lady Who Was Castrated" ("La Dame escoilée"),[15] concerns a shrewish wife who constantly contradicts her husband in everything, always getting the upper hand. Her son-in-law, a count, in her husband's absence, has her spread-eagled by his strong servants, slices into her loins with a knife, and pretends to remove her testicles—actually cut from one of the count's bulls. The count shows them to her, explaining over her cries that these were what was making her so masculine, so domineering. The count not only improves the lot of his father-in-law by making his mother-in-law promise never again to contradict her husband, but he also uses this incident as a warning to his own wife never to act in the way her mother acted. His wife vows never to contradict him: "I assure you," she says, "I will do whatever you want and desire. If I don't, you can cut off my head" (p. 34). Even this tale, which brings sex in in a most bizarre and gruesome way, is told completely in the courtly manner. The count observes all the courtly rules of behavior; he falls in love with the young girl in the way prescribed by the rules of courtly love: "Love struck him in the breast" (p. 27) when he first sees her; he speaks to her parents in the most proper of terms and desires the girl for her beauty and breeding; he cannot sleep just thinking about her; and, after returning to his own home with his new bride, when his in-laws visit him, the mother-in-law announces her coming to the count, and he is upset at her lack of propriety: "The count thought she was insane with pride to notify him herself instead of her lord, who he heard had also come" (p. 31). These few examples (in the last two paragraphs) show that the use of sex in the fabliaux can be traced in one way or another to the courtly world, ostensibly purer than the world of the fabliau. Paul Brians, speaking of "The Lady Who Was Castrated," says, " . . . the milieu is distinctly noble, the author addresses himself to lords embroiled in marital difficulties, and many of the descriptions and much of the terminology belong to the courtly style . . . . It is clear that such a tale is in no way foreign to the spirit of the medieval court. The tale is a vigorous, infuriated reassertion of the traditional male dominance of women in the face of the growing cult of courtly love" (p. 36). So the authors drew directly from courtly love or in strong opposition to it. One way or another, the courtly love system was the source of most of the fabliaux.

One of the component characteristics of the genre is its overstatement. Just as the love in courtly literature is often expressed in exaggerated terms,[16] so the sex in the literature of the medieval period is frequently related with certain areas of exaggeration. The husband is not merely protective of his wife and worried about his own reputation, he is usually insanely jealous (like January in *The Merchant's Tale*). The lovers do not merely make love and go to sleep, they do it for hours, tirelessly, as if neither of them ever wearied of it or got sore.[17] The wife is always wonderfully clever—so clever that she can normally save her skin by coming up with some outrageous line concerning the sexual activities her husband has (nearly?) caught her in to dupe him thoroughly. The husband is not merely dupable, he is usually either so simple-minded as to be practically senile, or he is so thoroughly outwitted by his wife that he retires in humiliation, nevermore to question his wife's faithfulness. Boccaccio, in the *Decameron* (sixth day, seventh story), tells of a woman who is caught by her husband in her lover's embraces. The husband demands that she be burned, as it was set down in the statutes of the city. But the wife—fully admitting her guilt and thus giving the magistrate full rights to condemn her to the pyre—asks her husband in front of the justice if she has ever denied her husband the sexual pleasures he has requested of her. He admits that she *always* satisfied him. Then the wife asks that if her husband had taken from her all that he ever needed to satisfy him, what was she to do with what was left over: throw it to the dogs? Was it not better to give it to someone else than to let it go to waste or spoil? The justice not only let her go free, he even changed the statute on her behalf. Her cleverness in freeing herself is one thing; the exaggeration comes in the justice's going so far as to change the law because of her case. In *The Merchant's Tale* May tells her doddering old husband January that the reason she was "struggling" in the tree (with her lover Damian) was that only in this manner could she restore his eyesight:

> I have yow holpe on bothe youre eyen blynde.
> Up peril of my soule, I shal nat lyen,
> As me was taught, to heele with youre eyen,
> Was no thyng bet, to make yow to see,
> Than strugle with a man upon a tree.
> God woot, I dide it in ful good entente.[18]

> [I have helped you in both your blind eyes.
> Upon peril of my soul, I shall not lie,
> As was taught to me, to heal your eyes with,
> There was no better thing, to permit you to see,
> Than to struggle with a man up in a tree.
> God knows, I did it with the best intention.]

As if this were not enough, she adds that his having recently regained his vision made him see fuzzily, so what he thought he saw (copulation) was merely "struggle." January is completely taken in by this. Her exceptional use of logic and rhetoric and his exaggerated gullibility are typical of the fabliaux.

One of the elements frequently attributed to the fabliaux is their realism. On a very simple level, realism may be seen as the use of sex, humiliation, or bawdy jokes—realistic because they are earthy and represent the human condition for most men. But the fabliau genre does not present life realistically (despite such statements as, the fabliaux "always maintain[ed] a realistic tone and manner"[19]). Charles Muscatine explains it this way:[20]

> The literature of the bourgeois tradition[21] is "realistic" or "naturalistic," but it neither attempts nor achieves the reportorial detail of the modern fiction describable by these labels . . . . I use the terms "realistic" and "naturalistic," then, loosely—for lack of better ones—to indicate that for the Middle Ages . . . this literature has a remarkable preoccupation with the animal facts of life. It takes, in the ordinary sense, a realistic view of things.

If the fabliaux lack realism in their use of exaggeration, they also lack it in their characterization, their plots, and even in their use of what Paul Theiner calls "the fableor's authentication of himself and his materials."[22] On characterization, D. W. Robertson, Jr. says, "'Realism' requires realistic characters, but the characters who animate the fabliaux are not, in a modern sense, 'realistic' at all. They are, rather, types."[23] On plots, Cooke states, "Granted that the overall style is realistic, there are almost no fabliaux that portray completely realistic actions, for they range on a spectrum that moves from the wild or far-fetched through the bizarre and incredible all the way to the impossible or supernatural."[24] The cruelty of the count in "The Lady Who was Castrated," the intervention of the gods in *The Merchant's Tale,* and the knight's ability to make vaginas and anuses speak are just a few cases in point. Paul Theiner's essay discusses some of the elements of setting that serve as the author's attempt to authenticate the entire tale. For example, "the authenticity of the fabliau is often sustained by appeals to universal knowledge, especially of a proverbial sort. If we all agree on the truth of the principle enunciated, we can scarcely find fault with the 'realism' of that individual feature that does not so much confirm the saying . . . as provide us with an instance."[25] Theiner shows how the use of proverbs and other "authenticating features" (p. 122) is just a game; it is what he calls "the game of authentication" (p. 123). He says, "Once we have joined [the author] in the game, we can follow his lead into the actual story, secure in the knowledge that the whole performance has been properly placed in the schema of reality" (p. 123).

Many critics concern themselves with the realism of the fabliaux. But Theiner's statements about the "game of authentication" should show us that such a preoccupation is unnecessary. We all willingly suspend our disbelief when we read any literary work. We can believe that May duped January in the same way that we believe that Superman can fly or that Beowulf was killed by a dragon.

Because we suspend our disbelief, sometimes the feelings we have for a character border on pity. This is not exactly a "constituent part," but a result of the part of the tale in which one character is humiliated. January's excessive fear of being cuckolded and his extensive and extreme actions to protect his own and his wife's virtue doom him from the start, and make him look so ludicrous and simple-minded as to be laughable. But there is something pitiable in this man's approaching senility. In a way, his lustiness— which he has indulged in until "he was passed his sixty yeer" (p. 115, l. 1253)—emphasizes his spiritual sterility and the dotage that comes with old age.[26] When he is cuckolded and then fooled into believing it was for his own good, we ought more to sympathize with him than to laugh at him. We must laugh, of course, at his hilarious preparations for his wedding night. He thinks he will shock and hurt May:

> Allas! O tendre creature,
> Now wolde God ye myghte wel endure
> Al my corage, it is so sharp and keene!
> I am agast ye shul it nat sustene.
> > (p. 120, ll. 1757–60)

> [Tender creature!
> Alas, God grant you may endure the nature
> Of my desires, they are so sharp and hot.
> I am aghast lest you sustain them not.]

Though on the surface the word "corage" in this instance means something like *ardor,* I am certain that January translates it in his mind into something more phallic. His preparations, with his aphrodisiacs ("He drynketh ypocras, clarree, and vernage/Of spices hoote, t'encreessen his corage"— p. 121, ll. 1808–9[27]), and Chaucer's description of May as " . . . broght abedde as stille as stoon" (p. 121, l. 1818) make us half pity and half ridicule this old man. At the heart of every fabliau, then, there is not merely laughter and fun, there is also a sober statement about man's condition. With January this condition is his old age and the loss of wits that comes with age.

Chaucer does not want us to take his lesson too seriously. He wants us to laugh and goes to considerable effort to this end. He has January begin his seduction, if you will, of his fresh young wife with the warning that this will take some time, but be patient; January tells May:

> There nys no werkman, whatsoevere he be,
> That may bothe werke wel and hastily.
> (p. 121, ll. 1832-33)

And Chaucer follows this with the observation:

> Thus laboureth he til that the day gan dawe.
> (p. 121, l. 1842)

It takes him until dawn to complete the act—which was more *labor* than fun. As if his attempt as thus described were not funny enough, Chaucer adds one brilliant touch to this scene—May's reaction to and observation of it all:

> But God woot what that May thoughte in hir herte,
> When she hym saugh up sittynge in his sherte,
> In his nyght-cappe, and with his nekke lene:
> She preyseth nat his pleyyng worth a bene.
> (p. 121, ll. 1851-54)

> [God knows what May was thinking in her heart
> Seeing him sit there in his shirt apart,
> Wearing his night-cap, with his scrawny throat.
> She didn't think his games were worth a groat.]

May and the audience listen to his crowing and singing and watch the slack skin on his neck wobble. Chaucer—like all the authors of the fabliaux—emphasizes the humorous, the ludicrous, the entertaining, with no more recognition of the morality of the situation or the pitiable nature of the old man than the characters themselves have.

I might add that May's position—from the audience's point of view—might be seen from two angles. From without, her situation is amusing. We have been told that January has insisted on marrying a virgin, or at least a girl no older than sixteen (l. 1417). [Considering how quickly May "takes to" Damian, it is doubtful that she was a virgin.] The picture of a young, beautiful, ripe girl sitting in bed watching her ancient husband prepare to take her is quite funny; May herself might have laughed. From within, however, her situation is dreadful. She is doomed to face this senile, wrinkled, cackling lecher for the rest of his life. This may be what Chaucer implies when he says she was brought to January on their wedding night "as stille as stoon." The situation is certainly loathsome to her, and despite our laughter at the entire situation, we must feel some pity for poor May. Her position is not atypical; that is, in almost all the fabliaux, someone gets taken advantage of—someone loses something—and if we can look beyond the humor of the tale for a moment, we can observe the sobering elements in the work.

Another element common to many fabliaux is the characters' preoccupation with their reputations. I have already mentioned this in connection with January. When men in the tales consider their reputations, it manifests itself in their jealousy and fear of being cuckolded. When women consider their reputations, it is usually false pretense of faithfulness to their husbands. In the earliest extant English fabliau, "Dame Sirith," we have the standard situation of a young, attractive woman whose husband is out of the house and who is propositioned by a young man. Her immediate response is:

> And ich am wif bothe god and treue—
> Treuer womon ne may no mon knowe
>   Then ich am.
> Thilke time ne shal never betide
> That mon for wowing ne thoru prude
>   Shal do me sham![28]

> [And I am both a good and faithful wife—
> A truer woman no man may know
>   Than I am.
> It shall never come to pass
> That a man, through propositioning or through pride,
>   Shall cause me shame!]

She will have nothing to do with him because of her reputation. She sends him away. The lover goes to Dame Sirith who promises to change the girl's mind. The old dame tells the lady that her (Dame Sirith's) dog is weeping because a young clerk propositioned the Dame's daughter, who rejected him; he then turned her into a bitch, and the dog weeps because of this metamorphosis. Margery sees the similarity between her position and that of Dame Sirith's daughter and asks for the Dame's help. The Dame arranges a meeting with the two, and the young girl eagerly greets the man with

> Welcome, Wilekin, swete thing!
> Thou art welcomere then the king!

> Wilekin the swete,
> My love I thee behete,
>   To don al thine wille.
> Turnd ich have my thout,
> For I ne wolde nout
>   That thou thee shuldest spille.

> [Welcome, Willikin, sweet thing!
> You are more welcome than the king!
> I promise my love to you,
>   To do all your will.

I have changed my mind,
For I wouldn't want
You to kill yourself.]
(ll. 425–32)

Her quick willingness to believe Dame Sirith's preposterous story about the weeping bitch shows that her former stance of faithfulness to her husband was pretence; she is willing to let *any* excuse convince her to do what she was already disposed to do—that is, to give in to Willikin. But even in her willingness to be seduced, she adds a little touch that takes the responsibility off her shoulders and places it on to Willikin's: she says, I am doing this so that you will not kill yourself over unrequited love. She turns her deed, which she knows is immoral, into a noble act of preserving the life of another. It is merely part of her stance of faithfulness.[29]

It ought to be pointed out also that the authors themselves were concerned with the public reputation of the characters. Almost every fableor, in setting forth his characters, makes some mention of the characters' social positions. Either the principal figure is a knight, or he is quite wealthy (as is the case with the brow-beaten husband of "The Lady Who Was Castrated"), or he is "very worthy and greatly beloved in his land" (said of Marie de France's Equitan[30]). The husband in "The Wife of Orleans"[31] "was a property owner, rich beyond measure" (p. 1). The central figures of "The Beaten Path" (see note 11) are a knight and a queen. Even a character of low social rank, like the Butcher of Abbeville[32] by Eustache d'Amiens, can be described as "an honest man, trustworthy and well bred, a good workman in his craft" (p. 31). In most of the fabliaux the rank or noble qualities of the characters as described by the authors is little more than window-dressing. It usually has little or nothing to do with the tale. It is part of the authenticating effects Theiner speaks of. Chaucer, on the other hand, can use it for humorous ends. When the Reeve says of the Miller's daughter that she was "ycomen of noble kyn;/The person of the toun hir fader was,"[33] the fact that she is the illegitimate daughter of a parson gives us a clear indication of the sarcasm of the speaker. This sarcasm is reinforced in the "marvelous" dowry the Reeve says she brought with her to the marriage:

> With hire he [the parson] yaf ful many a panne of bras.
> (p. 56, l. 3944)

The dowry consisted of brass pennies. And the wife shows her own preoccupation with her "high" lineage in her bearing:

> She was as digne as water in a dich,
> And ful of hoker and of bisemare.
> Hir thoughte that a lady sholde hire spare,

What for hire kynrede and hir nortelrie
That she hadde lerned in the nonnerie.

[She was as scornful as water in a ditch,
And full of derision and of scorn.
To her it seemed that a lady should treat her with consideration,
What with her (high) birth and her education
Which she had gotten in a nunnery.]

(p. 56, ll. 3964–68.)

The Reeve is about to humiliate the Miller who is on the pilgrimage by tell-ing a story of the humiliation of the Miller and his family in the tale. By set-ting up the Miller's wife as supposedly of high birth, he can make her "fall" (when she engages in intercourse with one of the clerks) seem great. It is something like the difference between seeing a hobo get a pie in the face and seeing a well-dressed, bejeweled, obviously quite wealthy and smug woman get hit with that pie. The hobo can raise within the audience a variety of emotions depending on the situation; the millionairess is humiliated. So the author's use of the public reputation of his characters can be worked into the tale thematically, preparing the reader for what Thomas Cooke calls the Comic Climax.[34]

Though several critics have commented on the structure of the fabliaux,[35] no one—to the best of my knowledge—has mentioned the possibility that the tales' structures are often like and may have been modeled on that of the medieval sermon. When a moral is present, it is often used in the same way as is the "text" of a sermon.[36] If the tale has an aphoristic opening—like the *text* or *theme* of the standard sermon—and if the main body of the fabliau sets about in one way or another to be an example of this text (or a proof of it), and if the author concludes with a reiteration of this text, we have at least three distinct sermon divisions: text, exemplum, and peroration.

The audience must certainly have been churchgoers; their training all their lives was to see things in terms of Christianity and its teachings. They would have been thoroughly familiar with the sermon structure, for they were preached to at least once a week, the sermons normally having as part of their structure an exemplum; many of the fabliaux are written in just this format. For example, "The Lady Who Was Castrated" begins with a gener-alized statement about men who have wives who rebel against their hus-bands and the trouble these wives could cause; the tale is an example of how to handle such a wife. "The Lay of Ignaurés" begins likewise with the "advice," "He who loves should never hide it," and so on for the first stanza, and then goes on to talk about Ignaurés, who loved twelve women at the same time and hid his love of the others from each.[37] Chaucer's *Pardoner's Tale* is an excellent example of the sermon structure, as can be expected from a man who makes his living by giving sermons. The text of the Par-doner's sermon is *Radix malorum est Cupiditas*—the root of evil is avarice.

He then tells a tale that proves this maxim; then, in his drunkenness, he tries to dupe his fellow travelers out of their money by selling them pardons. He practices what he preaches; the moral applies both to his story and to his own activities. Though not properly a fabliau, this tale demonstrates the common usage of the sermon structure in the recitation of tales in the medieval period.

So the moral tags at the ends of many fabliaux are nothing more than what preachers called the "closing formulae," which reiterated the original theme of the sermon. If these characteristics of the sermon (theme, exemplum, and closing formula—and perhaps other parts of sermon structure) were present, then we must see the structure of the tale as carrying some meaning. Given the religious training or exposure that the audience must certainly have had, we can see that this audience would have perceived the meaning carried in the structure of the tale. The "meaning" of which I speak is the moral that they would have been expected to draw from the tales themselves, independent of the morals that were given by the authors—for, admittedly, many of the morals given by the authors had nothing to do with the stories they had just told.[38]

Purposes and Effects

The main functions of literature are to teach and to entertain. Unquestionably, the fabliaux are entertaining. Theiner says, " . . . the world view of the fabliau . . . is a strategy for eliciting laughter."[39] If the aim of the fabliau is to entertain, it is understandable why the authors chose themes, stereotypical figures, and motifs that would naturally bring smiles to the faces of their audience. There is the old, lusty, half-impotent man with his young, even-more-lusty wife—who invariably finds a young lover who can satisfy her needs. There is the woman who wishes to keep her reputation [see pages 170–172 above], but who can be convinced, for one reason or another, to give her body to a man.[40] We see the lusty monks, the jealous, maniacally overprotective husbands, the oversexed, clever wives, the eager lovers, frequent adultery, and a marked disinterest in the legal or moral implications of their acts. We also see copulating in the most bizarre fashions, under the most dangerous or ludicrous circumstances. The focal point of all this is humor: the more unusual the lovemaking, the cleverer the wife is in explaining her actions to her gullible husband; the more dangerous the circumstances of the lovers, the funnier the story is likely to be.

Chaucer's *Merchant's Tale* presents one of the stereotyped situations of the genre: the old man (January) who, in his dotage, takes on a young, lovely wife (May), who in turn takes for herself a young, lusty lover (Damian). This brings up an important point. The young lover is a much better match for the girl than is her husband, not only because Damian can satisfy May sexually, but also because they are on the same social level. The point is that January, a knight, is badly duped (mostly by his own faulty reason in opting for a young, fresh maid), with the implication that the nobility—of which January is a rather low and ignoble example—is inferior in some ways to the classes beneath them.[41] The genre is a great leveler: the highest are not immune to ridicule, the meanest can often get the upper hand and bring about the humiliation of their social superiors. No one is exempt from ridicule in the fabliaux. Hence, the purpose of the genre may be to amuse, but it could arrive at this amusement through ridicule, satire, or burlesque.

If the goal of the genre was to amuse by means of unrestrained narrative, blunt language, coarse characters, and obscene action, then how do we explain the moralizing we get in most fabliaux? What *is* the aim of these ribald tales? The best treatment of this problem is Jürgen Beyer's essay "The Morality of the Amoral" (see note 1). Among other things, Beyer says that from the brief, humorous, often bawdy exempla of the early twelfth century came the more expanded genre of fabliau; then he says:

> This expansion into complete narrative inhibits the moralistic, didactic power of the genre to convince, however, since it lends the stories too much independent weight and consequently causes the demonstrative norms to recede somewhat into the background. (p. 29)

The point is a matter of emphasis. If the moralistic material were of great enough quantity in the stories, it could genuinely teach the audience something. But more often than not, the moral statements are little more than tags added to a tale to give it the air of didacticism, or to make us think that the author himself would never indulge in such "low" literature unless he had some high-minded intentions. The moral always comes off as a rather weak justification for writing the tale. The octosyllabic rhymed couplet—used by the romancers in their more elevated genre—was adopted by the writers of fabliaux partially to give their compositions a sense of propriety. Beyer puts it this way:

> [The writers of fabliaux] did not hesitate to dress this worldly subject matter in literary forms that sometimes . . . came from the sacral sphere . . . . It is rhyme which endows the oral comic tale with the dignity of art . . . . It is truly remarkable that the use of rhyme alone made the comic tale fit for polite society and worthy of literary treatment . . . . From approximately 1150, a certain liberalization must have spread through society, for the comic tale now is freer from the earlier constraints . . . . It [the fabliau] opens itself up to the common and vulgar and especially to the obscene and scatological to a degree hitherto unknown, and it almost completely renounces any sort of moral or didactic obligation, so the "poetics of the ugly" practiced in the fabliau now receives full emphasis. (pp. 32–33)

Beyer then points out that the fabliaux writers themselves saw their genre as one which is designed to bring pleasure to its audience and to take their minds off the drudgery of their lives.

If this is so, that the primary function of the fabliau is to etertain, how does one explain the fact that more than two-thirds of these tales draw some moral? The use of the moral may be to "get the piece past the censors," so to speak, and to protect the author. Or it may be, as Theiner suggests, a means of authenticating the realism of the work.[42] But as Beyer says, " . . . in the fabliau the farcical reduction does not stop short of the lesson, but in most cases destroys it . . . . [Often] the 'truth' of the proverbial moral is cleverly made absurd . . . . Many of these fabliaux omit any type of concluding moral reference, with which they document their lack of interest in a moralization of what they have presented, or they draw a different and totally unpredictable lesson from the tale, so it can be said: The moral actually documents the unfitness of the fabliau for moralization" (p. 39). Norris J. Lacy[43] says simply that the moral "must have been related with tongue in cheek" (p. 110). He says later that the esthetic distance created in a variety of ways in this genre "enables the reader or audience to suspend moral judgment" (p. 117). Lacy goes too far here; and I think Beyer is slightly on the wrong track when he says that the reader is able to suspend moral judgment because the moral tags used by the authors do not seem to fit. We may not learn from the morals used by the authors, but the structure of the work — as I have discussed above — strongly suggests how the tales might be didactic.

The point I am trying to make here is that too often critics narrow-mindedly state that the sole purpose of the genre is to entertain. I claim that we can learn (if only by negative example) from these tales as much as we can be entertained by them. The effects they have on us are more complex than merely causing us to laugh. Thomas Cooke says that "There is no way that an author can avoid infusing values into a story."[44] The audience, even in their laughter, would have seen these values.

The fabliaux were primarily written to make us laugh. I do not want to do what Chaucer's Miller advises us against: to make earnest out of game (to take too seriously what is intended in jest; see *The Miller's Prologue*, p. 48, l. 3186). I cannot help feeling, however, that — considering when these pieces were written — the audience did learn something from them, regardless of what the authors' intentions were. We do learn by parody, burlesque, and satire, words often used in describing the fabliaux. We learn that medieval people, even the clerics, did not always adhere to the rather rigid teachings of the Church about sex. But perhaps the most important thing we learn from these tales is how to laugh at ourselves.

16

Prostitution in the Later Middle Ages

Vern L. Bullough

Medieval canon lawyers, as James Brundage pointed out in an earlier chapter, accepted prostitution as a fact of life. The problem that medieval authorities faced was how to contain it. Their solution was undoubtedly influenced by Saint Thomas Aquinas, who compared the existence of prostitution with that of a sewer in a palace. If the sewer did not exist, according to Saint Thomas, the palace would be filled with pollution. Similarly if prostitutes disappeared, the world would be filled with "sodomy" and other crimes.[1] The difficulty was in channeling the sewer.

Adding to the dimensions of their problems was a growing urban population, increasing concentrations of fighting men, a shortage of women in many areas,[2] and more frequent travel. Traditionally, wherever there have been large concentrations of men, prostitutes have made an appearance. Even the Crusades were not exempt. During the first Crusade we have reports of prostitutes being driven out of the Crusaders' camps as early as 1097.[3] On the pilgrimages that both predated and coincided with the Crusades, women "pilgrims" are said to have supported themselves by selling sex in towns along the route.[4] On both Crusades and pilgrimages, prostitutes sometimes traveled disguised as men, and even Louis IX, the saintly King of France who felt prostitution was sinful, could not prevent prostitutes from establishing themselves near the royal tent on the Crusades that he led.[5]

So ubiquitous were prostitutes on the Crusades that the canon lawyer Henry de Susa (Hostiensis) posed a tantalizing moral question about whether a crusading harlot should be encouraged. He hypothesized that

176

such a woman could recruit numerous men, and that the men so recruited would clearly bolster the defensive forces of the Holy Land, something that was much needed. He wondered whether the great good brought about by the prostitute could outweigh the evil of a prostitute taking the cross. He finally concluded that it would not, because the motivation of the men recruited by the prostitute was not likely to be spiritual. Thus, he concluded, it would be best if prostitutes stayed clear of the Crusades, regardless of their motives.[6]

Though lawyers could pose such moral questions, the church officials seemed unable to deal with prostitutes in their midst. In Paris, for example, prostitutes were so numerous that according to tradition they organized into a guild with Mary Magdalene as their patron saint. Though this tradition is suspect, there was a chapel dedicated to Saint Mary the Egyptian (the prostitute saint mentioned in an earlier chapter). Allegedly, St. Mary's chapel had a window depicting the saint, her skirt pulled up to her thighs, about to embark in a boat, with an inscription reading: "How the saint offered her body to a boatman to pay for her passage."[7]

The first reaction of some secular rulers to the growing number of prostitutes was to try to eliminate them all together. As early as 1158, the Holy Roman Emperor Frederick Barbarossa, upset at the number of prostitutes traveling with his army, had ordered the punishment of both the prostitute and her customer. According to the *Lex Pacis Castrensis,* soldiers caught fornicating with prostitutes were to be severely punished and the prostitutes themselves were to have their noses cut off.[8] The justification for such a punishment is that slitting or cutting of a woman's nose would make her less attractive, but Frederick's legislation was not particularly effective and it was not repeated.

Saint Louis (Louis IX) made the most concentrated effort to banish prostitutes. According to tradition, Saint Louis had become concerned about Paris prostitutes when a prostitute sat next to the queen in church, and the queen, as was her custom, bestowed a kiss on her. Though the incident might well be apocryphal, Louis in 1254 decreed that all prostitutes, as well as all persons making a living from prostitution, be classed as outlaws, that is, denied protection of the king's law. In addition, all their personal goods, clothing, furs, tunics, and linen chemises were to be seized.[9] Louis soon had second thoughts about his action when complaints began to reach his ears that it was increasingly difficult to protect "honest" wives and "virtuous" daughters from lecherous attacks. Louis then temporarily turned from banning prostitutes to regulating them.

Prostitutes were forbidden to live in certain sections of Paris, prohibited from wearing certain types of jewelry or fine cloth dresses, and placed under the supervision of a police-type magistrate whose popular title was *roi des ribauds,* king of the bawds, beggars, and vagabonds. This official had the power to arrest and confine prostitutes who infringed upon the law by their dress, domicile, or behavior. Though the regulations seemed to be effective in dealing with some of the abuses associated with prostitution, Louis worried that his tolerance of evil was a sin, and he apparently contemplated returning to an outright ban. He died before such a ban could be enacted, but he instructed his son and successor, Philip, to carry through on this ban. Philip dutifully followed his father's request by declaring prostitution a legal misdemeanor and established a formidable array of penalties to bear against the offending women and their accomplices. The program was soon abandoned, and instead, cities were left to establish their own methods of control.[10]

Among the most detailed of the early regulations were those issued by Alfonso IX of Castile (1188–1230). He was primarily concerned with those who profited from prostitution. These he classified into five categories: (1) those who trafficked in prostitutes; (2) landlords who let their premises to whores; (3) men or women who kept brothels; (4) husbands who prostituted their wives; and (5) pimps who solicited or recruited women. Those involved in selling prostitutes were to be exiled from the kingdom; landlords who rented rooms to prostitutes were to have their houses impounded and pay a fine as well; brothelkeepers had to free the women found in their brothels (an implication that the prostitutes in such houses might have been slaves) and find them husbands or else suffer the possibility of execution; husbands who prostituted their wives were to be flogged for a first offense, and if they persisted were to be sent to the galleys as convicts. Women found supporting pimps were to be publicly whipped and have their clothes destroyed.[11]

Medieval authorities were particularly desirous of regulating brothels because they were regarded as centers of public disturbance as well as covers for criminal activity. Some cities attempted to meet the problem of banning prostitution within their walls, as did Leicester and Cambridge in England. Bristol, for a time, classed prostitutes with lepers and prohibited both from within the city walls. What worked for a smaller city, however, did not necessarily work out for the larger ones. London at first tried to follow the example of the more provincial cities by excluding prostitutes, but when this proved impractical, it set aside certain areas within the cities in which prostitutes could settle. Brothels found outside the stipulated districts had their doors and windows removed; if this was not enough to force the prostitute to leave, the beadle of London then had the authority to dismantle the whole house.

Though the prostitute herself might be accepted as a necessary evil, and therefore tolerated, there was almost universal hostility to those who lived on the earnings of prostitutes. A male procurer discovered inside the city of London was to be tonsured, shaved, and exhibited in the pillory for a first offense; a second offense resulted in imprisonment, while a third was to lead to expulsion from the city. A woman procurer had her hair cut "round her head" for the first offense, after which she was to be exhibited in the stocks; penalties for subsequent infractions were the same as those for males. Understandably, with the ever-present possibility of such harsh punishments many of those associated with prostitution attempted to cloak their activities with some respectable trade. In the process some trades, particularly that of barber and bathkeeper, became almost synonymous with prostitution. Stewkeepers (bathhouse keepers), in fact, came to be so intimately connected with prostitution that the very term "stew" came to be synonymous with a house of prostitution. To rid the baths of prostitutes, stews were periodically examined to see that prostitutes were not present; similarly, the premises of barber surgeons were inspected monthly in order to ferret out prostitutes.[12]

Gradually, medieval authorities developed a two-pronged approach for dealing with prostitution: (1) the establishment of segregated districts, and (2) specific wardrobes for prostitutes. In Bristol, the hoods of prostitutes had to be made with striped fur, and this distinguished them from "respectable" women. Though prostitutes were allowed entrance into sections of the city outside their district, once they left their quarters, they were closely watched to make certain that they did not enter with a customer any house other than a designated brothel in the segregated area. Some cities, such as London, specifically prohibited prostitutes from "parading" anywhere except in the regulated districts; those women who violated the law were liable to expulsion from the city.[13] In Paris, most prostitutes lived in a section of the city known as the Clapier,[14] a name perpetuated in the slang term *clap* describing gonorrhea, which then and now was associated with prostitution. Since the prostitute was so confined in her activity, there were few actual streetwalkers. Generally the medieval prostitutes lived in a brothel, and if she did entice customers through expeditions outside of the segregated district, her sexual activities had to take place within the specified quarters. One of the reasons that prostitutes had to wear a distinctive costume was so the authorities could be sure the rules were being enforced.[15]

Antonio Beccadelli (Panormita) (1394–1471) encouraged travelers to seek out the center of the city in his *Hermaphroditus*. Roughly translated, he wrote:

Look for the magnificent temple of Santa Reparata . . . . Arriving there take a right, then proceeding a little stop and ask . . . [for directions] to the Mercato Vecchio. Near the obelisk, betraying itself by its odor, is the genial bordello. Enter and say "hello" to the procuress and whores for me; you will be welcomed by all . . . . Elena, the blond will approach you [along] with sweet Matilda, both gifted in stimulating; they really have it. Giannetta will come, and with her, her Cagnolina. The latter is gracious with [Giannetta], her patroness, [but] with men she is a dear. Clodia will quickly come running, her painted breasts exposed, [and she is] a girl valued for her caresses. Galla will reach for your penis with her hands and her cunt without blushing, so that you can have both together. Anna, with wine on her breath, will come up to you and offer you a song in German. Pitto, too, will come, [and she] is unequalled at humping, and Ursa, [full of] joy of whoring, will be with her. Taide will tell you to come up the nearby Street, which received its name from the slaughtered cow, so that she can greet you. All the whores of this so famous city will come to you, swarming joyfully together because of your arrival. Here you can say and do whatever pleases you, and a refusal will never redden your cheeks. Since you've lusted for so long a time, here, you can fuck as much as you can . . . and have yourself fucked.[16]

Regulating prostitution proved difficult. Jacques de Vitry, writing in the first half of the thirteenth century, described the Parisian prostitutes as being everywhere, soliciting even passing clerics to sample "their" delights. To those males who passed them by without greeting, they cried out "Sodomite," to embarrass them. De Vitry reported that a brothel and scholars' hall often occupied the same premises and that while the master was delivering his lectures in an upper room, the prostitutes were plying their trade in the room below. Occasionally, he added, the arguments between the prostitutes and their pimps rose to mingle with the disputations of the scholars.

One of the reasons that students and prostitutes were in close proximity is because the students were often patrons. De Vitry reported that the Parisian students were more dissolute than the regular population since unlike most, they "counted fornication as no sin."[17] Paris was not alone among university towns in having problems with prostitutes. One of the jobs assigned to the university chancellor at Cambridge (as well as those at universities elsewhere) was to deal with the town prostitutes.[18] Sometimes the association between the prostitute and the university was even closer. In Toulouse, for example, the profits from the town brothel were divided between the city and the university.[19]

Such a collaborative relationship was perhaps inevitable, since, once the state accepted the necessity for regulating prostitution, it was not difficult to rationalize that the state should get remunerated for its efforts. In rather rapid succession the effort of the state changed from efforts to abolish prostitution, to regulating it, to seeing it as a source of revenue. Some cities even set up official brothels. Florence, for example, established an Office of Decency in 1403, the duty of which was to acquire a building suitable for a brothel, to recruit foreign prostitutes to work in it, and to assure them remuneration and protection.[20] The nominal reason for this action was the belief that an officially sponsored brothel would effectively combat the dangers of male homosexuality and thus remedy the decline in legitimate population resulting from an insufficient number of marriages.[31]

One of the most controversial set of regulations comes from the city of Avignon where a public house of ill fame was set up under the official patronage of Queen Joanna, ruler of Naples and of Provence, in 1347. Though there is some doubt about their authenticity, hence the controversy, the regulations are only slightly different from other surviving statutes. The ordinance stipulated that a public brothel be set up in order to keep the prostitutes off the streets. If the prostitutes left the brothel for any reason, they had to wear a red knot on their left shoulder. Any prostitute failing to abide by the regulations was to be led through the city with drums playing and a red knot hanging at her shoulder and, subsequently, publicly whipped. If she persisted in her offenses, she was to be turned out of the city. The official brothel was established near the Convent of the Augustinian Friars near Bridge Street, and it was stipulated that the door always be kept locked so that no person could gain admittance without permission of the abbess or governess (the title of the brothel keeper), chosen by the city fathers who held office for a year. Men admitted to the brothel were warned that if they created a disturbance, frightened the women, or violated the house rules in any way, they would be turned over to the beadles of the city for punishment. The aspect of regulation that has aroused the most controversy is one stipulating that the abbess and surgeon examine the prostitutes every Saturday to see if they had any illness and to determine whether they were pregnant. A pregnant prostitute was to be put under special care in order that there not be a spontaneous abortion. Regulations called for the brothel to be closed on Good Friday, Holy Saturday, and Easter Sunday, and if per chance the abbess was found to have admitted customers on these religious days, she was to be publicly whipped and dismissed from her job. The abbess was also to make certain that Jews were not admitted into the brothel. Any Jew found to be a customer was to be whipped.[22] The brothel continued to function after Joanna sold the town to Pope Clement VI, the only difference being that it now operated under papal sponsorship. The old laws were enforced, and a Jew was publicly whipped in 1498 for entering the brothel.

The passing reference to Jews in houses of prostitution was more or less uniform throughout Christian Europe. The medieval church saw a danger to Christianity in sexual intimacies between Jews and Christians, although the danger was not so much one of morality as apostasy. A Gentile prostitute who recognized her customer as Jewish was to withdraw from contact. If, however, intimacies did occur between a Jew and a Christian prostitute, the Jew could be put to death. Jews did not particularly object to this prohibition against sexual relationships but accepted it. Rabbi Judah he-Hasid, for example, advised Jewish women who found themselves in the presence of potentially "immoral" young Jewish men to conceal their Jewish identity and claim to be Christian, even to the extent of displaying a crucifix on her chest. This, he felt, would intimidate Jewish men and prevent them from molesting her. In other areas Jewish writers were as hostile to intercourse between Christians and Jews as the Christians were. Talmudic writers taught that the Jewish male who consorted with a Gentile woman would not be released from Gehenna after death, and to emphasize the dangers, they also imposed a this-world punishment of flogging. In fourteenth-century Spain, a Jewish widow charged with having sexual relations with a Gentile man was condemned by a Jewish court to have her nose cut off.[23] This was not an unusual punishment.

Avignon and Florence were just two of the many cities to establish more or less officially sponsored brothels as a way of adding to the municipal coffers. Ordinances for such brothels are extant from Nuremberg, Strasbourg, Munich, Constance, Nimes, Ulm, Florence, Venice, and many other cities. Not infrequently, the local executioner doubled as supervisor of whorehouses. This would give him an ongoing income since executions were not that plentiful.[24] The holy city of Rome was not different from other cities, and the marshals of the pope were careful to collect their brothel fees.[25] Usually, however, ecclesiastical officials tried to avoid direct connection with the operation of a brothel. This did not mean that there was no connection. For example, in 1321 an English cardinal purchased a house with a brothel as tenants for investment purposes, and he had no qualms about allowing it to continue in operation.[26]

As indicated above, prostitutes had to wear special signs of their trade but there was no uniform agreement as to what these might be. In areas under the jurisdiction of the king of France, they usually wore a red shoulder knot but there were exceptions. In Toulouse, they wore a white knot; in Leipzig, they wore yellow cloaks trimmed with blue; in Vienna, a yellow handkerchief was attached to their shoulder; and in Bern and Zurich, prostitutes wore a red cap. In Parma prostitutes wore white cloaks, in Bergamo yellow, and in Milan black wool. Any citizen meeting prostitutes who were not properly identified by their clothing had the right to strip them of their clothes.[27]

Once a street was set apart for prostitution, it often continued to be so identified centuries later. Henry Mayhew, a nineteenth-century authority on prostitution, found that the Paris streets then set apart for brothels, such as the Rue Froidmantel, la Court Robert de Paris, Rue Charon, Rue Tyron, and Champs Fleury, had served the same purpose in the Middle Ages.[28] In those towns where there had been a shifting of the district, old streets still carried names associated with their previous tenants, such as Frauengasse Strasse, Frauenpforte Strasse, or Frauenfleck Strasse in German-speaking areas. Most streets bearing the name Rose, regardless of language, probably originally had been streets for prostitutes, since the euphemism to pluck a rose was a common term meaning to copulate with a prostitute.

Medieval prostitutes were mobile, not only moving from house to house, but appearing wherever there were large masses of males. A good example of this mobility is the influx of prostitutes at the Council of Constance, held in the small city of Constance between 1414 and 1418 and called to end the Great Schism and deal with heresy and reform. Contemporary chroniclers report that hundreds of prostitutes flocked to Constance in order to entertain the delegates.[29] Prostitutes also followed the armies and, in fact, were regarded as essential for taking care of the wounded and for doing most of the necessary chores for the fighting men such as cooking, laundry, and keeping the camp in order.

The ubiquity of prostitution is indicated in part through the vast number of terms associated with brothels. Translating these terms into English, we find references to women's house, friendship house, daughter house, aunt's house, rose garden, "Stockhaus" (jailhouse), temple house or temple, joy house, clap house, common house, abbey, lupanaria, great house, public house, bordello, stew, brothel, bagnio, and many others.[30] Bloch, in his pioneering study of prostitution, found some seventy-five towns and cities in medieval Germany with brothels;[31] other countries had a similar number.

In spite of this ubiquity, there were continuing efforts throughout the medieval period to reclaim the prostitute. As James Brundage mentioned in an earlier chapter, one of the favored methods was to encourage the prostitute to enter the religious life, to become a nun. From at least the twelfth century onward, if not earlier, religious houses had been established with the specific purpose of being an asylum for reformed prostitutes.[32] Emphasizing this was the establishment of a special religious order of penitential nuns organized in 1224, and sanctioned in 1227 by Pope Gregory IX, as the Order of Saint Mary Magdalene. Since the sisters wore a white habit, they were often called the "White Ladies,"[33] and the order was encouraged by both secular and ecclesiastical officials.[34] Magdalene houses, however, were not always successful in the long run. A good example is the Vienna Magdalene house, established at the beginning of the fourteenth century although it was not officially chartered until 1384. Popularly known as the Soul House, the women were organized as if they belonged to a convent, although they were not required to take an oath of either poverty or chastity. Instead the women, after a suitable period of residence in the house to repent of their past, were encouraged to marry and many left the house as brides. Difficulties came in 1480 when the Emperor Frederick III granted the inmates the right to sell the produce of their vineyards, in an effort to defray some of the costs of the house. Unfortunately, some of the women began selling sex on the side as an inducement to increasing the sale of wine, and the end result was the closing down of the house and the deeding of the property to the local Franciscans.[35]

Although the church for a time had been reluctant to encourage marriage with a prostitute, by the twelfth century the popes were officially encouraging such action. Pope Innocent II in 1109 lauded those who married harlots in order to reform them and described their actions as not the "least among the works of charity."[36]

One of the more original ways to rescue women from prostitution was that advocated by Fulk of Neuilly, one of the preachers associated with the Fourth Crusade. Fulk secured an agreement with the Parisian authorities whereby they would give 1,000 livres, the University of Paris agreed to supplement this with 250 livres, and the total amount was to be given to any former prostitute who contracted an honorable marriage.[37] Generally, however, church officials were reluctant to sanction such marriages unless the prostitute had done public penance and obtained a special dispensation.[38]

Prostitution throughout most of the medieval period lacked the romanticizing present in some of the Greek classics. Also during much of the Middle Ages, prostitution was not quite so hierarchically organized as it was in the Greek and Roman world. Towards the end of the Middle Ages, however, the high-class prostitute had again made an appearance. There are at least two explanations for this reappearance, one economic, the other cultural. Prostitution, it should be emphasized, is usually a hard life, unless and until the prostitute is able to be selective in her choice of clientele. If somehow she can become a mysterious or romantic figure, if she can gain wealth and status by her accomplishments, then she becomes something more than an ordinary whore. Though early medieval kings had their mistresses, the market for high-class courtesans was limited. This changed with the growing prosperity in the later medieval period, with the growth of urbanization, and with the new mystique associated with romantic love as it developed in the twelfth and thirteenth centuries. The courtesan mistress reached her height in France under Francis I (1494-1547) at the end of the medieval period. Francis adored women; he enjoyed their company, admired their beauty, appreciated their wit, delighted in their perfume, and sought their favors. He is reported to have said that a court without women was like a year without spring, or like a spring without roses. According to the Abbé de Brantôme, the sixteenth-century chronicler of the lives of fair and gallant ladies, Francis held that all noblemen of his court should be pursuing at least one courtesan; those men who did not were regarded as simpletons without taste.[39] Many stories, probably mostly apocryphal, are told about the courtesans in his court.[40]

Some of the predecessors of Francis I also had famous mistresses. Agnes Sorel, the mistress of Charles VII (1403-1461), dominated him until her death in 1450. She is remembered today for introducing a dress style that exposed the breasts. Not all mistresses and courtesans were young. Diane de Poitiers, the companion of Henry II, the son of Francis I, was twenty years older than her young lover.[41] A woman known as the "Greek" was a famous courtesan in Rome,[42] as was another known as Faustina.[43]

The concept of courtesan, however, did not extend below the level of the upper classes. The world itself originally meant one who was attached to the court and is derived from the word courtier. It soon became synonymous with a high-class prostitute who restricted her attention to men of the upper classes. By so doing, she also fitted into some of the stereotypes of Andrew the Chaplain, the codifier of courtly love. Andrew taught that love was an emotion confined only to the nobility, and he apparently believed that it was unlikely that anyone in the lower classes would have the virtues necessary for love. If a nobleman desired a peasant woman so strongly that he could not resist the temptation, he was free to rape her on the spot since a courteous approach would only be wasted on a woman who could not possibly feel love.[44] Andrew argued that the ordinary prostitute should be shunned. If occasionally a gentleman had need for her service, he should not waste his time courting her, nor should he find it necessary to instruct her in the art of love.[45]

These ideas were not confined to Andrew. Baldassare Castiglione, the author of the *Book of the Courtier,* taught that it was essential for the courtier to love apart from the common, ignorant sort of people.[46] Needless to say, the lower-class male who tried to have intercourse with an upper-class female found himself in deep trouble, much the same as a black man in the American South did in any relationship with a white woman.

Though upper-class writers tended to neglect the lower-status prostitute, even to profane her character, she also found her way into literature primarily through the writings of François Villon (1431–?), master of arts, thief, pimp, pickpocket, frequenter of brothels, recorder of the lower levels of Parisian life. Villon, in his various poems and testaments, has left us some of the most moving portrayals of prostitutes in literature. In the *Lament of Belle Heaulmière,* Villon records the advice of an old whore to six would-be prostitutes. *Heaulmière* means the helmetmaker's girl, and we know that prostitutes were often known by the trades at which they worked or had worked. The six novitiates are indicative of this. Belle Gauntière sold gloves in her spare time; Blanchela Savetière was the wife of a cobbler; Gente Saulcissière worked in a sausage shop; Guillemette la Tapissière was in tapestry; Jehanneton le Chaperonnière made hoods and horns; and Katherine l'Esponnière was married to a man who belonged to the spur-making guild. To all of them, Belle offered the same advice: Make your money while you can, spare no man, for an aged prostitute is of no more use than a worn-out coin.[47]

Villon seems rather jaundiced in his views toward women. He was convinced that love of women was the work of the devil, if only because for every moment of pleasure one has to suffer so many moments of sadness. He believed that women loved only for money, a belief that might have been derived from the fact that he once loved a prostitute. In a poem about his love, he reported that as soon as his pocketbook had been exhausted, his whore had cast him aside for a rich, old man who was more "foul, ugly, and hideous" than one could imagine. Each part of this poem ends with the refrain that poverty counts you out, for the rich always have the advantage in love. In John Payne's translation of this poem, "Ballad of Ladies' Love," the refrain "Riche amoureux a toujours l'advantage" is translated as "The wealthy gallant always gains the day." This is the second verse in the Payne translation:

> So chanced it that, whilst coin my purse did fill,
> The world went merry as a marriage bell
> And I was all in all with her, until,
> Without a word said, my wanton's loose eyes fell
> Upon a graybeard, rich but foul as hell:
> A man more hideous never woman bore.
> But what of that? He had his will and more:
> And I, confounded, stricken with dismay,
> Upon this text went glossing passing sore:
> The wealthy gallant always gains the day.[48]

Despite his cynical attitude, Villon had a deep-seated sympathy for many of the women of the street, and in one of his poems he described both his life as a pimp and that of his girlfriend, the prostitute Margo, who after satisfying her customers,

> claps me on the head,
> says I'm cute and whacks my thigh.
> Then both drunk, we sleep like logs
> When we awake, her belly starts to quiver,
> and she mounts me, to spare love's fruit;
> I groan, squashed beneath her weight—
> this lechery of hers will ruin me,
> in this brothel where we ply our trade.[49]

The other verses in this poem also end with the refrain "in this brothel where we ply our trade."

In the Paris where Villon lived and wrote, then a city of approximately one hundred thousand, prostitutes were numerous. One fifteenth-century observer claimed that there were five or six thousand women engaged in prostitution,[50] and though this number is probably an exaggeration, the numbers must still have been in the thousands. By the end of the Middle Ages prostitution was not only accepted, but the cult of the courtesan had romanticized it, at least at some levels. The status of women was changing slightly, but women still had a long way to go for any semblance of equality. They were regarded as sex objects, but to be regarded as a sex object was not as bad as some of the alternatives. Leone Battista Alberti, one of the learned men of the Renaissance, said that all women were "crazy and full of fleas." Prostitution was tolerated, even regulated in most of the areas of Europe, and all attempts to eliminate it had been more or less abandoned. Prostitution was still often condemned but the prostitute herself was not. There was always hope that she would abandon her ways, but other than joining a convent or getting married, there was little a respectable woman could do to support herself. Ordinary women worked in the shops of their husbands or fathers, but even these opportunities were restricted, and many, even married women, found prostitution a profitable sideline.

17

Human Sexuality in Twelfth- through Fifteenth-Century Scientific Writings

Helen Rodnite Lemay

Introduction

The lively interest in the sensible world and its workings that we witness from the twelfth century on did not exclude the human reproductive cycle, and medieval scientists often present us with detailed accounts of the sexual act and of the forces controlling it. This chapter will examine the treatment of human sexuality in medical, astrological, and related natural-philosophical works written or translated into Latin between the twelfth and fifteenth centuries.

Gynecology and urology are important branches of medicine today, and the functioning of the reproductive organs was obviously central to the study of the human body during the Middle Ages as well. What is perhaps not so obvious is the importance of astrological texts in an examination of medieval scientific treatment of sexuality. Treatises on the science of the stars were an integral part of the Arabic scientific corpus that was so decisive in transforming Western intellectual life in the twelfth and thirteenth centuries; Arabic astrological works were imported along with purely Aristotelian writings, expanding considerably the sources of scientific information available to the Latin West. Astrological treatises give extensive consideration to sexual behavior, for the science of astrology examines all aspects of man in his social context, thus it is appropriate to include here an account of the Arabic ideas.

Not only did Western scientists receive Arab astrology as part of the baggage that contained Aristotelian science, but they eagerly embraced the study of the stars and their effects on man. Arabic astrological works were widely translated and copied; the *Centiloquium,* for example, an astrological handbook designed primarily for the use of physicians, was translated into Latin six times during the twelfth century by many of the central figures of this period, and over one hundred fifty manuscripts have been identified so far.[1] Further, there exists an entire genre of Latin derivative writings based on the Arabic sources. In the thirteenth, fourteenth, and fifteenth centuries, Latin authors became uneasy about citing the doctrinally dangerous Arab works, and for this reason they often composed their own summaries of astrology. Finally, astrologers often played an important role in the cultural life of the West. For example, Michael Scot served as court astrologer for Frederick II and wrote on medicine as well; Blasius of Parma, the outstanding fourteenth-century Italian naturalist, carried on intensive study of Arabic astrology;[2] and Giovanni Pontano, the renowned Italian humanist, composed a commentary on the *Centiloquium* as well as a major astrological treatise. Sexual matters take up an important part of these Latin writings; indeed, they often provide us with a record of specifically how the astrologer dealt with his clients' sexual questions.

Sexuality was treated in a matter-of-fact way by both doctors and astrologers. Medical writers describe without embarrassment methods for improving erection in the male member, exciting a woman to desire, disguising a girl's loss of virginity. The astrologers, too, show no uneasiness about this subject; they treat human sexual functioning along with marriage, health, and success in one's chosen career as an important part of life and therefore a proper subject for consideration by astrology. Further, although certain sexual acts may be judged perverse, and although some are clearly stated to be against the law, astrological and medical writings do not discuss sexual ethics. The authors that I have read may note in passing their societies' censure of homosexuality, prostitution, and rape, but they do not deal in their scientific treatises with the moral issues connected with these practices.

Aside from the obvious reason that ethical discussion has no place in a tract on disorders of the womb or the casting of horoscopes, the absence of moral overtones in the astrological treatises in particular may be explained by the deterministic stance of the authors. Although the problem of the freedom of the will versus divine power was not so easily solved for Muslim theologians, the astrologers resolved the issue by concluding that the heavens control human sexuality. They considered that the stars were a natural force directly dependent upon God, just as individual human beings also derived their powers directly from Allah. Thus, according to the Arab astrologers, one's sexual behavior is, to a large degree, beyond one's control. The astrological texts underline this notion of divine omnipotence by constantly repeating the clause "insha'llah," if god wills it, rendered by the Latins as "si Deus voluerit" or "nutu Dei."

The *Centiloquium,* composed in Cairo in the late ninth or early tenth century, provides us with perhaps the clearest formulation of Arabic astrological thinking on the issue of determinism. Verba 1 and 2 state that the stars are animate beings of a higher order than man. They operate according to immutable laws, and it is up to man to discern these laws, to reach the level of perception where his soul becomes one with the intelligences.[3] The relation between man and these higher powers is one of relative subservience, however. Although an individual can come to know the rules by which the stars operate, he can do nothing to change them. At best he can work around the inevitable,[4] choosing favorable moments for his acts, or fabricating amulets in the shape of a constellation to capture a certain position of the sky and prolong its effect.[5]

Although man has a certain leeway in manipulating externals, however, his basic nature, and therefore his sexuality, is determined by the stars. This is poignantly demonstrated in Verbum 95 where we are privy to the confession of a man who suffers from secret desires. "Although you see me dressed in clean clothes," he tells us, "I do this for the eyes of men . . . I am in great tension, for my inclination is otherwise." His desire, it turns out, is to spend the night with a Negress or a Negro, preferably the latter, wrapped in a coarse blanket of goat's hair. This urge springs directly from the constellation Aries that determined his nativity, or horoscope, and he is powerless to change it. Although the poor man swears by God that he has always hated homosexuality, this desire continues to torment him. He does not act on it, however, nor does he reveal it to his soldiers and familiars.[6] For this individual, his sexual complexion is predetermined by the heavens, and he can conform to the mores of society only with a good deal of inner turmoil.

Not all the astrological writings state as clearly as the *Centiloquium* that the stars are actually the causes of an individual's sexual makeup. Many Arabs and their Latin interpreters are more ambivalent; Abu Ma 'shar, for example, the ninth-century Arab whose *Introductorium maius in astronomiam* was the most influential astrological writing for Western scientific development, alternates between this position and the stance that the heavens are merely indicators of what already exists. Indeed, the Latin manuscripts of the *Introductorium* clearly divide into two groups, one using *facere* and the other *significare quod,*[7] and the same disagreement is found among the Latin interpreters of Alchabitius, the tenth-century summarizer of Abu Ma 'shar. John of Seville, the twelfth-century Latin translator of Alchabitius's treatise on astrological judgments, renders the Arabic by referring to the planet Venus as the *"significatrix"* of women, wives, and mothers; however, a later commentator, perhaps John of Saxony, adds the remark that Venus has an influence over the humors, especially the genitalia and private parts of women.[8]

The question of determinism was, of course, of particular importance for the Latins, given the ecclesiastical context of the medieval university. The long apologies for astrology, such as the one found in the beginning of Guido Bonatti's thirteenth-century Latin astrological treatise, provide us with clear evidence of contemporary theological opposition to this science.[9] Although Bonatti does offer the argument that, because it was used by the holy fathers, astrology should not be shunned, his basic position on determinism, taken from Abu Ma 'shar, is naturalistic. The stars are noble, perfect beings who rule over the creatures in the corruptible world of the four elements. But, says Bonatti, they do not rule a man or a horse or a ship in the same way that a man would; rather, they govern them by controlling the elements of which corruptible beings are composed.[10] The Latin author is not clear on the degree of free will left to man as a result of this, nor does he treat to any significant degree the problem of conflict with divine omnipotence.[11] Basically he, like other Latin astrologers, accepts the Arabic astrological interpretation of Aristotle's statements in his *Treatise on Generation and Corruption* and his *Meteorology* that inferior things are subject to superior ones.[12] Thus, on the subject of human sexuality, we find Bonatti repeating the statement of the ninth-century Arab astrologer Albubather that the stars act directly on the seed, at times corrupting the womb or semen, as well as Ahmad ibn Yusuf's assertion in the *Centiloquium* that masculine planets cause males, and feminine planets females.[13]

The medical and natural-philosophical writers grant a more limited power to the stars. Many medical works do not mention extraterrestrial control over human sexuality, and Latin treatises on human generation limit their discussion of stellar influence to the section on embryological development. During the fifth month of fetal life, state the thirteenth-century author of the *De secretis mulierum* and the fifteenth-century humanist Peter Candidus Decembrius, Venus is in control. This planet is responsible for the configuration of the exterior members — the ears, nose, fingers, and sexual organs. It bestows as well upon the individual the capacity for physical desire. The signs of the Zodiac also control the members of the forming body, these authors add. Scorpio rules over the place of desire in both males and females. Besides determining fetal development, the planets also bestow certain characteristics upon the individual who has been conceived under their domination. Thus the child born under Venus will be beautiful and voluptuous, obviously affecting his or her future sexual life.[14]

Although there is some kind of general agreement among the sources, then, that the stars influence terrestrial events, astrologers, doctors, and natural philosophers are not in accord over the degree of this influence. Furthermore, there is a basic difference of approach among the groups. When seeking to understand particular events, astrologers look first at the configuration of the heavens, and they are very precise about how information can be derived from the sky. Astrological writings are divided into a number of branches, and each of these categories serves a specific purpose in the practitioner's attempt to understand human sexual behavior. The *Introductoria* or Judgements are general works setting down rules and principles; the Nativities apply these rules to individuals, explaining the proper manner for casting horoscopes; Interrogations use the stars to find the answer to questions; and Elections concentrate on choosing the right moment to act. Thus, a general writing will tell us that the sperm receives its power directly from the firmament;[15] a Nativities will spell out precisely the position of Venus, Mars, and the moon that will cause large genitals or sickness in these organs;[16] a treatise on Interrogations will give instructions on how to determine if a woman is a virgin;[17] and a work on Elections will indicate when an individual is most likely to experience great desire.

Medical and natural-philosophical writers turn first to terrestrial phenomena in their explanations of human sexuality. Having outlined planetary influence on fetal development, they prefer to discuss adult sexual conduct in terms of natural causes. Hot or cold complexions, deformities in reproductive organs, diet, and climate are some of the factors that physicians and natural philosophers list as determinants of sexual behavior.

Nevertheless, despite their divergence of method, the astrological and medical traditions sometimes become mixed. One of the most striking examples of this mixture is found in the *Book on Nativities* by Albubather, translated during the twelfth century by Plato of Tivoli and again in 1218 by Salio at Padua.[18] Albubather's treatment of fetal development includes a good deal of medical material. According to the astrologer, the root of feminine matter is cold and humidity, and this is warmed by the natural heat of the womb during sexual intercourse. At this point matter descends to this seven-chambered matrix from all parts of the body. When the male seed fertilizes one or more of these chambers, the newly conceived child will be nourished by the feminine substance, which is really menstrual blood.

This account, which is standard in the medical works, is followed by a detailed explanation of planetary direction of the growing fetus. For the first month, according to Albubather, the male and female seed do not mix but remain as separate as the white and yolk of an egg, under the rule of the planet Saturn. In the second month, Jupiter, the planet of wind, takes over and causes the seeds to become one, producing nausea in the woman, whose whole body is transformed by the wind of Jupiter and the seed within her. The child who has much of this wind will be wise, for it is even subtler than the soul, and produces the child's thoughts, just as the soul gives the five senses.[19]

Albubather continues his description through the nine months, but what is significant here is that he links astrological and medical theory. That is, he does not merely repeat the statement of Aristotle that superior things act on inferiors, but he outlines for us precisely how the planets directly cause biological phenomena, such as nausea in early pregnancy as well as functions of the brain. We see a parallel attempt to combine the two disciplines in the

Compilation on the Science of the Stars by the thirteenth-century Latin astrologer, Leopold of Austria. Following Ahmad ibn Yusuf and Abu Ma 'shar, Leopold integrates medical theory into his discussion of a fundamental astrological problem: how to determine the exact moment of conception for the purpose of casting a horoscope. The time of birth informs us of the moment of conception and vice versa, he tells us, and conception can be noted by certain biological signs. Leopold then lists the standard indicators taken directly from Abu Ma 'shar's *Introduction to Astrology*— changes in the breast, eyes, and body tone—and he gets carried away with his source to the point of including which signs foretell a male or female child.[20] For this author, then, medicine is basic to astrological practice.

The inclusion of medical material in astrological writings is not limited to these two examples, nor is it surprising in view of the overlap of the two disciplines in society. Astrological works were formally incorporated in the curricula of medieval medical faculties,[21] and many practicing physicians wrote treatises on astrology. Furthermore, the documentary evidence for the connection between astrology and medicine is considerable. Both Arabs and Latins present us with clear statements of the necessity for doctors to be trained in astrology, and fourteenth- and fifteenth-century manuscripts of the *Centiloquium,* for example, testify that this was carried out in practice, for these codices are filled with marginal notes by physicians trying to adjust the "Ptolemaic" rules to their everyday observations.[22] Furthermore, the famous physician Arnold of Villanova insists that phlebotomy be performed and pharmaceutical preparations be administered only when the planets are favorable,[23] and Michael Scot notes, in the midst of his discussion of human generation, that the woman who is planning to become pregnant should record the exact moment of sexual intercourse so that astrological judgment regarding her offspring will be accurate.[24]

Although these examples can be multiplied, it is nevertheless necessary to comb the literature with a good deal of care to uncover texts that include both disciplines in their discussion of a problem. Medieval scientific understanding of human sexuality, at least as recorded in astrological, medical, and natural-philosophical writings, tended to be compartmentalized; doctors and natural philosophers, for the most part, wrote about the human body and its relation to terrestrial phenomena, and astrologers treated man as he was influenced by the stars. Although all groups agreed that ultimate responsibility for physical phenomena lay in the supercelestial world, each looked to its own assumptions and training when dealing with man's sexual life.

Virginity

A question that preoccupied Arabs and Latins, astrologers, doctors, and natural philosophers was how to determine if a woman's virginity had been corrupted. This aspect of sexuality obviously possessed a social significance that was not limited to the Middle Ages, and the topic was consequently well developed in the scientific sources. For astrologers it fell logically under the category of interrogations, the use of the planets as indicators of all things hidden to men, and Zahel in his ninth-century treatise *De interrogationibus*, translated from the Arabic by John of Seville, includes a section on how to determine from the stars whether a woman is a virgin.[25] Abenragel's eleventh-century treatise on judgments, translated into Latin c. 1256, is also concerned with this problem. If the ascendent and the moon are in fixed signs, he tells us, the woman is a virgin and free from all suspicion; if they are in mobile signs, she is corrupt. The planets can tell us as well whether she was propositioned, what she answered, and whether she really sent him away.[26]

Latin astrologers were just as eager to make use of the stars to inquire into a girl's purity. John of Saxony in the fourteenth century copies Abenragel practically word for word on this question;[27] however, the fullest treatment of corruption of virginity by a Latin astrologer was given a century earlier by Guido Bonatti. By looking at the stars Bonatti was determined to establish exactly how far the woman had progressed toward final penetration by the male; while the Arabs gave indications of how one could make judgments, he worked out the full details on his own. Thus he states that if the lord of the ascendent and the moon are in fixed signs and the angles are in mobile signs, she was tempted and did not give in. If the moon is joined to Venus or Mercury, another woman delivered the man's message but she still remained steadfast in virtue. If the ascendent and the moon are in mobile signs, she was tempted and is still thinking it over. Further refinements of these planetary positions indicate that the man touched the female subject's private parts; that he placed his organs on top of hers, causing her to believe mistakenly that her virginity had been lost; or that he ejaculated without penetration.[28]

Bonatti's discussion of virginity gives us evidence of how the practitioner of the science of the stars could have functioned as an arbiter of sexual disputes within the society. Having set down detailed information about how to determine the truth about a girl's corruption from the configuration of the heavens, he continues his exposition by giving instructions on how this information should be presented. If you find that a woman is truly a virgin, Bonatti declares, tell the questioner that nothing can be said against her. However, he continues, corruption of virginity is a complex matter. A female's virginity can expire without her engaging in sexual intercourse with a man. She can be devirginized by her own hands or someone else's; titillation of the fingers can cause her to ejaculate (or emit her own seed) and therefore leave the condition of purity. In this case, the astrologer can rationalize that, although the girl may have laughed or played with another, she was not known by a man in the way she has been accused, and therefore he should not tell his client the full truth. He should say simply that the stars indicate that she is excused before her interrogator, because if he gives the full information, the girl will be taken as corrupt, as if she had actually been with a man.[29]

The medical and natural-philosophical discussions of virginity make much less interesting reading. Averroës tells us that the vulva of a virgin is wrinkled,[30] and according to the *De secretis mulierum* and its commentators the signs of chastity are a sense of shame, a modest gait and glance, and good manners. When the man gets closer to the woman, he can tell if he was the first to do so by the size of the vaginal opening; if she is tight and hard to penetrate, he can be reasonably assured. All of these signs may be feigned, however, caution the authors. A woman can pretend to be modest and mannerly, and she may apply certain ointments to herself that have the power to constrict the skin. The only sure sign, then, is found in the urine (although the authors give no indication of how the man should go about collecting it). The urine of virgins is clear and sparkling white; if it is clear and golden, the woman is still pure but won't remain so for long, as the golden color indicates heat in her body and therefore a strong desire for sex. Once a girl has lost her maidenhead, her urine is turbid because of the broken membrane, and male sperm appear in the bottom of it.[31]

The thirteenth-century physician William of Saliceto adds to these signs. A virgin urinates with a more subtle hiss than a nonvirgin; it takes her longer to finish than it does a small boy. Obstetrical examination will indicate whether a woman has been corrupted, for it will disclose whether the knot of virginity is tightly tied and wrinkled with veins and arteries that stand out like the creases on a chickpea, and whether the mouth of the womb is firmly closed. William cautions that simply the fact of bleeding with sexual intercourse does not prove that this is the girl's first time: she may be having her menstrual period, so one should examine the blood. The blood of corruption of virginity flows in much less quantity than the menses; it is lighter in color and exits with greater force. William's position, like that of Guido Bonatti, however, is sympathetic to the female who is being accused. He provides a detailed "cure" to make a corrupt woman appear to be a virgin. She must wash the mouth of the vulva, sit in a hot bath, rub on certain prescribed ointments, and place in the vulva a dove's intestine that she has filled with blood.[32]

Sexual Proclivities

Arab astrologers took a great deal of interest in the varieties of sexual expression, and in their discussions of sexual proclivities they grant a large degree of control to the stars. Indeed, they are convinced that the precise manner in which the individual will perform the carnal act is fixed at the moment of conception. They rely on the outline in the basic work of Greek astrology, Ptolemy's *Quadripartitum,* composed approximately 150 A.D. in Alexandria, which was an important source for Arabic understanding of the science of the stars. Ptolemy states that if the luminaries are alone in the masculine signs (for certain parts of the sky are considered to be masculine and others feminine), women possess an exceeding amount of unnatural quality. This stellar configuration increases the virility of their souls and makes them lustful for unnatural congresses, when they act as if their female friends were their wives. Depending upon the position of Mars and Venus they may perform these acts either secretly or openly. The stars can also cause women to become harlots, and they can produce similar aberrations in men.[33]

In his eleventh-century commentary on the *Quadripartitum,* 'Ali ibn Ridwan gives us his interpretation of this passage. Relying most probably on the pseudo-Ptolemaic *Centiloquium,* Ibn Ridwan tells us that when Ptolemy states that women act as if their female friends were their wives, he means that they rub one another as if they were men.[34] A detailed account of the effect of the stars on sexual proclivities is found as well in Albubather, Ibn Ezra, Albohali, Abenragel, and Alchabitius. For example, Albohali tells us that the planets can cause a woman to be sexually aggressive;[35] Ibn Ezra relates that Venus in the twelfth or seventh house leads to daily sexual intercourse;[36] Albubather asserts that certain signs produce sodomy, excessive sexual appetite, impotence, sterility, and hermaphroditism. (Albubather is so detailed on stellar influences that he even informs his reader when the individual will suffer hemorrhoids or bad breath.)[37] According to Abenragel, it is even possible to satisfy one's curiosity about a neighbor's sex life by means of astrology; he outlines a method for determining whether the people next door will have sexual intercourse on a certain night.[38]

The Latin astrologers, for the most part, follow the Arabs on this subject. Although he cannot resist adding extra details, such as the fact that if Venus is in a certain position when a male child is conceived, his future sexual intercourse will be in the woman-above position, Guido Bonatti extensively quotes the Arab writers. For example, he cites the late eighth- or early ninth-century astrologer Aomar, who was translated by John of Seville, to the effect that the stars can cause a woman to be insatiable, virile, or, presumably, both.[39] Leopold of Austria explains this phenomenon: masculine tendencies are determined by humidity, feminine by dryness; the oriental stars control the former and the occidental the latter.[40] Giovanni Pontano tells us that not only can planetary conjunctions cause perversions, but they can cause sex changes as well. He cites by name a number of women in Italy who changed into men—one after twelve years of marriage, and another, forty years old, who was so ridiculed that she joined a monastery.[41]

The physicians and natural philosophers do not spell out as clearly the variations of sexual activity, and they emphasize natural causes in their discussions of sexual proclivities. Thus Averroës states that if a man's testicles are cold, he will be sluggish in coitus; if they are both cold and dry, he will be impotent.[42] The physician Arnold of Villanova, who died in 1311, agrees with the Arab medical writer that a man's sexual appetite is largely dependent upon the complexion of the testicles. If these are hot, he tells us in his *Liber de coitu,* the man will have a great desire for sexual intercourse, beget many males, and grow an abundance of pubic hair.[43] Arnold does not have a similar discussion of female reproductive organs, but Michael Scot in his *Liber physiognomiae* describes a woman with a hot and therefore lustful nature as having small, hard breasts, little menses, and plenty of hair in the appropriate places,[44] and the author of the *De secretis mulierum* and his follower Candidus Decembrius note that female desire is greatest during youth and pregnancy.[45]

Diet is also an important determinant of sexual behavior, according to these authors. Arnold of Villanova and Michael Scot relate that raw eggs and sweet cheese stimulate desire,[46] and therapy for sexual disorders usually begins with a corrective diet. For example, William of Saliceto states that if a man's ability to engage in sexual intercourse is diminished because of general weakness of the body, he should see to it that he chooses foods that cause him to put on weight and that are well tolerated in the first, second, and third digestions. If diminution of coitus is caused by sperm that becomes too cold and cannot be ejaculated because it has frozen, hot foods should be consumed.[47]

William is one of the few medical writers to deal with homosexuality, and his treatment of this topic is extremely limited. He mentions only lesbianism that results from a growth called a *ragadia* that bleeds easily and is sometimes caused by difficult childbirth. The *ragadia* arises from the mouth of the womb, and flesh continues to be added until sometimes it appears outside the vagina in the form of a penis. In this case, states the famous Bolognese surgeon, women will sometimes act with other women as they normally do with men during coitus.[48] The only other mention of homosexuality that I have found in the medical and natural-philosophical writings is Michael Scot's statement in the *Liber physiognomiae* that a young man dressed as a girl is an incitement to sodomy.[49]

An interesting overlap between the astrological and medical traditions is found in the pseudo-Ptolemaic *Centiloquium* and Anthonius Guainerius's fifteenth-century treatise *De matricibus.* Both of these deal with the problem posed by a desire for foul odors during sexual intercourse. Ahmad ibn Yusuf states that if Mars is in the ascendent at a person's conception, he will take delight in terrible odors, and if Saturn should also be in his nativity, he will want to smell feces during coitus. "I once knew a rich man," he continues, "who swore that when he was with beautiful and pleasant-smelling women, he was unable to have an erection." When he was with a vile, stinking one, however, this problem was solved.[50] The Arab offers no remedy for his impotence; in the *Centiloquium* it is clearly stated that one should simply follow one's natural inclinations.[51]

Anthonius Guainerius takes an entirely different approach to this situation. Chapter 24 of his *Treatise on the Womb* is devoted to those things that help bring about pleasure in coitus, for, he states, if both male and female enjoy sexual intercourse, this is a great help to conception. Among the things that can prevent this delectation is a desire for foul-smelling odors. In this case, the Renaissance physician prescribes a number of ointments to be applied to the penis, one of which is made with honey and, he says, will work wonderfully to produce long-lasting erections.[52] Unlike the astrologer, Guainerius attempts to cure this condition by natural remedies.

Marital Fidelity and Illegitimate Progeny

Sexual loyalty to one's spouse is another topic treated in detail in the astrological literature. According to practitioners of the science of the stars, the heavens are divided into twelve houses, and the seventh of these controls marriage. Leopold of Austria outlines for us all sixteen parts of this house, which include the marriage of men, the marriage of women, male cunning used against women, and sexual intercourse. The fifth part is of particular importance: it controls licentiousness and coitus of men. If this part is in a good position, states Leopold, the marriage will be successful; if not, it will fail.[53]

The tenth-century Arab Alchabitius gives us more specific information on how to determine the character of a future husband, and, in particular, his sexual behavior. In his treatise on astrological judgments, translated during the twelfth century by John of Seville, Alchabitius states that we must determine the position of the sun at the hour of a woman's nativity. If it is in the two eastern quarters, her husband will either be very young himself, or after a few days he will copulate with a young boy. If it is in the two western quarters, either he will begin to have sexual intercourse late in life, or he will choose an old woman as a sexual partner soon after the marriage. If the sun is joined with Saturn, he will be a man of the law who likes to work; if it participates with Jupiter, he will be prone to abstinence and have a good and noble heart; and if it is linked with Mars, he will be brave in heart but bear her no love.[54] The twelfth-century Jewish astrologer Abraham ibn Ezra, whose book on *Nativities* was translated in 1293 by John of Seville, adds that if Venus is in the twelfth or seventh house of a man's nativity, he will have sexual intercourse with his wife daily.[55]

Almost all the Arabic astrological treatises include a description of the configuration of the heavens that will produce an adulterous spouse. Ibn Ezra states that if Jupiter does not face Mars the individual will be adulterous,[56] and the ninth-century Arab Albubather outlines the positions of Venus, Mercury, and Mars that indicate whether a newborn child will become a fornicator and whether children will result from his illicit sexual activity.[57] Albubather's contemporary, Albohali, also considers that Venus can cause an individual to be unstable in marriage, with straying sexual desires.[58] Abenragel in the eleventh century devotes a chapter of his book on Judgments to the method for determining whether a woman will be faithful to her husband,[59] and Zahel, another ninth-century Arab, gives instructions on how to tell from the planets whether a woman has a lover.[60] These statements became part of Western scientific literature in the twelfth and thirteenth centuries, and were adopted by the Latin astrologers. For example, Giovanni Pontano in his fifteenth-century treatise *On Celestial Matters* also stresses the importance of Venus in causing a woman to become adulterous.[61]

The question of marital fidelity is directly related to legitimacy of children, and the astrologers also believed that they could determine paternity by the position of the planets. Thus, Zahel and Abenragel each devote a chapter of their astrological works to the topic of how to tell whether a pregnancy is legitimate or a result of fornication.[62] I have seen no attempt in these writings to decide this question after the child has been born, nor have I seen any mention in the medical or natural-philosophical literature of how to tell whether a particular man is the father of a child, although the question of hereditary characteristics is discussed in a general sense in the treatises on the development of the embryo.[63] On the basis of the material I have examined, medieval scientists did no better than modern ones in deciding this important question.

Another topic that interested the astrologers was whether a spouse was guilty of incest. The three ninth-century Arabs, Zahel, Aomar, and Alkindi, whose writings were translated into Latin in the twelfth century, give directions on how to tell whether suspicion of incest is well founded.[64] According to Alkindi, the position of the sun and moon with respect to Mars tells us whether an individual has an incestuous relationship, and variations in the places of these planets will indicate whether the incest has taken place publicly or privately. Incest is another topic that does not find a place in the medical or natural-philosophical literature, and indeed the only comment I have seen on marital sexual relations in this group of writings is a statement by Michael Scot that some spouses always hate one another because they are extremely dissimilar in complexion, for example, one will be choleric and another sanguine in temperament.[65]

Sterility

Causes of sterility are outlined in great detail in all three groups of writings;

however, only the medical and natural-philosophical works provide cures for this condition. According to Albubather, Gemini, Leo, and Virgo are sterile signs, and if Venus and the moon should be situated in these signs in a newborn's horoscope, and if Mars and Saturn are in a bad position with relation to them, he or she will never have any offspring.[66] Ibn Ezra states that the sperm is universally controlled by Venus, and judgments concerning the seed should therefore be made according to its strength or depression. He quotes the astrologer "Hermes"[67] to the effect that if Venus is in Leo or Scorpio, the individual will not have sons because of an impediment in his member.[68] The Latin astrologer Giovanni Pontano also stresses the importance of Venus in causing male sterility, and he notes as well that certain stars make a woman sterile and cause a man to lose interest in coitus. Pontano also lists some physical causes of sterility normally cited in the medical and natural-philosophical writings; he states, for example, that extreme obesity will make a woman incapable of bearing children.[69]

One of the most detailed medical treatments of sterility is found in Averroës's *Colliget.* The Arab physician discusses both male and female impediments to conception. Male infertility can be caused by a diminution of the digestive power in the testicles, which renders the sperm unfit for generation. If the testicles become too hot, the sperm burns; if they are too cold, it is not cooked well enough. Another problem that can arise in men is that weakness, lassitude, or bad form can deprive the penis of its expulsive power. The penis will also be unable to ejaculate when the cord that sustains the erection is cut.

Women, too, can suffer a loss of their expulsive power, and their seed can also be harmed by extreme heat or cold. Ailments of the womb are another factor that affects ability to conceive and to carry a child to term. An attribute of the female that is essential to bearing children is the conservative virtue, and when it is diminished or absent, the embryo can no longer be conserved in the womb. This deprivation is caused by a bad complexion, either material or nonmaterial in nature, and nonmaterial complexions of this sort that arise from the beginning of generation are called sterility. "Although some say that this complexion can be caused by the disposition of the celestial bodies," states Averroës, "I neither see nor affirm this."[70]

The other medical treatments of this topic that I have seen do not mention the planets at all. William of Saliceto lists twelve reasons for difficulty of impregnation, all of which center on the complexion of the reproductive organs. A woman can be too fat, too weak, too hot or cold, too lubricated. She can move about too much after coitus, expelling the sperm from her womb. Her womb can be ulcerated, or she can have hemorrhoids. The man can have a penis that is too small and cannot send the sperm far enough; or it can be too long, with the result that the generative spirit of the seed is weakened during the long trip to the end. Another possible deformity of the penis that can lead to infertility involves the ligaments on the head of the organ; if they are too small, causing it to bend towards the testicles, the sperm does not exit all at the same time and does not survive the trip through the bent passageway. Finally, male and female can both be either hot or cold, and this will lead to a distemperate state in the womb.[71]

William gives advice on how to cure many of these conditions: a fat person can go on a diet, for example, and heat and cold can be tempered somewhat by eating foods that have the opposite characteristics. Ulcers and hemorrhoids can be cured by medicines, and ligaments on the head of the penis can be stretched by the use of ointments or cut to straighten out the organ. Some problems, however, can be solved only by judicious choice of a partner. A man with a short penis should choose a small woman and remain tightly attached to her during sexual intercourse, and a man with a long penis should choose a big woman with long thighs. If the choice has already been made, for example, in the case of two married people of the same complexion, two alternatives are possible. Either the man can find another partner of the opposite type, for it is more fitting that the man make this change than the woman, or else they can attempt to alter the wife's condition by diet. It is better to work to change the woman than the man, states William, because the woman provides the matter in generation, and when the male emits his seed she should have ready for him a place that has been properly prepared for this generative substance.[72]

In the course of his discussion of sterility, William includes directions for preventing conception and inducing abortion. He recognizes that the chapter is not according to law; however, he claims to include it because of the danger that pregnancy can pose for a woman who is unhealthy, weak, or very young. Birth control can be practiced by having the man ejaculate first; then the woman is to open her thighs, stand on her feet, jump hard for seven or eight paces, and descend a flight of stairs. Another method is to have the woman coat the womb with certain oils, or for the man to anoint the head of the penis with these same oils. If these methods fail, William prescribes a medicine that, if taken for ten days, will cause the woman to eject a dead fetus.[73]

William's other methods for provoking abortion are the same as those for curing the retention of menses, and understandably, he and the other medical writers deal extensively with sterility caused by diseases of the testicles or the womb. The natural philosophers are more concerned with determining which partner is the cause of inability to conceive; Michael Scot cites the eleventh-century Salernitan Constantinus Africanus to the effect that the form of a woman's foot indicates whether her vulva is too small, [74] and the thirteenth-century author of the *De secretis mulierum* describes a test to show whether male or female is the cause of infertility. A urine specimen should be obtained from each of them; bran of wheat should be added to this; and the pots should then be closed up for nine days or longer. If the defect is in the man, there will be worms in his pot; if the fault is the woman's, menses will be found in hers. If both are to blame, both tests will give positive results.

To cure this condition in the female, the *Secrets of Women* advises that the womb and testicles of a hare should be pulverized and mixed with wine, and that the woman should consume this potion at the end of her menstrual period. This will not only produce a pregnancy, but the child that is born will be of the favored male sex. A similar remedy applies to infertile males and females alike; in this case, the potion is made from the liver and testicles of a small pig. The fourteenth-century commentators attempted to interpret these prescriptions in terms of scientific principles; the mixture of powder and wine, speculates one of these natural philosophers, must be designed to cure sterility in a woman whose seed contains too much cold gross matter by making it hot. One could also interpret this as an aid to the entire process of conception, he continues, and in this case it would benefit any sterile woman of the proper age.[75]

Although one might tend to dismiss these remedies as mere superstition,[76] they are found as well in William of Saliceto's rather sophisticated treatise on medicine. He lists an infertility test involving urine and grain that is similar to the one in the *De secretis mulierum,* another involving urine and lettuce, and a third instructing the experimenter to place sperm on water and see if it floats.[77] They are not present in Guainerius's fifteenth-century treatise on the womb; however, this is probably due to the more limited scope of his topic rather than to any progress in Renaissance medicine. Guainerius's discussion of failure to conceive is much less detailed and much more concerned with causes than with cures.[78] The treatment of sterility in the medical sources remains essentially the same from the thirteenth to the fifteenth centuries.

Coitus

Instructions for the proper method for performing sexual intercourse, which abound in the medical material, are not found in the astrological writings. Perhaps the astrologers thought that this was one area of human action where man did not need the guidance of the stars. Only Peter of Abano's *Conciliator,* composed in about 1303 to reconcile the conflicting opinions of medical men and astrologers, treats stellar influence on the coital act.[79] The other sources that I have seen emphasize method; they are unanimous in the point of view that there is only one correct way to conduct conjugal relations. If they are performed in any other fashion, their main purpose, that of procreation, will remain unfulfilled, or, if a child is conceived, it will suffer deformities because of its parents' aberrant practices.

William of Saliceto's instructions are inserted in a chapter entitled "On those things that aid conception." He begins by describing the conditions under which the act should be performed. The two individuals should have contrary complexions; they should have undergone a long period of abstinence beforehand; neither of them should be inebriated; and the woman should have prepared herself. This means that she should have had a hot bath, placed medication in the vulva every day, and should be in the middle of her menstrual cycle.[80] According to a fourteenth-century commentator on the *De secretis mulierum,* the couple should see that their food is digested and that they have had a bowel movement before the day begins.[81] Peter of Abano states that the man must be young, but not a child, have well-distributed flesh, and a large quantity of sperm that is sufficiently gross and hot. He should also have an immense appetite that is not weakened by coitus; his testicles should be large with the veins manifest in them; and the right testicle should inflate first.[82]

When a proper sex partner has been chosen and preparations have been made, the sources then leave the initiative up to the man. Arnold of Villanova explains in the *De regimine sanitatis,* composed before 1311, that this is because women are modest.[83] The suggested approaches vary with each author, however. The commentator on the *Secrets of Women* instructs the man to begin by speaking lightly to the woman;[84] Anthonius Guainerius would have him start by placing himself in her familiar embrace and giving her kisses with sweet sucking of the lips and sweet words;[85] and Arnold of Villanova and William of Saliceto prefer that he begin with the breasts. Arnold states that he should begin caressing them when the woman is in the first stages of sleep because of her natural shyness.[86]

The next step involves what the commentator on the *De secretis mulierum* calls the woman's *"inferior"* (or lower) parts.[87] Guainerius instructs the man to rub the place between the anus and the vulva because in the act of coitus it is right to do all kinds of things,[88] and William quotes Avicenna to the effect that this wall of hair around the vulva is the place of greatest delectation in women, and the man should not only rub it but at the same time he should make different motions in his face and eyes.[89] When the proper moment is reached, that is, according to Arnold of Villanova[90] and the commentator, when the woman's heat level has been raised enough, she will give signs that she is ready for entry. The commentator tells us that she will begin to speak as if she were babbling;[91] Guainerius explains that her words will be cut short because she will be too tired to finish them,[92] and William notes that different motions of her eyes and a faster breathing rate will give the man the idea.[93]

At this point most sources simply state that the man should become erect and mix with her.[94] For Guainerius, however, the procedure is not that simple. The fifteenth-century physician would have the male partner stop and chew pepper to produce saliva, which he should then spread on the penis before entry. He can also use other ointments that cause "incredible delectation" to the woman. When he penetrates her, Guainerius continues, the woman's head should be lowered, her left thigh elevated with her left foot underneath it, and her right leg extended. This procedure will ensure that male and female seed will be ejected at the same time, which is necessary for conception.[95]

There is some disagreement about what the woman should do once intercourse has actually begun. The commentator thinks that at this moment she should lie still, for if she should move, the seed might be divided and a defective child conceived.[96] The doctors, however, are more concerned that the woman have an orgasm and thus emit her seed. Guainerius recommends that she "strenuously resolve her debt to the lord Venus" along with the man,[97] and William counsels the man to save his ejaculation until he knows that the woman has fulfilled her desire. Only at this point should he push violently with his genitals and emit his sperm.[98]

The doctors' concern for the woman's pleasure is not limited to their attempts to ensure conception. Arnold of Villanova, Guainerius, and William of Saliceto all include prescriptions for augmenting desire and delight in intercourse and for producing an erection in the man.[99] William devotes a chapter to methods for increasing the length and thickness of the virile member beyond its natural state, and he admits in the beginning of this section that the subject has nothing whatever to do with human virtue. He maintains that it does pertain to medical practice, however, and proceeds to instruct his reader to wash his member daily with very hot water in which pepper has been cooked, and to rub it vigorously until it becomes reddened and a kind of tumor appears. He should then use special oils, and apply a plaster two or three times a day for thirty to forty days. Frequent coitus with a soft woman whose vulva is hot and somewhat rough will also be beneficial.[100]

William is also concerned with disorders of coitus, and he devotes a great deal of space to their cure. There are nine causes for diminution of coitus in a man, and of these eight can be helped by medicines and other remedies. Excessive desire can also be a problem; a person suffering from one form of this malady can be recognized by his reddish color and fleshy body, and he should apply a special ointment to his kidneys, penis, and testicles in order to temper the excess amount of blood in these areas. Priapismus is a disease that men and women both can suffer. It involves involuntary tension of the sex organs without desire: women experience itching and men have a constant erection. The worst disorder, however, states William, is that suffered by men who undergo a weakness of the intestinal sphincter immediately after intercourse. A man who is prone to have this involuntary bowel movement in bed tends to have a soft body, experience great desire for a woman, take exceeding pleasure in sexual intercourse, and occasionally soil himself before coitus as well. He should see to it that he uses a suppository before approaching his partner.[101]

Orgasm

Orgasm is often treated separately from coitus in medieval scientific texts, although once again I have not seen the subject mentioned in the astrological treatises. A common statement by natural philosophers is that women experience two delights in coitus, one at the emission of their own seed, and a second at the reception of the man's. The commentator on the *De secretis mulierum* states that if we understand the term *"delectatio"* intensively, the man's pleasure is greater because his seed is hotter; however, if we take the term extensively, the woman has more enjoyment because she has two delights. The commentator refers to Aristotle's statements on this question in the first book of *On the Generation of Animals*; however, the philosopher did not adhere to the two-seed theory of human reproduction and, consequently, does not share this view on female orgasm.

The most influential text on this subject is found in the chapter on the generation of the embryo in Avicenna's *Canon of Medicine,* translated into Latin during the twelfth century, which is mostly repeated by William of Saliceto, Peter of Abano, and by the fourteenth-century Bolognese physician, James of Forli.[103] A woman has three delights in intercourse, according to the early eleventh-century Arabic physician: one from the motion of her own sperm, a second from the motion of the male sperm, and a third from the motion or rubbing that takes place in coitus. These orgasms are not individual impulses, but each is composed of a number of motions, and none is complete until several titillations have passed, followed by a certain quiet. If a male should ejaculate before the woman has experienced her own movements of the matrix, she will have a small delectation similar to what the man feels before the emission of his own seed. But he should be aware that this will not satisfy her. The only way that her fire will be extinguished in a manner that resembles cold water being poured on boiling water is if she first expels her own seed as described and then swallows the male seed when it is ejaculated.[104]

Conclusion

Medieval astrologers, doctors, and natural philosophers devoted a great deal of effort to analyzing and describing the various facets of human sexuality. A central part of human activity, the sexual act and the forces controlling it were treated in copious detail by these scientists, who frequently included in their discussions an evaluation of its effect upon participants. For the astrologers sex was somewhat neutral; just like health and wealth, it was controlled by the stars and man could do little but wait to experience what the heavens had prepared for him. For the doctors and natural philosophers, on the other hand, sexual activity had its dangers, although most of these take a less negative view than Averroës, who clearly disputes the notion that sperm is a superfluity that must be evacuated and emphatically agrees with "many wise men" who prohibit the use of coitus in conserving health.[105] Although it poses fewer dangers for women, who have more excess humidity, than it does for men, who are in danger of drying up,[106] sexual intercourse is, for medieval scientists, a normal part of life that should be examined, discussed, and treated like any other human activity.

18

Postscript: Heresy, Witchcraft, and Sexuality

Vern L. Bullough

Church sexual ideals remained much the same at the end of the Middle Ages as they were at the beginning. Although, as the various contributors to this book have indicated, Church officials dealt with the world as they found it, the ascetic ideal still dominated, and at best, sexual activity was only to be tolerated providing it resulted in procreation. Prostitution in Florence, for example, was justified in just such terms. Some indication of just how deeply rooted hostility to nonprocreative sex was, is indicated by the sexual charges alleged against heretics and witches. Gerhard Ladner has explained that the cultural revolution of the twelfth and thirteenth centuries encouraged a desire for material pleasure that was in conflict with traditional Christian values—resulting in psychological dissonance and widespread alienation.[1] The Church attempted to channel many of the alienated into orthodox reform movements, such as the Franciscans, but not all could be so directed, and the result was a turn to unorthodox religious movements, even among some of the followers of Saint Francis. Inevitably also, the repressed desire for material pleasure on the part of the orthodox led them to attribute to the heretics enjoyment of the very materialistic pleasures they were denying themselves. By implication then, a person who engaged in forbidden kinds of sexual pleasure must be a heretic—and a heretic must engage in "deviant" sexual activity.

There is, however, another factor to be considered in the association of forbidden sexuality with heresy and witchcraft. Many of the twelfth and thirteenth century heresies can be traced to the dualistic concepts of the ancient Manichaeans, while others seem to have had strong pantheistic tendencies that were also present in early Christian heresies. Ernest Werner has argued that both dualism and pantheism have the same religious motivation, namely, an attempt to escape from the bonds of worldly unrighteousness and inadequacy, an escape also coupled with a quest for godly purity. To this end, libertinism could be regarded as a decisive way of taking a stand against the hypocrisy of the world, a way of making a drastic assertion of the holiness of the believers. To emphasize this dedicated purpose, the break with established order could be marked by an act of desecration, by undertaking conduct that the establishment would regard as blasphemous.[2] If this argument has validity, sexual promiscuity of whatever nature became a way of denying the validity of current societal standards.

In confronting the alleged overactive sexual activity of the heretics (and witches), we are left then with at least two alternatives: either the heretics and others condemned by society engaged in the sexual conduct they are accused of or else such conduct was attributed to them regardless of whether they engaged in it or not. In either case the Church had an opportunity to reemphasize its code of sexual morality, to teach the ideal Christian sexual code in a world that often ignored it.

The association of stigmatized sexual conduct with heretical thought is effectively illustrated by the use of the term buggery to imply forbidden sexual conduct. Originally, the term buggery was used to describe Albigensian or Manichaean heretics of the latter Middle Ages. The term is believed to be a corruption of the term Bulgars, another name for the Albigensians who were believed to have originated in Bulgaria. Fairly early it also implied sexual "deviation." One of the earliest uses of the term in English in a possible sexual connotation is in the writing of Robert Mannyng of Brunne (1288–1388). In Mannyng's *Langtoft's Chronicle,* one of the characters states that the pope was a heretic who "lyved in bugerie."[3] Though the meaning is ambiguous many scholars, including the compilers of the *Oxford English Dictionary,* took the reference to imply a sexual sin. Similar meanings were read into it by the compilers of English law.

Buggery, however, did not always mean a sexual act, and attempts to read sexual activities into the term have led to a serious misreading of history. The pioneering sexologist, Havelock Ellis, for example, wrote that Louis IX (1226–1270) handed sodomists over to the Church to be burned.[4] He was wrong on several counts. First, the medieval Church never burned anyone; such matters were left up to the state although the Church might well have found them guilty of a criminal activity for which burning was the penalty. More importantly, Ellis confused buggery with sodomy. An English translation of the statute in question reads:

If anyone is suspected of bougerie the magistrate must seize him and send him to the bishop: and if he is convicted, he must be burnt, and all his goods confiscated to the baron. And the heretic ought to be dealt with in the same way, when his offence has been proven, and all his goods confiscated to the baron.[5]

The purpose obviously was to stamp out heresy,[6] not list sexual sins.[7] Proof for this claim comes from an examination of the contemporary documents of the period that always use the word sodomy when sexual acts are described, never the term buggery. For example, a legal collection made about 1260 at Orleans includes several passages dealing with *bogerie* (the word is spelled in several different ways) in the sense of heresy,[8] as well as one passage dealing specifically with sexual practices. In this later case, however, the term sodomy is used, although what is meant by sodomy is ambiguous since men as well as women could commit sodomy.

> Those who have been proved to be sodomites must lost their c_____[?]. And if anyone commits this offence a second time, he must undergo mutilation [il doit perdre membre]. And if he does it a third time he must be burnt.[9]

Though the statute required that third time offenders be burnt, there is no evidence that sodomists were in fact burned in France during this period, or even that sodomy was of great concern. Of the fifteen hundred judgments pronounced in the French Parliament during the reign of Saint Louis, only one refers to sodomists, and this concerns a disputed jurisdiction between the Bishop of Amiens and the town of Amiens on the right to judge sodomists. The French Parliament ruled in favor of the town.[10] Probably, the statutory provision for burning was not a medieval innovation but a pro forma one based on the provisions of the Theodosian Code, which entered medieval law through the Carolingian legislation of the ninth century.

Even though *bogrerie* in this instance referred to heresy and not sexual activity, the two are usually equated. This appears in the description of the heretical Waldensians by the twelfth-century Alan of Lille.

> In their assemblies they indulge in gluttony and devote themselves to excesses, as those who have ceased to consort with them testify . . . lovers of pleasures, putting carnal delights before the spiritual. These are they who creep into the house of widows and lead them astray.[11]

Contrary to Alan of Lille's charge, the Waldensians as a group earned a justified reputation of being extremely ascetic-minded. Obviously if such charges could be made against an ascetic group like the Waldensians, they could also be made against almost any other group. Robert E. Lerner, in his study of the Brethren of the Free Spirit, for example, concluded that most of the stories about sexual promiscuity and deviation failed the basic historical test of corroboration. Close examination revealed that only a handful were based upon eyewitness accounts and only rarely was there an independent corroborating witness. Moreover, once a story made its appearance it was repeated with various slight alterations in numerous different situations.[12]

The Cathars or Albigensians were most often associated with stigmatized sexual behavior, probably because of their dualistic theology. They had a horror of procreation and taught that the *perfecti,* those who most fully accepted the Cathar way of life, were to avoid procreation, even the ingestion of foods such as meat, eggs, cheese, and milk engendered by sexual procreation. Insemination, they taught, led to the imprisonment of spirits in the material flesh while salvation involved the removal of the material. Since medieval people recognized the essentially sexual nature of man, and, in fact, struggled to overcome it, they could accept the aversion to sex ascribed to the Cathars as resulting only from a turn to nonprocreative sexual activities.

In this they echoed Saint Augustine and the other early Church Fathers who had taught that the Manichaeans, the dualistic predecessors of the Albigensians, had indulged in all kinds of forbidden sexual conduct. Many of the stories repeated about the Cathars in the later Middle Ages seem to be repetitions of similar stories about the Manichaeans in the early Middle Ages. Perhaps typical of such charges is that of Guibert of Nogent, who described a group of heretics (probably Cathars) near Soissons in the early twelfth century.

> They condemn marriage and the begetting of offspring through intercourse. And surely, wherever they are scattered throughout the Latin world, you may see men living with women but not under the name of husband and wife, and in such fashion that man does not dwell with woman, male with female, but men are known to lie with men, women with women; for among them it is unlawful for men to approach women. They reject foods of all sorts which are the product of coition.
>
> They hold meetings in cellars and secret places, the sexes mingling freely. When candles have been lighted, in the sight of all, light women with bare buttocks (it is said) offer themselves to a certain one lying behind them. Directly the candles are extinguished, they all cry out together "Chaos!" and each one lies with her who first comes to hand.
>
> Now it so happens that a woman has there been gotten with child, as soon as the offspring is delivered, it is brought back to the same place. A great fire is lit, and the child is thrown from hand to hand through the flames by those sitting around the fire until it is dead. It is then reduced to ashes; from the ashes bread is made, of which a morsel is given to each as a sacrament. Once that has been eaten, it is very rarely that one is brought back to his sense from that heresy.[13]

In spite of the contradictory nature of Guibert's account, since he implies in one place there is no intercourse leading to procreation and in another states that a baby is born, his list of sexual and other crimes attributed to the heretics may be regarded as a more or less standard listing: sodomy, intercourse

in the wrong position, coitus interruptus, infanticide. Obviously, he seems
to imply, no good Christian would engage in such activities.

Similar descriptions exist that emphasize that Guibert is not alone. An
early twelfth-century writer, Henry of Le Mans or Lausanne, wrote that a
certain heretic enjoyed the pandering of both matrons and adolescent boys
who, in their attendance upon him,

> avowed openly their aberrations and increased them, caressed his feet, his but-
> tocks, his groin, with tender hands. Completely carried away by this fellow's
> wantonness and by the enormity of adultery, they publicly proclaimed that
> they had never touched a man of such strength, such humanity, such power.[14]

Walter Map, towards the end of the same century, described another group
of heretics as living together but not having children. During their services,
he added, a black cat represented their God, and they caressed the cat, and
the feet, the tail, and the genitals of the cat, and then,

> as if drawing license for lasciviousness from the place of foulness, each seizes
> the man or woman next to him and they co-mingle as long as each is able to
> prolong the wantonness. The masters also say, and teach the novices, that it is
> perfect charity to do or suffer what a brother or sister may have desired or
> sought, namely to soothe one another when burning with passion; and from
> submitting they are called Patarines.[15]

Once the medieval equation of active sexuality with religious deviation is
accepted, it is understandable why it could be extended to other fields. Some
times even modern scholars do much the same thing. For example, D. Stanley Jones, in an interesting but misleading and inaccurate study, equated the
struggle over the introduction of Aristotle at the University of Paris in the
thirteenth century with a hidden battle over homosexuality. Jones viewed
the controversy over Aristotle as a struggle with Platonism, which he in turn
equated with homosexuality. To Jones, the temporary defeat of Aristotle
allowed that "hidden strain" of homosexuality that lies "endemic in all cen-
tres of population" to temporarily emerge. The only way these homosexual
victors were vanquished was to enact a death penalty for all those caught in
engaging in sexual intercourse with persons of the same sex. This also allowed
Aristotle to win acceptance over Plato.[16]

Jones's explanation has little correlation with the facts of the case. To
begin with, Plato was known primarily through the neo-Platonism of Saint
Augustine and others who had acted as purifiers and eliminated much of the
homoerotic elements inherent in Plato's writings. Aristotle, at the time of
the controversy, was just beginning to make his appearance and his views
were disseminated largely by Arabic commentators. In spite of the errors of
Jones, however, there were some sexual connotations in the debate, and
charges of sexual deviation were made. The Averroist commentators on

Aristotle were, in fact, charged with teaching that continence was not a virtue, that perfect abstinence from sexual activity corrupted virtue, and that a delight in the act of sex in no way impeded intellectual progress. It was even alleged that some Averroists stated that simple fornication among two unmarried people was not sinful.[17]

In retrospect, charging someone with sexual sins in the later Middle Ages was like charging someone with being a Communist during the McCarthy era in the United States. The simple charge, if it involved anything other than simple fornication, was enough to discredit that person. Inevitably, as heresy increased, so did the condemnation of sexuality. The Amalricians, another heretical group, for example, were said to teach that true believers need obey no law. Instead, since all things are of God there can be no evil, and those who followed their lustful urges were simply doing God's will. To resist such lustful desires was to resist God. As one contemporary chronicler reported:

> If anyone was "in the Spirit," they said, even if he were to commit fornication or to be fouled by any other filthiness, there would be no sin in him, because that Spirit, who is God, being entirely distinct from the body, cannot sin.[18]

The thirteenth-century pseudo-Apostles led by Gerard Segarelli and Colcino of Novaro taught that holy poverty was the only perfect state, one in which all human restraint on religious expression was lifted. In the ceremony to become an apostle, these roving evangelists allegedly had their followers shed all clothing, don a special garb, and then go out preaching. According to the chronicler Salimbene, Segarelli had a horde of boy followers who submitted to sodomy. Salimbene in fact shows great concern over homosexuality and comments on the diffusion of this vice among scholars and clerks and mentions that nuns also practiced it.[19]

As long as heresy remained a minor threat, efforts at control were left in the hands of the local bishops. Often in fact some of the heretics, such as Segarelli, originally were tolerated as harmless. As the number of dissenters grew, there was a demand for greater centralization. In the thirteenth century this led to the papacy itself taking over control of heresy through the establishment of the Inquisition. The newly founded Dominicans were appointed to ferret out the heretics in the pope's name. By the middle of the century inquisitors were authorized to seize the goods of suspected heretics, imprison and torture them, and upon conviction turn them over to the secular officials for execution, all on minimal evidence. Once heresy hunting became institutionalized, the charges against the heretic became more or less uniform and sinful sexual activities remained an important aspect of such charges.

Witchcraft too was associated with certain kinds of sexual deviance. Male transvestism, for example, was regarded as witchcraft and one of the earliest references to this is to be found in the *Canon Episcopi* of Regino of Prum written about 906. Regino reports that bishops were requested to be on the lookout for, among other things, women claiming to ride out at night on a beast and accompanied by a throng of demons transformed into women.[20] This reference of demons transformed into females is somewhat unusual since, in later charges of witchcraft, the typical transformation is from humans into animals such as a cat, dog, or hare, and not a changing of sex. A later example of the association of witchcraft and transvestism took place in the thirteenth century when the Inquisitor in Southern France, Stephen of Bourbon, reported in the 1250s an incident of males who dressed themselves as women entering the house of a rich farmer, dancing and singing, "We take one and give back a hundred." The verse referred to a popular belief in the powers of the good people *(bonae)* to confer prosperity upon any house in which they had been given presents. The suspicious wife of the farmer did not accept the female impersonators' claim to be *bonae* and tried to put an end to their revel. They, nonetheless, began carrying all the goods out of her house repeating, "Be quiet and close your eyes. You shall be rich, because we are the bonae res, and your goods will be multiplied."[21]

Jeffrey Russell in his study of witchcraft attempted to establish the first time specific sexual activities were reported in either heresy or witchcraft trials. He believed that the first equation of homosexual intercourse with heresy was in 1114 and, after this time, variations on the phrases "vir cum viris" and "femina cum feminis" (or, in English, men with men, women with women) appear again and again.[22] The first hint of the *osculum infame,* or the infamous kiss, in which the participants in heretical or witchcraft ceremonies are reported to kiss the buttocks or anus of an animal or human appears in the thirteenth century in the writings of David of Augsburg. Official sanction was given to such a belief by a bull of Pope Gregory IX issued in 1233 which reported such practices. The bull, based on the statement of an inquisitor, claimed that heretics had secret meetings in which the postulant who wanted to become a member is supposed to kiss the devil on the mouth or anus. At such times the devil appeared in the form of a toad, goose, duck, black cat, or as a thin, pale man, with black shining eyes. All adherents of the sect were supposed to follow the postulant in giving the obscene kiss.[23]

Numerous variations of the obscene kiss were reported. A heretic named Lepzet reported that the believers, supposedly Albigensians in this case, practiced their secret rituals in a cave and that during the ceremony the "bishop" of the sect bared his buttock and inserted a silver spoon into his anus upon which he then offered an oblation. The congregation then kissed the bishop's backside, after which they gathered around a pillar on which there was a huge cat. As the cat clung to the pillar, each believer kissed its anus. The lights were then put out and everyone embraced the person next to him, *masculi in masculo et feminae in feminas,* or male in male and female in female. Lepzet claimed that the sect taught sodomy was a perfectly acceptable form of intercourse while marriage was regarded as a sin of fornication.[24] Similar charges were made in the fourteenth century against the Brethren of the Free Spirit who were accused among other things of practicing incest, adultery, sodomy, and coitus interruptus.[25]

Probably the most notorious attempt to equate deviant sexuality with heretical conduct was the trial of the Knights Templar. On the order of the French king, Philip IV, all the Templars in France, including the Grand Master Jacques de Molay, were arrested on the night of October 13, 1307, and charged with heresy and sodomy. How valid the charges of sodomy were has been a matter of debate. Gershon Legman has argued that the Templars in fact practiced homosexuality and that Jacques de Molay, the leader of the Templars, was a homosexual.[26] At the opposite end of the spectrum is Julius Gmelin who believed that the Templars were as "pure as the Holy Father himself."[27] Few writers have remained neutral about this most colorful, most powerful, and most widely known of the crusading orders.[28]

Henry C. Lea, the nineteenth-century collector of information on witchcraft and the Inquisition, felt that the condemnation of the Templars constituted the "great crime of the Middle Ages."[29] Though one of the reasons for moving against the Templars was their great wealth and power, this nowhere appears in the charges against them. Instead other charges, including sexual ones, were made. The original accusation was made by a certain Esquiu de Floyran, a former member of the Order who had been charged by the Order with murdering a Templar official. When Esquiu, perhaps in an effort to save himself, made his charges against the Templars to King James II of Aragon, his charges were ignored. He persisted in his charges, however, until he reached the ear of Philip. Philip, already angered by the Templars, had requested Pope Clement V to investigate but before the Pope did so Philip denounced the Templars to the Inquisition. Two of the eight charges against them had sexual connotations. It was claimed that novices on admission had to spit on the cross, renounce Christ, and take part in a mock ceremonial involving the *osculum infame* in which the initiate had to kiss either the buttocks (anus?) or the navel (penis?) of a Templar official. It was also charged that the Templars were addicted to sodomy and the initiates were taught that they might have carnal copulation with each other.[30]

The most important facet of the trial was that concerned with Jacques de Molay, and it is instructive both for what de Molay admitted and what he denied. Under torture, the Grand Master confessed that he had denied Christ depicted on the cross when he was accepted into the order and that he had even spat on the cross as part of his initiation. He denied, however, that he had ever been told to unite himself carnally with another brother and claimed that he had never done such a thing. Why admit part of the charge and deny the other? One historian of the order wrote:

If the confession is genuine, and doubt has been thrown on it—the only explanation consistent with his innocence is fear of the consequences for himself
and the Templars if he denied the charges. He is said to have especially feared
the charge of homosexuality brought against him and had been promised that
this part of the indictment would not be pressed if he acknowledged other
charges.[31]

This defense of de Molay sounds almost as if the writer believed in the
charges of homosexuality, but the only evidence that de Molay might have
engaged in homosexual activities was the accusation of a certain Hugh
de Narsac that de Molay had engaged in sodomy with his valet. De Molay
never admitted the charge and neither did several thousand Templars examined over a seven-year period admit similar charges. In fact only three, even
after torture, confessed to engaging in sodomy, although several hundred
confessed that they had heard homosexuality might be permitted but they
swore that they had not engaged in it themselves.[32] Since the torture was
severe, and many knights died under torture, it would seem that sodomy
was more a trumped-up charge than a real one. Large numbers admitted
engaging in the "obscene kiss" as part of their initiation but it is difficult to
read any homosexual conduct into such actions or even any license to engage
in licentious acts.[33]

Edith Simon, in her popular history of the Templars, felt that all the sexual charges may have resulted from the fact that medieval asceticism, by
denying sex, led to an obsession about sex. Moreover the

insistence that the fighting monks were to shun women even more stringently
than most other religious fraternities lent added fuel to the train of thought; it
was seriously submitted that the injunction to sodomy had been designed to
clinch the Templar's aversion to all feminine contact. So the train of thought
sped on to the final point of arrival; for a group of men obviously more sinful
than the generality to be more privileged than anybody else, could not be just.
Envy and greed call themselves righteous.[34]

In short the Templars became a scapegoat and, in the medieval mind, as sinners they were inevitably involved in forbidden sexual activities.

The same kind of scapegoating appears in other areas of medieval life. In
the *Divine Comedy* of Dante Alighieri, several persons are listed as residing
in the seventh level of the Inferno. This level, reserved for those who had
committed crimes of violence, included among them the "sodomists" Brunetto Latino, Priscian, Francesco d'Accorso, Andrea de Mozzi, Guido Guerra,
Tegghiaio Aldrobandi, Jacopo Rusticucci, and Guiuglielmo Borsiers.[35]

Though Dante seemed to imply that homosexuality was prevalent among
men of letters, there is still the question of why Dante chose the people he
did to represent the crime of sodomy. Upon examination it becomes clear
that many of those put in this particular level of the Inferno were political

enemies of Dante. In the case of Priscian, Dante might have confused the grammarian with the fourth-century bishop of Avilla, Priscillian, who was charged by his contemporaries with committing certain unnatural sins,[36] but he also might have been put there, as was Brunetto Latino, because he belonged to the literary group Dante equated with homosexuality. Guido Guerra, Jacopo Rusticicucci, Tegghiaio Aldrobandi, Brunetto Latini, and quite possibly Guiglielmo Borsiere were Guelphs, those responsible for the exile of the Ghibelline Dante from Florence. This was his revenge. Dante also places some sodomists in purgatory, but only one is mentioned by name, Julius Caesar.[37]

When witchcraft became an issue in medieval Europe, it too took on sexual connotations. H. C. Lea wrote that the curiosity of judges at witchcraft trials became almost insatiable when it came to learning all the possible details about sexual intercourse, and their industry in seeking this information was rewarded by an "abundance of foul imaginations."[38] The nature of this sexual material has been the subject of some scholarly discussion, with scholars falling into two camps, namely, the supporters of the late Margaret Murray and her opponents, with her opponents generally having the best of the argument. Professor Murray was struck by the fact that the sexual acts to which witches confessed followed a rather consistent pattern. From this as well as other evidence, she concluded that witchcraft actually represented the last traces of an ancient fertility religion.[39]

Jeffrey Russell represents the view of most scholars when he regards witchcraft as in part due to a decay of ideas and institutions that earlier had held society together. Deprived of their old securities, people responded in a panic that found vent in the terror of witchcraft. Also important was the growing influence of Neoplatonism, which emphasized a magical world view, and in turn led to the growth of magic. Inevitably the Inquisition, originally established to deal with heresy, became active against magicians and diviners.[40] Sexual activity also made a person suspect. The most important papal contribution to the witch phenomenon was a bull of Innocent VIII (1484–1495) issued on December 5, 1484. The bull stated:

It has come to our ears that members of both sexes do not avoid having intercourse with demons, incubi and succubi; and that by their sorceries and by their incantations, charms and conjuration, they suffocate, extinguish and cause to perish the births of women, the increase of animals, the corn of the ground, the grapes of the vineyard and the fruit of the trees, as well as men, women, flocks, herbs and other various kinds of animals, vines and apple trees, corn and other fruits of the earth; making and procuring that men and women, flocks and herds and other animals suffer and are tormented both from within and without so that men beget not nor women conceive; and they impede the conjugal action of men and women.[41]

The bull had been issued at the request of Heinrich Institoris (1430–1505) and Jakob Sprenger (1436–95), who requested the support of the pope in order to overcome opposition to their witchhunting activities. The two incorporated the bull as a prefatory justification in their *Malleus Male-ficarum*, the handbook for all future witchhunters. The *Malleus* or *Hammer of Witches*, printed in 1486, achieved broad popularity. Institoris is regarded as the chief author of the work while Sprenger is relegated to a more minor role. The purpose of the *Malleus* was to refute in systematic fashion all arguments against the reality of witchcraft, and in the process of doing this it crystallized previous folklore about black magic into a stringent code and gathered church dogma on heresy together in popular form. Witchcraft was defined as the most abominable of heresies. It was characterized as having four essentials: (1) renunciation of the Christian faith, (2) the sacrifice of unbaptized infants to Satan, (3) the devotion of body and soul to evil, and (4) sexual relations with incubi or succubi.[42] Usually the orgies are regarded as heterosexual, and charges of any kind of activity that could be interpreted as homosexual were only rarely lodged against those accused of witchcraft.[43]

The sexual activity most often described is that with incubi or succubi, lewd demons or goblins who sought intercourse with humans. Incubi and succubi were not so much real demons in themselves as the manifestation of demons who assumed the form of a male (incubus) and female (succubus) for the purpose of intercourse. Since technically they were angels who had fallen from their status because of their lust, intercourse with such creatures raised several problems, not the least of which was a kind of transsexual change as the demons changed their sex from male to female and back again. Moreover, since by definition the incubus was a member of a species different than man, intercourse with them could be condemned as bestiality or buggery. One Church authority wrote that to sin with a succubus or incubus was bestiality, "to which sin is added also malice against religion, sodomy, adultery, and incest." To bolster such arguments the witchhunters gathered together many accounts of monsters, half human and half animal, born of such unions.[44]

One of the interesting theological problems involved in intercourse with demons was to explain how the demons, particularly the incubi who took the male form, could have humanlike organs and give forth semen. Some authorities, such as Caesarius of Heisterbach who wrote in the thirteenth century, believed that such devils collected the human semen emitted during nocturnal emissions or as a result of masturbation and used it to create new bodies for themselves.[45] Most authorities followed the example of Saint Thomas Aquinas,[46] who argued that the devils in the form of succubi seduced males and received their semen and then later, assuming the role of incubi, poured this semen into the female repositories.[46] This was also the view of the authors of the *Malleus Maleficarum*.[47]

Usually, the sexual practices equated with witchcraft are described in the most generalized kinds of terms, although occasionally terms such as sodomy or statements such as intercourse "after the manner of beasts" are utilized. Sometimes the devil appeared in animal form, particularly that of a bull, a fox, or even sometimes a hare, but his most likely form was as an incubus and he was far more likely to have intercourse with women than with men. This is because women were regarded as far more licentious as men. One authority has estimated that the male incubus appears about nine times as frequently in the works on demonology as does the female succubus.[48]

Witchcraft and sorcery were also believed to be responsible for impotence, infertility, and a whole series of other sex-connected activities. One of the supposed powers of a witch was her ability to make the penis disappear by casting a "glamour" over it. Once this happened, only the witch herself could restore normal sexual activity by making it reappear. A witch was also regarded as the main cause of the male failure to achieve an erection, and it was witchcraft that prevented women from conceiving or caused them to miscarry. Impotence was believed to be caused by a ligature, that is, the witch, by tying knots in threads or hanks of leather, would cause impotence until the hidden knot was discovered or untied or until the witch lifted her spell. Generally, however, the believer in witchcraft held that the devil wished to encourage, not discourage, fornication, and so ligature was believed to be less common than the other forms of *malefica* or evils a witch might impose.[49]

In conclusion, the medieval ascetic ideals remained influential throughout the medieval period. Church officials were realists, however, and they dealt with people as they found them. Generally, as in the case of prostitutes and others who engaged in "sinful" activities, there was compassion and hope for ultimate salvation; with others, such as homosexuals, there was less tolerance.[50] The influence of the ascetic ideal is probably best exemplified at the end of the Middle Ages by the Church's attempt to equate many forms of sexual activity with heresy or witchcraft or other forms of stigmatized social activity. This equation served as a means of warning society about its own sexual urges and at the same time offered society a way of deflecting its own anxieties about sex onto other groups who served as convenient scapegoats. This book, however, only begins to examine sexual activity in the medieval period, and sexuality in any period of history remains largely unexplored and uncharted. If this book encourages others to begin to explore in greater depth what has previously been a forbidden topic, it will have served its purpose. Perhaps readers will now realize, if they have not before, that medieval people were as much interested in sex as their modern descendants.

Appendix: Medieval Canon Law and Its Sources

The medieval Church's legal system, known as the canon law, touched virtually every aspect of life in Western Europe during the Middle Ages. Sexual activity in particular was rigorously monitored by the officials and the courts of the Church. As a consequence of this, it is scarcely possible to deal with medieval sexual life without paying a great deal of attention to the ideas, policies, and provisions of canon law on this matter.

Medieval canon law comprised a large and complex body of regulations, and no single collection or series of books adequately reflects the whole apparatus of canonical jurisdiction. The most important sources, however, are those in the *Corpus iuris canonici,* a collection of canonical rules and regulations that includes the major texts studied in the law faculties of the medieval universities. This collection comprises six different works: the *Decretum Gratiani,* the *Liber Extra,* the *Liber Sextus,* the *Constitutiones Clementinae,* the *Extravagantes Johannis XXII,* and the *Extravagantes Communes.*

Decretum Gratiani

The foundation of the *Corpus iuris canonici* is the *Decretum* of Gratian, first published sometime about 1140. Gratian himself, about whom very little is known, apparently called his work the *Concordantia discordantium*

219

canonum, or *Harmony of Conflicting Rules.* This is both a massive collection of earlier Church law, as well as an attempt to reconcile laws that conflicted with one another by a process of logical analysis and differentiation. The text of the *Decretum* is divided into three major sections. Part I consists of 101 Distinctions, each made up of *capitula,* or citations from authorities, and *dicta,* or Gratian's remarks about the texts. Each Distinction deals with a single topic or a closely related group of subjects. Thus, for example, Distinction I deals with the species of law in general, Distinction 2 with the various types and sources of law in the Roman legal system, Distinction 3 with the nature and functions of ecclesiastical law, and so forth. There are, all told, some 973 chapters in Part I. The first twenty Distinctions deal with the foundations of law, especially ecclesiastical law. The remaining Distinctions of Part I deal with the different kinds of ministries within the Church, with the problems of ordination, the qualifications that the Church's ministers should have, the hierarchy of authority within the Church, and the relationship of ecclesiastical to secular power.

Part II is divided into thirty-six Cases, each of which states a situation and then develops one or more questions concerning the case. Each question is discussed in turn, and Gratian cites the *capitula,* or authoritative canonical statements, that bear upon the problem at issue. In his *dicta* Gratian also comments upon the issues in each question and on the problems arising from conflicting authorities in dealing with those issues. Question 3 of Case 33 stands apart from the rest of Part II, however, since this question is subdivided into seven Distinctions. This section of Part II is known as the *Tractatus de penitentia,* since it deals with the penitential system of the Church. The topics treated in the remainder of Part II are quite diverse and include such subjects as simony, the choosing of bishops, excommunication, oaths and perjury, warfare, and many other matters. Cases 27 to 36 deal with the law of marriage and sexual offenses, and this is the most important section of the *Decretum* for historians of those matters, although references to sexual behavior crop up occasionally in other sections of the work. Part II is by far the longest part of the *Decretum* and contains nearly 2,600 chapters.

Part III, the shortest major division of the *Decretum,* is known as the *Tractatus de consecratione.* This section is divided into five Distinctions, dealing with liturgical and sacramental law. It has been suggested by some scholars that this section was added to the *Decretum,* perhaps by one of Gratian's disciples, after the appearance of Parts I and II. There are about 400 chapters in Part III.

The *Liber Extra*

Following the appearance of the *Decretum Gratiani,* popes, councils, and other Church authorities continued to add to the body of rules and regulations that governed the activities of the Church's members. As the law continued to grow, it became necessary to add supplements to the *Decretum* if it was to be kept up to date. There are a great many collections of this new law, commonly referred to as decretal law, since a great deal of it was contained in decretal letters of the popes. Decretal letters are decisions that establish a central point of law applicable to cases other than the one at issue in the decision. Gradually, it became apparent that some effort ought to be made to create a comprehensive collection of the thousands of decretals and other new legislation that had appeared in Gratian's time. Finally, on 5 September 1234 Pope Gregory IX promulgated a major official collection of the new law. This collection is known as the *Liber Extra* or *Decretales Gregorii IX*. It was put together by Raymond of Penyafort, a Catalan canonist commissioned by the Pope to undertake the work. The *Liber Extra* (conventionally abbreviated *X*) is divided into five books. Each book is subdivided into Title (of which there are 185 all told), and each Title consists of one or more chapters. The whole work comprises 1,971 chapters.

The *Liber Sextus* and Later Decretal Collections

New legislation continued to appear after the publication of the *Liber Extra,* and once again legal scholars and authorities of various kinds began compiling collections of this new law. By the end of the thirteenth century, these collections were outmoded by a new official collection, the *Liber Sextus,* put together at the direction of Pope Boniface VIII and formally promulgated on 3 March 1298. Like the *Liber Extra,* the *Liber Sextus* is divided into five books, comprising 76 titles and 359 chapters. Two decades later a further compilation of decretals was officially promulgated by Pope John XXII on 25 October 1317. This is the *Constitutiones Clementinae,* the last official decretal collection issued by a medieval pontiff. It is much smaller than its predecessors but follows the same organizational scheme, with five books, 52 titles, and 106 chapters. This collection is known as the *Constitutiones Clementinae* because most of the decretals contained in it were issued by Pope Clement V (1305–1314). A few years later in 1325 a small, private collection of twenty decretals of Pope John XXII was assembled by Zenzelinus de Cassanis (d. 1334), a professor of canon law at the University of Montpellier. This collection was entitled the *Extravagantes Johannis XXII.* The final segment of the *Corpus iuris canonici,* known as the *Extravagantes Communes,* was a small collection of 69 chapters compiled by Jean Chappuis, a Parisian canon lawyer, in 1500.

Canonical Citation System

The various portions of the *Corpus iuris canonici* are cited by modern scholars according to a simple citation system that enables students and scholars to refer quickly and accurately to the texts of the medieval canon law and also to the commentaries on those texts. The system works this way:

Decretum Gratiani

D.1 c.1	Distinctio 1, capitulum (chapter) 1 (in Parts I and III)
C.1 q.1 c.1	Causa (Case) 1, questio (question) 1, cap 1 (in Part II)
De pen.	Causa 33, questio 3
De cons.	Tractatus de consecratione (Part III)
d.a.c.	"Dictum Gratiani ante capitulum . . ." (that is, Gratian's comment before the cited chapter.)
d.p.c.	"Dictum Gratiani post capitulum . . ." (that is, Gratian's comment after the cited chapter.)
Glos. ord. to c.1.2.1.c.1 ad V si non gratis datur	The ordinary gloss, that is, the interpretation of C.1 q.1. c.1 and particularly of the words "If it is not given freely," commonly taught in the law schools.

Decretal collections

X 1.1.1	Liber Extra, Book 1, Title 1, Chapter 1
VI 1.2.2.2	Liber Sextus, Book 1, Title 1, Chapter 1
Clem.	Constitutiones Clementinae
Extrav. Jo. XXII	Extravagantes Johannis XXII
Extrav. Comm.	Extravagantes communes
Comp I 1.1.1	Compilatio prima, Liber 1, titulus 1, capitulum

Corpus iuris civilis

Cod. 1.1.1	Codex Justianus, Liber (Book) 1, titulus (title) 1, lex (law) 1
Dig. 1.1.1	Digestum, Liber 1, titulus 1, fragmentum 1
Inst.	Institutiones Justiani
Nov.	Novellae
Auth.	Authenticum
pr.	principium

Decretists and Decretalists

In addition to studying the law itself, it is necessary for students of medieval history to pay attention to the ways in which the law was interpreted, particularly if they wish to understand the workings of medieval society. The teachers in the law faculties of the medieval universities produced a vast body of commentary on the texts of the *Corpus iuris canonici*. In recent decades historians have come to recognize that these commentaries are critically important sources and, since many of them have never been published, a great deal of work has gone into effort to make these sources available. Medieval canon lawyers who wrote and lectured primarily on the *Decretum* of Gratian are commonly known as decretists, while those who wrote about the *Liber Extra* are referred to as decretalists. The decretists and decretalists are our best sources of information about the ways in which the canon law was applied and the way in which those who worked with it understood its provisions. The work of these lawyers is also important for other reasons. Historians have come to recognize that many of the ablest minds of the twelfth and thirteenth centuries were attracted to the study of law, and in the writings of the law professors of that period one can discover not only technical information about the law itself, but also intriguing and sometimes highly original discussions of basic social problems. Hence, many of the chapters in this book have drawn heavily both upon the texts of the medieval canon law and upon the canonistic literature produced by the decretists and decretalists.

Bibliography

Few book-length monographs have been written about medieval sexuality. Readers of this book might consult the following books in English that deal with some of the material discussed in this book.

Bailey, Derrick Sherwin. *Homosexuality and the Western Tradition*. London: Longmans, Green and Company.

———. *Sexual Relation in Christian Thought*. New York: Harper and Brothers, 1959.

Boswell, John. *Christianity, Social Tolerance, and Homosexuality*. Chicago: University of Chicago Press, 1980.

Bullough, Vern L. *Sexual Variance in Society and History*. 1976. Reprinted. Chicago: University of Chicago Press, 1980.

Goodich, Michael. *The Unmentionable Vice: Homosexuality in the Later Medieval Period*. Santa Barbara: ABC-Clio, 1979.

Noonan, John T. *Contraception: A History of Its Treatment by Catholic Theologians and Canonists*. Cambridge, Mass.: Belknap Press of Harvard University, 1966.

Radcliff-Umstead, Douglas. *Human Sexuality in the Middle Ages and Renaissance*. Pittsburgh: University of Pittsburgh Publications on the Middle Ages and the Renaissance, 1978.

Ross, Thomas W. *Chaucer's Bawdy*. New York: E.P. Dutton, 1972.

Readers who want to go beyond the level of these books or of this book are advised to consult the notes of the various chapters for references. The following abbreviations and editions are used.

CCSL   *Corpus Christianorum,* Series Latina, Turnholt, Belgium, 1954 ff.
CG   *Concilia Galliae,* ed. C. Munier in CCSL, Turnholt, Belgium, 1963, vol. 148 ff.
COD   *Conciliorum oecumenicorum decreta,* ed. G. Alberigo et al., 2nd ed., Freiburg i/br., 1962.
        Corpus iuris canonici, Ed. E. Friedberg, 2 vols., Leipzig, 1879–81.
        Corpus iuris civilis, ed. T. Mommsen et al., 3 vols., Berlin, 1872.
CSEL   *Corpus Scriptorum Ecclesiasticorum Latinorum,* Vienna, 1886 ff.
CVH   *Concilios Visigoticos e Hispano Ramanos,* ed. J. Vives. Barcelona, 1963.
DACL   *Dictionnaire d'archéologie chrétienne et de liturgie,* ed. F. Cabrol et al. Paris, 1907–53.
DDC   *Dictionnaire de droit canonique,* ed. R. Naz. Paris, 1935–65.
DHGE   *Dictionnaire d'histoire et de géographie ecclesiastique,* ed. A. Baudrillart et al. Paris, 1912 ff.
DTC   *Dictionnaire de théologie catholique,* ed. A. Vacant et al. Paris, 1903–50.
glos ord cited from
        Corpus iuris canonici una cum glossis, 4 vols., Venice, 1605.
        and
        Corpus iuris civilis una cum glossis, 5 vols., Lyon, 1584.
Grágás *Grágás Islaendernes lovbo i fristaten tid,* ed. by Vilhalmur Finsen for Det nordiske Literatur-Samfund, 4 vols., Copenhagen, 1852–57.
KLNM   *Kulturhistorisk Leksikon for Nordisk Middelalder,* Oslo, 1956 ff.
MGH   *Monumenta Germaniae historica,* ed. G. H. Pertz, T. Mommsen, et al. Berlin, Hannover, Leipzig, et al., 1826 ff.
NCE   *New Catholic Encyclopedia.* New York, 1967.
NPNF   *Nicene and Post Nicene Fathers,* ed. P. Schaff and F. Wace, 2 series, 14 vols. each. New York, 1886–90, 1890–1900.
PG   *Patrologia Graeca,* ed. J. P. Migne, 161 vols. in 165. Paris, Garnier Fratres, 1857–86.
PL   *Patrologia Latina,* ed. J. P. Migne, 221 vols., Paris, Garnier Fratres, 1844–64.
Sac Conc *Sacrorum conciliorum nova et amplissima collectio,* ed. J. D. Mansi et al. 31 vols. Florence and Venice, 1759–98.
SC   *Sources Chrétiennes,* ed. H. De Lubac, J. Daniélou, and (currently) C. Mondesert. Les Editions du Cerf: Paris, ongoing collection.

Notes

Preface

1. Norman F. Cantor, Medieval History (New York: Macmillan, 1963), p. 31.

Chapter 1

Introduction: The Christian Inheritance

1. Matt. 5:31-32; Mark 10:11-12; Matt. 19:3-9.
2. Matt. 19:11-12 (Vulgate).
3. Eusebius, Ecclesiastical History, VI, viii, ed. and trans. Kirsopp Lake (London: William Heinemann, 1926).
4. See the discussion in Derrick Sherwin Bailey, Sexual Relation in Christian Thought (New York: Harper and Brothers, 1959), p. 72, n. 11.
5. Luke 14:26
6. Matt. 10:37, 19:29; Mark 10:29.
7. Luke 21:23.
8. Matt. 5:228.
9. I Cor. 7:1.
10. I Cor. 7:1-12 (Vulgate).
11. I Cor. 7:28, 32-34.
12. I Tim. 4:3.
13. II Thess. 2:2.
14. See Robert M. Grant, Augustus to Constantine: The Thrust of the Christian Movement into the Roman World (New York: Harper & Row, 1970), p. 69.
15. I Thess. 4:3-5.
16. I Cor. 5:11 (Vulgate).
17. I Cor. 6:9-10 (Revised Standard Version).

18. I Tim. 1:9-10.

19. Rom. 1:26-27 (Revised Standard Version).

20. For discussion of these see, Vern Bullough, *Sexual Variance in Society and History* (New York: Wiley Interscience, 1976), chap. VIII.

21. R. Walzer, *Galen on Jews and Christians* (London: Oxford University Press, 1949), p. 65.

22. For discussion of these pre-Christian precursors see Bullough, *Sexual Variance,* chap. VII. For the Gnostic writings themselves see, James M. Robinson, ed., *The Nag Hammadi Library in English* (New York: Harper & Row, 1977).

23. See John T. Noonan, Jr., *Contraception: A History of Its Treatment by Catholic Theologians and Canonists* (Cambridge: Harvard University Press, 1966), p. 58.

24. Acts 8:9-24.

25. Rev. 2:6, 14-15.

26. Clement, *Stromata,* III, cap 3 (12) in vol. II, NPNF, Series 1. In this particular edition of Clement, the editors hesitated to translate this section because of its sexual overtones. There is an English translation of the third book in John F. L. Oulton and Henry Chadwick, *Alexandrian Christianity* (Philadelphia: Westminster Press, 1954).

27. Tertullian, *On the Flesh of Christ,* cap. 1, in vol. III, NPNF, Series 1.

28. Tertullian, *Against Marcion,* IV, cap. vii, in vol. III, NPNF, Series 1.

29. Ibid., V, cap. vii.

30. Ibid., IV, cap. xxiv.

31. Clement, *Stromata,* III, cap. 17 (102).

32. Justin Martyr, *Dialogue with Trypho,* cap. ii, in vol. I, NPNF, Series 1; also, Arthur C. McGiffert, *A History of Christian Thought,* 2 vols. (New York: Charles Scribner's Sons, 1932), I, 100.

33. Justin Martyr, *Apology,* I, cap. 29, in vol. I, NPNF, Series 1.

34. Justin Martyr, *Dialogue with Trypho,* 100; also Erwin R. Goodenough, *The Theology of Justin Martyr* (reprinted Amsterdam: Philo Press, 1923), pp. 181-82, 235-39.

35. Justin Martyr, *Apology,* I, xxix. See also Noonan, *Contraception, passim.*

36. Clement, *Stromata,* II, vii.

37. See Athenagoras, *A Plea for Christians,* chaps. xxxii-xxxiv, in vol. II, NPNF, Series 1.

38. Tertullian, *To His Wife,* I, ii-iii in vol. IV, NPNF, Series 1.

39. Clement, *Stromata,* III, cap. 12 (81).

40. Arthur Vööbus, *History of Asceticism in the Syrian Orient* (Louvain: *Corpus Scriptorum Christianorum Orientalium,* 1958), I, 69.

41. Tertullian, *On Monogamy,* cap. 3, in vol. IV, *The Ante-Nicene Fathers.*

42. Soranus, *Gynecology,* I, vii (32), trans. Owsei Temkin (Baltimore: The Johns Hopkins Press, 1956).

43. Saint Gregory of Nyssa, *On Virginity,* trans. Virginia Woods Callahan in vol. LVIII of *The Fathers of the Church* (Washington, D.C.: The Catholic University of America, 1948 f.).

44. St. Jerome, *Against Helvidius,* 21-22, trans. John H. Hritza, vol. LIII, *The Fathers of the Church,* and St. Jerome, *Letters,* xxii, 2, ed. and trans. Charles Christoper Mierow in vol. XXXIII, *Ancient Christian Writers* (Westminster: The Newman Press, 1963). See also Jerome, *Letters,* xlvii, ed. and trans. Jerome Labourt (Paris: Société Les Belles Lettres, 1949 ff), and *Select Letters,* LIV, 4, ed. and trans. F. A. Wright (London: William Heinemann, 1933).

45. St. Jerome, *Select Letters,* XXII, 20.

46. St. Ambrose, *De Vidius,* cap. XIII, xxxi, and *De Virginitate,* I, cap. 6 in vol. VII, *Omnia Opera,* ed. D. A. B. Caillau (Paris: Paul Mellier, 1844).

47. St. Ambrose, *De Vidius,* cap. XV, lxxxviii, and cap XI, lxix.

48. Bailey, *Sexual Relation in Christian Thought,* p. 24.

49. St. Jerome, *Contre Jovinien, Contre Vigilantius* in *Oeuvres de Saint Jerome,* ed. M. B. de Matougues (Paris: Soulte de Pantheon Litteraire, 1841), and *Against Helvidius,* op. cit.

50. Sozomen, *Ecclesiastical History,* I, xxiii, trans. Edward Walford (London: Henry G. Bohn, 1855); Socrates, *Ecclesiastical History,* I, xi (London: Henry G. Bohn, 1904).

51. . Bailey, *Sexual Relation in Christian Thought,* p. 30.

52. See Henri-Charles Puech, *Le Manicheisme* (Paris: Civilisations du sud, S. AEP, 1949). The best extant source for the teachings of Mani are the various writings of St. Augustine, but also invaluable is the *Fihrist, or the Register of the Sciences of Muhammad ibn Ishaq ibn al-Nadim,* written in the tenth century in Arabic. It was edited and translated by Bayard Dodge under the title of *The Fihrist of al-Nadim,* 2 vols. (New York: Columbia University Press, 1970). See also Noonan, *Contraception,* pp. 107–30.

53. St. Augustine, *Confessions,* VIII, vii, ed. and trans. William Watts (London: William Heinemann, 1919).

54. Ibid., VI, xii; also St. Augustine, *The Happy Life* (de beata vita), I (4), ed. and trans. Ludwig Schopp in vol. I, *The Fathers of the Church.*

55. Rom. 13:13–14 (Vulgate).

56. St. Augustine, *Confessions,* VIII, xii.

57. St. Augustine, *Concerning the Nature of Good,* cap. xvii, trans. A. H. Newman in *Basic Writings of St. Augustine,* ed. Whitney J. Oates (New York: Random House, 1948), p. 455.

58. St. Augustine, *De Gratia Christi, et de Peccato originali contra Pelagium,* cap. 43, xxxviii, trans. Marcus Dodd in vol. II, *The Works of St. Augustine* (Edinburgh: T. & T. Clark, 1885).

59. St. Augustine, *City of God,* XIV, 26, trans. Demetrius B. Zema and Gerald G. Walsh, *Fathers of the Church.*

60. Ibid, XIV, 17, 19.

61. Ibid, XIV, 26, and also 23, 24; St. Augustine, *De nuptiis et concupiscentia,* II, cap. 14 (v), trans. Marcus Dodd, in vol. II, *The Works of St. Augustine.*

62. Bailey, *Sexual Relation in Christian Thought,* p. 54.

63. St. Augustine, *De peccatorium meritis et remissione,* cap. 57 (XXIX), trans. Marcus Dodd, in vol. IV, *The Works of St. Augustine.*

64. St. Augustine, *De nuptiis et Concupiscentia,* I, cap. 4 (iii).

65. Ibid, I, cap. 8 (vii).

66. Ibid, I, cap. 9 (viii).

67. St. Augustine, *De bono conjugali,* X, 10, in vol. XL, *PL,* and St. Augustine, *Sermones,* CCCLI, iii (5), in vol. XXXIX, *PL.*

68. St. Augustine, *Against Two Letters of the Pelagians,* I, cap. 27 (xiii), cap. 30 (xv) in vol. XV, *The Works of St. Augustine.*

69. St. Augustine, *De nuptiis et concupiscentia,* I, 17 (xv).

70. St. Augustine, *De bono conjugali,* V.

71. St. Augustine, *Soliloquies,* I, 10 (17), trans. Thomas F. Gilligan in vol. I, *Fathers of the Church.*

Chapter 2

Formation of Medieval Ideals: Christian Theory and Christian Practice

1. *Concilius Eliberitanum,* Canon XXXIII, in *Sac Conc,* II, 246–52.

2. Sozomen, *Ecclesiastical History,* I, 23 (London: Henry G. Bohn, 1855), and Socrates, *Ecclesiastical History,* I, ii (London: Henry G. Bohn, 1855).

3. Siricius, *Epistolae et Decreta, Epistola I, ad Himer, passim* in vol. XIII, *PL*.

4. See Derrick Sherwin Bailey, *Sexual Relation in Christian Thought* (New York: Harper and Brothers, 1959), p. 30.

5. Leo I, *Epistola* CLXVII, *inquis,* iv, v, vi, in vol. LIV, *PL*.

6. For a comprehensive, although somewhat dated discussion, see Henry C. Lea, *History of Sacerdotal Celibacy in the Christian Church* 4th ed., revised and reprinted (London: Watts and Company, 1932).

7. *Council in Trulo* (692) in Charles Joseph Hefele, *A History of the Councils of the Church* (Edinburgh: T.T. Clark, 1896), V, vi, and for the episcopate, xlviii.

8. St. John Chrysostom, "On Account of Fornication," in *On Those Words of the Apostle,* vol. LI, *PG,* col. 213, and "Messenger," II, col. 143–144.

9. St. John Chrysostom, "On Account of Fornication," in *Words of the Apostle,* LI, 213. See also John T. Noonan, *Contraception* (Cambridge: Harvard Univeristy Press, 1966), p. 79.

10. Norman E. Himes, *Medical History of Contraception,* reprinted (New York: Schocken Books, 1970), pp. 94–96. Himes gives a translation of the pertinent parts of Aetius, *On Medicine in Sixteen Books,* XVI, xvi and xvii.

11. Paulus Aegineta, *Seven Books of Medicine,* Book I, sect. xxxv, trans. from Greek with commentary Francis Adams, 3 vols. (London: Sydenham Society, 1844–47), I, 44–45.

12. *Concilius Nicaenum* (325), Canon I, *Sac conc,* II, 668.

13. William L. Westermann, *The Slave Systems of Greek and Roman Antiquity* (Philadelphia: American Philosophical Society, 1955), p. 118 n, 88. For an account of the various legislative enactments, see W. W. Buckland, *The Roman Law of Slavery,* reprinted (New York: AMS Press, 1969), pp. 37, 40–41, 80 n, 7, 602–03.

14. Steven Runciman, *Byzantine Civilization,* reprinted (New York: Meridian Books, 1956), p. 162.

15. Steven Runciman, *The Emperor Romanus Lecapenus and His Reign* (Cambridge: University Press, 1963), p. 30. For a breakdown of the offices, see J. B. Burty, *The Imperial Administrative System in the Ninth Century,* reprinted (New York: Burt Franklin, 1958), pp. 120–29, the section entitled "Dignities and Offices of the Eunuchs." There were eight orders of eunuchs. Bury's account is based upon the *Keltorologion* of Philotheos. See also Wilhelm Ensslin, "The Emperor and Imperial Administration," in *Byzantium,* ed. Norman H. Baynes and H. St. L. B. Moss (Oxford: Clarendon Press, 1948), p. 286.

16. A. H. M. Jones, *The Later Roman Empire,* 2 vols. (Norman: University of Oklahoma Press, 1964), II, 1232–33 n, 7.

17. The most complete account of sexual activities in the Byzantine Empire can be found in P. Koukoules, *The Private Life of the Byzantines* (in Greek), 8 vols. (Athens: Institut Français, 1947–1957).

18. St. John Chrysostom, *Homilies,* LXXIII, 3 in vol. VII, *Oeuvres Complètes* (Nantes and Mazear: Libraire-Editeur, 1865). For further discussion of Chrysostom, see Derrick Sherwin Bailey, *Homosexuality and the Western Christian Tradition* (London: Longmans Green and Company, 1955), pp. 83–83.

19. For discussion see M. L. Laistner, *Christianity and Pagan Culture in the Later Roman Empire* (Ithaca: Cornell University Press, 1951), p. 87 n, 3, 94, 111 n, 57, 136 n, 11, 110 n, 56.

20. St. Basil, *Letters,* CCXVII, 62, in *The Fathers of the Church,* trans. Agnes Clare Way (New York: Fathers of the Church, 1955), vol. 28.

21. St. Gregory of Nyssa, *Epistula Canonica,* 4, in *PG,* XLV, 227.

22. Laistner, *Christianity and Pagan Culture,* p. 81.

23. *The Theodosian Code,* trans. Clyde Pharr (Princeton: Princeton University Press, 1952), pp. 231–32.

24. For discussion see Derrick Sherwin Bailey, *Homosexuality and the Western Christian Tradition,* p. 70, and Vern L. Bullough, *Sexual Variance in Society and History* (New York: Wiley Interscience, 1976).

25. W. G. Holmes, *The Age of Justinian and Theodora*, 2 vols. (London: G. Bell and Company, 1912), I, 121.

26. *The Theodosian Code*, p. 232.

27. Evagrius, *Ecclesiastical History*, III, 39–41 (London: Henry G. Bohn, 1854).

28. See, for example, *Codex*, IX, ix, *"Ad Legem de Adulteriis et de Stupro"*; *Digest*, XLVIII, v. 35.1 *"stuprum . . . puero;"* *Digest*, XLVIII, v. 9 *"cum masculo"*; *Institutes*, IV, xviii, 4, and *Novellae* 77 and 141, in the *Corpus Juris Civilis*, 3 vols. (Berlin: Weidmann, 1959).

29. *Institutes*, IV, xviii, 4. There are several English translations, including one by J. B. Moyle (Oxford: Clarendon Press, 1937), and by Thomas Collett Sandars (London: Longmans, Green and Company, 1910).

30. See Bailey, *Homosexuality and the Western Christian Tradition*, pp. 66–67.

31. *Novel* 77.

32. *Novel* 141.

33. Procopius, *Anecdota*, XI, 36, trans. H. B. Dewing (London: William Heinemann, 1940).

34. *Basilicorum*, LX, 36.46 (Amsterdam: A. M. Hakkert, 1962).

35. Ernest Barker, *Social and Political Thought in Byzantium* (Oxford: Clarendon Press, 1957), p. 124. See also Pletho, *On Laws*, Book III.

36. The texts of the Visigothic laws are in *MGH*, *Leges* I. For other laws dealing with sex, see *Lex Ribuaria*, *MGH*, *Leges*, V, 216–31; *Leges Almanorum, Lex Baiwariorum, MGH, Leges*, Sectio I, V, pars. 1 & 2; *Lex Salica, MGH, Leges*, Sectio VIII, IV, par. II; *Pactus Legis Saliciae, MGH, Leges*, Sectio VIII, IV, par. 1; *Lex Ribuaria, MGH, Leges*, Sectio VIII, II, par. 2; *Lex Frisonum*, and *Lex Burgundionum*, in *MGH, Leges*, III; *Leges Saxonum*, and *Lex Thuringorum, MGH, Leges*, V (Hannover: Hahn, 1875), and *Ancient Laws and Institutes of England*, ed. B. Thorpe (London: Commissioners of the Public Records, 1840), pp. 1–189.

37. Jean Brissaud, *A History of French Private Law*, trans. Rapelje Howell (Boston: Little, Brown and Company, 1912), p. 136.

38. See, for example, the Laws of King Alfred, c. 42, in *Ancient Laws and Institutes of England*, p. 40.

Chapter 3

Chaste Marriage and Clerical Celibacy

1. A shorter version of this paper was presented at the meeting of the Medieval Institute of Western Michigan, Kalamazoo, in May 1974.

2. J. E. Lynch, "Marriage and Celibacy of the Clergy: The Discipline of the Western Church, a Historico-canonical Synopsis," *The Jurist*, 32 (1972), Part I, 14–38; Part II, 189–212, and J. P. Caudet, *Mariage et célibat dans le service pastoral de l'église* (Paris: Ed. de l'Orante, 1967).

3. *Didascalia et Constitutiones Apostolorum*, II, 2, ed. F. X. Funk (Paderborn, 1905), 33–34.

4. Eusebius of Caesarea, *Historia Ecclesiastica*, V, 24, 6 in *Sources Chrétiennes*, ed. Sagnard 41, 68. Henceforth cited as *SC*. R. Gryson, *Les origines du célibat écclésiastique du première au septième siècles* (Gembloux, ed. J. Duculot, SA., 1970), 34–56, has combined the available sources to demonstrate that examples of unmarried clergy are rare in the first three centuries and that many of the clergy can be shown to have fathered children.

5. *NPNF*, series 1, VII, 461. The translator (Gifford) points out that whether or not the lady can be identified as the wife of Gregory of Nyssa, she was indubitably married to a priest.

6. Gregory the Great, *Regula Pastoralis*, 27, *PL*, 77.

232   Notes

7. *Penitential of Theodore of Tarsus,* XIV, 4, in John T. McNeill and Helen M. Gamer, *Medieval Handbooks of Penance* (New York: Columbia University Press, 1938).

8. *Dialogus,* I, 10, *PL,* 77.

9. The various forms of ritual purity in use throughout the world have been surveyed by John Main, *Religious Chastity, an ethnological study* (New York, 1913). Chapter 16 on temporary continence for cult purposes is particularly useful. R. Gryson, *Les origines du célibat,* has been the most thorough investigator for our period, though J. E. Lynch, "Marriage and Celibacy," and E. Schillebeeckx, *Celibacy* (New York: Sheed and Ward, 1968) pursue the same line of thought.

10. Gryson, *Les origines du célibat,* 42.

11. *Refutations of All Heresies,* IX, 8, *ANF,* V, 131.

12. F. Bouché-Leclerq, "Les lois demographiques d'Auguste," *Revu Historique* 57 (1895), 241-92.

13. Tertullian, *Exhortatio Castitatis,* 7 in *CCSL,* II, 2, 10, stated that the practice of marital rights numbs the mind to spiritual experience. Jerome, *Contra Jovinianum,* I, 41, went so far as to claim that only virgins receive the counsel of God. Epiphanius of Salamine, *Abrégé de la foi catholique* 21, 3-11, was one of the first to rank virgins at the top of the Christian hierarchy, followed by chaste widows and then faithful married persons. See Gryson, *Les origines du célibat,* 113.

14. Elvira, c. 33; clergy were forbidden to live with any woman but a sister, mother, or virgin daughter consecrate to God. *Concilios Visigóticos e Hispano-Romanos* (henceforth *CVH*), ed. J. Vives (Barcelona-Madrid, 1963), 7; S. Laeuchli, *Power and Sexuality: the Emergence of Canon Law at the Synod of Elvira* (Philadelphia: Temple University Press, 1972), 162, presents the action as part of a larger psychological crisis. Both Lynch, "Marriage and Celibacy" and Gryson, *Les origines du célibat,* reject these extreme views and implicitly emphasize ritual purity.

15. Socrates, *Ecclesiastical History,* I, 11, trans. A. C. Zenos, *NPNF,* 50.

16. *Demonstratio evangelica,* I, 9, trans. W. J. Ferrar in Eusebius, *Proof of the Gospel* (London, 1920).

17. *De officiis ministrorum,* I, 50, *PL* 16, 21, 107.

18. Paulinus, *Epistolae,* ed. Hartel, *CSEL,* 39. See also letters 38, 44, 51 addressed to similar couples and 20 and 30 to Sulpicius Severus who formed a spiritual marriage with his mother-in-law after the death of his wife.

19. Augustine, *Epistolae,* no. 27, 33, ed. S. W. Parsons, *Fathers of the Church* (New York, 1951), p. 88.

20. For example, the Council of Tours (567 A.D.), c. 14, in *Concilia Galliae* (hereafter cited as *CG*), I, ed. C. Munier, in *CCSL* 148 and 148A et al. (Turnhoet, Belg., 1963), 191 and a grant by the Bishop of Lucca in 725, presenting a small monastery and hospice to a priest named Romuald and his wife in *Antiquitates Italicae Medii Aevi Dissert,* ed. Muratori (Milan, 1738-42), 74: see also *PL,* 61, 895-96.

21. Andrieu, *Les Ordines Romani* (Louvain, 1956), 4, 140-41. See also the texts compiled by Lynch in "Marriage and Celibacy," 30.

22. *Ad Gallos Episcopos, Epistola* 10, 3, *PL* 13, 1187. The standard attribution to Siricius is defended by Lynch in "Marriage and Celibacy" against Gryson's suggestion that it was written by Pope Damasus, *Les origines du célibat,* 127-31.

23. Letter to Rusticus of Narbonne, 3, *PL* 54, 1204.

24. *Epistola* 2, to Vitricius of Rouen, 9, *PL* 20, 475-77; also to Exsuperius of Toulouse, *Epistola* 6, 1, 2-4, *PL* 20, 496-498.

25. *Epistola* 1, 20, in *MGH Epist.* 1-1, 76, 31-32; 9, 110; *Epistola* 2, 1; 116, 21-24.

26. Agde (506 A.D.), c. 16, in *Concilia Galliae (CG)* in *CCSL* 148, 125; Epaone (517 A.D.), c. 37, *CG* II, ed. C. De Clercq, *CCSL,* 148A, 34, 233; Arles III, c. 2, *CG* II, 43, 16; 44, 23.

27. Orleans I (511 A.D.) c. 13, *CG* II, 8, 102-105.

28. Orleans IV (541 A.D.), c. 17, *CG* II, 136, 103-105; deposed priests were suspected of occupying the same chamber as their wives.

29. *Epistola* 105, *PG,* 66, 1485, cited by Gryson, *Les origines du célibat,* 50.

30. c. 17 *CG,* 148A, 136.

31. *Libri octo miraculorum in gloria confessorum,* 77, ed. Krusch, *MGH SS Mer.* 1, 794.

32. c. 6, *CVH* 40, and texts gathered by Gryson, *Les origines du célibat,* p. 29.

33. *Vita S. Remigii,* 42–43, *PL* 125.

34. Lynch, "Marriage and Celibacy," 31.

36. The Council of Worms (868 A.D.) c. 9, *Sac Conc.* 15, 871, and *MGH Capit.* I, 95–96 n, 22, forbade any priest or deacon to have a woman living in the house except under canonical license.

36. Saint Boniface, *Epistolae 50–51, MGH Epist.* Selec. 1, 80–92.

37. Mantionis, Episcopus Catalaunensis, *Epistola ad Fulconem Remenses, PL* 131, 23.

38. Adalbert of Bremen urged his clergy to free themselves if they could and, if not, to live modestly with their wives (11th century), Magister Adam, *Gesta Hamburgensis,* 29, schol. 77, ed. Lappenberg, *MGH SS* 7, 3, 346.

39. I Cor. 7:36. The debate as to whether or not the Corinthians were practicing spiritual marriage turns on the almost incomprehensible statement that appears to give some man the power to determine whether or not a girl might remain a virgin. Achelis, *Virgines subintroductae* (Leipzig: 1902) argued that it referred to spiritual marriage but de Labriolle, "Le mariage spirituel dans l'antiquité chrétienne," *Revue Historique* 137 (1921):204–225, denied that Paul or any of the Church Fathers approved the dangerous practice. See also von Allmen, *Maris et femmes d'après Saint Paul* (Paris: Delachaux et Niestlé, 1951) and, by the same author, *Le mariage chrétien selon Saint Paul* (Paris: Ed. Levain, 1953.)

40. Achelis, *Virgines Subintroductae,* collected a series of texts demonstrating the existence of the practice in Spain, Syria, Persia, Gaul, and elsewhere. He believed that the practices stemmed from Paul's time, but de Labriolle, "Le mariage spirituel," showed that it was new to the third and fourth centuries.

41. *Adversus Haereses* I, 13, 7, trans. Roberts and Donaldson, *ANF,* I, I, 336, and I, 6, 3; 324.

42. *Exhortatio Castitatis,* 12, *CCSL* II, 2.

43. Canon 27, *CVH* 6.

44. Eusebius, *Historia Ecclesiastica,* 7, 30, 12–41, *SC* 41, 217.

45. *Epistola* 4, 1, 1; 3, 3; 4, 1: ed. Hartel, *CSEL,* 3–2, 472; 22, 473; 5:475.

46. *Epistola* 169, trans. Agnes C. Way, *Fathers of the Church* (New York, 1951), vol. 13.

47. *Les Cohabitations suspects,* ed. and trans. J. Dumortier, *Nouvelle Collection de Textes et Documents* (Paris: Société du Guillaume Budé, 1955).

48. *Demonstratio* VI, 4, *NPNF* XIII, 366.

49. Sulpicius Severus, *Dialogus* I, *CSEL,* ed. Halm, 1–2.

50. *Dialogus* III, 7, *PL* 77.

51. *Codex Justinianus,* Novella 6, 5, ed. Schoell-Kroll, 42–43. The phraseology has been explored by A. Guillamont, "Le nom des agapètes," *Vigiliae Christianae* 23 (1969):30–37.

52. Ibid, 6, 30.

53. Clerics were forbidden to live with virgins, and both virgins and consecrated widows were forbidden to marry by the Councils of Agde, c. 10–11, *CG,* I, 199; 152–200; Orléans, c. 29 *CG,* II, 12, 170–72; Epaone, c. 20–29, *CG* II, 159–62; Clermont, c. 16, *CG* II, 109–94–111; Orléans V, c. 3, *CG* II, 149, 26–35. They were even forbidden to marry if they claimed that they had taken the veil in order to avoid forcible abduction, Tours II, c. 19, *CG* II, 20 (alluding to laws of Childebert, Clotair, and Charibert on the same subject). Visigothic law punished nuns for marrying, III, 1, 2, ed. Zeumer, *MGH Leges* I, 209 (Hannover, 1902). In 721, Gregory II called a synod for the special purpose of condemning incestuous unions, in which he included the marriages of nuns and priests' widows, C. J. Hefele and H. Leclercq, *Histoire des Conciles* (Paris: 1909), vol. 3[1], 597. In 774, the Duke of Benevento, *Capitulare Arechis Principia Beneventi,* c. 12, ed. P. Canciani, *Barbarorum Leges Antiquas* (Venice, 1781), I, 262, ordered the cloistering of widows who had taken a vow of chastity to prevent them from

leading a debauched life under cover of the vow ("quaedam muliercule, defunctis viris, maritalis dominatire soluti, licentius proprii arbitrii libertatum iruentur").

54. Palladius, *Lausiac History,* 41, 5. A. Meyer mentioned husbands and wives in the convent at Rome, though Mary Bateson thought he might have been referring to couples living at home, "Origin and early history of double monasteries," *Royal Historical Society Transactions* 13 (1899):141.

55. Justin Martyr, *Apologia* I, 15, trans. Roberts and Donaldson, *ANF,* Series I, 167; Athengoras, *Supplique pour les Chrétiennes,* 33, *SC* 3, 161; Minucius, *Octavius,* 31, 5, *CSEL* 2, 45.

56. *Pastor,* Vision II, 3, *SC* 53, 89.

57. *Exhortatio Castitatis,* XIII, 4, *CSEL* II, 2, 1035.

58. *Letter to Polycarp* 5, *SC,* 10, 171.

59. Palladius, *Lausiac History,* 41–43.

60. Paulinus, *Epistolae,* no. 18, to Victicius, Bishop of Rouen.

61. *Expositio Evangelii secundum Lucam,* 1, 44, *CSEL* 32–34, 39.

62. Hugo Koch, *Adhuc Virgo: Mariens Jungfrauschaft und Ehe in der alt kirchlichen überlieferung bis zum Ende des 4. Jahrhunderts.* (Tübingen, 1929), attributes that argument not only to Tertullian, *De Carne Christi,* 23, *CCSL* II, pt. 2, 886–89, where it is clearly stated, but also to Irenaeus, *Adversus Haeresus* III, 22.4, *SC,* 34.

63. *Adversus Helvidium: Liber de perpetua virginitate B. Mariae,* 17, *PL,* 23, 193.

64. *De Sancta Virginitate,* 4, ed. J. Zycha, *CSEL* 34², 28.

65. Ambrose, *De Institutione Virginibus,* 42, *PL* 16, 331.

66. *De Nuptiis et Concupiscentiae,* 11, 12, *PL* 44, 420.

67. *Etymologies,* 9, 7, *PL* 82, 365.

68. *Adversus Helvidium, PL* 23, 214.

69. *De Conjugiis Adulterinus,* 1, 3, *PL* 40, 453; *De Bono Conjugali,* 1, 6, *PL* 40, 377; *De Sermone Dominum in Monte secundum Mattheum* 1, 15, *CCSL* 35, 43.

70. *De Continentia,* 26, 27, *PL* 42, 367.

71. *Ad Uxorem,* 1, 6, *CCSL,* 1, 380.

72. *Epistolae* 2, *PL* 61, 733.

73. *Epistolae,* 127, *PL* 33, 483.

74. *De Fide,* 1, 3–44, *PL* 65, 733.

75. *Epistolae* 45 and 50, *PL* 33, 483. For praise of chaste marriage, see *Regula Pastoralis,* 3, 27, *PL* 77, 1025; *Homilies, PL* 76, 1273.

76. Bede, *Historia Ecclesiasticae,* 6, 11, *PL* 95, 188.

77. *Theodosiani Libri XVI,* ed. Mommsen and Meyer (Berlin, 1954), 18, 16.1, p. 418. See also 9, 25.2, p. 479.

78. Gregory of Nyssa, *Life of Macrina,* trans. V. W. Callahan *Fathers of the Church,* 58.

79. *Lausiac History,* 148. Also, Ibid., 137, on Olympias who was also believed to have preserved her virginity throughout her brief marriage by unknown devices.

80. Ibid., 142. The author of the *Vie de Sainte Mélanie,* trans. D. Gorce (Paris, 1962), c. 8, was convinced that the initiative was always hers.

81. Bede, *Historiae Ecclesiasticae,* 4, 19, *PL* 85, 201.

82. Leonard J. Friedman, *Virgin Wives: a study of unconsummated marriages* (London: Tavistock Publications, 1962). Introduction, ix.

83. Jo Ann McNamara, "Sexual Equality and the Cult of Virginity in Early Christian Thought," *Feminist Studies* 3 (1976):145–158.

84. Jo Ann McNamara and Suzanne F. Wemple, "Marriage and Divorce in the Frankish Kingdom," in *Women in Medieval Society,* ed. Susan M. Stuard (Philadelphia: University of Pennsylvania Press, 1976), 95–124.

85. The Councils of Verberie (756), c. 21 and Compiègne, c. 5 and 16, *MGH Leges II,* 39.

86. The letter of Gregory II to Saint Boniface in 726, *MGH Epist.* 3, 276, suggesting that a marriage that lacked conjugal relations as a result of the wife's illness might be dissolved was

interpreted by Rolandus (later Alexander III) in the twelfth century to mean that the marriage had in fact never been consummated: *Summa Magister Rolandus,* c. 32, ed. Thaner (Innsbruck, 1874), 181.

87. *De nuptiis Stephani, PL* 126, 145.

88. *Responsa ad Consulta Bulgarorum,* ed. Hardouin, *Concilia,* V, 354.

89. *De divortio, PL* 125, 717 ABC. For further discussion, see J. Calmette, *La diplomatie carolingienne* (Paris, 1901) *Bibliothèque École des Hautes Études,* 35.

90. William of Malmesbury, *Gesta Regum Anglorum,* 2, c. 197, *Rerum Britannicarum Medii Aevi Scriptores,* 239.

91. *Chronicon, MGH SS* 7, 62. Hugo Koch, *Die Ehe Kaiser Heinrichs II mit Kunigunde* (Köln, 1908), argued that Henry hoped to have children and only gradually came to accept that he would not. The argument was based on Koch's interpretation of a letter to the Bishop of Wurzburg, Jaffé, *Biblioteca Rerum Germanicarum* 5, 478, and of a remark in the *Chronicon* of Thietmar von Merseburg, ed. Kurze, 3¹, 152. The evidence is, however, highly equivocal and at most might show no more than that Henry did not wish to make his private circumstances public and therefore avoided questions about the disposition of his inheritance. See also, Philipp Oppenheim, *Die Consecratio Virginum als Geistesgeschichtlichen Probleme* (Rome, 1943), 70.

92. *Vita Sanctae Cunegundis, MGH SS* 4, 105.

93. The councils of Bourges (1031), *Sac Conc* 19, 503; Compostella (1056), *Sac Conc* 19, 858; Tours (1060), *Sac Conc* 19, 927, adopted such measures and Leo IX was said to have ordered that the "concubines of Roman priests" be made slaves in the Lateran palace: Bernold, *Chronicon, MGH SS,* 5, 426.

94. Mansi, *Sac Conc* 19, 897.

95. c. 21, *Sac Conc* 21.

96. c. 7, *Sac Conc* 21; the tests to support the decision were supplied by Gratian, *Decretum. Corpus Iuris Canonici (CIC),* ed. Friedberg (Leipzig, 1876–81). Secunda pars, causa 27, q. 1, c. 1–43.

97. A. Esmein, *Le mariage en droit canonique* (Paris, 1891), 269, believed that this marked the last appearance of virgins and consecrated widows who lived in the world without their families (or even with them) unregulated by ecclesiastical authority.

98. *Epistola* 14, *PL* 145, 451–54.

99. A. Overmann, *Gräfin Mathilde von Tuscien* (Innsbruck: Minerva GMBH, 1895) 241–46, examined the dubious and muddy texts that relate the story of this first marriage without reaching a satisfactory conclusion. The pope simply told her not to abandon those who belonged to her, which Overmann, Ibid., 244, interpreted as a refusal of divorce.

100. *Opuscula* 56, 5, *PL* 145, 815. R. Bezzola, *Les origines et la formation de la littérature courtoise en occident (500–1200),* (Paris, 1944), 293–94.

101. *Epistolae collectae,* 11, ed. Jaffé, 532, December 16, 1074, *PL* 145.

Chapter 4

The Prostitute in the Early Middle Ages

This paper was presented at Kalamazoo, Michigan, at a conference sponsored by the Medieval Institute of Western Michigan University. It was printed in *Studies in Medieval Culture,* X (1977), 9–17, and reprinted with permission with slight changes.

1. Horace, *Satires,* I, ii, 32–37, ed. and trans. H. Rushton Fairclough, reprinted (London: Heinemann, 1966).

2. See also Hans Licht, *Sexual Life in Ancient Greece,* trans. J. H. Freese (London: Routledge & Kegan Paul, 1932), p. 337. The statement appears in a scholiast of Horace's works.

3. Cicero, *Pro Caelio,* XX, 48, ed. and trans. by R. Radner, rev. (London: William Heinemann, 1965).

4. See Vern L. Bullough and Bonnie Bullough, *Prostitution* (New York: Crown Publishers, 1978), pp. 47-57.

5. Propertius, *Elegies,* IV, 5, 11, ed. and trans. by H. F. Butler, reprinted (London: William Heinemann, 1962).

6. See Propertius, and Catullus, and Tibullus, *Elegies,* trans. J. P. Postgate, rev. (London: William Heinemann, 1962).

7. Juvenal, *Satires,* VI, 114-129, ed. and trans. G. J. Ramsay, reprinted (London: William Heinemann, 1940).

8. Livy, *History,* I, 57-60, ed. and trans. B. O. Foster, Evan T. Sage, and F. G. Moore, 14 vols. (London: William Heinemann, 1935-1959).

9. Lucretius, *De Rerum Natura,* ed. and trans. by W. H. D. Rouse (London: William Heinemann, 1924).

10. Tacitus, *Annals,* 85, ed. and trans. John Jackson (London: William Heinemann, 1956); Suetonius, "Tiberius," XXXV, 2, *Lives of the Caesars,* ed. and trans. by J. C. Rolfe, 2 vols. (London: William Heinemann, 1950-51). Suetonius implies the legislation dated only from the reign of Tiberius.

11. Livy, *History,* XXV, ii.

12. *Pauly Wissowa Real Encyclopaedie der classischen Altertumswissenschaft* (Stuttgart: J. B. Metzler, 1914-1961), XII, 1942 f., XV, 1023-1025.

13. Aulius Gellius, *Attic Nights,* IV, iii, ed. and trans. by John C. Rolfe, 3 vols. (reprinted London: William Heinemann, 1952-1960).

14. Carl G. Burns, *Fontes Juris Romani,* ed. Otto Gradenwitz, 7th ed. (Tubingen: I. C. B. Mohrii, 1909), 1, 18, 23, 123.

15. P. D. King, *Law and Society in the Visigothic Kingdom* (Cambridge: University Press, 1972), p. 118.

16. Ibid., p. 202 n, 5.

17. Ibid., p. 241.

18. *The Lombard Laws,* trans. with an introduction Katherine Fischer Drew (Philadelphia: University of Pennsylvania Press, 1973), "Rothair's Edict," 198, p. 90.

19. *The Burgundian Code,* XXXIII, trans. by Katherine Fischer Drew (Philadelphia: University of Pennsylvania Press, 1972), p. 45.

20. St. Augustine, *De Ordine,* II, iv, 12, in Migne, *PL* vol. XXXII.

21. *Constitutiones Apostolicae,* II, xxvi, in Migne, *PG* vol. I.

22. Thomas Aquinas, *Summa Theologiae,* II-II, Q.X, Art. II; II-II, Q. LX, 2 and 5; LXXXVII, 2, ad 2, and II-II, CXVIII, 8, ad 4, in the edition trans. the English Dominicans, 22 vols. (London: Burns, Oates, and Washburne, 1922).

23. For a treatment of some of the quandaries involved in this see James Brundage, "The Crusader's Wife: A Canonistic Quandary," *Studia Gratiana* XII (1967):425-442; Brundage has also written on prostitution later in this book.

24. Hostiensis (Henricus de Segusio), *In quinque Decretalium libri commentaria,* 5 vols. in 2 (Venice: apud Iuntas, 1581, reprinted Turin: Bottega d'Erasmo, 1965), *Lectura* to *X* 4.13.11, no. 2 (in vol. IV, fol. 27ra)

25. Ibid., *Lectura* to *X* 3.30.23, no. 3 (vol. III, vol. 100vb) and 4.1.20, no. 5 (IV., fol. 6^{nb}). See also *The Summa Parisiensis on the Decretum Gratiani,* c. 32, c. 1 ad. v. tolerabiliùs, ed. Terrence P. McLaughlin (Toronto: Pontifical Institute of Medieval Studies, 1952). See also Brundage's chapter in this book, pp. 118-128.

26. *The Theodosian Code,* Book XV, titulus 8, "De Lenonibus (procurers)." See the edition translated by Clyde Pharr in collaboration with Theresa S. Davidson and Mary B. Pharr (Princeton: Princeton University Press, 1952), p. 435.

27. *Digest, Lib.* XII, titulus v, and *Novella,* XIV, Collatio, III, titulus i, "De Lenonibus," in *Corpus Juris Civilis,* ed. Rudolf Shoel and Juilelem Kroll, 3 vols. (Berlin: Weidmann, 1959).

28. *Novella,* XIV, "Proemium," and Joannes Malalas, *Chronographia,* XVII, 5-6, ed. Ludwig Dindorf (Bonn: Impensis Ed. Weberi, 1831), pp. 440-41; Procopius, *Anecdota,* trans. H. B. Dewing (London: William Heinemann, 1935), and Procopius, *Buildings,* I, 9, ed. and trans. H. B. Dewing and Glanville Downey (London: William Heinemann, 1954).

29. For a discussion of these institutions, see Demetrious J. Consantelos, *Byzantine Philanthropy and Social Welfare* (New Brunswick, N.J.: Rutgers University Press, 1968), pp. 196, 233.

30. Michael Psellus, *Chronographia,* Book IV, "Michael IV," 36, trans. E. R. A. Sewter (New Haven: Yale University Press, 1953), pp. 73-74.

31. Luke 7:37.

32. Matt. 21:31.

33. Jerome, *Vita Pauli,* in *PL,* XXIII.

34. Ambrose, *De Virginibus,* II, 4, in *PL,* XVI.

35. See his life by Gregory of Nyssa.

36. The story is rather delightfully translated by Helen Waddell, *The Desert Fathers,* reprinted (Ann Arbor: University of Michigan Press, 1957), pp. 190-201.

37. *Butler's Lives of the Saints,* edited, revised and supplemented by Herbert Thurston and Donald Attwater, 4 vols. (London: Burns and Oates, 1956), II, 14-15.

38. Ibid., III, 267-68.

39. Waddell, *Desert Fathers,* pp. 171-88; Butler, *Lives of Saints,* IV, 59-61.

40. Ibid., IV, 426-28.

41. Hroswitha, "Paphnutius" *The Plays of Hroswitha,* trans. Christopher St. John (London: Chatto and Winters, 1923), pp. 75-100.

42. Jacques de Vitry, *Historia occidentalis,* ed. Hinnebusch, c. 8, pp. 99-100; See also Milton R. Gutsch, "A Twelfth-Century Preacher—Fulk of Neuilly," *The Crusades and Other Essays in Honor of Dana C. Munro* (New York: Appleton-Century-Crofts, 1928), pp. 190-91.

43. Max Heimbucher, *Die Orden und Kongregationen der katholischen Kirche,* 2 vols., 3rd ed. (Munich: F. Schovingh, 1965), I, 646-648.

44. Bernard Guillemain, *La court pontifical d'Avignon, 1309-1376: étude d'une société* (Paris: E. De Boccard, 1966), pp. 485-86.

45. John of Joinville, *Life of St. Louis,* CXLII, 725, trans. Rene Hague (New York: Sheed and Ward, 1955).

46. Richard Lewinsohn, *A History of Sexual Customs,* trans. Alexander Mayce (New York: Harper & Brothers, 1958), pp. 147-48.

47. Gratian, *Decretum,* Causa 32, quaestio 1, canon 2, and C. 33, 8.2, C.11-12, in *Corpus Juris Canonici,* ed. Emil Friedberg, 2. vols. (Leipzig: B. Tauschnitz, 1879; reprinted Graz: Akademische Druck-und-Verlagsantalt, 1959).

48. *Decretalis D. Gregorii pape IX suae integrati una cum glossi,* Liber 4, Titulus 1, canon 20 in *Corpus Juris Canonici* and see also Brundage on prostitution, Chapter 14 of this book.

49. George F. Fort, *History of Medical Economy during the Middle Ages* (New York: J. W. Bouton, 1883), p. 344.

Chapter 5

Transvestism in the Middle Ages

Originally published as "Transvestism in the Middle Ages: A Sociological Analysis," *American Journal of Sociology* 79 (1974), 1381-1394. Reprinted with some modifications by permission of the University of Chicago Press.

1. Magnus Hirschfeld, *Die Transvestiten* (Berlin: Alfred Pulvermacher, 1910).

2. Havelock Ellis, *Studies in the Psychology of Sex*, 2 vols. (New York: Random House, 1936). He includes a long study on eonism in vol. 2.

3. David O. Cauldwell, *Transvestism* (New York: Sexology Corporation, 1956); Eugene de Savitsch, *Homosexuality, Transvestism and Change of Sex* (London: William Heinemann, 1958); Robert J. Stoller, *Sex and Gender* (New York: Science House, 1968). The most recent study is Deborah Heller Feinbloom, *Transvestites and Transsexuals* (New York: Dell Publishing Company, 1976).

4. Stoller, *Sex and Gender,* pp. 183–87.

5. Edward Sagarin, *Odd Man In: Societies of Deviants in America* (Chicago: Quadrangle, 1969) and H. Taylor Buckner, *Deviant Group Organizations,* (M.A. thesis, University of California, 1964).

6. Deut. 22:5.

7. See Vern L. Bullough, *The Subordinate Sex* (Champagne-Urbana: University of Illinois Press, 1973), and especially "Medieval Medical and Scientific Views of Women," *Viator* 4 (1973):485–501.

8. Thomas Aquinas, *Summa Theologica,* I, Part I, 92, "The Production of Women," I, ii (New York: Benziger Brothers, 1947).

9. Philo, *On the Creation,* ed. and trans. F. H. Colson and G. H. Whittaker (London: William Heinemann, 1963), pp. 69–70, 151, 162, and *Questions and Answers on Genesis,* ed. and trans. by Ralph Marcus (London: William Heinemann, 1961), I, 40. See also Richard A. Baer, Jr., *Philo's Use of the Categories Male and Female* (Leiden: E. J. Brill, 1970), pp. 46, 51.

10. Jerome, *Commentarius in Epistolam ad Ephesios,* III, v (658), in *PL,* XXVI, 567.

11. Ambrose, *Expositionis in Evangelius secundum Lucum libri X,* 161 (1539) in *PL* XV, 1938.

12. H. Delehaye, *The Legends of the Saints,* trans. V. M. Crawford (Notre Dame: University of Notre Dame Press, 1961), p. 189.

13. Gregory of Tours, *History of the Franks,* Book X, cap. 16, trans. with an introduction by O. M. Dalton, 2. vols. (Oxford: Clarendon Press, 1927), II, 449.

14. Where possible I have utilized *Butler's Lives of the Saints,* edited, revised and supplemented by Herbert Thurston and Donald Attwater, 4 vols. (New York: P. J. Kennedy & Sons, 1956), for references since it is readily available to most readers. For more scholarly readers I have referred to the massive collection of saints' lives in original languages published under the title of *Acta Sanctorum* (Antwerp: 1643, in progress), which is arranged according to saints' days. The story of St. Pelagia can be found in *Butler's Lives of the Saints,* IV, 59–61; *Acta Sanctorum,* October IV, 248, and there is also an interesting account in Helen Waddell, *The Desert Fathers,* reprinted (Ann Arbor: University of Michigan Press, 1957), pp. 178-88.

15. *Butler's Lives of the Saints,* IV, 59–61; *Acta Sanctorum,* July IV, 287, October IV, 24, and Delehaye, *Legends of Saints,* 197–99.

16. *Butler's Lives of the Saints,* I, 313–14, and *Acta Sanctorum,* July IV, 149.

17. Herman Usener, *Legenden der heiligen Pelagia* (Bonn, 1879), p. 20.

18. Delehaye, *Legends of Saints,* pp. 204–06.

19. Marie Delcourt, *Hermaphrodite,* trans. from the French by Jennifer Nicholson (London: Studio Books, 1956), pp. 90–99.

20. *Butler's Lives of the Saints,* I, 33, and *Acta Sanctorum,* January I, 258.

21. Ibid., October IV, 99, and *Butler's Lives of the Saints,* IV, 69–70.

22. Ibid., IV, 612.

23. Ibid., I, 4–5, and *Acta Sanctorum,* February II, 535.

24. Ibid., September IV, 546, and *Butler's Lives of the Saints,* III, 623–25.

25. Ibid., II, 546–47, and *Acta Sanctorum,* March, II.

26. Ibid., September IV, 546, and *Butler's Lives of the Saints,* III, 623–25.

27. Ibid., III, 538, and *Acta Sanctorum,* September, III.

28. *Butler's Lives of the Saints,* II, 135.

29. Ibid., III, 151–52, and *Acta Sanctorum*, July IV, 50.

30. For a popular discussion of the saint, see Gillian Edward, *Uncumber and Pantaloon* (New York: E. P. Dutton, 1969).

31. *Butler's Lives of the Saints*, IV, 36–37, *Acta Sanctorum*, October III, 162.

32. Ibid., February III, 174.

33. There is a massive literature on Pope Joan, divided generally into pro-Joan, anti-Joan, and scholarly. Among the pro-Joan advocates was Alexander Cooke, *Pope Joan* (London: Blunt and Baring, 1610), who is also anti-Catholic. A more recent pro-Joan account is Clement Wood, *The Woman Who Was Pope* (New York: William Faro, 1931). A tongue-in-cheek pro-Joan appears in the semi-fictionalized retelling of her story by Ira Glackens, *Pope Joan* (New York: Coleridge Press). A good, brief summary of the scholarship and sources of the legend can be found in *The New Catholic Encyclopedia*, 15 vols. (New York, 1967). Horace K. Mann, *The Lives of the Popes* (London: Kegan Paul, 1925), II, 325, includes a brief summary of the coinage evidence against her existence. Perhaps the most complete scholarly examination was by Johann Dollinger, *Papstfabeln des Mittelalters*, 2nd ed. (Stuttgart, 1890).

34. *Trial of Jeanne d'Arc*, trans. W. P. Barrett (London: George Routledge and Sons, 1931), p. 152.

35. Ibid., p. 158.

36. *The Trial of Joan of Arc, the verbatim reports of the proceedings from the Orléans Manuscript*, trans. with an introduction and notes by W. S. Scott (Westport, Conn.: Associated Booksellers, 1956), p. 14. For the most complete examination of Joan of Arc, see the series of volumes under the title of *Documents et Recherches Relatifs à Jeanne la Pucelle* (Paris: Descel de Brouwer, ongoing).

37. For a discussion of this and references, see Joseph S. Tunison, *Dramatic Traditions of the Dark Ages*, reprinted (Folcroft, Pa.: Folcroft Press, 1969).

38. Quoted in Karl Mantzius, *A History of Theatrical Art*, II, *The Middle Ages*, trans. Louise von Cossell (New York: Peter Smith, 1937), p. 89.

39. See J. J. Jusserand, *English Wayfaring Life in the Middle Ages*, trans. Lucy Toulmin Smith (London: T. Fisher Unwin, n.d.), pp. 177–218.

40. Rosamond Gilder, *Enter the Actress: The First Women in the Theatre*, reprinted (New York: Theatre Arts Books, 1960), pp. 46 ff.

41. Quoted in Mantzius, *History of Theatrical Art*, II, pp. 270–71.

42. See Samuel L. Sumberg, *The Nuremberg Schembart Carnival* (New York: AMS Press, 1966), pp. 82–84, 104, 167.

43. Vern Bullough and Bonnie Bullough, *Care of the Sick: The Emergence of Modern Nursing* (New York: Prodist Press, 1978).

Chapter 6

The Sin against Nature and Homosexuality

1. For some background on this, see Derrick Sherwin Bailey, *Homosexuality and the Western Christian Tradition* (London: Longmans, Green and Company, 1955), and John T. Noonan, *Contraception: A History of Its Treatment by the Catholic Theologians and Canonists* (Cambridge: the Belknap Press of Harvard University Press, 1966). Both of these works are invaluable. For the carry-over of medieval definitions into modern law, see Alex K. Gigeroff, *Sexual Deviations in the Criminal Law* (Toronto: University of Toronto Press for the Clarke Institute of Psychiatry, 1968), and for a specific example, see William Blackstone, *Commentaries on the Laws of England*, new edition in four volumes with notes by John Frederick Archibold (London: William Reed, 1811), IV, 215. For a more specialized study, see Michael Goodich, *The Unmentionable Vice: Homosexuality in the Late Medieval Period* (Santa Barbara, Calif.: ABC CLIO, 1979).

2. Rom. 1:24-27. The translation is from the Authorized Version. The Douay translation differs only slightly and both use the term "against nature," which appears in the Vulgate. Italics are mine.

3. Matthew Black and H. H. Rowley, *Peake's Commentary on the Bible* (London: Thomas Nelson, 1962), par. 817 b, hold that the passage refers to homosexuality as does Otto Michael, *Der Brief an die Romer* (Gottingen: Van de Hoeck & Ruprecht, 1955), p. 59. A much broader interpretation that would include all sexual activities not leading to procreation is given by Herman L. Strack and Paul Billerbeck, *Kommentar zum Neuen Testament auf Talmud und Midrash,* 3rd ed. (Munich: Beck, 1961), III, *Die Brief des Neuen Testament und die Offenbarun Johannis,* 68-69.

4. For Stoic ideas, see Epictetus, *Encheiridion,* 41, in *Discourses,* ed. and trans. W. A. Oldfather, 2 vols. (London: William Heinemann, 1956, 1959). Aristotle had similar ideas. See Aristotle, *Historia Animalium,* 6088, trans. D'Arcy W. Thompson, *The Works of Aristotle,* IV (Oxford: Clarendon Press, 1910), and *Politics,* I, 2 (1252B), 7, ed. and trans. by H. Rackham (London: William Heinemann, 1944).

5. See, for example, A. C. Van Geytenbeck, *Musonius Rufus and Greek Diatribe,* trans. B. L. Hijamans, Jr., (Assen, Netherlands: Van Gorcum & Company, 1963), pp. 71-77; Seneca, *Fragments,* in vol. III of the *Opera,* ed. Frederich G. Haase (Leipzig: Teubner, 1853), no. 85. The passage is only found in St. Jerome, *Against Jovinian* (1:3), although Haase believes it derives from a lost treatise on marriage entitled *De Matrimonio.* See also Noonan, *Contraception,* p. 46.

6. Philo, *On the Special Laws (De Specialibus Legibus)* ed. and trans. F. H. Colson (London: William Heinemann, 1958), III, 113.

7. Philo, *On Special Laws,* VII, 37-42, and also Richard A. Baer, Jr., *Philo's Use of the Categories Male and Female* (Leiden: E. J. Brill, 1970), p. 46.

8. See Ocellus Lucanus, *De universi natura,* text and commentary by Richard Harder (Berlin: Weidmannsche, 1926), sec. 44, pp. 121-26, and Soranus, *Gynecology,* trans. by Owsei Temkin (Baltimore: The Johns Hopkins Press, 1956), I, vii (32).

9. Noonan, *Contraception,* p. 75.

10. Justin Martyr, *Apology,* I, xxix in *Ante-Nicene Fathers,* ed. Alexander Roberts and James Donaldson (American reprint: Grand Rapids: W. B. Erdmans, 1966), I, 172.

11. Clement of Alexandria, *Stromata,* III, vii, in *Ante-Nicene Fathers,* II, 391.

12. Clement of Alexandria, *Pedagogue or Instructor,* II, x, in *Ante-Nicene Fathers,* I, 260.

13. Tertullian, *On Modesty (De Pudicitia)* IV, in *Ante-Nicene Fathers,* IV, 77.

14. *Didascalia* or *Apostolic Constitutions,* VI, sec. v, 28, in *Ante-Nicene Fathers,* VII, pp. 462-63.

15. St. John Chrysostom, *Homilies on the Epistle of St. Paul to the Romans,* trans. J. B. Morris and W. H. Simcox, revised by George Stevens, in *Nicene and Post-Nicene Fathers of the Christian Church,* ed. Philip Schaff, Series no. 1, 14 vols. (New York: Charles Scribner, 1899-1909), Homily IV in vol. XI, 355-59. See also *Homilies on Epistle to Titus,* in *NPNF,* in vol. XIII, 536-37. He uses terms contrary to nature.

16. St. Augustine, *Soliloquies,* I, 10 (17), trans. Thomas F. Gilligan in vol. I, *Fathers of the Church* (New York: Cima Publishing Company, 1948).

17. St. Augustine, *The Good of Marriage,* 16:18, trans. Charles T. Wilcox in *Fathers of the Church* (New York: Fathers of the Church, 1955), vol. 15.

18. Ibid., 11:12.

19. St. Augustine, *Confessions,* III, cap. viii, ed. and trans. William Watts, 2 vols. (London: William Heinemann, 1950).

20. *The Theodosian Code,* IX, vii 3, ed. and trans. Clyde Pharr (Princeton, N.J.: Princeton University Press, 1952), pp. 231-32.

21. Ibid., IX, vii, 6, p. 232.

22. Novel 77, in *Corpus Juris Civilis,* 3 vols. (Berlin: Weidmann, 1959). Translation is that of Bailey, *Homomsexuality and Western Tradition,* pp. 73-74.

23. Ibid., Novel 141.

24. *Lex Visigoth,* Book III, titulus v. cap. 4, "De masculorum stupris," in *MGH Legum* section I, *Legum nationum Germanicorum,* I, 163, ed. Karl Zeumer.

25. J. Mansi, *Sac Conc* (Florence, 1766), XII, col. 71.

26. *Capitularium Karoli M. et Lvodvici Pii Libri VII,* Book V, cap. LXXXIII, "De his qui contra naturam peccant," in Mansi, *Sac Conc,* XVII B, col. 839. For other Carolingian legislation, see *Canones Isaac Episcopi Linonensis,* Titulus IV, "De incestis," cap. XI, in *Sac Conc,* XVII B., col. 1259; *Capitulare octarum anni* in *Sac Conc,* XVII B, col. 412; *Capitulare Tertium,* cap. ii, in *Sac Conc,* XVII B, col. 526; *Capitularium Karoli et Lvodvici pii Libri* VII Titulus 143, *Sac Conc,* XVII B, col. 1055; "additio secunda," cap. XXI, "De deversis malorum flagitis," *Sac Conc,* XVII B, col. 1143, and *Karoli Magni Capitulare primum anni,* Titulus XVII, "Ut monachus secundam regulam vivant," in *Sac Conc,* XVII B. col. 368. Most of the Carolingian enactments are fairly specific.

27. For a discussion of change see Lester K. Little, "Pride Goes before Avarice: Social Change and Vices in Latin Christendom," *American Historical Review* 76 (1971):16-49.

28. *Historia Ecclesiastica gentis Anglorum: Venerabilis Baedae opera historica,* ed. with an introduction by Charles Plummer, 2 vols. (Oxford: Clarendon Press, 1896), I, cclvii f.

29. The quotation is from the *Pseudo Roman Penitential* collected by Halitgar, bishop of Cambrai. The pertinent section, part of the prologue, can be found in *Medieval Handbooks of Penance,* ed. and trans. John T. McNeill and Helena M. Gamer (New York: Columbia University Press, 1938), p. 297.

30. Ibid., pp. 170, nos. 1 & 2. The penitential can also be found in *The Irish Penitentials,* ed. and trans. Ludwig Bieler (Dublin: Dublin Institute for Advanced Studies, 1963), pp. 66-67. Beiler includes the Latin text.

31. McNeill and Gamer, *Medieval Handbook,* pp. 171-72, and Beiler, *Irish Penitentials,* pp. 68-69, Nos. 3, 6, 7, 8.

32. McNeill and Gamer, *Medieval Handbook,* pp. 260-67, and Beiler, *Irish Penitentials,* pp. 96-107, nos. 2, 4, 10, 11, 15, 16, 17.

33. Beiler, *Irish Penitentials,* pp. 112-117, 126-129, and McNeill and Gamer, *Medieval Handbook,* pp. 102-105, 112-114, Section II, nos. 1, 2.

34. For a discussion of the seven deadly sins see Morton W. Bloomfield, *The Seven Deadly Sins* (East Lansing: Michigan State University Press, 1952).

35. Peter Damian, *Liber Gomorrhianus,* cap. I, in *Opera Omnia,* ed. Constantine Cajetan in Migne, *PL* CXLV, col. 161.

36. Damian, cap. xxii, col. 183.

37. For a brief discussion of this see Horace K. Mann, *The Lives of the Popes in the Middle Ages* (London: Kegan Paul, Trench Trubner & Company, 1925), VI, 49-53.

38. See J. Joseph Ryan, *Saint Peter Damiani and His Canonical Sources* (Toronto: Institute of Medieval Studies, 1956), pp. 154-55.

39. Ivo, *Decretum,* Par. IX, cap. 110, 128 in Migne, *PL* CLXI, 686. This section deals with activities *contra naturam.* He also deals with *De stupratoribus puerorum,* cap. 109, col. 686. For St. Augustine, *Confessions,* see above.

40. *Decretum,* IX, 106 in Migne, *PL* CLXI, 685-686.

41. Noonan, *Contraception,* p. 173.

42. Burchard, *Decretum,* Libri XX, xix, cap. v, "Interrogatory," in Migne, *PL* CXL, 951-76, esp. 967-68, "Item de fornication."

43. For a brief popular discussion of the origins of canon law see Stephen G. Kuttner, *Harmony from Dissonance,* Wimmer Lecture X, Saint Vincent College (Latrobe, Penn.: The Archabbey Press, 1960).

44. Gratian, *Decretum, Pars Secunda,* Causa XXXII, Questio vii, c. 13, "Graviora sunt flagica, que contra naturam probantur," in *Corpus Canonica,* ed. Emil Friedberg, 2 vols.

(Leipzig: Bernard Tauchnitz, 1879-81), I, col. 1143. See St. Augustine, *Confessions,* III, viii, and the citations above.

45. Gratian, *Decretum, Pars Secunda,* Causa XXXII, questio vii, c. 14, Friedberg, *Corpus Canonica,* I, col. 1144.

46. Gratian, *Decretum, Pars Secunda,* Causa XXXII, Questio vii, c. 11 in Friedberg, *Corpus Canonica,* I, 1143.

47. Gratian, *Decretum, Pars Secunda,* Causa XXXIII, Tractatus de Penitencia, Questio iii, distinctio cap. xv, in Friedberg, *Corpus Canonica,* II, 1161.

48. Bailey, *Homosexuality and Western Tradition,* p. 69.

49. For example, see R. Brouillard, "Bestialité" in *Dictionnaire de Droit Canonique,* 7 vols. (Paris: Librairie Letouzey et Ano, 1935-65), 793-99. Gratian included it under crime against nature, and most of the later councils refer only to "incontinentia quae contra naturam est," which Brouillard believed included bestiality.

50. *Concilium Londoniense,* cap. XXVIII, in Mansi, *Sac Conc,* XX, 1152.

51. *Concilium Londoniense,* XXIX, Mansi, *Sac Conc,* XX, col. 1152.

52. *Concilium Neapolitanum,* cap. XI, in Mansi, *Sac Conc,* XXI, col. 624. Canons 8, 9, 10 also deal with sodomy and spontaneous pollution. Mansi has some discussion on the subject in his Introduction, *Sac Conc,* col. 261-62.

53. *Concilium Lateranense,* III, cap. xi, in Mansi, *Sac Conc,* XXII, col. 224-225.

54. *Concilium Parisiense,* Par. II, xxi, in Mansi, *Sac Conc,* XXII, col. 831. It uses the Third Lateran statute as a source.

55. Ibid., Par. III, ii, in Mansi, *Sac Conc,* col. 849.

56. *Concilium Magistri Roberti apud Rotomagum* (1214), xxiii, xxiv, xxxii, in Mansi, *Sac Conc,* cols. 910 and 912.

57. *Concilium Lateranense,* IV (1215), XIV, "De incontinentia clericorum punienda," in Mansi, *Sac Conc,* XXII, col. 1003.

58. Included among later actions would be that of the Second Council of Rouen in 1235, which repeats the statement of the Third Lateran. See *Concilium Ramense,* XL, in Mansi, *Sac Conc,* XXIII, col. 379, although the term "contra naturam" is not used. The council of Bezier in 1246, Le Mans in 1247, and Clermont in 1268 repeat the Fourth Lateran but do not use the term against nature. See *Concilium Biterrense,* XIX, in Mansi, *Sac Conc,* XXIII, col. 696; *Statuta Sinodalia Ecclesiae Canomanensis,* Par. III (i), Mansi, *Sac Conc,* XXIII, col. 755, and *Incipiunt Statuta Synodalia Clarmontensis Ecclesiae,* Par. II, i, in Mansi, *Sac Conc,* XXIII, col. 1203. Others used the term against nature including *Odonis Episcopi Parisiensis Synodicae Constitutiones,* cap. VI, 4, 5, in Mansi, *Sac Conc,* XXIII, col. 578; *Concilium Provinciale Fritzlariae,* IV, in Mansi, *Sac Conc,* XXIII, col. 726; *Statuta Synodalia Johannis Episcopi Leodiensis,* Par IV, xi, Mansi, *Sac Conc,* XXIV, col. 891, and *Ad Remense Concilium,* Mansi, *Sac Conc,* XXVI, col. 1073. There are no numbered paragraphs in the last. Dates for these last Councils are Paris in 1196, the others in 1246, 1287, and 1408.

59. *Decretales Gregori IX,* Liber Quintus, Titulus XXXI, cap. iv, in *Corpus Juris Canonici,* II, col. 836. This was based on the Third Lateran Council.

60. Peter Lombard, *Libri IV Sententiarum,* ed. the Fathers of the College of St. Bonaventure (n.p., 1916), Liber IV, Distinctio XXXVIII, cap. ii, in vol. II, 970.

61. Albertus Magnus, *Summa Theologiae,* Liber II, Tractatus XVIII, Questio 122, Membrum I, articulus iv, in *Opera Omnia,* ed. S. C. A. Bornet, vols. XXXI-XXXIV (Paris: Ludovium Vives, 1895).

62. Albertus Magnus, *Commentarii in IV Sententiarum,* Distinctio III, 27, in *Opera Omnia,* XXIX.

63. Albertus Magnus, *In Evangelium Lucam,* XVII, 29, in *Opera Omnia,* XXII, XXIII.

64. St. Thomas Aquinas, *Summa Theologica,* II, II, Q. cliv, 1, trans. Fathers of English Dominican Province (New York: Benziger Brothers, 1947). See all the section on virginity, II, II, q. clii, 2, 3.

65. Ibid., II II, q. cliv, 11.

66. Ibid., II–II, Q. cliv, 11 and 12.

67. Ibid., II, q. cliv, 12.

68. Ibid., II II, Q. cliv, 4.

69. Bernardine of Sienna, *Quadragesimale de Evangelio Aeterno,* Sermo XIX, Articulus II, cap. 4, Articulus II, cap. 3, in *Opera Omnia,* ed. the College of St. Bonaventure (Florence: Collegii S. Bonavaenturae, 1956), III, 334, 337–338. Also *Contra Soddomian in Selecta ex Autographo Budapestimensi,* cap. 27, in *Opera Omnia,* IX, 427–430.

70. Bernardine, Sermo XV, "De horren peccato contra naturam," I, 1, in *Quadragesimale, Opera Omnia,* III, 267–84.

71. Peter Cantor, *Verbum Abbreviatum,* cap. CXXXVIII, De vito Sodomitico, in Migne, *Patrologia Latina,* CCV, col. 333–35, esp. 335.

72. John Gerson, *Regulae Morales,* XCIX, "De Luxuria," in *Opera Omnia,* ed. L. Elliss du Pin (Antwerp, 1706), III, col. 95.

73. St. Antonino, *Confessionale* (Venice: 1514), cap. 57, pp. 57–58. He also equates it with the sin against nature.

74. Geoffrey Chaucer, *The Parson's Tale,* Line 577 in *The Canterbury Tales,* ed. F. N. Robinson, 2nd ed. (Boston: Houghton Mifflin, 1961).

75. Chaucer, *The Merchant's Tale,* 1839–1840.

76. Henrici de Seguso (Cardinal Hostiensis) *Summa Aurea,* (Venice 1574, reprinted Turin: Bottega d'Erasmo, 1963), Liber V, Summa de Penitentiis et remissionibus, cap. 49, Interrogationes que debent fieri in confessione, col. 1808.

77. John Myrc, *Instructions for Parish Priests,* ed. Edward Peacock, Early English Text Society, vol. XXXI (reprinted New York: Greenwood Press, n.d.).

78. *The Book of Vices and Virtues,* ed. W. Nelson Francis, Early English Text Society, vol. CCXVII (London: Oxford University Press, 1942), p. 43a. This book was edited from three extant texts of a translation from the French of Lorens d'Orléans, *Somme le Roi.*

79. Ibid., p. 46.

80. Ibid., p. 244.

81. Ibid., p. 248.

82. *Hali Maidenhad,* ed. F. J. Furnivall, revised from the edition edited by Oswald Cockayne, Early English Text Society, vol. XVIII (reprinted New York: Greenwood Press, 1969), p. 35.

83. Ibid., pp. 34–35. Translation is by Furnivall.

84. William Langland, *Piers the Plowman,* trans. by Margaret Williams (New York: Random House, 1971), Passus XI, lines 326–330, p. 195.

85. Ibid., Passus XIV, lines 74–78.

86. Ibid., Passus XII, lines 68–72, pp. 210–12. Langland put the italicized line in Latin.

87. *The Ancren Riwle,* ed. James Morton (reprinted New York: Cooper Square Publishers, 1966), p. 153.

88. Ibid., pp. 154–55.

89. Ibid., pp. 199–200.

90. "Cleanness," in the *Pearl Poet,* trans. by Margaret Williams (New York: Random House, 1967), p. 131.

91. Ibid., pp. 147–52.

92. The subject of sexuality and the sin against nature in Chaucer has received some attention. See Paul F. Baum, "Chaucer's Puns," *PMLA* 71 (1956):232; P. J. C. Field, "Chaucer's Merchant and the Sin Against Nature," *Notes and Queries,* March 1970, p. 84; George Williams, *A New View of Chaucer* (Durham, N.C.: Duke University Press, 1965), Chapter VIII, "Chaucer's Best Joke—The Tale of Sir Thopas," and Helen Storm Corsa, *Chaucer, Poet of Mirth and Morality* (Notre Dame: University of Notre Dame Press, 1964).

93. Chaucer, *The Parson's Tale,* pp. 909–10.

94. Dante Alighieri, *Inferno,* Canto XV, 106–108. There are many editions and translations. A readily available one is by Dorothy L. Sayers.

95. Dante, *Purgatory,* Canto XXVI, 40–42, 76–93.

96. Dennis de Rougemont, *Love in the Western World,* trans. Montgomery Belgion (New York: Pantheon Books, 1956), pp. 98–99.

97. Jeffrey Burton Russell, *Witchcraft in the Middle Ages* (Ithaca: Cornell University Press, 1972), pp. 126–27.

98. This equation was popularized by Havelock Ellis, "The Nature of Sexual Inversion," in *Studies in the Psychology of Sex,* 2 vols. (New York: Random House, 1936), I, Part IV, 347. Ellis misread the original French statute. See P. Viollet, *Les Establissment de St. Louis,* Livre I, cx, 4 vols. (Paris: Renouard, 1881–1886), II, 147–48, and *Ordonnances de Roys de France,* ed. Eusebe Jacob de Lauriere, Denis François Secousse, et al., 21 vols. (Paris, 1723–1849), I, Chap. lxxxv, 175, (1270). The confusion is also continued in the usually reliable *Oxford English Dictionary.*

99. See Samuel A. Tissot, *L'onanisme, dissertatione sur les maladies produites par la masturbation,* 4th ed. (Lausanne, 1769). See also Vern L. Bullough and Martha Voght, "Homosexuality and Its Confusion with the 'Secret Sin' in Pre-Freudian America," *Journal of the History of Medicine and Allied Sciences* 28 (1973):143–155. See also E. H. Hare, "Masturbatory Insanity: the History of an Idea," *Journal of Mental Sciences* 108 (1962):1–25; R. H. MacDonald, "The Frightful Consequences of Onanism," *Journal of the History of Ideas* 28 (1967):423–31, and Alex Comfort, *The Anxiety Makers* (New York: Delta Books, 1969).

100. Noonan, *Contraception, passim.*

Chapter 7

Sexual Irregularities in Medieval Scandinavia

1. For a discussion of the legal position of women in medieval Scandinavia, see my "The Position of Women in Scandinavia during the Viking Period," (M.A. Thesis, University of Wisconsin, 1978).

2. This view is found in Lizzie Carlsson, *"Jag giver dig min dotter." Trolovning och äktenskap i den svenska kvinnans äldre historia.* (Skrifter utgivna av Institut for Rättshistorisk Forskning, ser. I: 8, 20), 2 vols. (Stockholm, 1965–68).

3. Poul Johs. Jorgensen, *Dansk retshistorie* (Copenhagen: Gad, 1947), pp. 134 ff.

4. Ibid., pp. 33 ff.

5. Gerhard Hafström, *De svenska rättslällornas historia* (Lund: Juridiska Föreningen; Studentlitteratur, 1970), pp. 36 ff.

6. Jacobsen, *The Position of Women.*

7. According to chapter 10 of the Íslendingabok by Ari fro i borgilsson (d. 1148).

8. Roberta Frank, "Marriage in Twelfth- and Thirteenth-Century Iceland," *Viator* 4 (1973), 473–84.

9. *Grágás,* chaps. 149 and 151.

10. If one spouse was suddenly burdened with an influx of poor relatives whom he or she was obliged to support, the other spouse could declare a divorce with the words: "I want to divorce my husband/wife for the reason that I do not want my spouse's poor relatives to consume my property." *Grágás,* chap. 149.

11. Ibid., chap. 149.

12. Ibid.

13. *KLNM,* "Lejermal. Island" by Magnus Mar Larusson.

14. *Grágás,* chap. 156.

15. A conviction meant exile for three years. If the convict left Iceland, and he/she was given fair time to make travel arrangements, he/she could not be killed. Only if the convict refused to leave the country did he/she lose the protection of the law and thus could be killed without punishment by her/his enemies (*KLNM* "Fredloshed" by Magnus Mar Larusson).

16. A man or a woman condemned to death had no protection and could legally be killed by anyone. No one was allowed to help him or her (Ibid.)

17. *Grágás,* chap. 161.

18. Chap. 127.

19. Chap. 157.

20. Ibid.

21. Chap. 159.

22. Chap. 142.

23. Chap. 118.

24. Chaps. 128, 143. If a debtor was unable to pay off his debts, he could satisfy his creditor by going to work for him or her as a slave. He was then considered a slave in relation to the creditor but kept his rights and status in relation to others (*KLNM* "Trael" by Peter Foote).

25. *Grágás,* chap. 158.

26. Chap. 159.

27. Chap. 264.

28. Chap. 149.

29. Chap. 118.

30. Ibid.

31. Chaps. 118, 143.

32. Chap. 118.

33. Chap. 254.

34. Chap. 156.

35. Chap. 111.

36. Chap. 112.

37. Chap. 111.

38. Chap. 156.

39. Sigurdur Nordal, "The historical element in the Icelandic family sagas," *Scripta Islandica* 10 (1959), 9–24.

40. *Droplaugarsona saga,* chap. 6 (in *Íslenzk Fornrit,* v. 11).

41. *Brennu-Njals saga,* chap. 87 (in *Íslenzk Fornrit,* v. 12).

42. Ibid., chap. 64. It was legal to sell the right to prosecute the case.

43. *Grettis saga Asmundarsonar,* chap. 67 (in Islenzk Fornrit, v. 7).

44. The two complete laws still extant from early medieval Norway are the Gulaping law (henceforth cited as GU), which dates from 1150, with amendments from 1164, and the Frostaping law (henceforth FR), redacted c. 1170. The edition cited is *Norges gamle love indtil 1387,* edited and compiled R. Keyser and P. A. Munch, 5 vols. (Christiania, 1846–1895), v. 1: *Norges love aeldre end kong Magnus Haakonssöns regjerings Tiltraedelse i 1263.*

45. *KLNM,* "AEgteskabsbrud. Noreg." by Gudmund Sandvik.

46. The *Bjarköret,* printed in *Norges gamle love,* v. 1, 301–336.

47. GU, chap. 32; FR, iv, 39.

48. GU, chap. 160; FR, iv, 39.

49. FR, i, 10.

50. GU, chap. 25.

51. FR, iii, 5, 7.

52. FR, xi, 14.

53. FR, xi, 13.

54. GU, chap. 198. FR does not mention this.

55. GU, chap. 57; FR, ii, 1.

56. GU chap. 104; FR, vii, 8.

57. *KLNM,* "Oäkta barn. Noreg" by Rigmor Frimannslund.

58. GU, chap. 58; FR, ix, 1.

59. Al Gazal's travel description is printed in Harris Birkeland, *Nordens historie i Middelalderen etter arabiske kilder* (Skrfiter udg. av. Det Norske Videnskaps Akademi i Oslo: hist.-filos.

klass, 1954:2, Oslo, 1954), pp. 83ff. This is a translation and revision of Alexander Seippel, *Rerum Normannicarum fontes Arabici* (Oslo: Brogger, 1896-1924).

60. *Adami Gesta Hammaburgensis ecclesiae pontificum,* liber 4, cap. 6, *MGH,* Scriptores, p. 158.

61. *KLNM, "AEgteskabsbrud. Danmark" by Jens Ulf Jorgensen.*

62. See *Skanske lov* (henceforth SK), 215-216, compiled c. 1200-1215: *Valdemars Sjællandske lov* (henceforth VSJ), ii:1-2, compiled 1200-1220; *Eriks Sjaellandske lov* (henceforth ESJ), ii:2-2, dating from the thirteenth century. It is a revision and supplement to VSJ. The edition cited is *Danmarks gamle love med krikelovene.* Udg . . . af Johs. Brondum Nielsen (8 vols., Copenhagen: Gyldendal, 1933-61). Text one of each law is cited.

63. Ander *Sunesons parafrase* of SK (henceforth cited SKSu), 126. This is also found in the Nielsen collection cited above. It dates from c. 1220.

64. Ibid., 127.

65. *Juske lov* (henceforth JY), iii:37 (from the same collection).

66. Ibid., i:24.

67. Jorgensen, *Dansk retshistorie,* pp. 33ff.

68. *KLNM,* "Lejermal. Danmark" by Stig Iuul.

69. SK. 219; VSJ, iii:15; ESJ, iii:38, JY, ii:18.

70. SK, 219.

71. SK, 221; JY, ii:20.

72. SK, 224.

73. JY, ii:18.

74. JY, i:18.

75. SK, 222; JY, ii:20; VSJ, iii:15; ESJ, iii:38.

76. SKSu, 24.

77. Absalon Taranger, "Det uegte barns retshistorie," *Samtiden* 16 (1905):214-221, 219.

78. SK and VSJ.

79. SK, iii:6; ESJ, i:50; JY, i:25.

80. SK, 59; ESJ, i:18; JY, i:22.

81. *KLNM,* "Oakta barn. Danmark," by Jens Ulk Jorgensen.

82. SK, 59: ESJ, i:18; JY, i:22.

83. ESJ, i:18; JY, i:21.

84. SK, 63; SKSu, 24.

85. *Adami Gesta Hammaburgensis,* liber 4, cap. 21 (p. 170).

86. Ibid., liber 2, cap. 72 (p. 90).

87. *Saxonis Gesta Danorum,* liber 11, cap. 7.1 (ed. J. Olrik and H. Ræder. Copenhagen: Levin et Munksgaard, 1931).

88. James A. Brundage, "Concubinage and Marriage in Medieval Canon Law," *Journal of Medaeval History* 1 (1975), 1-17.

89. JY, 1:27.

90. GU, chap. 125.

91. *Adami Gesta Hammaburgensis,* liber 4, cap. 21 (p. 170).

92. The nine medieval Swedish laws were redacted c. 1220 to 1320. The edition consulted is *Svenska landskapslagar.* Tolkade . . . av Ake Holmback och Elias Wessen. 5 vols. (Stockholm: Geber, 1933-46).

93. *Östgötabalk.* Ärvdabalk, chap. 13, as in the collection cited in fn. 92.

94. *KLNM,* "AEgteskabsbrud. Sverige" by Gunnel Hedberg.

95. *Upplandslag,* Ärvdabalk, chap. 6; *Västmannalag,* Ärvdabalk, chap. 6.

96. *Östgötabalk,* Kyrkobalk, chap. 27.

97. *Upplandslag,* Ärvdabalk, chap. 6.

98. *KLNM,* "Lejermal. Sverige" by Per-Edwin Wallen.

99. *Östgötalag.* Ärvdabalk, chap. 16, e.g.

100. *Upplandslag.* Ärvdabalk, chap. 22, same in *Dalalag, Västmannalag.*
101. *Upplandslag.* Ärvdabalk, chap. 23.
102. *Östgötalag.* Ärvdabalk, chap. 4.
103. This was compiled about 1220. The edition cited is *Gutalag och Gutasaga.* Jämte ordbok. Utgifna . . . af Hugo Pipping. (Copenhagen, 1905-07).
104. Ibid., chap. 21.
105. Chap. 20a.
106. Ibid.
107. Chap. 20:14.
108. Chap. 23.
109. Richard F. Tomasson, "Premarital Sexual Permissiveness and Illegitimacy in the Nordic Countries," *Comparative Studies in Society and History* 18 (1976), 252-270.

Chapter 8

Sex and Canon Law: A Statistical Analysis of Samples of Canon and Civil Law

1. The subjects analyzed for this study were: occurrence of sexual topic, treatment of sexual crime, clerical status, status in religious life, treatment of lawyers, sacramental law, liturgical law, vows, penalties, marriage dowry, bastardy, law of war, infamia, ecclesiastical property law, simony, testamentary disposition, corporate bodies, contract, debt, sale, servile status, law concerning lepers, women's status, sources of law, councils, customary law, elections, guardianship, doctrinal deviation (i.e., heresy, schism, etc.), procedural law, law of evidence, witnesses, prostitution, concubinage, status of widows, orphans, children's status, intestate succession, law of privileges, dispensations, *quod omnes tangit* doctrine, appellate procedure, arbitration, pilgrim's status, *patria potestas,* bankruptcy, loans, vexatious litigation, possession *(dominium),* and manumission. A note was made on each of these categories for each of the texts examined. The notes, for the most part, simply indicated whether or not the topic was mentioned in each text. Some categories, however, were broken down into subcategories; thus, under sacramental law, for example, a separate note indicated which sacrament was dealt with by a given text or whether the text dealt with more than one sacrament. At some stages of the analysis it was necessary for technical reasons to collapse some categories, e.g., by transforming the separate mentions of individual sacraments into simple binary ("yes" or "no") categories.

2. For this analysis I have used the standard editions of the two bodies of law: the *Corpus iuris canonici,* ed. E. Friedberg, 2 vols. (Leipzig, 1879; rpt. Graz, 1959), and the *Corpus iuris civilis,* ed. P. Krueger, T. Mommsen, R. Schoell, and W. Kroll, 17th ed., 3 vols. (Berlin, 1963). The total number of canons in the Friedberg edition of the canon law amounts to 6,752. There seems to be no count of the number of texts in the civil law *Corpus.* A simple estimate, based on the mean number of texts per page from a tiny sample of ten randomly selected pages from each of the main collections (Digest, Codex, Novels, and Institutes), indicates that there are probably something on the order of 17,000 individual texts (fragments, laws, or sections) in the *Corpus iuris civilis.*

3. The selection of the 95 percent confidence interval is not quite so arbitrary as it may seem, nor are its implications quite so simple as they may appear. The 95 percent confidence interval is commonly used in social science literature as an acceptable margin of error, which is certainly one reason for selecting it. More important, however, the confidence interval is directly related to sample size, and moving the confidence interval, say to the 99 percent level, would require a considerable increase in the size of the sample required for the study. This, in turn, would require a sizeable increase in investment to carry out the study. The 95 percent level represents, in my judgment, a reasonable compromise between the need for a high degree of accuracy and the need for a limited sample size in order to make the project feasible. For

discussions of the statistical implications of the confidence interval see H. M. Blalock, Jr., *Social Statistics,* 2d ed. (New York, 1972), pp. 205–209; D. Raj, *Sampling Theory* (New York, 1968), pp. 27–30; W. G. Cochran, *Sampling Techniques,* 2d ed. (New York, 1963), pp. 12–15; M. H. Hansen, W. N. Harwitz, and W. G. Madow, *Sample Survey Methods and Theory,* 2 vols. (New York, 1953) 1:20–26, 124–129.

4. The distribution of the sample texts is:

	Number	% of sample
CANON LAW		
Decretum	200	25.0
Liber extra	144	18.0
Liber sextus	32	4.0
Clementines	8	1.0
Extravagantes Johannis XXII	6	0.7
CIVIL LAW		
Digest	150	18.8
Codex	125	15.5
Novels	100	12.5
Institutes	25	3.1
	800	100.0

5. The analysis was run on a UNIVAC 1106 electronic computer, using programs from N. H. Nie, C. H. Hull, J. G. Jenkins, K. Steinbrenner, and D. H. Bent, *Statistical Package for the Social Sciences,* 2d ed. (New York, 1975), 6.02 (released 20 April 1976). I should like here to acknowledge the technical assistance that I have received from the Social Science Research Facility of the University of Wisconsin–Milwaukee and especially the helpful advice of Ms. Carla Garnham, Consultant to the SSRF.

6. Crosstabulating the two variables yields a chi-square of 30.562 with six degrees of freedom (significance = .0000); Cramer's $V = .19545$; $C = .26642$. The asymmetric uncertainty coefficient for the two variables is .057 with clerical status dependent and .054 with sexual topic dependent.

7. For these variables chi-square = 206.99 with fourteen degrees of freedom (significance = .0000); $V = .509$; $C = .584$; asymmetric $U = .084$ with clergy dependent, but .135 with sexual crimes dependent.

8. The chi-square test for these variables yields 142.478 with nine degrees of freedom (significant above .0000); $V = .34457$; $C = .51249$; asymmetric $U = .11679$ with clerical status dependent and .21882 with sexual topic dependent.

9. Chi-square = 108.074 with 18 d.f. (significant above .0000); $V = .3$; $C = .461$; asymmetric $U = .07667$ with clerical status dependent and .16863 with sexual crime dependent.

10. For the association of sexual topics with the individual legal collections, chi-square = 29.97972 with 9 d.f. (significance = .0004); $V = .19258$; $C = .19$; asymmetric $U = .08262$ with sexual topic dependent. For the association of sexual crimes with specific legal collections, chi-square = 22.355 with 9 d.f. (significance = .0078); $V = .167$; $C = .165$; asymmetric $U = .087$ with sexual crimes dependent.

11. Chi-square for this association is 161.832 with 9 d.f. (significance = .0000); $V = .44977$; $C = .41019$; asymmetric $U = .22851$ with clerical status dependent.

12. A straightforward and relatively uncomplicated description of the procedures can be found in Blalock, *Social Statistics,* pp. 317–357. More mathematically demanding treatments may be found in M. L. Puri and P. K. Sen, *Nonparametric Methods in Multivariate Analysis* (New York, 1971), pp. 221–259; W. W. Cooley and P. R. Lohnes, *Multivariate Procedures for the Behavioral Sciences* (New York, 1962), pp. 60–91.

13. Discriminant analysis requires some mathematical sophistication for its interpretation, and I have not attempted here to do more than indicate in outline the conclusions that this analysis leads to. For discussions of the techniques and their interpretation see John P. Van de Geer, *Introduction to Multivariate Analysis for the Social Sciences* (San Francisco, 1971), pp. 243–272; also Cooley and Lohnes, *Multivariate Procedures,* pp. 116–123.

Chapter 9

The Marriage of Mary and Joseph in the Twelfth-Century Ideology of Marriage

*An earlier version of this essay was delivered at the annual meeting of the Medieval Association of the Pacific in 1974. I would like to acknowledge my indebtedness to John T. Noonan, Jr., who helped me in the formulation of the topic, and to Alan E. Bernstein, for his many valuable suggestions. I would also like to thank Paul Remac and James Brundage for biographical help, and David Amor for editorial assistance.

1. There are several works that describe the basic principles of medieval marriage law: Gabriel Le Bras, "Mariage: la doctrine du mariage chez les théologiens et les canonistes depuis l'an mille," *Dictionnaire de théologie catholique,* ed. A. Vacant et al. (Paris: 1903–50) 9^2:2123–2317; A. Esmein, *Le mariage en droit canonique,* 2 vols. (Paris, 1891); Jean Dauvillier, *Le mariage dans le droit classique de l'église depuis le Decrét de Gratian (1140) jusqu'à la mort de Clément V (1314)* (Paris, 1933); George Hayward Joyce, S.J., *Christian Marriage: An Historical and Doctrinal Study* (London, 1948); Joseph Freisen, *Geschichte des canonischen Eherechts,* 2nd ed. (1893; rpt. Paderborn, 1963). The specific topic of this paper is dealt with most extensively in a chapter of this last work (pp. 83–90), and in John T. Noonan, Jr., *Power to Dissolve: Lawyers and Marriages in the Courts of the Roman Curia* (Cambridge, Mass., 1972). For a summary of the problems involved in analyzing twelfth-century marriage law, see Gerard Fransen, "La formation du lien matrimonial au moyen-âge," *Revue de droit canonique* 21 (1971): 106–126.

2. The disagreement extended beyond the works of these men and is usually described as the conflict between the French and Roman churches, or the Parisian and Bolognese schools. See Esmein, *Le mariage canonique,* 1:119–125, and T. P. McLaughlin, C.S.B., "The Formation of the Marriage Bond according to the *Summa Parisiensis,"* *Mediaeval Studies* 15 (1953): 208–212. The varying opinions are also related to the differences between the Hebraic, Roman, and Germanic conceptions of marriage. For a useful discussion of this background, see J. Gaudemet, "Le lien matrimonial: les incertitudes du haut moyen-âge," *Revue du droit canonique* 21 (1971):81–105. For another example of canonistic ambivalence on the place of sexuality in marriage, see Elizabeth M. Makowski, "The Conjugal Debt and Medieval Canon Law," *Journal of Medieval History* 3 (1977):99–114.

3. A recent work by Georges Duby analyzes the conflict between the aristocratic and ecclesiastical models of marriage: *Medieval Marriage: Two Models from Twelfth-Century France* (Baltimore and London, 1978). Duby argues that a reconciliation between the two models began to develop in the second half of the twelfth century. Charles Donahue emphasizes the conflict between Alexander III's fundamental contribution to the canon law of marriage (that a marriage is formed either by words of present consent, with or without consummation, or by future consent followed by consummation) and the exercise of familial and feudal control over marriage: "The Policy of Alexander the Third's Consent Theory of Marriage," in the *Proceedings of the Fourth International Congress of Medieval Canon Law,* ed. Stephan Kuttner (Vatican City, 1976; Monumenta iuris canonici, Ser. C, vol. 5), 251–281. Father Michael Sheehan has suggested that the accommodation of secular and ecclesiastical views of marriage was a development of the later Middle Ages. He has shown that in fourteenth-century England, marriage practice was quite close to the individualistic view of twelfth-century marriage law, there being a notable lack of familial and seignorial concerns in the records he has used. The matter

of class must also be considered in this question, for it is easier to imagine a noble family making a decision for the inheritor of a patrimony than a peasant family for a child without such responsibilities. Unfortunately, or importantly, Sheehan notes that the well-to-do seem to be underrepresented in the register: "The Formation and Stability of Marriage in Fourteenth-Century England: Evidence of an Ely Register," *Mediaeval Studies* 33 (1971):228–263. An article by Juliette M. Turlan suggests that marital practice in the Middle Ages was quite distant from the doctrines of the law, especially with regard to the marriage of underage children (for whom the criterion of consummation seems to have been essential to the validity of the marriage) and clandestine marriage: "Recherches sur le mariage dans la pratique coutumière (XIIe–XVIe s.)," *Revue historique de droit français et étranger* 35 (1957):477–528. John T. Noonan, Jr. has explored the possible relationships between contemporary heretical movements and the development of church doctrine on marriage: *Contraception: A History of Its Treatment by the Catholic Theologians and Canonists* (New York, 1965).

4. Pars 2, Causa 27, Quaestio 2.

5. All quotations from the *Decretum* are taken from the translation of the marriage canons by John T. Noonan, Jr.: *Marriage Canons from the Decretum* (mimeographed, 1967). The standard edition of the *Corpus Iuris Canonici* by Aemilius Friedburg (Leipzig, 1879). All quotations are from C. 27, q. 2.

6. See canons 6, 12, d.p.c. 34, d.p.c. 39, c. 40.

7. Eph. 5:22–32. Emphasis added.

8. One other passage would seem to affirm the marriage of Mary and Joseph. In his *dictum post canonem* 39, Gratian states that Joseph is called the husband of Mary not by the effect of marriage, but by the management of necessities and by affection of an undivided mind. When put in its context, however, it seems that this statement is not actually corroborating the marriage of Mary and Joseph, but rather describing their state of betrothal, by which they are *called* spouses. As described above, the whole of the paragraph in which this statement is set is a discussion of the fact that although some are called married, they do not have the present effect of marriage but are called married by reason of future hope. For a different interpretation of this passage, see John T. Noonan, Jr., "Marital Affection in the Canonists," *Studia Gratiana* 12 (1967):495–496.

9. *De beatae Mariae virginitate, PL* 176.857–876; *De sacramentis christianae fidei, PL* 176.173–618. *De sacramentis* was written about five years before Gratian's *Decretum*. The precise date of the treatise on virginity cannot be ascertained. It is in the form of a letter to a certain bishop G., who in one manuscript is identified as Geoffrey, bishop of Châlons-sur-Marne. Geoffrey was bishop from 1131 to 1140. (See B. Hauréau, *Les oeuvres de Hugues de Saint-Victor* [Paris, 1886], 112–115.)

10. *PL* 176.857.

11. *PL* 176.857. Translations from this treatise are my own.

12. *PL* 176.859, 860, 873. Hugh does not cite Augustine, nor does he use Augustine's phrase *(individua vitae consuetudo)*, but the contents of their definitions are very similar. Hugh's definition is *PL* 176.873. In *De sacramentis* Hugh adopts the Augustinian definition explicitly (2.11.4).

13. Gen. 2:24 and Eph. 5:31 (which repeats Genesis).

14. *PL* 176.860, 863, 864, 874.

15. *PL* 176.870. The fourth chapter of the treatise repeats Hugh's definition of marriage in which sexual union is not necessary. An interesting objection is then raised: If marriage is so defined, why cannot there be marriage between two people of the same sex? Here Hugh relies on his concept of the sacrament of marriage in which the spouses symbolize the union between God and the soul. This is obviously not a union of equals, God being greater than the soul. Thus a union of two men or two women would not be suitable, but a union of man and woman is, since men and women are not equal, women being by nature subject to men (*PL* 176.873–876). The treatise then ends with a discussion of the different needs and contributions of the man and the woman within marriage. Yet in his treatise on the sacraments, Hugh, in explaining

marriage as "an undivided way of life," speaks of the equality of man and woman; woman was, after all, created from the side of man, rather than from his feet or head, and so was meant to share his life, rather than be his servant or lord (2.11.4).

16. See Seamus P. Heaney, *The Development of the Sacramentality of Marriage from Anselm of Laon to Thomas Aquinas* (Washington, D.C., 1963), 14–16. Heaney also discusses Peter Lombard (pp. 29–31) and Thomas Aquinas (pp. 65–68, 187–196).

17. The translations given are from *On the Sacraments of the Christian Faith*, trans. Roy J. Deferrari (Cambridge, Mass., 1951).

18. For a detailed discussion of the place of sexuality among the purposes of marriage, see Rudolf Weigand, "Die Lehre der Kanonisten des 12. und 13. Jahrhunderts von der Ehzwecken," *Studia Gratiana* 12 (1967):443–478.

19. p. 106.

20. This explanation is found in both *De beatae Mariae virginitate* (*PL* 176.870–872), and *De sacramentis* 2.1.8.

21. For a much less idealized treatment of marriage by Hugh, see his two treatises: *De vanitate mundi*, translated by a Religious of C.S.M.V., in *Selected Spiritual Writings* (New York, 1962), pp. 165–167; and *De nuptiis, PL* 176.1201–1218. Concerning the later, B. Hauréau has written, "Les femmes ont été rarement plus mal traitées qu'elles ne le sont ici" (Hauréau, *Oeuvres de Hugues,* p. 168). He defends Hugh of St. Victor as the author of this treatise against the attribution to Hugo de Folieto (pp. 167–168).

22. The modern edition of the Lombard's work is *Libri IV Sententiarum,* studio et cura PP. Collegii S. Bonaventurae, ed. 2, 2 vols. (Quaracchi, 1916). Elizabeth Rogers has translated Distinction 26 of Book 4 of the *Sentences,* and quotations from that Distinction are from her translation: *Peter Lombard and the Sacramental System* (New York, 1917). Quotations from other Distinctions are my own translations. All passages cited are from Book 4.

23. I have changed Roger's translation here from "harmony of their spirits." The Latin is *consensum animorum.*

24. Both Hugh and Thomas Aquinas also deal with the special reasons for Mary's marriage; see Hugh, *De beatae Mariae virginitate* (*PL* 176.867–869); Thomas Aquinas, *Summa Theologiae,* 3a.29.1.

25. Thomas's *Commentum in Quator Libros Sententiarum Magistri Petri Lombardi* can be found in *Opera Omnia,* vol. 7² (Parma, 1857). Translation, unless noted otherwise, is from the Dominican translation of the *Summa Theologica* (the Supplement) (New York, 1948). The people to whom Thomas refers, who were "mad enough to assert that corruptible things were created by an evil god" were the Cathars.

26. For full treatment of the role of nature in Thomas's consideration of marriage, see James P. Lyon, *The Essential Structure of Marriage: A Study of the Thomistic Teaching on the Natural Institution* (Washington, D.C., 1950). For a comparison with his contemporary, Saint Bonaventure, see John Francis Quinn, "Saint Bonaventure and the Sacrament of Matrimony," *Franciscan Studies* 34 (1974):101–143.

27. This translation is my own; the passage is not included in the Supplement of the *Summa.*

28. See above, pp. 103–104.

29. Lillian M. Randall, *Images in the Margins of Gothic Manuscripts,* California Studies in the History of Art, No. 4 (Berkeley: Univ. of California Press, 1966).

30. *Summa Theologiae,* la. 76.3.

31. Heaney notes that Eph. 5:32 was "the starting point for all attributions of the word *sacramentum* to marriage" (p. 4).

Chapter 10

Concubinage and Marriage in Medieval Canon Law

1. Eccles. 19:2. A version of this chapter appeared in *Journal of Medieval History* 1 (1975), 1–17. Reprinted and revised with permission.

2. J. T. Noonan, "Power to Choose," *Viator* 4 (1973):431.

3. For other definitions of concubinage see J. M. Buckley, "Concubinage," in *NCE*, 4: 120–121E; E. Jombart, "Concubinage," in *DDC*, 3:1514; B. Dolhagaray, "Concubinage," in *DTC*, 3:1.796–97; W. Plöchl, *Das Eherecht des Magisters Gratianus* in *Winer Staats–und Rechtswissenschaftliche Studien* (Leipzig, 1935), pp. 49–50; G. A. Bossert, *Concubinato: Doctrina, legislación, jurisprudencia* (Rosario, Argentina: 1968), p. 33; E. Bittencourt, *O concubinato no direito*, 2d ed., 4 vols. (Rio de Janeiro, 1969), 104–5, 109, 117; P. M. Meyer, *Der Römische Konkubinat nach den Rechtsquellen und den Inschriften* (Leipzig, 1895), p. 89. Although some canonists conceded that a man might legitimately have a single concubine, plural relationships were something else again. Constantine had explicitly forbidden married men to have concubines (*Cod*, 5.26.1). This rule had prevailed up to the early imperial period as well, but plural concubinage became common during the second and third centuries — witness, for example, Gordian II, who had twenty-two acknowledged concubines (Meyer, *Der Römische Konkubinat*, p. 89). Constantine reinstated the earlier prohibition of plural concubinage and medieval Romanists insisted that civil law allowed unmarried men to have only one concubine at a time [Odofredus, *Lectura super Codice*, 3 vols. in 2 (Lyon: 1550–52), 289ra to *Code* 5:26 and Odofredus, *Lectura super Digesto Novo* (Lyon, 1552), 192ra to *Digest* 24.2.11]. The canonists evidently considered plural concubinage a relatively minor matter, for they commented on it only briefly, presumably because they believed simultaneous plural concubinage was self-evidently wrong. Given this attitude, however, it is rather startling to find a provision in the *Liber Extra* that explicitly decrees that serial concubinage did not disqualify a man for clerical ordination, although successive marriages might do so (X 1.21.6). The *glos. ord.* to this decretal *ad v. bigami* remarked wonderingly on this ruling: Nota mirabile quod plus habet hic luxuria quam castitas, arg. 34. dist. fraternitas (D.34.c.7). Joannes Andreas, *In quinque decretalism libros novella commentaria*, 5 vols. in 4 (Venice, 1581), 186vb to X 1.26.6 added that a man who had several concubines was not a bigamist, save perhaps by interpretation. For the prohibition of ordination for a twice-married man see D. 34 c. 14.

4. Jerome, *Select Letters of St. Jerome*, ed. and trans. F. A. Wright (London: William Heinemann, 1933), Ep. 22, par. 14, p. 81. See also St. Augustine, *Sermo* 224.3 in J. P. Migne, *Patrologia Latina*, 221 vols. (Paris, 1844–1900), 38:1095.

5. L. M. Epstein, *Marriage Laws in the Bible and the Talmud* (Cambridge: Harvard University Press, 1942), pp. 35–37, 53–54.

6. Augustine, *De civitate Dei* 16:34 in Migne, *PL*, 41:512–13, and *Questiones in Heptatuecham* 1.90 in Migne, *PL* 34:571; see also J. Freisen, *Geschichte des kanonischen Eherechts bis zum Verfall der Glossenliteratur*, 2d ed. (Paderborn, 1893), pp. 46–47.

7. Freisen, *Geschichte des kanonischen Eherechts*, pp. 47–48 and J. P. Lacombe, *La famille dans la société romaine: étude de moralité comparée* (Paris: Bibliotheque anthropologique, 1889), pp. 390–91.

8. *Dig*. 25.7.1.2. See also G. C. Caselli, "Concubina pro uxore: Osservazioni in merito al C. 17 del primo Concilio de Toledo," *Revista di storia del diritto Italiano* 37–38 (1964–65):163–220, esp. 105–7 and Meyer, *Der Römische Konkubinat*, p. 60. Probably the commonest reason for concubinage among Romans legally able to marry each other was the inability of the woman's family to provide an adequate dowry. See J. P. V. D. Balsdon, *Roman Women, Their History and Habits* (New York, 1963).

9. *Cod*. 5.17.11 pr.; *Dig*. 32.49.4; 48.5.14[13]4; 48.20.5.1; *Nov*. 22.3; 117.5–6. See also A. Esmein, *Le mariage en droit canonique: Études sur l'histoire du droit canonique privé*, 2 vols. (Paris, 1891), 2, 107 n, 4; Noonan, "Power to Choose," p. 425, and J. T. Noonan, "Marital affection in the canonists," *Studia Gratiana* 12 (1967):479–509.

10. *Dig*. 34.9.16.1; R. Orestano, *La struttura giuridica del matrimonio romano dal diritto classico al diritto giustinianco* (Milano, 1951).

11. Augustine, *Confessions* 2.2 in *PL* 38:675–677.

12. Augustine, *De bono conjugali* 5.5, *PL* 40, 376–377; *Epist.* 259.1, *PL* 33; 1073–1075; *Sermones App.* 288.5 and 289.4, *PL* 39:2291–93.

13. Leclercq, "Concubinat," *DACL* 3/2, 2494-2500; Lacombe, *La famille dans la société*, pp. 392-94.

14. Esmein, *La mariage en droit canonique*, 2:109-12.

15. P. Bonfante, "Nota sulla riforma giustinianea del concubinato," *Studi in onore di Silvio Perozzli* (Palermo, 1925), pp. 281-286, esp. p. 284; Esmein, *La mariage en droit canonique*, 2:108-10; Jombart, "Concubinage," pp. 1513-14; Caselli, "Concubina pro uxore," pp. 171-72; P. E. Corbett, *The Roman Law of Marriage* (Oxford, 1930), p. 92; Bossert, *Concubinato*, p. 21; O. Robleda, *El matrimonio en derecho roman. Essencia, requisitos de validez, efectos, disolubilidad* (Roma, 1970), p. 280.

16. Freisen, *Geschichte des kanonischen Eherechts*, p. 53; H. Hermann, *Die Stellung unehelicher Kinder nach kanonischem recht*, in *Kanonistische Studien und Texte* (Amsterdam, 1971), p. 51; C. Gellenick, "Marriage by Consent in Literary Sources of Medieval Germany," *Studia Gratiana* 12 (1967):555-79, esp. p. 559; V. Stückradt, *Rechtswirkungen eheähnlicher Verhältnisse* (Köln, 1964), p. 14.

17. D.34 d.p.c.3; Plöchl, *Das Eherecht*, p. 51; Freisen, *Geschichte des kanonischen Eherechts*, p. 65.

18. The decretist commentators on Gratian's text followed his definition of concubinage very closely. See Paucapalea to D. 34 in J. F. von Schulte, ed., *Die Summa des Paucapalea über das Decretum Gratiani* (Giessen, 1890), pp. 27-28; Rufinus to D. 33. c. 1 in H. Singer, ed., *Die Summa magistri Rufini zum Decretum Gratiani* (Paderborn, 1902), p. 77; Stephen of Tournai to D.33 pr. in F. J. von Schulte, *Die Summa des Stephanus Tornacensis über das Decretum Gratiani* (Giessen, 1891), p. 50 as well as *glos. ord* to D. 33 d.a.c. 1 ad v. *sed queritar* and to D. 34 c.5 *ad v. christiano*. The *Summa Parisiensis* to D. 33 pr. in T. P. McLaughlin, ed., *The Summa Parisiensis on the Decretum Gratiani* (Toronto, 1952), p. 32, distinguished explicitly between the concubine and the harlot; later commenting on D. 34 c. 4 *ad v. is qui* (McLaughlin, *Summa Parisiensis*, p. 33), the anonymous author invoked the authority of the Salic law and added that concubinage was no sin. Huguccio in his *Summa* to D. 34 c. 3 (BN MS. lat. 3892. fol 41vb) identified concubinage with clandestine marriage.

19. Thus *glos. ord* to C. 32 q. 2 d.p.c. 2 ad v. *sine ardore*.

20. C. 32 q.2 d.p.c. 5 and c. 6.

21. Hugh of St. Victor 2.11.9 in R. J. Deferrari, trans., *On the Sacraments of the Christian Faith* (Cambridge: Medieval Academy of America, 1951); Thomas Aquinas, *Summa Theologica* III Supp. 2.49 a 6 ad i; W. Boulting, *Woman in Italy, from the Introduction of the Chivalrous Service of Love to the Appearance of the Professional Actress* (London, 1910), pp. 134-35.

22. C. 32 q.2.c.1; *Summa Parisiensis* to C. 32 q.2 d.p.c. 2 *ad v item immoderatus* and C. 32 q. 4 c. 14 in McLaughlin, *Summa Parisiensis*, pp. 241, 244; Rolandus, *Summa* to C. 32 q.2 in F. Thaner, ed., *Die Summa magistri Rolandi nachmals Papstes Alexander III* (Innsbruck, 1874), p. 164; *Summa 'Elegantius in iure diuino'* 1.35 in G. Fransen and S. Kuttner, eds., *Summa 'Elegantius in iure diuino' seu Coloniensis*, in *Monumenta iuris canonici* (New York, 1969), p. 9; Raymond de Peñafort, St. *Summa sancti Raymundi de Peniafort de poenitentia et matrimonio una cum glossis Ioannis de Friburgo* (Roma, 1603), 516-17. lib. 4 *tit.* de matrimonio, 10; *glos. ord* to D. 13 d.a.c. 1 *ad v. item adversus;* D. 13 c. 2 ad v. *et quia* and *maiora* C. 27 q. 2 c. 10 *ad v. non poterat;* R. Weigand, "Kanonistische Ehetraktate aus dem 12. Jahrhundert," *Proceedings of the Third International Congress of Medieval Canon Law* (1971):65.

23. *Glos. ord.* to D. 33 q.4.c.7 *ad v. voluptate* and D. 25 d.p.c. 3 *ad v. excerto*.

24. J.-L. Flandrin, "Contraception, mariage et relations amoureuses dans l'Occident chrétien," *Annales, Économies, sociétés, civilisations* 24 (1969):1379.

25. C.32 q.2.c.5.

26. Augustine, *Sermo* 392.2 in Migne, *PL* 39, 710.

27. Thus *Summa Parisiensis* to D. 32 c. 2 *ad v. concubinam* in McLaughlin, *Summa Parisiensis*, p. 32; Bernardus Papiensis, *Summa Decretalium* 3.2.2-3 in E. A. T. Laspeyres, ed., *Bernardus Papiensis, Summa Decretalium* (Regensburg, 1860), p. 68; William of Pagula,

Summa summarum 3.2 (Cambridge: Pembroke College. MS. 201. fol. 139rb). Note also the comments in Buckley, "Concubinage," p. 121; Dolhagaray, "Concubinage," p. 798; Esmein, *Le mariage en droit,* 2:104, 114–15, and M. Boelens, *Die Klerikerehe in der Gestzgebung der Kirche unter besonderer Berüksichtigung der Strafe. Eine rechtsgeschichtliche Untersuchung von den Anfängen der Kirche bis zum Jahre 1139* (Paderborn, 1968), pp. 88, 161.

28. Rufinus, *Summa* to C. 30 q.5 c.1 *ad v. adulteria* in Singer, *Summa magistri Rufini,* p. 469. A late medieval polemicist went so far as to proclaim concubinage a more serious moral offense than murder: *Directorium concubinarum saluberrimum quo quedam studenda et quasi inaudita pericula quam apertissime resoluuntur nedum clericis aut etiam laicis hoc crimine pollutis necessariu* (Köln, 1509), 14^r; see also *Cod.* 9.9.22.

29. Thus Joannes Faventinus, *Summa* to D. 33 c. 1 (BL MS. Add. 18,369,fol. 13va).

30. D. 34 c. 4. See also D. 34 c. 5; C. 32 q.2 c. 11; C. 32 q. 4 c.9; compare D. 34 c. 6.

31. The canon law probably intended to legitimize as marriages for ecclesiastical purposes certain unions that the civil law would not recognize as marriages; Caselli, "Concubina pro uxore," pp. 218–20.

32. C. 32. q. 2 c. 12. See also J. Gaudemet, "Le lien matrimonial: Les incertitudes du haut moyen-âge," *Revue de droit canonique* 21 (1971):88–89. Similar positions were sometimes taken in secular law as well. See *Las siete partidas* 4.14.1–2 in D. J. Vargas y Ponce, ed., *Las siete partidas del don Alfonso et Sabio,* 2d ed., 5 vols. (Paris, 1851), 3:127–29.

33. Esmein, *Le mariage en droit,* 2:113–114; Plöchl, *Das Eherecht,* p. 51. Gratian was by no means the first to assimilate concubinage to marriage. Nearly a century earlier, for example, the Roman Synod of 1059 had equated all consorts of priests, whether formally married or not, with concubines (Boelens, *Die Klerikerehe,* pp. 126, 134). The intention of these two cases, however, was totally different: the synod wanted to downgrade the wives of clerics to the lesser status of concubines, while Gratian wished to raise the concubine to something like the status of a wife. The effect of both endeavors, however, was to accentuate the notion that concubinage and marriage were in essence two species of the same genus.

34. Thus, among others, Stephen of Tournai, *Summa* to D. 33 d.p.c. 6 in Schulte, *Summa des Paucapalea,* p. 51; *Summa Parisiensis* to D. 32 d.p.c. 6. D. 33 pr., C. 32 q. 2 d.p.c. 10 and c. 11 in McLaughlin, *Summa Parisiensis,* pp. 32, 33, 242; *Summa 'Magister Gratianus uolens compilare'* (Cambridge, Peterhouse, MS. 169, fol. 4va).

35. Rufinus, *Summa* to D. 34 d.a.c. 7 *ad v. ceterum* in Singer, *Summa magistri Rufini,* p. 81.

36. Huguccio, *Summa* to C. 27 q. 2 c. 10 in J. Roman, "Summa d'Huguccio sur le Décret de Gratien d'après le manuscrit 3891 de la Bibliothèque Nationale. Causa XXVII. Questio II," *Revue historique de droit français et étranger* 27 (1903):759. This sort of approach to the relationship between concubinage and marriage is hardly unique either to the medieval period or to European society. In modern Latin America, for example, Bolivia, Cuba, Guatemala, and Panama all have established rather similar parities between concubinage and marriage (Bossert, *Concubinato,* p. 28). Similarly in the People's Republic of China a branch court of the Supreme Court for Southwestern China has ruled that: "A man and woman who have the intention of living together forever must be regarded as having marital relations [i.e., a marital relationship] regardless of whether they have performed marriage rites or not" (J. M. Meijer, "Problems of Translating the Marriage Law," in J. A. Cohen, ed., *Contemporary Chinese Law: Research Problems and Perspectives* (Cambridge, Mass.: Harvard Univ. Press, 1970), p. 218. This position probably reflects some survival of the traditional Chinese law on concubinage; D. C. Buxbaum, ed., *Family Law and Customary Law in Asia: A Contemporary Legal Perspective* (New York: International Publication Service, 1968), pp. 47–48.

37. Rolandus, *Summa* to C. 32 q. 4 c. 4 in Thaner, *Summa magistri Rolandi,* p. 171; Hostiensis, *In quinque Decretalium libri commentaria,* 5 vols. in 2 (Venezia, 1581), 35rb to X.4.17.5.

38. Thus, for example, the *glos ord.* to C. 31 q. 1 c. 3 *ad v. claudatur* states that if a man swears not to copulate with his concubine and then subsequently marries her, he has not committed perjury. The glossator here obviously assumed that there was an essential change in the

relationship by reason of the celebration of the marriage rite. Hostiensis' statement in his *Lectura to X 1.21.6 ad v. non incurrint (In quinque Decretalium)*, 123va that the marriage sacrament does not exist in concubinage was presumably intended to apply only to a relationship in which *affectio maritalis* was lacking.

39. Plöchl, *Das Eherecht*, p. 50; F. E. Adami, "Precizazioni in tema die consenso matrimoniale nel pensiero patristico," *Il diritto ecclesiastico* 76 (1965):209. Maitland's remarks in F. Pollock and F. W. Maitland, *The History of English Law before the Time of Edward I*, 2d ed., 2 vols. (Cambridge: Cambridge Univ. Press, 1968), 2:385 on the distinction between *de facto* marriage and concubinage are based on assumptions foreign to twelfth- and thirteenth-century canonistic thought.

40. H. Finke, *Die Frau im Mittelalter* (Kempten, 1913), pp. 52–53, and Noonan, "Marital Affection in the Canonists," p. 509.

41. Plöchl, *Das Eherecht*, p. 50.

42. *Cod.* 5.17.11 pr.; *Dig.* 32.49.4; 39.5.31 pr.; *Nov.* 117–6.

43. P. Gide, *Étude sur la condition privée de la femme dans le droit ancien et moderne et en particulier sur le sénatus-consulte velléien*, 2d ed. (Paris, 1885), p. 551; Caselli, "Concubina pro uxore," pp. 173–74; Corbett, *Roman Law*, p. 95.

44. Noonan, "Marital Affection in the Canonists," pp. 482–489.

45. *Dig.* 48.20.5.1; *Nov.* 22.3; Adami, "Precizazioni in tema," pp. 211–12.

46. J. Guademet, "Originalité et destin du mariage romain," *L'Europa e il diritto romano* 2 (Milano, 1954), p. 517.

47. *Summa* to C. 27 q. 2 c. 36 *ad v. quam conjunctionem* in Roman, "Summa d'Huguccio," p. 793.

48. *Summa Parisiensis* to D. 33 c. 1 *ad v. concubinam* in McLaughlin, *Summa Parisiensis*, p. 32; Rufinus, *Summa* to D. 34 d.a.c. 4 *ad v. coniugale affectu asciscitur* in Singer, *Summa magistri Rufini*, p. 80; Sicard of Cremona, *Summa* to D. 33 *ad v. concubina ducitur* (BL MS. Add. 18.367, fol. 8[ra]). Even more explicit is Joannes Faventinus, *Summa* to D. 34 d.p.c. 3 *ad v. coniugale affectus asciscitur* (BL MS Add. 18.369, fol. 14[rb]).

49. *Summa Parisiensis* to D. 34 d.p.c. 6 *ad v. ceterum* in McLaughlin, *Summa Parisiensis*, p. 33.

50. Rufinus, *Summa* to D. 34 d.p.c. 6 *ad v. ceterum* in Singer, *Summa magistri Rufini*, p. 81, repeated verbatim by Joannes Faventinus in BL MS. Add. 18.369, fol. 14[rb]; Huguccio, *Summa* to C. 27 q. 2 c. 51 in Roman, "Summa d'Huguccio," p. 803.

51. Huguccio, *Summa* to C. 27 q. 2 c. 17 *ad v. nuptiale misterium* in Roman, "Summa d'Huguccio," p. 766.

52. Pollock and Maitland, *History of English Law*, 2:368, 385. Also G. E. Howard, *A History of Matrimonial Institutions, Chiefly in England and the United States*, 3 vols. (Chicago, 1904), I:324, and D. M. Stenton, *The English Woman in History* (London, 1957), pp. 44–46. For a twelfth-century comment see Huguccio, *Summa* to C. 27 q. 2 d.p.c. 45 *ad v. ex his omnibus* in Roman, "Summa d'Huguccio," p. 799.

53. Corbett, *Roman Law*, p. 68; Howard, *History of Matrimonial Institutions*, I:291.

54. Howard, *History of Matrimonial Institutions*, I:334; Orestano, *La struttura giuridica*, pp. 187–88.

55. *Dig.* 23.1.1–2; *Inst.* 1.9 pr.; also *Dig.* 1.5.11:1.1.1.3.

56. *Dig.* 24.1.32.13.

57. J. Mullenders, *Le marriage présumé* (Roma: Analecta Gregoriana, 1971), p. 10.

58. Ibid., pp. 11–12; Noonan, "Power to Choose," p. 424; J. Gaudemet, "La Définition romano-canonique du marriage," *Speculum iuris et ecclesiarum* (Wien, 1967), pp. 107–14.

59. See Chapter 9, this book, by Penny Gold; see also G. Fransen, "La formation du lien matrimonial au moyen âge," *Revue de droit canonique* 21 (1971):106–26, esp. 108.

60. Huguccio, *Summa* to C. 27 q. 2 pr. *ad v. matrimonium est coniunctio* in Roman, "Summa d'Huguccio," p. 747; also *Summa* to D. 1 c. 7 *ad v. ut uiri et femine coniunctio*, BN MS. lat. 3892, fol. 2va.

61. Raymond of Peñafort, *Summa sancti Raymundi,* p. 511.

62. Hostiensis, *In quinque Decretalium,* 34ʳᵃ to X 4.16.7. In some isolated regions, however, this consensual theory apparently did not prevail in practice. See R. Frank, "Marriage in Twelfth- and Thirteenth-Century Iceland," *Viator* 4 (1973):473–84.

63. Mullenders, *Le marriage présumé,* p. 13.

64. Pollock and Maitland, *History of English Law,* 2:368–69.

65. Huguccio, *Summa* to C. 27 q. 2 pr. in Roman, "Summa d'Huguccio," p. 746; Howard, *History of Matrimonial Institutions,* 1:315; C. Nani, *Storia del diritto privato italiano* (Torino, 1902), pp. 175–76.

66. S. P. Heany, *The Development of the Sacramentality of Marriage from Anselm of Laon to Thomas Aquinas* (Washington, D.C.: Catholic University of America, 1963), and D. S. Bailey, *Sexual Relation in Christian Thought* (New York, 1959), pp. 139–41. Huguccio considered the unity and inseparabilty of the married couple to be the marriage sacrament and held that their consent to this unity brought the sacrament into being: *Summa* to C. 27 q. 2 pr. and c. 10 in Roman, "Summa d'Huguccio," pp. 749, 758. On Hugh of St. Victor's theory of two sacraments see Gold above, and Mullenders, *Le marriage présumé,* p. 14.

67. Huguccio, *Summa* to C. 27 q. 2 c. 2 in Roman, "Summa d'Huguccio," p. 751.

68. Gaudamet, *Originalité et destin du marriage romain,* p. 541, and A. Marongiu, "La forma religiosa del matrimonio nel diritto bizantino, normanno e svevo," *Archivio storico per la Calabria e la Lucania* 30 (1961):3–10.

69. K. Ritzer, *Le marriage dans les églises chrétiennes du Iᵉʳ aux XIᵉ siècle* (Paris: Lex Orandi, 1970), and M. M. Sheehan, "The Formation and Stability of Marriage in Fourteenth-Century England: Evidence of an Ely Register," *Mediaeval Studies* 33 (1971):228–63.

70. Huguccio, *Summa* to C. 27 q. 2 c. 2 *ad v. solus* in Roman, "Summa d'Huguccio," pp. 750–51; Fransen, "Formation au moyen âge," p. 125. Secular law in south Italy, however, demanded formal marriage ceremonies as a condition of validity: Marongiu, "Forma matrimonio bizantino," pp. 10–11, and A. Marongiu, "La forma religiosa del matrimonio nel regno di Napoli," *Studi in memoria di Romualdo Trifone* (Sapri, 1963), 1:1–10.

71. C. 30 q. 5 c. 6; Rufinus, *Summa* to D. 34 d.p.c. 3 *ad v. que cessantibus legalibus instrumentis* in Singer, *Summa magistri Rufini,* p. 80. Joannes Faventinus, commenting on D. 34 d.p.c. 3 *ad v. que cessantibus legalibus instrumentis* echoes the words of Rufinus almost verbatim (BL MS. Add 18.369, fol. 14ʳᵇ).

72. *COD,* 234 c. 51. The requirement was reiterated later by local synods, as for example in the statutes of Coventry c. 13; see F. M. Powicke and C. R. Cheney, ed., *Councils and Synods with Other Documents Relating to the English Church,* 2 vols. (Oxford, 1964), p. 212.

73. X 4.3.3.; Esmein, *Le mariage en droit,* I:180.

74. J. Dauvillier, *Le marriage dans le droit classique de l'église depui le Décret de Gratien (1140) jusqu'à mort de Clément V (1314)* (Paris, 1933), p. 102; Plöchl, *Das Eherecht,* p. 46; Esmein, *Le mariage en droit,* 2:127; Sheehan, "Formation and Stability of Marriage," pp. 253–55.

75. *Summa* to C. 30 q. 5 pr. in Singer, *Summa magistri Rufini,* p. 468.

76. Sheehan, "Formation and Stability of Marriage," pp. 228–63; H. A. Kelly, "Clandestine Marriage and Chaucer's *Troilus,*" *Viator* 4 (1973):435–57.

77. Thus Huguccio, *Summa* to d. 33 d.p.c. 1 *ad v. concubina* BN MS. Lat. 3892, fol. 41ʳᵃ. Also Joannes Faventinus, *Summa* to D. 34 c. 4 *ad v. aut concubine* (BL MS Add. 18.369, fol. 14ʳᵇ).

78. The Roman law theory of presumptive marriage held essentially that where a free woman was living with a man, their relationship was presumed to be a marriage unless proof of the contrary were shown; where a man of senatorial rank was living with a freedwoman, on the other hand, the relationship was presumed to be concubinage; *Dig.* 23.2.24.27; Freisen, *Geschichte des kanonischen Eherechts,* p. 49.

79. *Summa* to C. 27 q. 2 in Dauvillier, *Le marriage classique,* p. 57.

80. X 4.1.30; Dauvillier, *Le marriage classique,* pp. 59, 61.

81. Odofredus, *Lectura super Digesto* 172va-vb to *Dig.* 23.2.24.

82. Dauvillier, *Le marriage classique,* p. 67.

83. For some examples of twelfth- and thirteenth-century puzzlement over these anomalies, see *glos. ord.* to C. 32 q. 4 c. 9 *ad v. illictus* and to D. 34 d.p.c. 3 *ad v. lex:* Placentinus, *Summa Codicis* (Mainz, 1536), 218 to *Cod* 5.26; *Summa 'Elegantius'* 2.36 in Fransen and Kuttner, *Summa seu Coloniensis,* pp. 58–59; Cino da Pistoia, *In Codicem et aliquot titulos primi Pandectarum tomi, id est Digesti Veteris, doctissima commentaria,* 2 vols. (Frankfurt A/M, 1578), 292va to *Cod.* 5.4.4.; Hostiensis, *In quinque Decretalium,* 79rb to X 3.26.16.

84. Vern L. Bullough, *The Subordinate Sex: A History of Attitudes Toward Women* (Urbana, Ill., 1973), p. 164.

85. Sheehan, "Formation and Stability of Marriage," pp. 253–55; P. Wolff, "Quelques acts notariés concernant famille et mariage (XIVe-XVe siècles)," *Annales du Midi* 78 (1966), 115–23; Boulting, *Woman in Italy,* pp. 278–79; P. Hair, ed., *Before the Bawdy Court. Selections from Church Court and Other Records Relating to the Correction of Moral Offences in England, Scotland, and New England, 1300–1800* (London, 1972), pp. 45, 177, 200; G. L. Barni, "Un contratto di concubinato in Corsica nel XIII secolo," *Revista di storia del diritto Italiano* 22 (1949), 131–35; Frank, "Marriage in Iceland," p. 480; G. Laribière, "Le mariage à Toulouse au XIVe et XVe siècles," *Annales du Midi* 79 (1967):341; *Leggi e memorie Venete sulla prostituzione fino alla cadutto della Republica* (Venezia, 1870–72), p. 203.

86. Benencasus, *Casus* to D. 81 c. 15 *ad v. si qui,* and *Distinctiones Monaccenses* to D. 28 c. 17, in F. Liotta, *La continenza dei chierici nel pensiero canonistico classico da Graziano a Gregorio IX* (Milano: Quaderni di 'Studi Senesi,' 1971), pp. 131, 190.

87. *Dig.* 23.2.56; 25.7.1.3–4; 27.3 pr., 1, 5; Gide, *Étude condition la femme,* pp. 355–59; S. Solazzi, "Il concubinato con l'obscuro loco nata," *Studia et documenta historiae et iuris* 13–14 (1947–48):269–77; R. Astolfi, "Femina probosa, concubina, mater solitaria," *Studia et documenta historiae et iuris* 31 (1965):15–60.

88. *Dig.* 23.2.4.; 25.2.17 pr.; 25.71. pr.; Gide, *Étude condition la femme,* p. 563; Leclercq, "Concubinat," p. 2497.

89. A. Marongiu, *La famiglia nell'Italia meridionale (sec. VIII-XIII).* (Milano: Biblioteca dell'Unione Cattolica per le Scienze Sociale, 1944), pp. 91–93 gives a dozen examples from Neapolitan archives of documents containing a clause whereby a man renounces his concubine. The renunciation was usually addressed to the man's fiancée or her family, and the man normally promised to give the concubine to his fiancée to dispose of as she pleased.

90. Odofredus, *Lectura super Digesto Novo,* 35rb to *Dig.* 39.5.31; also *Dig.* 24.1.1; 24.1.3.; Boulting, *Woman in Italy,* p. 279.

91. *Nov.* 18.5; 89.12.2, 4,5; *X* 4.17.12. She could not receive a bequest from her lover if he were a cleric, according to William of Pagula, *Summa summarum* 3.2 (Cambridge: Pembroke College MS 201, fol. 139va). Simone de Borsano, in his *Lectura in Clem., proem, pars prima,* taught that those who held the doctoral degree were also forbidden to leave legacies to their concubines; see D. Maffei, "Dottori e studenti nel pensiro di Simone da Borsano, *Studia Gratiana* 15 (1972):229–50, esp. 242.

92. *Glos. ord.* to X 1.17.13 *ad v. consisterit;* Esmein, *Le mariage en droit,* 2:31, 38.

93. Bernardus Papiensis, *Summa decretalium* 4.18.3 in Laspeyres, *Bernardus Papiensis,* p. 183; Azo, *Summa super Codicem* (Pavia, 1506), 193 to *Cod.* 5.26.1; Odofredus, *Lectura super Codice,* 52:289ra to *Cod.* 5.26; Meyer, *Der Römische Konkubinat,* pp. 52–55; Hermann, *Stellung unehelicher Kinder,* pp. 45–47.

94. X 4.17.9.

95. Joannes Faventinus, *Summa* to C. 32 q. 2 c. 12 *ad. v. non omnis* (BL MS. Add. 18.369, fol. 145rb). Also X 4.17.12.

96. A seventh-century Spanish canon, incorporated in Gratian's *Decretum,* provided that the children of such unions were to become slaves of the Church: C. 15 q. 8 c. 3. By the last half of the twelfth century such savage rules had fallen totally into disuse and Rufinus labeled them "ridiculous" in his *Summa* to D. 81 c. 30 (Singer, *Summa magistri Rufini,* p. 172).

Nonetheless, the children of a cleric's concubine suffered special disadvantages; see H. Winterer, "Zur Priesterehe in Spanien bis zum Ausgang des Mittelalters," *Zeitschrift der Savigny-Stiftung für Rechtsgeschichte, kanonistische Abteilung* 52 (1966):370–83, esp. p. 372; R. C. Trexler, *Synodal Law in Florence and Fiesole 1306–1518, Studi e testi* (Vatican, 1971), 235–36.

97. *COD*, 599; *Constituion Supernae dispensationis,* par. 36; Freisen, *Geschichte des kanonischen Eherechts,* pp. 70–71.

98. *Sess.* 24 c. 8 in *COD* 1962:734–35; Esmein, *Le mariage en droit,* 2:310–14; local ordinances previously had sometimes prohibited lay concubinage as, for example, the Avignonese ordinances in L. Lepileur, ed., *La prostitution du XIIIe au XVIIe siècle. Documents tirès des archives d'Avignon, Comtat Venaissin, de la principauté d'Orange, et de la ville impériale de Besançon* (Paris, 1908), pp. 10, 13, and the Forli statutes in E. Rinaldi, "La donna negli statuti del commune di Forli, sec. XIV," *Studi storici* 18 (1909):185–200. Even a quarter of a century later, however, a jurist writing an opinion for Count Fugger spoke of concubinage as a *crimen mere ecclesiasticum* (Philadelphia: University of Pennsylvania. MS. Lea 376, fol 1^v).

99. *Sess.* 24 c. 1 in *COD,* 731–33; For an enlightening discussion and analysis of the controversies leading up to Trent's decisions on marriage reforms see R. Lettman, *Die Diskussion über di klandestinen Ehen und die Einführung einer zur Gültigkeit verptlichtenden Eheschliessungsform auf den Konzil von Trient* (Münster: Münsterische Beiträge zur Theologie, 1967); clandestine marriage persisted in England, however, down to 1753; see C. Lasch, "The Suppression of Clandestine Marriage in England: The Marriage Act of 1753," *Salmagundi* 26 (1974):90–109.

100. Pollock and Maitland, *History of English Law,* 2:385; Sheehan, "Formation and Stability of Marriage," pp. 261–63.

Chapter 11

Adultery and Fornication: A Study in Legal Theology

1. John 8:7.

2. Among many others, one might cite St. Jerome, *Adversus Jovinianum* 1.20 (*PL* 23:249); Arnobius, *Adversus gentes* 3.9–10, 4.19 (*PL* 5:947–50, 1039); Tertullian, *Ad uxorem* 1 (*PL* 1:1385–89); Hugh of St. Victor, *On the Sacraments of the Christian Faith* 2.11.9, trans. Roy J. Deferrari (Cambridge, Mass.: Mediaeval Academy of America, 1951), p. 342. Similar attitudes were expressed by the canonists, among whom one might cite, by way of example only, Joannes Teutonicus, *Glossa ordinaria* to D. 13 d.a.c. 1 ad v. *Item adversus; Summa 'Elegantius in iure diuino' seu Coloniensis* 1.35, ed. Gérard Fransen and Stephan Kuttner, Monumenta iuris canonici, ser. A. vol. 1 (New York: Fordham University Press, 1969), 1:39.

3. Joseph Freisen, *Geschichte des kanonischen Eherechts bis zum Verfall der Glossenliteratur,* 2d ed. (Paderborn: F. Schöningh, 1893; rpt. Aalen: Scientia Verlag, 1963), p. 45.

4. W. E. H. Lecky, *History of European Morals,* 2 vols. (New York: George Braziller, 1955), 2:282; Bronislaw Malinowski, "Parenthood, The Basis of Social Structure," in *The Family: Its Structure and Function,* ed. Rose Laub Cross (New York: St. Martin's Press, 1964), pp. 18–19.

5. Again, by way of example only, Lévy's study of the fourteenth-century register of the *officialis* of Paris reports twenty-one adultery cases and ten other cases of illicit intercourse; Kelly, dealing with the records of the *officialis* of Rochester, states that unlawful intercourse is shown in at least 124 of the 190 cases he examined; and Pearson's publication of the cases of a Worcester ruridecanal court shows that adultery or fornication figured in 88 percent of the preserved cases. See Jean-Philippe Lévy, "L'officialité de Paris et les questions familiales à la fin du XIVe siècle," *Études d'histoire du droit canonique dédiées à Gabriel Le Bras,* 2 vols. (Paris:

Sirey, 1965), 2:1277 n. 85; Henry Ansgar Kelly, "Clandestine Marriage and Chaucer's *Troilus*" *Viator* 4 (1973):440; Frank S. Pearson, "Records of a Ruridecanal Court of 1300" in *Collectanea of the Worcestershire Historical Society,* ed. S. G. Hamilton (London: Worcestershire Historical Society, 1912), pp. 69–80.

6. C. 36 q. 1 d.p.c. 2 §1: Fornicatio autem, licet videatur esse genus cuiuslibet illiciti coitus, qui fit extra uxorem legitimam, tamen specialiter intelligitur in usu viduarum, vel meretricum, vel concubinarum.

7. C. 32 q. 4 d.p.c. 10.

8. C. 32 q. 4 c. 12, citing Jerome on Gal. 5:19.

9. C. 34 q. 2 d.p.c. 7.

10. C. 32 q. 2 d.p.c. 1.

11. *Glos. ord.* to D. 13 c. 2 ad v. *maiora.*

12. C. 32 q. 2 c. 7; cf. John T. Noonan, Jr., *Contraception: A History of Its Treatment by the Catholic Theologians and Canonists* (Cambridge, Mass.: Belknap Press, 1965), pp. 129–30.

13. Huguccio to C. 15 q. 8 c. 1 pr. (BN, ms. lat. 3892, fol. 225va); Joannes Andreae, *In quinque decretalium libros novella commentaria* to X 4.13.6, no. 5 (Venetiis: Apud Franciscum Franciscium, 1581; rpt. Torino: Bottega d'Erasmo, 1963) fol. 41rb; A. Esmein, *Le mariage en droit canonique,* 2 vols. (Paris: Sirey, 1891; rpt. New York: Ben Franklin, 1968), 2:104.

14. C. 28 q. 1 c. 5.

15. X 3.32.20.

16. X 4.19.2.

17. C. 28 q. 1 c. 5.

18. C. 27 q. 1 c. 20.

19. C. 14 q. 6 c. 4.

20. *Glos. ord.* to X 4.15.6 ad v. *fornicario modo.*

21. *Glos. ord.* to D. 34 c. 7 ad v. *non patitur.*

22. X 3.2.7, 10.

23. C. 27 q. 2 c. 24.

24. Y.-B. Brissaud, "L'infanticide à la fin du moyen âge, ses motivations psychologiques et sa répression," *Revue historique de droit français et étranger,* 4th ser. 50 (1972):232. Likewise Jerome of Ascoli accused the Greeks of holding that simple fornication was no sin, a charge that Albertus Magnus repeated: Deno Geanakoplis, "Bonaventura, The Two Mendicant Orders, and the Greeks" (Paper delivered at the annual meeting of the American Historical Association, Chicago, 1974).

25. Azo, *Summa super Codicem* 9.9 (Pavia: Per Bernardum et Ambrosium fratres de Rouellis, 1506; rpt. Torino: Bottega d'Erasmo, 1966), p. 329.

26. J. A. C. Thomas, "Lex Julia de adulteriis coercendis," *Études offertes à Jean Macqueron* (Aix-en-Provence, 1970), p. 637.

27. C. 36 q. 1 d.p.c. 2 §3; C. 32 q. 1 c. 11.

28. C. 32 q. 5 d.p.c. 14, c. 16.

29. C. 32 q. 4 c. 4; likewise Azo, *Summa* to Cod. 9.9 (pp. 329–30).

30. C. 32 q. 5 c. 13; *glos. ord.* to C. 27 q. 1 c. 20 ad v. *peiores.*

31. Justina Ruiz de Conde, *El amor y el matrimonio secreto en los libros caballerias* (Madrid: Aguilar, 1948), p. 21.

32. C. 30 q. 1 c. 9.

33. C. 32 q. 2 c. 2; C. 32 q. 7 c. 27.

34. Rufinus, *Summa decretorum* to C. 30 q. 5 c. 1 ad v. *adulteria,* ed. H. Singer (Paderborn: F. Schöningh, 1902; rpt. Aalen: Scientia Verlag, 1963), p. 469.

35. C. 32 q. 7. c. 7.

36. C. 34 q. 2 c. 6.

37. *Glos. ord.* to X 4.15.6.

38. C. 32 q. 5 c. 4.

39. Thomas, "Lex Julia," p. 637.

40. C. 32 q. 4 c. 4; C. 32 q. 5 c. 23.

41. C. 32 q. 6 c. 4–5.

42. C. 32 q. 7 c. 15.

43. C. 32 q. 7 d.p.c. 10 and c. 11, 14.

44. *Summa Parisiensis* to C. 6 q. 1 pr. ad v. *notati,* ed. T. P. McLaughlin (Toronto: Pontifical Institute of Mediaeval Studies, 1952), p. 130; C. 6 q. 1 c. 17.

45. Lévy, "L'officialité de Paris," 1277; Robert C. Trexler, *Synodal Law in Florence and Fiesole, 1306–1518* (Città del Vaticano: Biblioteca Apostolica Vaticana, 1971; Studi e testi, vol. 268), p. 50.

46. *Glos. ord.* to D. 32 c. 5 ad v. *audiat.*

47. Michael M. Sheehan, "The Formation and Stability of Marriage in Fourteenth-Century England: Evidence of an Ely Register" *Mediaeval Studies* 33 (1971):253–55; Richard H. Helmholz, "Abjuration *sub pena nubendi* in the Church Courts of Medieval England," *The Jurist* 32 (1972):80–90.

48. Thomas, "Lex Julia," p. 638.

49. Thomas, "Lex Julia," pp. 640–41.

50. E.g., *The Lombard Laws,* Rothair 212, trans. Katherine Fisher Drew (Philadelphia: University of Pennsylvania Press, 1973), p. 93.

51. C. 33 q. 2 c. 9.

52. E.g., Frederick II, Constitutiones regni Siciliae 3.74(52) in *Historia diplomatica Friderici secundi,* ed. J. L. A. Huillard-Bréholles, 6 vols. (Paris: Plon, 1852–61; rpt. Torino: Bottega d'Erasmo, 1963) 4/1:168; A. H. de Oliveira Marques, *Daily Life in Portugal in the Middle Ages* (Madison: University of Wisconsin Press, 1971), pp. 177–78; and cf. the stark summary of the so-called Doctor Raymundus von Wiener-Neustadt, *Summa legum brevis, levis et utilis* 1.30, ed. Alexander Gál (Weimar: Böhlaus, 1926): Hoc rerum secundum canones. Secundum leges autem mulier deprehensa in adulterio insaccatur vel viva sepeliatur.

53. Thus Richard H. Helmholz, "Infanticide in the Province of Canterbury during the Fifteenth Century," *History of Childhood Quarterly* 2 (1975):384; Evelina Rinaldi, "La donna negli statuti del commune di Forli, sec. XIV," *Studi storici* 18 (1909):189; *glos. ord.* to c. 32 q. 1 c. 5 ad v. *et calvatos.*

54. *Cod.* 9.9.2; 9.9.17.1; *Dig.* 48.5.2.2, 6. The medieval civilians also taught that the condoning partner might be subject to the same penalties as the adulterous spouse: *glos. ord.* to *Cod.* 9.9.2 ad v. *crimen lenocinii;* cf. Frederick II, *Constitutiones* 3.76(54) in Huillard-Bréholles 4/1:169; and *glos. ord.* to X 5.16.3 ad v. *reus sit.*

55. D. 34 c. 11.

56. C. 32 q. 7 c. 1.

57. C. 32 q. 1 c. 2; C. 32 q. 5 c. 18; C. 32 q. 7 c. 10.

58. C. 32 q. 5. c. 19–22.

59. C. 32 q. 6 d.p.c. 5; *glos. ord.* to X 5.16.6 ad v. *mutua* compensatione.

60. X 4.19.5.

61. C. 32 q. 7 c. 3; C. 27 q. 2 d.p.c. 32; X 4.7.4.

62. X 2.16.2.

63. C. 32 q. 1 c. 5–8.

64. C. 32 q. 1 c. 6.

65. *Glos. ord.* to X 5.16.3 ad v. *sed non saepe.*

66. Lévy, "L'officialité de Paris," pp. 1277–78; Sheehan, "Fornication and Stability of Marriage" found only one adultery case in the register he examined—but forty-nine bigamy cases.

67. The law on this point was slow to crystallize. Ivo of Chartres found it extremely difficult to settle such a question on the basis of the late eleventh-century law and even Gratian in the mid-twelfth century was not really clear on the matter, although he discussed it at two points in the *Decretum.* By the beginning of the thirteenth century a doctrine of legal affinity was beginning to emerge: Esmein, *Le mariage,* 1:208–10; C. 31 q. 1 c. 1–5; X 4.7.1, 3, 5, 6; 4.13.8.

68. D. 56, c. 5-8.
69. D. 56 d.p.c. 13.
70. See the remarks of Michael M. Sheehan, "Marriage and Family in English Conciliar and Synodal Legislation," in *Essays in Honor of Anton Charles Pegis*, ed. J. Reginald O'Donnell (Toronto: Pontifical Institute of Mediaeval Studies, 1974), pp. 211-12.
71. Cf. the remarks of Lecky, *History of European Morals*, 2:351.

Chapter 12

The Problem of Impotence

1. On the theoretical views of the canonists concerning the role of sexual relations in marriage, see the chapter by J. A. Brundage, "Carnal Delight: The Sexual Theories of the Medieval Canonists" in *Proceedings of the Fifth International Congress of Medieval Canon Law* (Vatican City, forthcoming).
2. *Glos. ord.* to C. 33 q. 1 pr. ad v. *quod autem.* Bernardus Papiensis, *Summa decretalium* 4.16.2, ed. E. A. T. Laspeyres (Regensburg, 1860; repr. Graz, 1956), p. 176.
3. C. 33 q. 1 c. 2; C. 27 q. 2 c. 29 and *dictum post.*
4. C. 33 q. 1 c. 2 and *glos. ord.* ad v. *innupti.*
5. C. 33 q. 1 c. 3.
6. *Glos. ord.* to C. 33 q. 1 c. 3 ad v. *tempore.*
7. C. 33 q. 1 c. 4.
8. *Glos. ord.* to C. 33 q. 1 c. 1 ad v. *probare;* C. 33 q. 1 c. 2; Vincentius Hispanus, *Lectura* to 1 Comp. 5.14.4 = X 5.17.6, in Salamanca, Biblioteca de la Universidad, MS. 2186, fol. 206rb.
9. *Glos. ord.* to C. 33 q. 1 c. 1 ad v. *per iustum.*
10. *Glos. ord.* to C. 33 q. 1 c. 1 ad v. *judicium* and to c. 2 ad v. *septima manu.* Johannes Faventinus, *Summa* to C. 27 q. 2 c. 29, in London, British Library, MS. Royal 9.E.VII, fol. 136ra.
11. C. 33 q. 1 c. 2.
12. 1 Comp. 4.16.2 (X--).
13. 1 Comp. 4.16.4 (X--).
14. 1 Comp. 4.16.1 = X 4.15.1; 1 Comp. 4.16.3 = X 4.15.2; 2 Comp. 4.19.1 = X 4.15.3; 5 Comp. 4.2. un. = X 4.15.7.
15. 2 Comp. 4.9.3. = X 4.15.5; 3 Comp. 4.11.un. = X 4.15.6.
16. 2 Comp. 4.9.2 = X 4.15.4.
17. 3 Comp. 4.11.un. = X 4.15.6.
18. *Glos. ord.* to X 4.15.2 ad v. *impotentes;* cf. Tancredus, *Apparatus* to 1 Comp. 4.16.3 = X 4.15.2 ad v. *impotentes,* in Cambridge, Gonville and Caius College, MS. 28/17, p. 101b.
19. *Glos. ord.* to X 4.15.7 ad v. *cognoscendi alias.* Cf. the gloss to C. 33 q. 1 c. 4 ad v. *prioribus* in Caius MS. 283/767, fol. 196va. Tancredus developed this distinction further in his *Apparatus* to 3 Comp. 4.11.un. = X 4.15.6 ad v. *perpetuum,* in Caius MS. 28/17, p. 290b. 4.9.3 = X 4.15.5 et C. 33 q. 1 c. 4.
20. Tancredus, *Apparatus* to 3 Comp. 4.11. un. = X 4.15.6 ad v. *fornicationis,* in Caius, MS 28/17, p. 290a.
21. Tancredus, *Apparatus* to 3 Comp. 4.11.un. = X 4.15.6 ad v. *cuius simili,* in Caius MS. 28/17, p. 290a.
22. Cambridge University Library, Ely Diocesan Records, D/21/1, fol. 100^r, 102^v, 105^v, 110^r, 130^r, 134^v, 136^r, 140^v, 142^{r-v}.
23. Cambridge University Library, E. D. R., D/2/1, fol. 91^r, 94^{r-v}, 99^{r-v}, 102^v, 106^r, 107^v, 109^v, 111^v, 129^v, 134^r, 140^r, 146^v, 154^r.

24. On Étienne d'Aufrere see Georg Friedrich von Schulte, *Geschichte der Quellen und Literatur des canonischen Rechts*, 3 vols. (Stuttgart, 1875–1880; rpt. Graz, 1956) 3/1:553.

25. Stephanus Aufferius, *Decisiones* (Lyon, 1508), fol. 94ᵛ-96ᵛ.

26. X 4.1.16; 4.1.26; 4.5.7. See also the extended discussion of this problem by John T. Noonan, Jr., *Power to Dissolve: Lawyers and Marriages in the Courts of the Roman Curia* (Cambridge, Mass., 1972), pp. 80–122.

27. C. 27 q. 2 c. 3 and *glos. ord.* to *voti virginitatis;* also *glos. ord.* to X 4.1.16 ad v. *tutius.*

Chapter 13

Rape and Seduction in the Medieval Canon Law

1. Cyril J. Smith, "History of Rape and Rape Laws," *Women Lawyers Journal* 60 (1974), pp. 188–189; Oliver v. United States (1916) 230 F. 971, cert. den. 241 U.S. 670.

2. Obviously, this statement cuts a wide swath, but it is, I think, supportable. For the Anglo-American common law jurisdictions the basic definition of rape was formulated by Sir William Blackstone, *Commentaries* 4.120, ed. St. George Tucker, 5 vols. (Philadelphia, 1803), 5:209, who defines the crime of rape as "the carnal knowledge of a woman forcibly and against her will." This classic statement has been incorporated, often verbatim, into modern statute law in many jurisdictions (e.g., Wis. Stats. Ann. 944.01) and widely accepted by the courts and legal commentators; Starr v. State (Wisconsin, 1931) 237 NW 96, 205 Wis. 310; People v. McIlwain (California, 1942) 130 P 2d 141 at 136, 55 Cal. App. 2d. 322; 75 *Corpus juris secundum,* "Rape" §1. Current English statute law concerning rape (Sexual Offences Act, 1956 §1) does not define the offense but relies upon the common law definition: *Sexual Offences: A Report of the Cambridge Department of Criminal Science* (London, 1957), p. 321. For Belgian law, see F. Dumon, "A Comparison between the Law Relating to Sexual Offences in Belgium and in England," in *Sexual Offences,* pp. 493–94. A. Nelson, "Sexual Offences and Sexual Offenders in Denmark," in *Sexual Offences,* p. 483, treats Danish law on the subject. Swedish and Norwegian treatments of rape are described by Sten Rudholm, "Swedish Legislation and Practice Concerning Sexual Offences," and J. Andenaes, "Norwegian Legislation and Practice Concerning Sexual Offences," both in *Sexual Offences,* pp. 449–51, 467. For definitions in current use elsewhere, see *The French Penal Code,* ed. Gerhard O. W. Mueller (London, 1960), pp. 332–33; *The German Penal Code of 1871,* ed. Gerhard O. W. Mueller et al. (London, 1961), §177; Adolf Schrönke and Horst Schröder, *Strafgesetzbuch Kommentar* (München, 1967), pp. 901–4. For current Spanish law, see *Código penal,* ed. José Marquez Azcarte (Madrid, 1964), §440; also O. Garcerán de Vall y Laredo, *El rapto y su jurisprudencia* (Havana, 1945). The legal concept of rape in Spanish law (which is closer than most others to late medieval canon law) has also been assimilated by a number of Latin American legal systems; see e.g., *Código penal de la Republica Argentina y sus leyes y decretos complementarios,* ed. Fernando Marcelo Zamora (Buenos Aires, 1970), §130–131; *Código penal, lei das contravenções penais, código de menores e legislação complementar,* ed. Rubens B. Minguzzi (São Paulo, 1969), §219–220; E. Magalhões Naronha, *Direito penal,* 4th ed., 4 vols. (São Paulo, 1968–69), 3:173–96; Vitorino Prata Castelo Branco, *O advogado diante dos crimes sexualis,* 2d ed. (São Paulo, 1969), pp. 137–53.

3. August Friedrich von Pauly and G. Wissowa, eds., *Realencyclopädie der classischen Altertumswissenschaft,* 24 vols. in 49 (Stuttgart, 1894–1974), 12/1:250; Adolf Berger, *Encyclopedic Dictionary of Roman Law* (Philadelphia, 1953), p. 667; Sarah B. Pomeroy, *Goddesses, Whores, Wives and Slaves: Women in Classical Antiquity* (New York, 1975), pp. 160–61. There is a striking similarity between *raptus* in Roman law and the treatment in Jewish law of the ravishment of women. The Torah prescribed the death penalty for ravishment (Deut. 22: 25–29), but treated the act primarily as an offense against the girl's family, an attitude accepted

and further elaborated by Talmudic law. See Lewis M. Epstein, *Sex Laws in Judaism* (New York, 1967), pp. 178–89.

4. *Codex Theodosianus,* 9.24.1.

5. *Cod.* 9.13.5.

6. *Cod.* 9.13.1.1.; 1.3.53(54) pr., 3–4.

7. *Cod.* 9.13.1. pr.

8. Simon Kalifa, "Singularités matrimoniales chez les anciens germains: le rapt et le droit de la femme à disponer d'elle-même," *Revue historique de droit français et étranger,* 4th ser. 48 (1970):212–13.

9. The literature on Gratian and his work is immense. Perhaps the best brief introductions to the man and his work are by Stephan Kuttner, *Harmony from Dissonance: An Interpretation of Medieval Canon Law* (Latrobe, Pa., 1960), and "The Father of the Science of Canon Law," *The Jurist* 1 (1941):2–19. More recently Stanley Chodorow, *Christian Political Theory and Church Politics in the Mid-Twelfth Century: The Ecclesiology of Gratian's Decretum* (Berkeley, 1972) has suggested a novel reinterpretation of Gratian's work in the context of the ecclesiastical and political struggles of his time.

10. C. 27 q. 2 c. 48 and C. 36 q. 1 c. 1, citing Isidore, *Etymologiae* 5.24. Canonistic citations throughout are to the standard edition of the *Corpus iuris canonici* by E. Friedberg, 2 vols. (Leipzig, 1879) and employ the conventional canonistic citation system.

11. C. 36 q. 1 d.p.c. 2 pr.

12. C. 36 q. 1 d.p.c. 2 §5; C. 27 q. 2 d.p.c. 47. It was another matter entirely, however, if formal negotiations for marriage had begun prior to the rape. For an example of such a plea as a defense against a rape charge, see Hubert Silvestre, "Dix plaidoires inédites du XIIe siècle," *Traditio* 10 (1954):385–88.

13. On Gratian's use of the Roman law, see Stephan Kuttner, "New Studies on the Roman Law in Gratian's Decretum," *Seminar* 11 (1953):12–50, and "Additional Notes on the Roman Law in Gratian," *Seminar* 12 (1954):68–74, as well as Jean Gaudemet, "Das römische Recht in Gratians Dekret," *Oesterreichisches Archiv für Kirchenrecht* 12 (1961):177–230, and Jacqueline Rambaud-Buhot, "Les Paleae dans le Décret de Gratien," in *Proceedings of the Second International Congress of Medieval Canon Law,* ed. Stephan Kuttner and J. J. Ryan (Città del Vaticano, 1965), pp. 23–44.

14. *The Summa Parisiensis on the Decretum Gratiani* to C. 36 q. 1 pr., ed. T. J. McLaughlin (Toronto, 1952), p. 272; Stephen of Tournai, *Die Summa über das Decretum Gratiani* to C. 36 q. 1 pr., ed. J. F. von Schulte (Giessen, 1891), pp. 256–57; Rufinus, *Summa Decretorum* to C. 36 q. 1 pr., ed. H. Singer (Paderborn, 1902), p. 534; Bernardus Papiensis, *Summa Decretalium* 5.14.1, ed. E. A. T. Laspeyres (Regensburg, 1860), p. 231; Raymond of Peñafort, *Summa de poenitentia et matromonio* 2.5.1 (Roma, 1603), p. 166.

15. C. 36 q. 1 d.p.c. 3.

16. Tomás Sánchez, *De sancto matrimonii sacramento disputationum libri tres* 12.17.7, 3 vols. in 1 (Lyon, 1621), 2:46. Although Sánchez wrote after the Council of Trent had wrought basic changes in many parts of the Church's sexual law, his mastery of the medieval law makes his commentary an enormously important *summa* of late medieval positions on this area of the law. On the magisterial character of Sánchez's work, see John T. Noonan, Jr., *Power to Dissolve: Lawyers and Marriages in the Courts of the Roman Curia* (Cambridge, Mass., 1972), pp. 31–32.

17. C. 36 q. 1 d.p.c. 2.

18. C. 36 q. 1 d.p.c. 3; Carcy Campos de Medeira and Arnoldo Moreira, *Do crima de sedução* (Rio de Janeiro, 1968), p. 14.

19. Epstein, *Sex Laws in Judaism,* pp. 182–83. Rape is not a crime in the Bible.

20. Croghan v. State (1868) 22 Wis. 424 at 425.

21. Hieronymus de Zanetinis, *Tractatus utilis et quotidianus de foro conscientie et contentioso* §137, in *Tractatus universi iuris,* 28 vols. (Venezia, 1584–86) 1:86[ra]; but cf. Alexander Tartagnus, *Consiliorum,* no. 62, 2 vols. (Venezia, 1488) 1:67[rb].

22. Eleanora of Arborea, *Commentaria et glossa in Carta de logu, legum et ordinationum Sardarum,* to c. 21 (Celari, 1708), p. 56.

23. D. 1 de pen. d.p.c. 18; *Summa Parisiensis* to C. 36 pr. (ed. McLaughlin, p. 271).

24. Petrus de Monte, *Repertorium utriusque iuris,* s.v. *raptor* (Padova, 1480), fol. 221[rb]; Egidio Bossi, *Tractatus varii, qui omnem fere criminalem materiam excellenti doctrina complectuntur,* tit. De raptu mulieris §1 (Venezia, 1574), fol. 181[vb]-182[ra].

25. Bossi, *Tractatus varii,* tit. De coitu damnato § 68 (1574 ed., fol. 188[va-vb]). The English common law, by contrast, did not create the crime of statutory rape until 1576; Mortimer Levine, "A More than Ordinary Case of 'Rape' 13 and 14 Elizabeth I," *American Journal of Legal History* 7 (1963):162-63.

26. Bernard R. Crick, *Crime, Rape and Gin: Reflections on Contemporary Attitudes to Violence, Pornography and Addiction* (London, 1974), p. 65; Roger B. Dworkin, "The Resistance Standard in Rape Legislation," *Stanford Law Review* 18 (1966):680; *Sexual Offences,* p. 323.

27. Rufinus, *Summa* to C. 22 q. 5 c. 1 (ed. Singer, p. 400); cf. *Dig.* 4.2.1-2.

28. Sánchez, *De sancto matrimonii* 12.7.5 (1621 ed., 2:44).

29. Sánchez, *De sancto matrimonii* 12.7.10, 11, 32 (1621 ed., 2:44-45, 50); Bossi, *Tractatus varii,* tit. De coitu damnato § 66; tit. De raptu mulieris §7 (1574 ed., fol. 182[rb-va], 188rb).

30. Raymond of Peñafort, *Summa de penitentia* 2.5.44 (1603 ed., p. 219).

31. C. 27 q. 2 d.p.c. 49; Bossi, *Tractatus varii,* tit. De raptu mulieris §15 (1574 ed., fol. 183[rb-va]): Sánchez, *De sancto matrimonii* 12.7.7-8 (1621 ed., 2:44); Giovanni Nevizzani, *Silva nuptialis* (Lyon, 1524), fol. 73vb. For the very different consent standards employed by some modern American courts, see State v. Marable, (1940) 103 P 2d 1082 at 1085, 4 Wash. 2d 367; People v. McIlwain, (1942) 130 P 2d 131 at 135, 55 Cal. App. 2d 322; People v. Bales, (1940) 169 P 2d 262 at 265, 74 Cal. App. 2d 732; Bulls v. State, (Oklahoma, 1926) 241 P. 605 at 606; People v. Norrington, (California, 1921) 202 P 932 at 935; State v. Neil, (Idaho, 1901) 90 P 860 at 862; State v. Hoffman (1938) 280 NW 357 at 359, 228 Wis 235. For a proposal to restructure this element of modern rape law see Dworkin, "Resistance Standard," p. 683.

32. C. 36 q. 1 d.p.c. 3; Stephen of Tournai, *Summa* to C. 36 q. 1 d.p.c. 2 ad v. *patre ad animam* (ed. Schulte, p. 257); *Summa Parisiensis* to C. 36 q. 1 d.p.c. 2 (ed. McLaughlin, p. 272).

33. Rufinus, *Summa* to C. 34 q. 1 & 2 c. 3 ad v. *Legat libros* (ed. Singer, p. 508); Bossi, *Tractatus varii,* tit. De raptu mulieris §21 (1574 ed., fol. 184rb).

34. C. 27 q. 2 c. 49 = C. 36 q. 1 c. 2.

35. *Dig.* 47.9.3.5; *Cod.* 9.20.1.

36. Nevizzani, *Silva nuptialis,* 1524 ed., fol. 74ra; Sánchez, *De sancto matrimonii* 12.7.13, 20-21 (1621 ed., 2:45-47); Bossi, *Tractatus varii,* tit. De raptu mulieris §3-4 (1574 ed., fol. 182ra).

37. X 5.17.6; Adhémar Esmein, *Le mariage en droit canonique,* 2 vols. (Paris, 1891), 1:392; Richard H. Helmholz, *Marriage Litigation in Medieval England* (Cambridge, 1974), pp. 109-110.

38. Sánchez, *De sancto matrimonii* 12.7.21 (1621 ed., 2:47).

39. Nevizzani, *Silva nuptialis,* 1524 ed., fol. 73vb; Sánchez, *De sancto matrimonii* 12.7.18 (1621 ed., 2:46); Bossi, *Tractatus varii,* tit. De raptu mulieris §16 (1574 ed., fol. 183va).

40. *Cod.* 9.13.1.1(b).

41. Stephen of Tournai, *Summa* to C. 36 q. 1 d.p.c. 2 (ed. Schulte, p. 257); Innocent IV, *Apparatus toto urbe celebrandus super V libris Decretalium* to X 5.6.17 §1 (Frankfurt, 1570), fol. 515[v]; Hostiensis, *In quinque Decretalium libros commentaria[= Lectura]* to X 5.17.6 ad v. *Dicatur admitti* (Venezia, 1581), fol. 54[r]. This rule is retained by the modern common law, both in England and America; People v. Pizzura, (Michigan, 1920) 178 NW 235; 75 *Corpus juris secundum* "Rape" §6; *Sexual Offences,* pp. 324-25.

42. Nevizzani, *Silva nuptialis,* 1524 ed., fol. 74ra; Sánchez, *De sancto matrimonii* 12.7.22 (1621 ed., 2:47).

43. Petrus de Monte, *Repertorium,* s.v. *Raptor* (1480 ed., fol. 221va); Nevizzani, *Silva nuptialis,* 1524 ed., fol. 74rb; Sánchez, *De sancto matrimonii* 12.7.23 (1621 ed., 2:47); Alberto dei Gandini, *Tractatus de maleficiis,* ed. H. Kantorowicz, *Albertus Gandinus und das Strafrecht der Scholastik,* 2 vols. (Berlin, 1907–26), 2:360–61. The kings of Sicily, by contrast, tried to protect prostitutes in their kingdom from such rude attacks; Frederick II, *Constitutiones regni Siciliae* [= *Liber Augustalis*] 1.21(24), ed. J. L. A. Huillard-Bréholles, *Historia Diplomatica Friderici II,* 6 vols. in 12 (Paris, 1852–61), 4/1:23–24.

44. Bossi, *Tractatus varii,* tit., De raptu mulieris §10 (1574 ed., fol. 182vb-183ra).

45. Petrus de Monte, *Repertorium,* s. v. "Meretrix" (1480 ed., fol. 55^{ra-rb}).

46. Eleanora of Arborea, *Commentaria* to *Carta de logu,* c. 21 (1708 ed., p. 57); cf. Blackstone, *Commentaries* 4.213 (Tucker ed., 5:212), relying upon Bracton, fol. 147.

47. Sánchez, *De sancto matrimonii* 12.7.24–25, 47 (1621 ed., 2:47–48, 52); Nevizzani, *Silva nuptialis,* 1524 ed., fol. 52rb. The estimate that this was a highly unusual occurrence is borne out by modern experience as well; Norman S. Goldner, "Rape as a Heinous, but Understudied Offence," *Journal of Criminal Law, Criminology and Police Science* 63 (1972):405. Modern law usually does not recognize the offense; 75 *Corpus juris secundum,* "Rape" §6; Garcerán de Vall y Laredo, *El rapto y su jurisprudencia,* p. 12.

48. *Cod.* 9.13.1.1; Rolandus Bandinelli, *Die Summa magistri Rolandi nachmals Papstes Alexander III.* to C. 15 q. 7, ed. Friedrich Thaner (Innsbruck, 1874), p. 36.

49. Complaints about the frequency of the offense are no rarity at various periods of the Middle Ages, but court actions on rape charges are not remarkably common; see e.g., Hincmar of Reims, *De coercendis raptu viduarum, puellarum et sancimonialium,* c. 4 (*PL* 125:1019–1020) for ninth-century France and John C. Bellamy, *Crime and Public Order in England in the Later Middle Ages* (London, 1973), pp. 34, 58, for fourteenth- and fifteenth-century England.

50. DeLloyd J. Guth, "Enforcing the Law: Economic and Social Regulations during Henry VII's Reign," typescript paper, delivered at the Conference on Legal History, Cambridge, 9 July 1975.

51. X 5.17.4; Georg May, *Die geistliche Gerichtsbarkeit des Erzbischoffs von Mainz im Thüringen des späten Mittelalters* (Leipzig, 1956), pp. 209–210.

52. *Cod.* 9.13.1, 4, 5; 1.c.53 (54). 1–4; *Dig.* 48.6.5.2.

53. Statute of Westminster I, c. 13, 3 Edw. I (1275); 6 Rich. II 1.6 (1382–83); Blackstone, *Commentaries* 4.211 (ed. Tucker, 5:210–211); Bellamy, *Crime and Public Order,* p. 181; Garcerán de Vall y Laredo, *El rapto y su jurisprudencia,* pp. 2–3; Eleanora of Arborea, *Commentaria* to *Carta de logu,* c. 21 (1708 ed., p. 56).

54. C. 27 q. 2 c. 33–34; C. 36 q. 2 c. 2, 5; *Summa Parisiensis* to C. 36 q. 1 c. 3 (ed. McLaughlin, p. 272); Bernardus Papiensis, *Summa Decretalium* 5.14.2 (ed. Laspeyres, p. 231); Raymond of Peñafort, *Summa de penitentia* 2.5.3 (1603 ed., p. 168).

55. C. 36 q. 1 c. 3.

56. C. 3 q. 5 c. 9; C. 6 q. 1 c. 15, 17. On the other consequences of *infamia,* see Peter Landau, *Die Entstehung des kanonischen Infamiabegriffs von Gratian bis zur Glossa Ordinaria* (Köln, 1966).

57. *Cod.* 9.13.1.2; *Nov.* 143, 150.

58. Esmein, *Le mariage en droit canonique,* 1:391–93.

59. Kalifa, "Singularités matrimoniales" treats this subject in detail. See also Pierre Lemercier, "Une curiosité judiciare au moyen âge: la grace par mariage subséquent," *Revue historique de droit français et étranger,* 4th ser. 33 (1955):464–74.

60. C. 36 q. 2 c. 1, 4.

61. C. 36 q. 2 d.p.c. 6, c. 9, 10, d.p.c. 11.

62. Stephen of Tournai, *Summa* to C. 36 q. 2 pr. (ed. Schulte, p. 257); Rolandus, *Summa* to c. 36 q. 2 (ed. Thaner, pp. 233–234); Rufinus, *Summa* to C. 34 q. 1 & 2 c. 3; C. 36 q. 2 pr., c. 9, 11 (ed. Singer, pp. 507–08, 535–36).

63. X 5.17.7.

64. Raymond of Peñafort, *Summa de penitentia* 4.9.1, 4.11.4 (1603 ed., pp. 544–45, 552); Hostiensis, *Lectura* to X 5.17.7 ad v. *Cum raptore* (1581 ed., fol. 54ᵛ-55ʳ).

65. Sánchez, *De sancto matrimonii* 12.7.16 (1621 ed., 2:46). Visigothic law much earlier had permitted this as well: Lemercier, "Une curiosité judiciaire," p. 471.

66. 79 *Corpus juris secundum* 955.

67. *German Penal Code* §179, 182; *Código penal* (Brasil) §217; *Código penal* (Spain) §434. Seduction is not a separate offense under the French penal code, however, nor is it a crime in thirteen states of the United States; Benjamin Karpman, *The Sexual Offender and His Offences: Etiology, Pathology, Psychodynamics and Treatment* (New York, 1954), p. 18.

68. *Dig.* 47.10.9.4; 48.5.6.1; 48.5.35(34); 50.16.101 pr.; Guglielmo Castelli, "Il concubinato e la legislazione augustea," *Bolletino dell'Istituto di diritto romano* 27 (1914):65–66; J. A. C. Thomas, "Lex Julia de adulteriis coercendis," *Études offertes à Jean Macqueron* (Aix-en-Provence, 1970), p. 637; Paul Gide, *Étude sur la condition privée de la femme dans le droit ancien et moderne et en particulier sur le sénatus-consult velléien*, 2d ed. (Paris, 1885), p. 553.

69. *Dig.* 48.5.14 (13).2; Castelli, "Il concubinato" p. 59.

70. D. 1 de pen. c. 12, citing *Dig.* 47.10.9.4; see also C. 32 q. 4 c. 4 and C. 36 q. 1 d.p.c. 2 §2.

71. Paucapalea, *Summa über das Decretum Gratiani* to D. 1 de pen. c. 15, ed. J. F. von Schulte (Giessen, 1890), p. 133; Stephen of Tournai, *Summa* to C. 36 q. 1 d.p.c. 2 ad v. *Proprie virginum* (ed. Schulte, p. 257); *Summa Parisiensis* to C. 32 q. 4 c. 4 ad v. *Nemo omne stuprum* (ed. McLaughlin, p. 243).

72. *Comp. I* 5.13.1–2 = X 5.16.1–2.

73. Hostiensis, *Lectura* to X 5.16.2 ad v. *Stupro* (1581 ed., fol. 52ʳᵇ); cf. his *Summa aurea*, lib. 5, tit. De adulteriis et stupro (Lyon, 1537), fol. 244ᵛᵇ. This notion may also be implied in the gloss of William of Rennes to Raymond of Peñafort, *Summa de penitentia* 2.5.4 ad v. *Contrahere potest* (1603 ed., p. 168), which was written at approximately the same time as the *Summa aurea*. The distinction, however, can be found in Gratian's treatment of forcible coitus: C. 36 q. 1 d.p.c. 3.

74. João Mestieri, *Estudo sôbre o tipo básico do delito de estupro* (Rio de Janeiro, 1968), pp. 11, 15; Medeiros and Moreira, *Do crime de sedução*, pp. 13–14.

75. Petrus de Monte, *Repertorium*, s.v. "Seduco" (1480 ed., fol. 200ᵛᵃ); Nevizzani, *Silva nuptialis*, fol. 73ʳᵇ, 80ʳᵇ⁻ᵛᵃ.

76. Bossi, *Tractatus varii*, tit. De coitu damnato §46 (1574 ed., fol. 187ᵛᵃ).

77. D. 1 de pen. c. 15, citing *Dig.* 47.11.1.

78. C. 36 q. 2 c. 6.

79. *Comp. I* 5.13.1 = X 5.16.1, based on Exod. 22:16–17; Bernardus Papiensis, *Summa decretalium* 5.13.7 (ed. Laspeyres, pp. 229–30), further explained and amplified by William of Rennes, gloss to Raymond of Peñafort, *Summa de penitentia* 2.5.4 ad v. *Contrahere potest* (1603 ed., p. 168).

80. Tancredus, *Apparatus* to *Comp. I* 5.13.2 = X 5.16.2 ad v. *Excommunicatus*, Cambridge, Gonville and Caius MS. 28/17, p. 118ᵇ.

81. Hostiensis, *Summa aurea*, lib . 5, tit. De adulteriis et stupro §11 (1537 ed., fol. 244ᵛᵇ-245ʳᵃ); *Lectura* to X 5.16.2 ad v. *Corporaliter* (1581 ed., fol. 52ʳ).

82. May, *Die geistliche Gerichtsbarkeit*, p. 223.

Chapter 14

Prostitution in the Medieval Canon Law

1. It has even been suggested that prostitution may be older than mankind: investigators have characterized some forms of sexual behavior among chimpanzees and other primates as prostitution. See Vern L. Bullough, *The History of Prostitution* (New Hyde Park, N.Y.: University Books, 1964), p. 4, and the literature therein cited. The antiquity and ubiquity of

prostitution among human societies has often been remarked upon, although Bullough points out (p. 14) that just how universal it may be depends upon one's definition of what behavior prostitution includes. It is clear that sexual promiscuity may be discovered in virtually every human society. Promiscuity and prostitution, however, are not necessarily synonymous, although the medieval canonists tended to identify the one with the other.

2. Thus, although forbidden in the Mosaic law (Lev. 19:29, 21:7), prostitution obviously was practiced in ancient Israel (e.g., Gen. 38:12-26, Judg. 11:2, I Kings 3:16-28, etc.). Sacral prostitution is implied, though not explicitly described, in the laws of Hammurabi: see *The Babylonian Laws*, ed. with translation and commentary by G. R. Driver and Sir John C. Miles, 2 vols. (Oxford: Clarendon Press, 1955), 1:360-361, 366-367.

3. Prostitution is, in fact, extremely difficult to define satisfactorily. The problem is discussed by Bullough, *History of Prostitution*, pp. 1-2. A classic definition is given by Iwan Bloch, *Die Prostitution*, 2 vols. (Berlin: Louis Marcus, 1912-1925; Handbuch der gesamten Sexualwissenschaft), 1:38. Fernando Henriques, *Prostitution in Europe and the Americas*, 2 vols. (New York: Citadel Press, 1962), 1:17, attempts a slightly more explicit definition. A common law definition of prostitution was set down by Darling, in Rex v. de Munck, (1918) 1 KB 635: "We are of the opinion that prostitution is proved if it be shown that a woman offers her body commonly for lewdness for payment in return"; cited by T. E. James, *Prostitution and the Law* (London: Heinemann, 1951), p. 2.

4. D. 34 c. 16, citing St. Jerome, *Epist.* 64.7 ad Fabiolam: "Vidua est, cuius maritus mortuus est. Eiecta, que a marito uiuente proicitur. Meretrix, que multorum libidini patet." The conventional canonistic citation system is employed throughout this paper. For explanations, see Javier Ochoa Sanz and Aloisio Diez, *Indices canonum, titulorom et capitulorum corporis iuris canonici* (Rome: Commentarium pro Religiosis, 1964; Universa Bibliotheca Iuris, Subsidia, vol. 1), pp. iv-v. The texts of the various parts of the *Corpus* are cited from the standard edition by Emil Friedberg, 2 vols. (Leipzig: B. Tauchnitz, 1879; rpt. Graz: Akademische Druck- und Verlagsanstalt, 1959). The *glossa ordinaria* will be cited from the Venice, 1605, edition in 4 vols.

5. C. 27 q. 1 c. 41 *glos. ord.* ad v. *promiscuum*. Also Rolandus (later Pope Alexander III), *Summa* to C. 27 q. 1 c. 41 ad v. *promiscuum*, ed. Friedrich Thaner (Innsbruck: Wagner, 1874), p. 125.

6. Hostiensis (Henricus de Segusio), *In quinque Decretalium libros commentaria (= Lectura)* to *X* 4.1.20, no. 4, 5 vols, in 2 (Venice: apud Iuntas, 1581; rpt. Turin: Bottega d'Erasmo, 1965), vol. 4, fol. 6vb.

7. Joannes Andrea, *In quinque Decretalium libros novella commentaria* to *X* 3.2.6, no. 2, 5 vols. in 4 (Venice: apud Franciscum Franciscium, 1581; rpt. Turin: Bottega d'Erasmo, 1963), vol. 3, fol. 8rb, following Hostiensis, *Lectura* to *X* 3.2.6, no. 2 (*ed. cit.*, vol. 3, fol. 6rb).

8. Esp. Ulpian in *Dig.* 23.2.43; cf. also Modestinus in *Dig.* 23.2.24 and Marcellinus in *Dig.* 23.2.42. The conventional Roman law citation system is employed throughout this paper. For explanations see Javier Ochoa Sanz and Aloisio Diez, *Indices titulorum et legum corporis iuris civilis* (Rome: Commentarium pro Religiosis, 1965; Universa Bibliotheca Iuris, Subsidia, vol. 2), pp. x-xi. The texts of the *Corpus* are cited from the standard critical edition by P. Kruger, T. Mommsen, R. Schoell, and G. Kroll, 3 vols. (Berlin: Weidmann, 1872; many times reprinted). The *glossa ordinaria* will be cited from the Lyons, 1584, edition in 5 vols. The basic definitions set forth in the Roman law texts cited here identify as prostitutes the inmates of brothels, those who offer their bodies for hire in taverns and elsewhere, those who make their living by furnishing sex for pay, and promiscuous women in general, whether they take remuneration for their services or not. Public display was an important ingredient in the Roman jurists' notions about prostitution. The medieval jurists tended to identify certain occupations with prostitution and to take the view that actresses, for example, could be presumed to be prostitutes: see *Cod.* 5.4.23.1 *glos. ord.* ad v. *scenicis*. This was not a view to which the classical jurists necessarily subscribed: See Riccardo Astolfi, "Femina probrosa, concubina, mater solitaria," *Studia et documenta historiae et iuris* 31 (1965):15-60 at p. 20. The theologians

sometimes attempted to define how many men a woman must have intercourse with to merit classification as a prostitute. Bloch, *Die Prostitution*, 1:18, mentions opinions ranging from a low minimum of forty to a high minimum of 23,000.

9. *Dig.* 25.7.1, 3, 4; 34.9.16.1; 50.16.144; *Cod.* 5.26. The various senses of the term *maritalis affectio* are discussed by John T. Noonan, Jr., "Marital Affection in the Canonists," *Studia Gratiana* 12 (1967):482–489.

10. *Nov.* 89.12.4–5; Noonan, "Marital Affection," p. 489.

11. Adhémar Esmein, *Le mariage en droit canonique*, 2 vols. (Paris: L. Larose et Forcel, 1891; rpt. New York: Burt Franklin, 1968), 2:114–115. J. A. Brundage, "Concubinage and Marriage in Medieval Canon Law," chap. 10, pp. 118–128.

12. D. 34 d.a.c. 4.

13. *Summa decretorum* to D. 33 d.p.c. 1 and D. 34 d.a.c. 7 ad v. *certum si non talis,* ed. Heinrich Singer (Paderborn: F. Schöningh, 1902; rpt. Aalen: Scientia Verlag, 1963), pp. 77, 81.

14. Huguccio, *Summa* to D. 34 c. 3 (Paris, Bibliothèque Nationale, ms. lat. 3892, fol. 41vb); *Summa* to D. 33 d.p.c. 1 (B.N. lat. 3892, fol. 41ra); *Summa* to D. 33 c. 6 ad v. *concubinam relicet* (B.N. lat. 3892, fol. 41rb). *Summa 'Elegantius in iure diuino' seu Coloniensis*, 2 §36, ed. Gérard Fransen and Stephan Kuttner (New York: Fordham University Press, 1969; Monumenta Iuris Canonici, Corpus Glossatorum, vol. 1), pp. 58–59.

15. *Summa Coloniensis* 2 §37, ed. Fransen and Kuttner, p. 59; *Summa Parisiensis* to D. 33 pr., ed. Terence P. McLaughlin (Toronto: Pontifical Institute of Mediaeval Studies, 1952), p. 32; Joseph Freisen, *Geschichte des kanonischen Eherechts bis zum Verfall der Glossenliteratur*, 2d ed. (Paderborn: F. Schöningh, 1893; rpt. Aalen: Scientia Verlag, 1963), p. 58.

16. Esp. in the Mosaic law, e.g. Deut. 23:17, Lev. 19:29, 21:7, 9. Cf. the scriptural *glossa ordinaria* to Deut. 23:17, *Biblia sacra, Pentateuchus cum glossis interlineari et ordinaria, Nicolai Lyrani Postilla et Moralitates* (Lyon, 1545), fol. 358ra. Also Huguccio, *Summa* to C. 32 q. 4 c. 11 (B.N. lat. 3892, fol. 313va).

17. D. 1 c. 7 *glos. ord.* ad v. *ius naturale.*

18. *Dig.* 48.5.11(10): *Cod.* 1.4.14, 33; *Nov.* 14.1.

19. Augustine, *De ordine*, 2.4, in *PL* 32:1000.

20. Bloch, *Die Prostitution*, 1:640. See e.g., N. M. Haring, "Peter Cantor's View on Ecclesiastical Excommunication and its Practical Consequences," *Mediaeval Studies* 11 (1949): 101; St. Thomas, *Summa Theologica* 2^a 2^{ae} q. 10 a. 11; Hostiensis, *Lectura* to X 4.1.20, no. 7 (*ed. cit.*, vol. 4, fol. 6vb).

21. Nicholas of Lyra, *Postilla* to Matt., proem, quoted by Gaines Post, *Studies in Medieval Legal Thought: Public Law and the State, 1100–1322* (Princeton: Princeton University Press, 1964), p. 553 n. 151. Similar views were current in the sixteenth century: see Joost de Damhouder, *Subhaustationum compendiosa exegesis*, c. 5, in Benvenuto Straccha, *De mercatura decisiones et tractatus varii* (Lyon, 1610; rpt. Turin: Bottega d'Erasmo, 1971), p. 763; A. W. Small, *The Cameralists: The Pioneers of German Social Policy* (Chicago, 1909; rpt. New York: Burt Franklin, 1967), p. 37.

22. *Dig.* 1.1.1; D. 1 c. 7; cf. *Summa Parisiensis* to D. 1 c. 7 ad v. *coniunctio*, ed. McLaughlin, p. 2; *Summa Coloniensis* 1 §5, ed. Fransen and Kuttner, 1:2.

23. D. 50 c. 16; C. 15 q. 8 c. 1 *glos. ord.* ad v. *caetera*; Huguccio, *Summa* to D. 25 d.p.c. 3 ad v. *sine peccato* (B.N. lat. 3892, fol. 29va).

24. D. 2 de pen. c. 5 *glos. ord.* ad v. *ex qua minus.*

25. D. 13 c. 2 *glos. ord.* ad v. *nervi, testiculorum*; C. 32 q. 2 d.p.c. 2 *glos. ord.* ad v. *sine ardore*; cf. Peter Lombard's views in his *Sententiae* 2.20.1 (*PL* 192:692).

26. D. 5 c. 2; *Summa Parisiensis* to C. 32 q. 4 c. 14, ed. McLaughlin, p. 244. See also Rudolf Weigand, "Die Lehre der Kanonisten von den Ehezwecken," *Studia Gratiana* 12 (1967):443–478.

27. D. 13 d.a.c. 1 *glos. ord.* ad v. *item adversus*; D. 13 c. 2 *glos. ord.* ad v. *et quia*; D. 25 d.p.c. 3 and *glos. ord.* ad v. *excepto*; C. 27 q. 1 c. 20 *glos. ord.* ad v. *peiores*; C. 27 q. 2 c. 10 *glos. ord.* ad v. *non poterat*; C. 33 q. 4 c. 7 *glos. ord.* ad v. *voluptate*; *Summa Parisiensis* to

D. 5 c. 4 ad v. *prava,* ed. McLaughlin, p. 5. For the view of St. Thomas, see *Summa Theologica* 3 Supp. q. 49 a. 2 ad. 1.

28. C. 32 q. 7 c. 11; the *Summa Parisiensis* to C. 32 q. 2 d.p.c. 2 ad v. *item immoderatus,* ed. McLaughlin, p. 241, equates it with adultery, while D. 13 c. 2 *glos. ord.* ad v. *maiora* treats it as fornication.

29. C. 32 q. 1 c. 11 *glos. ord.* ad v. *usus mali.*

30. *X.* 1.33.12 *glos. ord.* ad v. *iurisdictionis.* Cf. Joannes Andrea, *Novella* to *X* 1.33.12, no. 6 (*ed. cit.,* vol. 1, fol. 267vb).

31. *X.* 3.32.18 *glos. ord.* ad v. *talis etas de qua suspicio.*

32. Hostiensis, *Lectura* to *X* 4.13.11, no. 1 (*ed. cit.,* vol. 4, fol. 27ra). Joannes Andrea, *Novella* to *X* 4.13.11, no. 5 (*ed. cit.,* vol. 4, vol. 42vb) follows Hostiensis virtually word-for-word.

33. Quoted in C. 27 q. 1 c. 2 *glos. ord.* ad v. *viae sunt.*

34. Hostiensis, *Lectura* to *X* 3.34.7, no. 15 (*ed. cit.,* vol. 3, fol. 127rb).

35. Thus, e.g., C. 33 q. 5 c. 3, 4, 11, d.p.c. 20; D. 5 c. 4 *glos. ord.* ad v. *ablactetur.* This was an especially acute problem for crusaders, whose extended absence might expose their wives to sexual temptations. On the canonists' treatment of this problem, see my study, "The Crusader's Wife: A Canonistic Quandary," *Studia Gratiana* 12 (1967):425–442.

36. This usage is common form, based on I Cor. 7:3–6; see Esmein, *Le mariage en droit canonique,* 1:84, 110; 2:8–13; John T. Noonan, Jr., *Contraception: A History of Its Treatment by the Catholic Theologians and Canonists* (Cambridge, Mass.: Belknap Press, 1965), pp. 283–285. Peter Herde, *Audientia litterarum contradictarum: Untersuchungen über die päpstlichen Justizbriefe und die päpstliche Delegationsgerichtsbarkeit vom 13, bis zum Beginn des 16, Jahrhunderts,* 2 vols. (Tübingen: Max Niemeyer, 1970; Bibliothek des deutschen historischen Instituts in Rom, vols. 31–32), 2:304, gives the form for delegation of trial on such a complaint.

37. Hostiensis, *Lectura* to *X* 4.15.6, no. 6 (*ed. cit.* vol. 4, fol. 33ra).

38. Hostiensis, *Lectura* to *X* 5.40.10 (*ed. cit.,* vol. 5, fol. 125vb).

39. Hostiensis, *Lectura* to *X* 3.33.2, no. 10 (*ed. cit.,* vol. 3, fol. 124rb).

40. C. 27 q. 1 c. 4; C. 32 q. 5 c. 11 *glos. ord.* ad v. *aliam:* Hostiensis, *Lectura* to *X* 2.13.10, no. 13 (*ed. cit.,* vol. 2, fol. 51rb).

41. Hostiensis, *Lectura* to *X* 4.2.1, no. 3 (*ed. cit.,* vol. 4, fol. 10ra).

42. Hostiensis, *Lectura* to *X* 4.2.4, no. 2 (*ed. cit.,* vol. 4, fol. 11rb).

43. Innocent IV, *Apparatus toto orbe celebrandus super V libris Decretalium* to *X* 1.21.5 §3 (Frankfurt, 1570), fol. 112^{v}.

44. Joannes Andrea, *Novella* to *X,* prol., no. 7 (*ed. cit.,* vol. 1, fol. 6ra).

45. Hostiensis, *Lectura* to *X* 4.13.11, no. 2 (*ed. cit.,* vol. 4, fol. 27ra), followed *ad litteram* by Joannes Andrea, *Novella* to *X* 4.13.11, no. 1.

46. C. 12 q. 2 d.p.c. 58 *glos. ord.* ad v. *capitali.*

47. Rufinus, *Summa* to C. 32 q. 2 d.p.c. 2 (ed. Singer, p. 479); *X* 5.39.25 *glos. ord.* ad v. *meretricali.*

48. E.g., Huguccio, *Summa* to D. 1 c. 7 ad v. *ut uiri et femine coniunctio* (B.N. lat. 3892, fol. 2va).

49. *Cod.* 5.27.1.1 *glos. ord.* ad v. *venenis.*

50. *Cod.* 9.9.28(29) *glos. ord.* ad v. *intemperantia vina.*

51. C. 24 q. 1 c. 28 *glos. ord.* ad v. *sed suas.*

52. Hostiensis, *Lectura* to *X* 2.23.15, no. 3 (*ed. cit.,* vol. 2, fol. 124va).

53. *X* 3.2.2 (= *Comp. I* 3.2.3): cf. D. 81 c. 22.

54. C. 11 q. 3 c. 14 *glos. ord.* ad v. *sinistrum.*

55. Hippolytus de Marsiliis, *Tractatus de fideiussoribus,* in Benvenuto Straccha, *De mercatura decisiones,* p. 689.

56. Punishment for those who frequented harlots, especially for clerics who did so, is frequently prescribed: e.g., D. 28 c. 9; D. 33 c. 6; D. 51 c. 5; Rufinus, *Summa* to D. 33 pr. (ed. Singer, p. 77); D. 32 *glos. ord.* ad v. *audiet;* Gulielmus Durantis, *Speculum iuris,* lib. 4,

partic. 4, De adulteriis et stupro, no. 5, 2 vols. in 1 (Frankfurt a/M.: Sumptibus heredum A. Wechli et J. Gymnici, 1592), 2:477. The law dealing with pimps, procurers, and brothel-keepers is extensive. See, *inter alia, Dig.* 3.2.4.2, 13.7.24.3, 48.5.2.6; *Cod.* 1.4.12, 14, 33; 4.56.1, 2, 3; 7.6.1.4; 9.9.2; 11.41.6; *Nov.* 14 (=*Auth.* coll. 3 tit. 1); Rolandus, *Summa* to C. 32 q. 1 c. 4 (ed. Thaner, p. 60); Goffredus de Trani, *Summa super titulis Decretalium* to X 5.16.4 (Lyon: Roman Morin, 1519; rpt., Aalen: Scientia Verlag, 1968), fol. 216ra; X 5.16.3 *glos. ord.* ad v. *reus sit;* Hostiensis, *Summa aurea una cum summariis et adnotationibus Nicolai Superantii,* lib. 5, De adulteriis et stupro, no. 14 (Lyon, 1537; rpt. Aalen: Scientia Verlag, 1962), fol. 245ra.

57. X 4.1.20 *glos. ord.* ad v. *publicas;* the opinions of Laurentius and Vincentius are given by Stephan Kuttner, *Kanonistische Schullehre von Gratian bis auf die Dekretalen Gregors IX.* (Vatican City: Biblioteca Apostolica Vaticana, 1935; rpt. 1961; Studi e testi, vol. 64), p. 298 n. 1.

58. Hostiensis, *Lectura* to X 4.1.20, no. 6, and 4.19.4, no. 3 (*ed. cit.,* vol. 4, fol. 6vb, 43vb).

59. Hostiensis, *Lectura* to X 5.18.3 no. 2–4, 9 (*ed. cit.,* vol. 5, fol. 55^{ra-rb}).

60. Hostiensis, *Lectura* to X 4.19.4, no. 3 (*ed. cit.,* vol. 4, fol. 43vb).

61. Leopold Brandl, *Die Sexualethik des heiligen Albertus Magnus: eine Moralgeschichtliche Untersuchung* (Regensburg: F. Putest, 1955; *Studien zur Geschichte der katholischen Moraltheologie,* vol. 2), p. 244; Dennis Doherty, *The Sexual Doctrine of Cardinal Cajetan* (Regensburg: F. Putest, 1966; Studien zur Geschichte der katholischen Moraltheologie, vol. 12), pp. 102–103.

62. St. Thomas Aquinas, *Summa Theologica,* 2^a 2^{ae} q. 118 a. 8 ad. 4; Jacques de Vitry, *Historia occidentalis,* c. 18, ed. John F. Hinnebusch (Frieburg: University Press, 1972; Spicilegium Friburgense, vol. 17), p. 99. Some modern writers have suggested that avarice is a factor in modern marriage and that the principal economic difference between marriage and prostitution lies in the nature of the return: prostitution involves the rendering of sexual services for a specified fee, while marriage provides continuous support in return for assured availability of sexual gratification: *Max Weber on Law in Economy and Society,* ed. Max Rheinstein (Cambridge, Mass.: Harvard University Press, 1954; Twentieth Century Legal Philosophy Series, vol. 6), p. 134.

63. *Dig.* 13.7.24.3; *Cod.* 1.4.12, 14, 33; 4.56.1–3; 7.6.1.4; 11.41.6; Azo, *Summa super Codicem* to *Cod.* 11.41 (Pavia: Per Bernardinum et Ambrosium fratres de Rouellis, 1506; rpt. Turin: Bottega d'Erasmo, 1966; Corpus glossatorum juris civilis, vol. 2), p. 437.

64. *Summa Parisiensis* to C. 32 q. 5 c. 1 ad v. *tolerabilius* (ed. McLaughlin, p. 245).

65. Hans Herter, "Die Soziologie der antiken Prostitution im Lichte des heidnischen und christlichen Schrifttums," *Jahrbuch für Antike und Christentum* 3 (1960):70–110; *Dig.* 9.9.28(29) *glos. ord.* ad v. *et stupri et adulterii; Dig.* 23.2.47.

66. Vern L. Bullough, "Problems and Methods for Research in Prostitution and the Behavioral Sciences," *Journal of the History of the Behavioral Sciences* 1 (1965):247.

67. Hostiensis, *Lectura* to X 3.30.23, no. 3 (*ed. cit.,* vol. 3, fol. 100vb) and 4.1.20, no. 5 (*ed. cit.,* vol. 4, fol. 6vb); *Cod.* 9.9.28(29).

68. C. 4 q. 1 c. 1.

69. C. 6 q. 1 d.a.c. 1, *glos. ord.* ad v. *quod autem.*

70. *Dig.* 29.1.41.1; 37.12.3 pr.

71. X 2.1.14 *glos. ord.* ad v. *factum proponat.*

72. *Dig.* 12.5.4, quoting Ulpian, who relies on the doctrines of Labeo and Marcellus in this passage.

73. Huguccio, *Summa* to C. 14 q. 5 d.a.c. 1 (B.N. lat. 3892, fol. 119ra); cf. D. 86 c. 7 *glos. ord.* ad v. *talibus;* Hostiensis, *Lectura* to X 3.30.23, no. 7 (*ed. cit.,* vol. 3, fol. 100vb).

74. Azo, *Summa Codicis* to *Cod.* 4.7 (*ed. cit.,* p. 115).

75. Doherty, *The Sexual Doctrine of Cardinal Cajetan,* p. 102 n. 35.

76. *Cod.* 5.3.5 *glos. ord.* ad v. *non potes;* Azo, *Summa Codicis* to *Cod.* 4.7 *(ed. cit.,* p. 115).

77. See Joannes Teutonicus, *Apparatus* to *Comp. III* 3.23.5 (=*X* 3.30.28). (Admont, Stiftsbibliothek, ms. 22, fol. 209ʳ. I wish to thank Professor Kenneth J. Pennington, Jr., for calling this passage to my attention and for his transcription of the ms.) Cf. the argument of Panormitanus, *Commentaria,* 9 vols. (Venice: Apud Iuntas, 1588) to *X* 3.30.23 (vol. 6, fol. 231ʳᵇ).

78. Hostiensis, *Lectura* to *X* 3.30.23, no. 2 *(ed. cit.),* vol. 3, fol. 100ᵛᵇ.

79. St. Thomas Aquinas, *Summa Theologica* 2ᵃ 2ᵃᵉ q. 87 a. 2 ad. 2.

80. Huguccio, *Summa* to C. 14 q. 5 d.a.c. 1 (B.N. lat. 3892, fol. 119ʳᵃ).

81. Rufinus, *Summa* to C. 14 q. 5 pr. (ed. Singer, pp. 342-343).

82. D. 90 c. 2 *glos. ord.* ad v. *dona,* ad fin.; C. 1 q. 1 c. 27 *glos. ord.* ad v. *ex illicitis rebus;* C. 14 q. 5 d.a.c. 1 *glos. ord.* ad v. *quod vero.*

83. Hostiensis, *Summa aurea,* lib. 3 tit. De voto et voti redemptione, no. 11 *(ed. cit.,* fol. 177ʳᵇ).

84. *X* 5.1.20 and *glos. ord.* ad v. *concubinarios.*

85. *Dig.* 47.2.39; 47.10.15.15; *Cod.* 9.9.22.

86. Alberto dei Gandini, *Tractatus de maleficiis,* ed. H. Kantorowicz, *Albertus Gandinus und das Stratfrecht der Scholastik,* 2 vols. (Berlin: J. Gutentag, 1907-1926), 2:360-361. In contrast, the monarchs of Sicily protected prostitutes in their kingdom from such attacks; see Frederick II, *Constitutiones regni Siciliae (=Liber Augustalis)* 1.21(24), ed. J. L. A. Huillard-Bréholles, *Historia diplomatica Friderici II,* 6 vols. in 12 (Paris: Plon, 1852-1861; rpt. Turin: Bottega d'Erasmo, 1963), 4/1:23-24.

87. Alberto dei Gandini, *Tractatus de maleficiis,* ed. Kantorowicz, 2:214.

88. E.g., Hostiensis, *Lectura* to *X* 5.6.15, no. 4 *(ed. cit.,* vol. 5, fol. 32ᵛᵇ).

89. Bullough, *History of Prostitution,* pp. 113-114; Richard Lewinsohn, *A History of Sexual Customs,* trans. A. Mayco (New York: Harper, 1958), p. 145.

90. Bullough, *History of Prostitution,* p. 112.

91. Bloch, *Die Prostitution,* 1:690.

92. Bloch, *Die Prostitution,* 1:740-745, lists seventy-five towns and cities in Germany that had brothels between the thirteenth and fifteenth centuries.

93. Bloch, *Die Prostitution,* 1:670. For a more detailed account of a slightly later period, see Ruth Pike, *Aristocrats and Traders: Sevillian Society in the Sixteenth Century* (Ithaca: Cornell University Press, 1972), pp. 195, 203-206.

94. E.g., Jean de Joinville, *The Life of St. Louis,* 36.171, trans. René Hague (New York: Sheed and Ward, 1955), p. 66; Alberto dei Gandini, *Tractatus de maleficiis,* ed. Kantorowicz, 1:243-244 (Urk. 30), 252-254 (Urk. 35); Bullough, *History of Prostitution,* p. 113. There were older — and equally ineffectual — precedents: see *Nov.* 14.1 (=*Auth. coll.* 3, tit. 1).

95. Bullough, *History of Prostitution,* p. 115; also *The Development of Medicine as a Profession: The Contribution of the Medieval University to Modern Medicine* (New York: Hafner, 1966), p. 88; Lewinsohn, *History of Sexual Customs,* p. 148. Bloch, *Die Prostitution,* 1:747-750, gives a lengthy — and eloquent — list of words used to designate brothels in the Middle Ages.

96. D. 81 c. 28 *glos. ord.* ad v. *omnino;* C. 24 q. 1 c. 24 *glos. ord.* ad v. *balneas;* Rufinus, *Summa* to D. 81 c. 20 (ed. Singer, p. 172).

97. *Historia occidentalis,* c. 7, ed. Hinnebusch, p. 91; cf. the harlots at the door of the tent of meeting: I Sam. 2:22 (=I Kings 2:22).

98. Matt. 21:31-33.

99. Luke 7:37.

100. Durantis, *Speculum iuris,* lib. 4, partic. 4, De adulteriis et stupro, no. 8-9 *(ed. cit.,* 2:377) gives examples of such petitions.

101. D. 34 d.p.c. 8; C. 32 q. 1 d.p.c. 13.

102. Jacques de Vitry, *Historia occidentalis,* c. 8, ed. Hinnebusch, pp. 99-100; Milton R. Gutsch, "A Twelfth-Century Preacher — Fulk of Neuilly," *The Crusades and Other Essays in*

Honor of Dana C. Munro (New York: Appleton-Century-Crofts, 1928), pp. 190–191; Bullough, *History of Prostitution,* p. 115.

103. Max Heimbucher, *Die Orden und Kongregationen der katholischen Kirche,* 3d. ed., 2 vols. (Munich: F. Schöningh, 1965), 1:646–648.

104. Bernard Guillemain, *La cour pontifical d'Avignon, 1309–1376: étude d'une société* (Paris: E. de Boccard, 1966), pp. 485–486.

105. Jean de Joinville, *Life of St. Louis* 142.725, trans. Hague, p. 210.

106. C. 32 q. 1 c. 1, taken from an apocryphal work ascribed to St. John Chrysostom. Gratian, in his *dictum* before this canon, appears to equate harlotry with adultery.

107. C. 33 q. 2 c. 11–12; Esmein, *Le mariage en droit canonique* 1:210.

108. *Cod.* 5.4.29.6; 9.9.20.

109. C. 32 q. 1 c. 14.

110. Peter Lombard, *Sententiae* 4.30 (*PL* 192:917); Esmein, *Le mariage en droit canonique* 1:312–313.

111. C. 32 q. 1 d.p.c. 13.

112. C. 32 q. 1 c. 10, again equating whores with adulteresses; C. 32 q. 1 d.p.c. 13; Freisen, *Geschichte des kanonischen Eherechts,* pp. 621–622.

113. E.g., Paucapalea, *Summa* to C. 32, ed. J. F. von Schulte (Giessen: E. Roth, 1890), p. 125; *Summa Parisiensis* to C. 32 q. 1 c. 1 ad v. *sicut crudelis,* ed. McLaughlin, p. 240; Rufinus, *Summa* to C. 32 q. 1 pr., ed. Singer, p. 475; Rolandus, *Summa* to C. 32 q. 1, ed. Thaner, pp. 158–159; Huguccio, *Summa* to C. 32 q. 1 d.a.c. 1 (B.N. lat. 3892, fol. 308ra).

114. Rolandus, *Summa* to C. 32 q. 1, ed. Thaner, p. 162.

115. *X.* 4.1.20 (= *Comp. II* 4.1.5).

116. *X* 4.1.20 *glos. ord.* ad v. *in uxores:* "Hic de ea, quae continere libenter vellet, si invenerit qui eam ducere vellet in uxorem. Ber."

117. E.g., Innocent IV, *Apparatus* to *X* 4.1.20 (*ed. cit.,* fol. 465v); Hostiensis, *Lectura* to *X* 3.32.19, no. 3, and *X* 4.1.20, no. 8 (*ed. cit.,* vol. 3, fol. 121vb; vol. 4, fol. 6vb).

118. C. 31 q. 1 c. 1–7; C. 32 q. 4 d.a.c. 1; Esmein, *Le mariage en droit canonique,* 1:208–210.

119. C. 32 q. 1 c. 1 *glos. ord.* ad v. *patronus.*

120. D. 33 c. 2; D. 34 c. 11, d.p.c. 14, c. 15.

121. Rufinus, *Summa* to D. 33 c. 2, ed. Singer, p. 77; D. 33 d.a.c. 1 *glos. ord.* ad v. *sed queritur;* D. 34 d.p.c. 8 *glos. ord.* ad v. *meretricari.*

122. Rufinus, *Summa* to D. 34 pr., ed. Singer, pp. 79–80.

123. *X* 1.21.1 *glos. ord.* ad v. *in bigamis.* Bigamy in the ecclesiastical law had a number of peculiarities: See Stephan Kuttner, "Pope Lucius III and the Bigamous Archbishop of Palermo," *Medieval Studies Presented to Aubrey Gwynn, S.J.* (Dublin, 1961), pp. 409–453.

Chapter 15

Sex in the Literature of the Middle Ages: The Fabliaux

1. The chapter does not go into the complex topics of who the audience and the authors of these tales were. Joseph Bédier, *Les Fabliaux: Études de littérature populaire et d'histoire littéraire du moyen âge* (Paris: Champion, 1964), argues that the fabliau is the product of the bourgeoisie. Per Nykrog, *Les Fabliaux: Étude d'histoire littéraire et de stylistique médiévale* (Copenhagen: Ejnar Munksgaard, 1957), says that the nobility, too, not only enjoyed these bawdy stories but often wrote them. Another view is expressed by Knud Togeby in his essay "The Nature of the Fabliaux" in *The Humor of the Fabliaux, A Collection of Critical Essays,* ed. by Thomas D. Cooke and Benjamin L. Honeycutt (Columbia, Missouri: University of Missouri Press, 1974), pp. 7–13. He writes, "If we are to venture into this delicate question of the relation between social classes and literary genres, I should like to suggest another social group

as a fertile milieu for the creation of the fabliau. A new social group was emerging throughout Europe in the second half of the twelfth century: the students of the cathedral schools, later of the universities" (p. 11). Regardless of which group authored the fabliaux, Jürgen Beyer says that the emergence of the genre "may be conceived of and interpreted as the spontaneity and literary self-realization of the farcical spirit." (Beyer, "The Morality of the Amoral," in *The Humor of the Fabliaux*, Cooke and Honeycutt, eds., pp. 15–42; this statement is on p. 17.)

    2. See Beyer in Cooke and Honeycutt, *The Humor of the Fabliaux*, p. 18.

    3. Ibid., p. 18 n. 9.

    4. See, for example, Per Nykrog's study cited in note 1; also see Thomas D. Cooke, *The Old French and Chaucerian Fabliaux: A Study of Their Comic Climax* (Columbia, Missouri and London: University of Missouri Press, 1978), pp. 142 ff.

    5. See Alexander Denomy, *The Heresy of Courtly Love* (Gloucester, Massachusetts: Peter Smith, 1965). Other useful treatments are C. S. Lewis, *The Allegory of Love* (Oxford University Press, 1959); William Allan Neilson, *Origins and Sources of the 'Court of Love'* (New York: Russell & Russell, 1967); F. X. Newman, ed. *The Meaning of Courtly Love* (Albany, New York: State University of New York Press, 1968). The Newman volume has an excellent selected bibliography (pp. 97–102) of works done in the last twenty years (up through 1968) on the topic.

    6. "Fabliau Settings," in Cooke and Honeycutt, *The Humor of the Fabliaux*, pp. 119–136.

    7. These are Chaucer's words in describing the Squire (*Canterbury Tales, General Prologue*, l. 80). All references to Chaucer will be to the edition by F. N. Robinson, *The Works of Geoffrey Chaucer* (Boston: Houghton Mifflin Company, 1961). This phrase is on page 18.

    8. "Le Chevalier Qui Fist Parler les Cons," in *Fabliaux, Ribald Tales from the Old French*, ed. and trans. by Robert Hellman and Richard O'Gorman (New York: Thomas Y. Crowell Company, 1966), pp. 105–121.

    9. Naturally this is a joke because her father is a parson, proving that she is illegitimate, having for a father a man who should be celibate. That she was brought up in a convent supports this suggestion. But this does not negate the point I am making. The author still wants us to see her as higher born than the clerk.

    10. "Béranger au Lonc Cul," in Hellman and O'Gorman, *Fabliaux*, pp. 59–66.

    11. "Le Sentier Battu," in Hellman and O'Gorman, *Fabliaux*, pp. 23–26.

    12. "Les Perdriz," in Hellman and O'Gorman, *Fabliaux*, pp. 123–127.

    13. Though, of course, the queen and the knight must needs be at odds here because of the insulting game they are playing. One nice touch in this story is in the structure. The opening line of the tale is homiletic: "It is not wise to make fun of others . . . ." This is like the opening of a sermon in which the priest states his 'text' and then gives his exemplum to illustrate this text. In this case, the exemplum is the exchange of insults. Frequently, religious figures as well play prominent roles in the fabliaux, partly because of the humor that can come from the incongruity of a priest's or friar's presence in a bawdy tale, partly because the corruption of the clergy is a good source of satire. For further discussion of the courtly elements in fabliaux, see Charles Muscatine, *Chaucer and the French Tradition* (Berkeley: University of California Press, 1966), pp. 66–71. In his section "Courtly Traits in the Bourgeois Tradition," Muscatine says that "the courtly elements are most often inoperative artistically, petrified fossils of expression that have been introduced for lack of something better" (p. 67); I claim that they could be vestiges of the source of the genre, not 'introduced,' but 'left over.'

    14. "Guillaume au Faucon," in Hellman and O'Gorman, *Fabliaux*, pp. 81–93.

    15. "La Dame escoilée," in *Bawdy Tales from the Courts of Medieval France*, ed. and trans. by Paul Brians (New York: Harper Torchbooks, 1973), pp. 24–35.

    16. Perhaps one of the sources of such love is in the real reactions some people have— exhibited in what we call "puppy love."

    17. Thomas D. Cooke, in his essay "Pornography and the Comic Spirit" (in Cooke and Honeycutt, *The Humor of the Fabliaux*, pp. 137–162), says: "The potency of the penis in the

fabliaux is generally enormous, the prize, I believe, going to the priest in *Le Prestre et Alison*, who has sex nine times in one night" (p. 147).

18. Robinson, *Works of Chaucer*, p. 126, 11. 2370-75.

19. See *A Handbook to Literature*, 3rd ed., by C. Hugh Holman, based on the original by William Flint Thrall and Addison Hibbard (New York: Odyssey Press, 1972), p. 218.

20. Muscatine, *Chaucer and the French Tradition*, p. 59.

21. As mentioned in note 3, the genre of fabliau is not necessarily in a bourgeois tradition; this is Muscatine's view. Note the title of this section of his book — "Courtly Traits in the Bourgeois Tradition."

22. Paul Theiner, "Fabliau Settings," in Cooke and Honeycutt, *The Humor of the Fabliaux*, pp. 119-136; this statement is on page 121.

23. D. W. Robertson, Jr., *A Preface to Chaucer: Studies in Medieval Perspectives* (Princeton, New Jersey: Princeton University Press, 1963), p. 206. Robertson here refers his readers to Nykrog's study, *Les Fabliaux*, pp. 108-9.

24. Thomas D. Cooke, "Pornography, The Comic Spirit, and the Fabliaux," in Cooke and Honeycutt, *The Humor of the Fabliaux*, pp. 137-162; this statement is on page 160.

25. Theiner, "Fabliau Settings," p. 122.

26. He was quite old, having far exceeded his life expectancy.

27. Perhaps here is another pun on 'corage.'

28. "Dame Sirith," in *Middle English Poetry, An Anthology*, ed. by Lewis J. Owen and Nancy H. Owen (New York: The Bobbs-Merrill Company, Inc., 1971), pp. 307-325; this passage is on p. 312, 11. 121-26.

29. Such a stance was not restricted to medieval fabliaux. In a Restoration play by Sir John Vanbrugh, *The Relapse*, one character, Berinthia, who has continually turned back the advances of Loveless, is finally hoisted onto his shoulder as he heads for a couch on which to ravish her. She has just said, " . . . I will not go." Loveless replies, "Then you must be carried." Berinthia then says, "Help! help! I'm ravished! ruined! undone! O Lord, I shall never be able to bear it." The stage direction puts this speech in perspective; it says merely: *"(Very softly)."* Berinthia goes through the motions of being pure, while her tone of voice betrays her real desires. She wants to do it, but she just does not want to admit that she wants to. Quoted from *Plays of the Restoration and Eighteenth Century*, ed. by Dougald MacMillan and Howard Mumford Jones (New York: Holt, Rinehart and Winston, 1931, repr. 1964), p. 382 [IV, iii]. The desire to keep one's reputation clean, likewise, was characteristic of other genres. For example, in the mystery play "The Woman Taken in Adultery" (from the N. Town Cycle, in *Everyman and Medieval Miracle Plays*, ed. by A. C. Cawley [New York: E. P. Dutton & Co., 1959], pp. 133-42), the woman who is confronted by the Scribe and the Pharisee says to them, " . . . Both gold and silver ye shall have,/So that in cleanness ye keep my name" (iii, 163-64). Incidentally, the marvelous picture of the whoring young man who "runs out in his doublet, with shoes untied and holding up his breeches with his hand" (p. 137) was almost certainly influenced by the fabliaux. The Bible does not even mention him (see John 8:3-11).

30. "Equitan," trans. by Brians, *Bawdy Tales*, p. 50.

31. "The Wife of Orleans," in Hellman and O'Gorman, *Fabliaux*, pp. 1-7.

32. "The Butcher of Abbeville," in Hellman and O'Gorman, *Fabliaux*, pp. 31-44.

33. Robinson, *Works of Chaucer*, p. 56, 11. 3942-3.

34. Cooke, *The Old French and Chaucerian Fabliaux;* see especially chapters 2, 3, and 4.

35. See, for example, Cooke, *The Old French and Chaucerian Fabliaux*; his chapters on the Preparation for the Climax: The Showing and the Telling (pp. 23-63; 64-106); Birney, Earle, "The Inhibited and the Uninhibited: Ironic Structure in the *Miller's Tale*," *Neophilologus* 44 (1960), 333-38; Pearcy, Roy J., "Structural Modes for the Fabliaux and the *Summoner's Tale* Analogues," *Fabula* 15 (1974), 103-13; Sedgewick, G. G., "The Structure of *The Merchant's Tale*," *University of Toronto Quarterly* 17 (1948), 337-45; Wentersdorf, Karl P., "Theme and Structure in The Merchant's Tale: The Function of the Pluto Episode," *PMLA* 80 (1965), 522-27.

36. For a thorough discussion of the six-part structure of a medieval sermon see, *Middle English Sermons,* ed. by Woodburn O. Ross (London: Oxford University Press for The Early English Text Society, 1960), pp. xliv-li. Robinson, *Works of Chaucer,* points out (p. 729) that "The Pardoner's sermon seems to have only three or four of these divisions"; the point is that a sermon may leave out several of the six parts and still be an acceptable sermon.

37. "The Lay of Ignaurés," in Brians, *Bawdy Tales,* pp. 37–48.

38. This is what Per Nykrog calls "a moral that is no moral" (see "Courtliness and the Townspeople: The Fabliaux as a Courtly Burlesque," in Cooke and Honeycutt, *The Humor of the Fabliaux,* pp. 59–73; this statement is on p. 71). A good example of this is in "The Peasant and His Two Donkeys" (in *Medieval Comic Tales,* trans. by Peter Rickard, et al. [Totowa, New Jersey: Rowman and Littlefield, 1973], pp. 3–4); the peasant, used to the constant odor of manure (his profession being a manure carrier and spreader), faints at the odor of the spices in a street in a town in front of an apothecary shop. It takes several whiffs of manure to revive him. The moral is, "he who puts aside all pride acts sensibly and reasonably. No man should be false to his origins" (p. 4). The relation of the moral to the brief tale is, at best, tenuous.

39. Theiner, "Fabliau Settings," p. 134.

40. One excellent example of this may be found in poem #24, "De Clerico et Puella," in *The Harley Lyrics,* ed. by G. L. Brook (Manchester: Manchester University Press, 1968), pp. 62–63. The poem is a debate between the cleric and the woman he desires. He tries his best to win her with lines like "you could cure my ailments," "if I die because of love, the guilt will be yours," "you fill me with great sorrow," "we once kissed fifty times at your window," and so on. When she is reminded of his kisses—though she had flatly rejected each of his arguments to this point—she weakens. He then says that when he was a scholar at school he learned much of lore, that he has suffered for her love-wounds much anguish far from his home in the forest, and that he desperately wants her pity. Despite the weakness of his arguments, but remembering his kisses, she gives in, remarking on his firm, quiet speech, on her own unwillingness to let him suffer on her account (the same excuse Margery uses in "Dame Sirith"), and (without coming right out and saying it) on her desire for him. This is not properly a fabliau; it is more a lovers' debate. But elements in this poem are clearly from the fabliau tradition. I cite this here to show that the writers of fabliaux were working with the same motifs and characters popular in the secular erotic verse of the time. Cooke, in his chapter on "Comic Climax" *(The Old French and Chaucerian Fabliaux)* shows the genre's relation to fables, ballads, and farces (pp. 110ff.).

41. That January is a knight is suspicious. His position among the lower nobility must have been acquired at a time when it took only wealth—not valor or service—to become a knight. The fact that he is a knight would lead us to expect some kind of exemplary behavior. Honeycutt comments on this in his essay "The Knight and His World as Instruments of Humor in the Fabliaux," in Cooke and Honeycutt, *The Humor of the Fabliaux,* pp. 75–92. He speaks of the elevated position of the knight in society, and "the juxtaposition of courtly ideals and crude reality" (p. 76) that we get in the behavior of the knights in the fabliaux. Later, he points out that "There are several fabliaux in which the humor is based on a character's manifestation of moral qualities totally incongruous with the knightly ideals of *courtoisie* and *prouesse* and with the noble role of the knight in other literary genres" (p. 90). This describes *The Merchant's Tale* accurately.

42. See the quotation from Theiner on page 167 of this essay.

43. Lacy, "Types of Esthetic Distances in the Fabliaux," in Cooke and Honeycutt, *The Humor of the Fabliaux,* pp. 107–117.

44. Cooke, *The Old French and Chaucerian Fabliaux,* p. 23. See also pp. 62-63 for Cooke's example of "the importance of values and norms in the fabliaux."

Chapter 16

Prostitution in the Later Middle Ages

1. Thomas Aquinas, *Summa Theologica,* II-II, Q.X, Art II and II-II Q. lx, 2 and 5, II-II,

LXXXVII, 2, ad. 2, and II–II, CXVIII, 8 ad. 4 in the edition translated by the English Dominicans, 22 vols. (Burns, Oates & Washburne, 1922).

2. Vern Bullough and Cameron Campbell, "Female Longevity and Diet in the Middle Ages," *Speculum* 55 (April 1980):317–325.

3. George F. Fort, *History of Medical Economy During the Middle Ages* (New York: J. W. Bouton, 1883), p. 340.

4. William E. Lecky, *History of European Morals.* 2 vols. (repr., New York: George Braziller, 1955), 2:152.

5. John of Joinville, *The Life of St. Louis,* trans. René Hague (New York: Sheed and Ward, 1955), XXXVI, par. 170–71.

6. Hostiensis, *Summa aurea* (Lyons: Joannes de Lambray, 1537; repr. Aalen: Scientia Verlag, 1962), lib. 3, no. 11 (fol. 177rb).

7. Paul LaCroix, *History of Prostitution,* trans. Samuel Putnam, 2 vols. (New York: Covici-Friede, 1931), 1:728–29.

8. *Monumenta Germaniae historica, Legum,* sec. 4. const. I (Hanover: Hahn, 1875–79), p. 240.

9. The ordinance is given in Joinville, *Life of St. Louis,* CXL, par. 702. See also *Ordonnances de rois de France,* ed. Eusébe Jacob de Lauriére, Denis François Secousse, et al. (Paris, 1728–1849), I, 74, 104.

10. Ibid., XX, 180.

11. Iwan Bloch, *Die Prostitution,* 2 vols. (Berlin: Louis Marcus, 1912), 1:676, 722.

12. G. T. Salusbury, *Street Life in Medieval England* (Oxford: Pen-In-Hand, 1948), pp. 148–55; John Stow, *The Survey of London* (1598) ed. Henry Wheatley (London: J. M. Dent, 1912), pp. 360–61.

13. Ibid.

14. Fort, *History of Medical Economy,* p. 339.

15. For a survey of some of this legislation, see Robert Ulysse, *Les signes d'infamie au moyen âge* (Paris: Honoré Champion, 1891), pp. 176–89.

16. Antonii Beccadelli (Panormita), *Hermaphroditus* (Frider. Carol. Forbergius-Coburgi Sumtibus Meuseliorum, 1824), Bk. II, cap. 37.

16. Jacques de Vitry, *Historia occidentalis,* c. 7., ed. Hinnebush, p. 91.

18. Ralph B. Pugh, *Imprisonment in Medieval England* (Cambridge: Cambridge University Press, 1968), p. 51.

19. *Ordonnances,* VII, 127.

20. The law was incorporated in the *Statuta populi et communis Florentiae,* 3 vols. (Friburgi, 1778–83), 3:41–45.

21. Ibid., 3:42, 44.

22. The Avignon regulations, because of the provision for medical inspection, have been much examined, and for this same reason are thought not to be genuine. See P. Pansier, "Histoire des prétendus statuts de la reine Jeanne," *Janus* VII (1902).

23. Louis M. Epstein, *Sex Laws and Customs in Judaism* (repr. New York: Ktav Publishing House, 1967), pp. 172–73.

24. For discussion see Iwan Bloch, *Die Prostitution,* 1:670, 767–70. Though I use Bloch in this chapter because he cites many inaccessible pamphlets and books, I should warn historians to be on guard when they do cite him. He has a lot of valuable information but his sources cannot always be traced, and when one does find them, they are often miscited.

25. G. G. Coulton, *Medieval Panorama* (Cambridge: Cambridge University Press, 1949), p. 172.

26. Fort, *History of Medical Economy,* pp. 336–47.

27. A. P. E. Rabutuax, *De la Prostitution en Europe depuis l'antiquité jusqu'à la fin du XVI siècle* (Paris: Libre-Duquesne Frères, 1851), p. 54; see also Henry Mayhew, *London*

Labour and the London Poor, 4 vols. (London: Griffin, Bohn; repr. Dover Publications, 1968), 4:187-88; Bloch, *Die Prostitution,* 1:814-15.

29. Ulrich Richental, *Chronicle of the Council of Florence,* in *The Council of Constance,* trans. Louise Rope Loomis, edited and annotated by John H. Mundy and Kennerly M. Woody (New York: Columbia University Press, 1961), Summary, p. 190. He reported there were so many prostitutes he could not count them all.

30. For a detailed listing see Bloch, *Die Prostitution,* 1:747-50.

31. Ibid., 1:740-45. His lists for other countries are not as complete as for Germany. For Paris and France, see pp. 745-46; for Italy, p. 747.

32. Jacques de Vitry, *Historia occidentalis,* c. 8, pp. 99-100; Milton R. Gutsch, "A Twelfth-Century Preacher—Fulk of Neuilly," *The Crusades and Other Essays in Honor of Dana C. Munro* (New York: Appleton-Century-Crofts, 1928), pp. 190-91.

33. Max Heimbucher, *Die Orden und Kogregationen der katholischen Kirche,* 3d ed., 2 vols. (Munich: F. Schöningh, 1965), 1:646-48.

34. Bernard Guillemain, *Le court pontifical d'Avignon 1309-1376* (Paris: E. DeBoccard, 1966), pp. 485-86, and Joinville, *Life of St. Louis,* XCLII, 725.

35. This is the account given by Richard Lewinsohn, *A History of Sexual Customs,* trans. Alexander Mayce (New York: Harper & Brothers, 1958), pp. 147-48. I was unable to check the Austrian sources.

36. Gratian, *Decretum,* Causa 32, quaestio 1, canon 1, and C. 33, q. 2. C. 11-12. in *Corpus Juris Canonici,* ed. Emil Friedberg, 2 vols. (Leipzig: B. Tauschnitz, 1879; reprinted, Graz: Akademische Druck-und Verlags-anstalt, 1959) and *Decretalis D. Gregorii papae IX suae integrati una cum glossi* Liber I, Titulus I, canon 20 in *Corpus Juris Canonici.*

37. Fort, *History of Medical Economy,* p. 344, and Gutsch, "A Twelfth-Century Preacher."

38. See the references in note 36.

39. There are numerous editions of Brantômes work. I have utilized the translation by A. R. Allinson, *Lives of Fair and Gallant Ladies* (New York: Liveright, 1933), bk. VI, chap. 2, p. 313.

40. Particularly by Brantôme, *Lives of Ladies,* bk. VI, chap. 2, p. 315, and *passim.*

41. Nina Epton, *Love and the French* (London: Cassell, 1959), pp. 93-95, 114, *passim,* gives accounts of the various mistresses and courtesans.

42. Brantôme, *Lives of Ladies,* bk. I, chap. 5, pp. 35-36.

43. Ibid., bk. I, chap. 12, p. 97.

44. Andreas Capellanus, *The Art of Courtly Love,* trans. J. J. Parry (New York: Columbia University Press, 1941), bk. I, chap. II.

45. Ibid., bk. I, chap. 12.

46. Baldassare Castiglioni, *The Courtier,* trans. Thomas Hoby (New York: National Alumni, 1907), bk. IV, chap. 6.

47. There are many translations of Villon. See D. B. Wyndham Lewis, *François Villon* (New York: Literary Guilt, 1928), pp. 276-77. This gives a survey of much of his life and of his poems. See also *François Villon, The Complete Works,* trans. Anthony Bonner (New York: David McKay Company, 1960), pp. 51 ff. Norman Cameron, *Poems of François Villon* (London: Jonathan Cape, 1952). Other translations are by John Payne, H. de Vere Stackpoole, J. Heron Lepper, and separate poems have been translated by Rossetti, Swinburne, Wilfred Thorley, and many others.

48. The French version of these are given by Lewis, *François Villon,* pp. 324-25. Not all scholars attribute the poem to Villon.

49. *Villon, Complete Works,* trans. Anthony Bonner, pp. 106-9.

50. Jean Hervez, *Ruffians et Ribaudes au moyen âge* (Paris: Bibliothèque des Curieux, 1913), pp. 112-113. Other visitors were also greatly impressed by the number of prostitutes.

Chapter 17

Human Sexuality in Twelfth- through Fifteenth-Century Scientific Writings

This chapter is an expanded form of an article that appeared in *Isis* in March 1980. Portions are taken from an article, "William of Saliceto on Human Sexuality," to appear in *Viator* 12 (1981).

1. The *Centiloquium (Kitab al-Thamara* or *Liber Fructus)* was composed by pseudo-Haly (Abu Ja'far Ahmad ibn Yusuf ibn Ibrahim al-Katib al Tuluni) in the late ninth or early tenth century in Cairo. It is being studied at present by a research group at the CUNY Graduate Center under the direction of Richard Lemay. See Richard Lemay, "Origin and Success of the Kitab Tamara . . .," Aleppo University, *Proceedings of the First International Symposium on the History of Arabic Science,* 5-12 April 1976. The author of this work will henceforth be referred to as Ahmad ibn Yusuf.

2. See Graziella Federici Vescovini, "Su uno scritto astrologico di Biagio Pelacani da Parma," *Rinascimento* 22 (Dec. 1971):79-93; "La dottrina astrologica di Biagio Pelacani da Parma e le sue connessioni con l'opera di Albumasar," *Rivista di Filosofia* 63, no. 4 (Oct.-Dec. 1972):300-317.

3. Ahmad ibn Yusuf, *Centiloquium,* tr. Plato of Tivoli, Verba 1 and 2 in *Liber Quadripartitus Ptolomaei* . . . (Venice: Ratdolt, 1484), f. 7a. See also ed. Venice (Locatellus), 1493, f. 107.

4. Ahmad ibn Yusuf, *Centiloquium,* tr. Plato of Tivoli, Verbum 5 in *Liber Quadripartitus Ptolomaei* (Venice, 1493), f. 107va.

5. Ahmad ibn Yusuf, *Centiloquium,* tr. Plato of Tivoli, Verbum 9 in *Liber Quadripartitus Ptolomaei* (Venice, 1493), f. 107vb.

6. Ahmad ibn Yusuf, *Centiloquium,* tr. Plato of Tivoli, Verbum 95 in *Liber Quadripartitus Ptolomaei* (Venice, 1493), f. 115vb-116ra.

7. See Richard Lemay, "Fautes et contresens dans les traductions arabolatines médiévales: *L'Introductorium in Astronomiam* d'Abou Ma'shar de Balkh," in *Colloques: Textes des Rapports, XIIe Congrès International d'Histoire des Sciences, (Revue de Synthèse,* Troisième Série, nos. 49-52, Année 1968), p. 122.

8. Additio. Venus habet influentiam super . . . humores superfluitates maxime circa genitalia et mulierum pudibunda. Alchabitius, *Astronomie iudiciarie principia,* tr. John of Seville (Lyons, 1521), f. xli. On Alchabitius, see Manfred Ullmann, *Die Natur- und Geheimwissenschaften im Islam* (Leiden, 1972), p. 332.

9. See Lynn Thorndike, *History of Magic and Experimental Science,* vol. II, p. 830.

10. Guido Bonatus, *Decem tractatus astronomie* (Venice, 1506), f. 147. See Lynn Thorndike, *History of Magic and Experimental Science,* 8 vols. (New York: Columbia University Press, 1923-1958), 2:825-828.

11. Bonatti does contend that fortune rules in everything, yet he attempts to save freedom of the will by limiting his nativities to "natural" occurrences. Lynn Thorndike, *History of Magic and Experimental Science,* 2:830-31, 833.

12. For a listing of Aristotelian statements on this point see Richard Lemay, *Abu Ma'shar and Latin Aristotelianism in the Twelfth Century* (Beirut, 1962), p. 60 n, 4.

13. Guido Bonatus, *Decem tractatus astronomie* (Venice, 1506), f. 242v f.306vb.

14. Pseudo-Albertus Magnus, *De secretis mulierum,* Lyons, 1580, pp. 52, 66; cf. Petrus Candidus Decembrius, *De genitura hominis* (Rome, ca. 1487). On the authorship of the *De secretis mulierum,* see Lynn Thorndike, "Further consideration of the *Experimenta, Speculum astronomiae,* and *De secretis mulierum* ascribed to Albertus Magnus," *Speculum* 30 (1955): 413-443. I am studying this treatise at present with the help of a grant from the SUNY Research Foundation. On Peter Candidus Decembrius, see Lynn Thorndike, *History of Magic and Experimental Science,* 4:398-399.

15. E.g., 'Ali ibn Ridwan, *Commentarium super Ptolomaei Quadripartitum* (Venice, 1493), f. 54rb.

16. E.g., Albubather, *De nativitatibus* (Venice, 1492), f. c3.

17. E.g., Zahel, *De interrogationibus* (Venice: Locatellus, 1493), f. 130rb.

18. On Albubather see Manfred Ullmann, *Die Medizin im Islam* (Leiden, 1970), p. 158.

19. Albubather, *De nativitatibus*, f. a3 verso.

20. Leopold of Austria, *Compilatio de astrorum scientia* (Venice and Augsburg: Ratdolt, 1489), f. g2 verso–g3. On Leopold of Austria, see Francis J. Carmody, *Arabic Astronomical and Astrological Sciences in Latin Translation* (Berkeley and Los Angeles, 1956), p. 170.

21. E.g., the Centiloquium was used in Paris (1358), Bologna (1405), and Cracow (mid-1400s). See Denifle-Châtelain, *Chartularium Universitatis Parisiensis, Auctarium* (Paris, 1889), vol. I, p. 235; Carlo Malagola, *Statuti delle Università e dei Collegi dello Studio Bolognese* (Bologna, 1888), pp. 276 and 214; A. Birkenmajer, *Études d'histoire des sciences en Pologne, Studia Copernicana* 4 (1972):469–485; Richard Lemay, "Origin and Success of the Kitab Tamara . . ." Aleppo University, *Proceedings of the First International Symposium on the History of Arabic Science,* 5–12 April 1976; Richard Lemay, "The Teaching of Astronomy in the Universities of the 14th–15th Century, Principally in Paris," in *Essays in Honor of Pearl Kibre, Manuscripta* 20 (1976):197–217; Richard Lemay, "The Late Medieval School of Astronomy at Cracow and the Copernican System," in *Science and History: Essays in Honor of Edward Rosen,* Warsaw-Krakow, Polish Academy of Sciences (*Studia Copernicana* XVI), 1978.

22. These marginal notes are found particularly in reference to Verbum 51 (duration of pregnancy) and Verbum 60 (critical days), which often appear separately. For example, for Verbum 60 see ms. Bergamo Bibl. Civica Angelo Mai 1177, f. 59–60 (Delta I sopra 11–14c.); Cambridge Pembroke 204, f. 69. Verba which have a medical significance are numerous, e.g., 10 (poisons), 19 (emetics), 20 (surgery), 21 (emetics), 37 (cause of sickness or death), 42 (Galen's theory of relation of sickness to stars), 44, 56 (humidity), 57 (choice of doctor), 68 (chronic and acute diseases), 69 (eye diseases), 70 (epilepsy, lunacy, manics), 71 (sex life), 73 (type of death), 74 (scars on the face), 76 (death by suffocation or submersion), 80 (sex perversions), 86 (various native powers of body and soul), 91 (diagnosis), 92 (Saturn and Mars on diseases).

23. Arnoldus de Villanova, *De regimine sanitatis* in *Opera* (Lyons, 1509), f. 151rb. On Arnold of Villanova, see Lynn Thorndike, *History of Magic and Experimental Science,* 2:846–847.

24. Michael Scotus, *Liber physiognomiae* (Venice, 1477), f. b7 verso. See Lynn Thorndike, *Michael Scot* (London and Edinburgh, 1965), chaps. 1 and 4.

25. Questio de muliere si sit virgo vel corrupta. Zahel, *De interrogationibus* (Venice: Locatellus, 1493), f. 130rb. On Zahel, see Manfred Ullmann, *Die Natur- und Geheimwissenschaften im Islam,* pp. 309–312.

26. Abenragel (Albohazen), *Liber in iudiciis astrorum* (Venice, 1485), f. 27. See Carlo A. Nallino, *Raccolta di scritti editi e inediti* (Rome, 1944), vol. V, pp. 340–341; Francis J. Carmody, *Arabic Astronomical and Astrological Sciences,* pp. 150–154.

27. Iohannes Saxonii, *Commentarium super Alchabitii Astronomie iudiciarie principia* (Lyons, 1520), f. xxxii.

28. Guido Bonatus, *Decem tractatus astronomie,* f. 203v–204.

29. Guido Bonatus, *Decem tractatus astronomie,* f. 204ra.

30. Averroës, *Colliget* (Venice, 1549), f. 49v.

31. Pseudo-Albertus Magnus, *De secretis mulierum* (Lyons, 1580), p. 119.

32. Guilielmus de Saliceto, *Summa conservationis et curationis* (Venice, 1489), f. i3ra.

33. Ptolemy, *Tetrabiblos* III, 14, ed. and trans. F. E. Robbins (London and Cambridge, Mass., 1971), pp. 368–369.

34. Ali ibn Ridwan, *Commentarium super Ptolemaei Quadripartitum* (Venice, 1493), f. 84ra. On 'Ali ibn Ridwan, see Manfred Ullmann, *Die Medizin im Islam,* p. 158.

35. Albohali, *De iudiciis nativitatum,* tr. Johannes Hispalensis, Nuremberg, 1546, f. k2 verso. See Carlo A. Nallino, *Raccolta,* vol. V, p. 330; Francis J. Carmody, *Arabic Astronomical and Astrological Sciences,* p. 49; Manfred Ullmann, *Die Natur- und Geheimwissenschaften im Islam,* pp. 312–313; Lynn Thorndike, "John of Seville," *Speculum* 34 (1959):20–38, esp. p. 32.

36. Abraham ben Meir Ibn Ezra, *Abrahe Avenaris Judei Astrologi peritissimi in re iudiciali opera,* tr. Petrus de Abano (Venice, 1507), f. D2 verso. This writing was composed during the twelfth century and translated by Peter of Abano in 1293. See Lynn Thorndike, *History of Magic and Experimental Science,* 2:917.

37. Albubather, *De nativitatibus,* f. c–c4.

38. Abenragel, *Liber in iudiciis astrorum* (Venice, 1485), f. 27v: Cap. 24, In questione si habuerit rem cum muliere hac nocte vel non.

39. Guido Bonatus, *Decem tractatus astronomie,* f. 312rb.

40. Leopold of Austria, *Compilatio de astrorum scientia,* f. h6 verso.

41. Iohannes Iovianus Pontanus, *De rebus coelestibus* in *Opera Omnia* (Venice, 1519), vol. III, f. 250.

42. Averroës, *Colliget* (Venice, 1549), f. 68v.

43. Arnoldus de Villanova, *De coitu* in *Hec sunt opera . . . nuperrime recognita ac emendata* (Lyons, 1509), f. 273.

44. Michael Scotus, *Liber physiognomiae* (Venice, 1477), f. b2 verso. See also ed. Lyons, 1580 (entitled *De secretis naturae),* p. 254.

45. Pseudo-Albertus Magnus, *De secretis mulierum* (Lyons, 1580), p. 24. cf. ed. Venice, 1508, f. B3.

46. Arnoldus de Villanova, *De coitu,* f. 213rb. Michael Scotus, *De secretis naturae (Liber physiognomiae)* (Lyons, 1580), pp. 246–247.

47. Guilielmus de Saliceto, *Summa conservations et curationis,* f. h6va–h6vb.

48. Guilielmus de Saliceto, *Summa conservationis et curationis,* f. i2rb.

49. Michael Scotus, *De secretis naturae (Liber physiognomiae)* (Lyons, 1580), p. 247.

50. Ahmad ibn Yusuf, *Centiloquium,* tr. Plato of Tivoli, Verbum 40 in *Liber Quadripartiti Ptolomaei* (Venice, 1493), f. 110va.

51. Ahmad ibn Yusuf, *Centiloquium,* tr. Plato of Tivoli, Verbum 95 in *Liber Quadripartiti Ptolomaei* (Venice, 1493), f. 115vb.

52. Antonio Guainerius, *Tractatus de matricibus,* Cap. 24 in *Opera Omnia* (Pavia, 1481).

53. Leopold of Austria, *Compilatio de astrorum scientia* (Venice and Augsburg: Ratdolt, 1489), f. 3 (numbered 31 in the Columbia University Library copy).

54. Alchabitius, *Astronomie iudiciarie principia,* tr. Johannes Hispalensis (Lyons, 1520), f. xxxi verso.

55. Abraham ben Meir Ibn Ezra, *Liber nativitatum et revolutionum eorum,* tr. Petrus de Abano, in *In re judiciali opera* (Venice, 1507), f. D2 verso.

56. Abraham ben Meir Ibn Ezra, *Liber nativitatum,* F. D2 verso.

57. Quando Venus in occidente vel medio celi et Mercurius cum ea in termino Martis fuerit, natus erit fornicator ac prolem in fornicatione habebit. Albubather, *De nativitatibus* (Venice, 1492), f. b6 verso.

58. Albohali, *De iudiciis nativitatum,* tr. Johannes Hispalensis, (Nuremberg, 1546), f. K. verso.

59. Cap. 30 pro muliere si erit fidelis viro suo de corpore vel non. Albohazen (Haly, filius Abenragel), *Liber in iudiciis astrorum* (Venice, 1485), f. 28v.

60. Zahel, *De interogationibus* (Venice, 1493), f. 130va.

61. Quod si Venus quoque et ipsa foemineo in signo constituta fuerit, eadem haec mulier et adultera erit . . . Iohannes Iovianus Pontanus, *De rebus coelestibus* in *Opera Omnia* (Venice, 1519), vol. III, f. 291.

62. Quaestio de pregnante si fit ex fornicatione vel non. Zahel, *De interrogationibus,* f. 130va. Cap. 28 in questione si pregnatio est legitima vel de fornicatione. Albohazen (Haly filius Abenragel), *Liber in iudiciis astrorum,* f. 28.

63. See Anthony M. Hewson, *Giles of Rome and the Medieval Theory of Conception: A Study of the De formatione corporis humani in utero,* University of London Historical Series no. 38 (Atlantic Highlands, N.J.: Humanities Press, 1975).

64. *Liber novum judicum in judiciis astrorum* (Venice, 1509), f. 34v–35.

65. Michael Scotus, *Liber physiognomiae* (Venice 1477), f. d verso. William of Saliceto presents the opposite view, that complexions should not be similar, in his discussion of infertility. See notes 71 and 72 below.

66. Albubather, *De nativitatibus* (Venice, 1492), f. c3 verso.

67. On "Hermes," see Francis J. Carmody, *Arabic Astronomical and Astrological Sciences,* pp. 52-70.

68. Abraham ben Meir Ibn Ezra, *Liber nativitatum,* f. D.

69. Iohannes Iovianus Pontanus, *De rebus coelestibus,* f. 248v.

70. Averroës, *Colliget* (Venice, 1549), f. 62-62v.

71. Guilielmus de Saliceto, *Summa conservationis et curationis,* f. i4rb-i4va.

72. Guilielmus de Saliceto, *Summa conservationis et curationis,* f. i4va-i5rb.

73. Guilielmus de Saliceto, *Summa conservationis et curationis,* f. i3vb.

74. Michael Scotus, *Liber physiognomiae,* f. b3v.

75. Pseudo-Albertus Magnus, *De secretis mulierum cum commento* (Venice, 1508), f. G-G2.

76. See Lynn Thorndike, *History of Magic and Experimental Science,* 2:744.

77. Guilielmus de Saliceto, *Summa conservationis,* f. i5va.

78. Antonio Guainerius, *Tractatus de matricibus,* cap. 20.

79. Lynn Thorndike, *History of Magic and Experimental Science,* 2:880.

80. Guilielmus de Saliceto, *Summa conservationis,* f. i3 verso.

81. Commentary on *De secretis mulierum* (Venice, 1508), f. E6 verso.

82. Petrus de Abano, *Conciliator differentiarum philosophorum et medicorum* (Venice, 1522), f. 39ra.

83. Arnoldus de Villanova, *De regimine sanitatis* in *Hec sunt opera . . . nuperrime recognita ac emendata* (Lyons, 1509), f. 213.

84. " . . . scilicet ei iocose loquendo . . . " Commentary on *De secretis mulierum* (Venice, 1508), f. E6 verso.

85. Antonio Guainerius, *Tractatus de matricibus,* f. z4 verso.

86. Arnoldus de Villanova, *De regimine sanitatis,* f. 213.

87. " . . . et partes inferiores digitis confricando . . . " Commentary on *De secretis mulierum* (Venice, 1508), f. E6 verso.

88. " . . . et quia in actu tali omnia facere fas est locum inter anum et vulvam leviter confricet" Antonio Guainerius, *Tractatus de matricibus,* f. z4 verso.

89. Guilielmus de Saliceto, *Summa conservationis,* f. i3vb.

90. Arnoldus de Villanova, *De regimine sanitatis,* f. 213.

91. "Unde cum foemina incipit loqui quasi balbuciendo . . . " (Commentary on *De secretis mulierum,* Venice, 1508, f. E6 verso).

92. Antonio Guainerius, *Tractatus de matricibus,* f. z4 verso.

93. Guilielmus de Saliceto, *Summa conservationis,* f. i3vb.

94. " . . . tunc mas debet se erigere et ei commiscere" Commentary on *De secretis mulierum* (Venice, 1508), f. E6 verso.

95. Antonio Guainerius, *Tractatus de matricibus,* f. z4 verso.

96. Commentary on *De secretis mulierum,* Venice, 1508, f. E6 verso.

97. Antonio Guainerius, *Tractatus de matricibus,* f. Z4 verso.

98. Guilielmus de Saliceto, *Summa conservationis,* f. i3vb.

99. Arnoldus de Villanova, *De coitu* in *Hec sunt opera . . . ,* (Lyons, 1509), f. 273rb; Antonio Guainerius, *Tractatus de matricibus,* f. z4 verso-z5; Guilielmus de Saliceto, *Summa conservationis,* f. 6r-7r.

100. Guilielmus de Saliceto, *Summa conservationis,* f. 6rb.

101. Guilielmus de Saliceto, *Summa conservationis,* f. 6va-7rb.

102. Commentary on *De secretis mulierum,* f. A7 recto.

103. Guilielmus de Saliceto, *Summa conservationis,* f. 16vb; Petrus de Abano, *Conciliator,*

f. 53; Jacopo da Forli, *Expositio supra capitulum [Avicennae] De generatione embrionis cum quaestionibus eiusdem* (Venice, 1518), f. 11r–v.

104. Avicenna, *De generatione embrionis* in Jacopo da Forli, *Expositio*, f. 11r.

105. Averroës, *Colliget* (Venice, 1549), f. 77v.

106. See commentary on *De secretis mulierum* (Venice, 1508), f. G7.

Chapter 18

Postscript: Heresy, Witchcraft, and Sexuality

1. Gerhart Ladner, "Homo Viator: Medieval Ideas of Alienation and Order," *Speculum* 42 (1967):233–59.

2. Ernst Werner, in Theodora Büttner and Ernst Werner, *Circumcellionem und Adamiten: Zwei Form mittelalterlich Haeresie* (Berlin: Akademie Verlag, 1959), pp. 93–116.

3. For references to early use of the term, including that of Robert de Brunne, see the discussion in the *Oxford English Dictionary*, 12 volumes, corrected (Oxford: Clarendon Press, 1933).

4. Havelock Ellis, "The Nature of Sexual Inversion," in *Studies in the Psychology of Sex*, 2 vols. (New York: Random House, 1936), I, pt. IV, 347.

5. P. Viollet, *Les Establissment de St. Louis*, Livre I, xc, 4 vols. (Paris: Renouard, 1881–1886), II, 147–48. It is also found in *Ordonnances de Roys de France*, ed. Eusèbe Jacob de Lauriére, Denis François Secousse, et al., 21 vols. (Paris, 1723–1849), I, chap. lxxxv, 175 (1270). See also Derrick Sherwin Bailey, *Homosexuality and the Western Christian Tradition* (London: Longmans, Green and Company, 1955), pp. 141–42.

6. See *Coutume de Touraine-Anjou*, 78, in Viollet, *Establissement de St. Louis*, III, 50.

7. Viollet, *Establissement de St. Louis*, Introduction, "Sodomie," I, 254, n. 1.

8. P. N. Rapetti, *Le Livres de Justice et de Plet* (Paris: Typographie de Firmin Didot fréres, 1850), I, iii.7, and X, xix.6–7, pp. 12–13, 215–16.

9. Ibid., XVIII, xxiv.22, pp. 179–80.

10. A. A. Beugnot, *Les Olims, ou Registres des Arrêts*, 3 vols. (Imprimerie Royale, 1849–1868), I, v, p. 136 (1261). Other references to sodomy come under Philippe IV in 1310, LXVII, Ibid., III, 3A, p. 572, where an unjust accusation is made, and under Philippe V in 1317, VIII, Ibid., III, 3 B p. 1202, where the man is found innocent.

11. Alan of Lille, De fide catholica contra haereticos sui temporis, II, 1, in *PL*, 221 vols. (Paris: 1844–1900), CCX, 80. A translation of this can be found in Walter Wakefield and Austin P. Evans, *Heresies of the High Middle Ages* (New York: Columbia University Press, 1969), pp. 219–20.

12. See Robert E. Lerner, *The Heresy of the Free Spirit in the Middle Ages* (Berkeley and Los Angeles: University of California Press, 1972), especially his first chapter entitled "Heresy and Fornication," pp. 10–34. See also Gordon Leff, *Heresy in the Later Middle Ages*, 2 vols. (Manchester: Manchester University Press, 1967); Norman Cohn, *The Pursuit of the Millennium* (Fairlawn, New Jersey: Essential Books, 1957), and I. von Döllinger, *Geschichte der gnostisch-manichäischen Sekten* in *Beiträge zur Sektengeschichte des Mittelalters*, reprinted 2 vols. (New York: Burt Franklin, 1970). A background study that is also valuable is Jeffrey Burton Russell, *Dissent and Reform in the Early Middle Ages* (Berkeley: University of California Press, 1965).

13. Guibert de Nugent, *Histoire de sa vie*, ed. George Bourgin (Paris: A. Picard et fils, 1907), pp. 212–15. This translation is based on Wakefield and Evans, *Heresies of High Middle Ages*, p. 103.

14. Henry of Le Mans, *Actus pontificum Cenomannis in urbe degentium*, ed. G. Busson and A. Ledru (*Archives historiques du Maine*, II, Le Mans: Société historique de la province

du Mans, 1901), pp. 407-15, and translated in Wakefield and Evans, *Heresies of High Middle Ages,* p. 109.

15. Walter Map, *De nugis curialium,* I, xxx, ed. Montague R. James (Oxford: Clarendon Press, 1914), pp. 57-59, and translated in Wakefield and Evans, *Heresies of High Middle Ages,* pp. 254-55.

16. D. Stanley-Jones, "Sexual Inversion and the English Law," *The Medical Press and Circular* CCXV, no. 5588 (12 June 1946), pp. 391-98.

16. *Chartularium Universitatis Parisiensis,* ed. Henricus Denifle and Aemelio Chatelain, 4 vols. (Paris; reprinted Brussells: Culture et Civilization, 1964), I, no. 473, pp. 543-558, pars. 166, 169, 170, 172, 176, 177, 183.

18. This is taken from Caesarius of Heisterbach, *Dialogus miraculorum,* v, xxii, ed. Joseph Strange, 2 vols. (Cologna: H. Lempertz & Company, 1851), I, 304-07, and is translated in Wakefield and Evans, *Heresies of High Middle Ages,* p. 259.

19. See *Cronica Fratris Salimbene de Adam,* ed. Oswald Holder-Egger, *Monumenta Germaniae Historica, Scriptores,* XXXII, pt. 1, (1248), 255-94, (1274), 489, (1284), 563, (1286), 619-20. There is an English summary in G. G. Coulton, *From St. Francis to Dante* (London: David Nutt, 1906).

20. There are two basic versions of the *Canon Episcopi,* a shorter and longer one, and they appear in Regino of Prüm, *De synodalibus causis et disciplinis ecclesiasticis libri duo,* II, 45, 364, in *PL,* CXXXII, and in Burchard of Worms, *Decretorium Libri Viginti,* I, 94, X, l. 29, and XIX, 70, 90, in *PL,* CXL. A more easily available copy of the documents as well as discussion about them can be found in Jeffrey Burton Russell, *Witchcraft in the Middle Ages* (Ithaca: Cornell University Press, 1972), app. I, p. 292.

21. This is reported in Stephen of Bourgon, *Anecdotes historiques,* ed. Albert Lecoy de la Marche (Paris: Librairie Renouard, 1877), pp. 319-325, and see also Russell, *Witchcraft,* p. 157. This equation of transvestism with witchcraft is a continuation of an old custom which tended to regard crossdressing as one aspect of paganism. Some of the references to this have been collected by Russell, *Witchcraft,* p. 315 n, 22.

22. Ibid., pp. 126-27.

23. Gregory IX, *Vox in Rama,* titulus vii, par. 363-69, in *Monumenta Germaniae Historica, Epp. saec.,* XIII, I, 413.

24. The document is printed in Ignaz Döllinger, *Geschichte der Sekten,* II, 369-73. See also Russell, *Witchcraft,* pp. 162-63.

25. For further discussion of this, see Lerner, *Heresy of Free Spirit,* pp. 109-50, *passim.* For a particular confession, namely that of John and Albert of Brunn, see Leff, *Heresy in Later Middle Ages,* app. I, especially pp. 714, 716, which deals with sodomy.

26. Gershon Legman, *The Guilt of the Templars* (New York: Basic Books, 1966).

27. Julius Gmelin, *Schuld oder Unschuld des Templerordens: Kritischer Versuch zur Lösung der Frage* (Stuttgart: W. Kohlhammer, 1893).

28. Thomas Parker, *The Knights Templars in England* (Tucson: University of Arizona Press, 1963), p. 1.

29. Henry C. Lea, *History of the Inquisition of the Middle Ages,* 3 vols., reprinted (New York: S. A. Russell, 1955), III, 238.

30. The charges are summarized in Edith Simon, *The Piebald Standard: A Biography of the Knights Templars* (Boston: Little, Brown and Company, 1959), pp. 284-85.

31. G. A. Campbell, *The Knights Templars, Their Rise and Fall* (New York: Robert McBride & Company, n.d. [1937]), p. 258.

32. Simon, *Piebald Standard,* p. 286.

33. For a statistical breakdown of some of the confessions, see Edward J. Martin, *The Trial of the Templars* (London: George Allen & Unwin, 1928), p. 65. He writes that in one sample of 138, 11 confessed to the renunciation of Jesus, 109 to kissing in some abnormal

form, 121 to spitting or other insults to the cross, 99 to license to vice, 8 having an idolatrous head, and 1 to omissions in the canon; 6 denied all charges.

34. Simon, *Piebald Standard,* p. 336.

35. There are many editions and translations of Dante. A readily available Italian edition is that edited by Natalino Sapegno, *La Divina Commedia* (Milan: Riccardo Ricciardi, 1957). The three-volume English translation by Dorothy L. Sayers (New York: Basic Books, 1962) was widely sold. The reference is to the *Inferno,* Canto XV, 106–08 and reads:

> In somma sappi che tutti fur cherci
> e litterati grandi e di gran fama,
> d'un peccato medesmo al mondo lerci.

36. Biographical and other information on the individuals concerned is summarized in Paget Toynbee, *A Dictionary of Proper Names and Notable Matters in the Works of Dante,* rev. Charles S. Singleton (Oxford: Clarendon Press, 1968). The revised edition includes a list of recent periodical articles about the individuals.

37. Dante, *Purgatory,* Canto XXVI, 77. The whole canto deals with the sin of lust, both heterosexual and homosexual. The only individual mentioned as being involved in homosexuality is Caesar.

38. Rossell Hope Robbins, *The Encyclopedia of Witchcraft and Demonology* (New York: Crown Publishers, 1959), p. 461. I am unable to find the exact page in Henry C. Lea, *Materials Toward a History of Witchcraft,* arr. and ed. Arthur C. Howland, 3 vols. (reprinted New York: Thomas Yoseloff, Inc., 1957), but any reading of Lea's material verifies the general intent of the quotation.

39. Margaret A. Murray, *The Witch-Cult in Western Europe* (Oxford: Clarendon Press, 1921).

40. Russell, *Witchcraft,* pp. 227–29.

41. For the sources see Joseph Hansen, *Quellen und Untersuchungen zur Geschichte des Hexenwahns und Hexenverfolgung im Mittelalter* (Bonn, 1901; reprinted Hildesheim, Olm, 1963), pp. 2403, and Hansen, *Zauberwahn, Inquisition, und Hexenprozess im Mittelalter und die Entstehung der grossen Hexenverfolgung* (Munich: R. Oldenbourgh, 1900), pp. 467–75. A translation of the bull appears in the introduction to the English translation of Henrich Kramer [Institoris] and James Sprenger, *The Malleus Maleficarum,* trans. Montagu Summers (New York: Dover Publications, 1971).

42. Kramer and Sprenger, *Malleus.* See also Russell, *Witchcraft,* pp. 226–264.

43. Ibid., pp. 219, 238.

44. Robbins, *Encyclopedia of Witchcraft,* p. 258.

45. For this and other beliefs see Lea, *Materials.* He includes an extract from Caesarius, *Dialogus,* I, 152.

46. St. Thomas Aquinas, *Summa Theologica* (New York: Benziger Brothers, 1947), I.1, q. 51, 3; 6. See Lea, *Materials,* I, 155–56. St. Bonaventure and Duns Scotus follow Aquinas.

47. Kramer and Sprenger, *Malleus,* pt. II, q. i, ch. 4, p. 112.

48. Ibid., pt. I, Q. 6, pp. 41–48.

49. For some examples see Lea, *Materials,* I, 162–170.

50. See "The Trial of Arnold of Verniolle for Heresy and Sodomy," in Michael Goodich, *The Unmentionable Vice: Homosexuality in the Later Medieval Period* (Santa Barbara: ABC-Clio, 1979), pp. 89–124.

Index

285